CW01667396

The Sufi Saints of the Indian Subcontinent

Sufi – a man of the people called *sufiyah* who profess the mystic principles of *tasawwuf* (mysticism). There are many *silsilas* (concatenations) in sufis, but they are all agreed in their principal tenet—submission to a *murshid* (inspired guide). The great object of the sufi mystic is to lose his own identity. The sole object of sufism is to lead the wandering soul onward, stage by stage, until it reaches the desired goal—perfect union with the Divine Being.

This book *The Sufi Saints of the Indian Subcontinent* is a short biographical sketch of *sufiya'-e-kiram* (the generous mystics) of Indian subcontinent. If we want *falaah wa behbood* (success and well-being) here *faani* (perishable) world and in *aakhirat* (the next world, life after death) which is *baqa'e-davam* (everlastingness), the teachings of sufis (described in this book) will be very useful because sufis have left a lasting legacy that will guide the people today and in future.

Hazrat Dr. Zahurul Hassan Sharib [(1914-96) Gudri Shah Baba IV, affectionately known as Zahur Miyan] was born in Moradabad, U.P. He received a doctorate in Political Science and thereafter pursued a legal career.

However, a deep interest in spiritual life steered him towards sufism (Islamic mysticism). He moved to Ajmer, the city of the renowned sufi saint Khwaja Moinuddin Hasan Chishti, where he spent many years in the love and service of his *pir-o-murshid* (spiritual guide) Hazrat Nawab Khadim Hasan Shah Sahib, Gudri Shah Baba III. In 1971, upon the demise of his spiritual guide, Dr. Sharib succeeded as the Head of the Gudri Shahi Order of sufis. Under his inspiring guidance, the Order gained momentum both in the East and the West.

Dr. Sharib was fluent in many languages, including some modern European languages. He has, to his credit, a vast number of publications in Urdu, English, Dutch, and Italian. Apart from writing books on mysticism, he has translated classical Persian poetry into other languages. He has also authored several books on rural sociology.

Dr. Sharib passed away into the Mercy of the Almighty on April 8, 1996. His tomb at the Usmani Chilla at Ajmer, Rajasthan, attracts scores of people throughout the year. His *'urs* (death ceremony) is celebrated according to the lunar calendar on Ziq'ada 19 and 20 at his tomb.

Dr. Zahurul Hassan Sharib (Gudri Shah Baba IV)

The Sufi Saints of the Indian Subcontinent

Zahurul Hassan Sharib

Munshiram Manoharlal
Publishers Pvt. Ltd.

ISBN 978-81-215-1052-3
Reprinted 2011
First published 2006

PRINTED IN INDIA
Published by Vikram Jain *for*
Munshiram Manoharlal Publishers Pvt. Ltd.
PO Box 5715, 54 Rani Jhansi Road, New Delhi 110 055, INDIA

www.mrmlbooks.com

Contents

Foreword

The subcontinent of India has been chosen by the Almighty as the home for the mystics and dervishes of various faiths and religious beliefs. Not only has the subcontinent seen the birth of saints, sufis and sannyasis, but even the fakirs and the dervishes from other countries have accepted it as their final abode. It is therefore not surprising to find a long list of accomplished sufi saints who made this subcontinent their final resting place.

Dr. Zahurul Hassan Sharib, or Zahur Miyan, as he was called affectionately, made it the purpose of his life to devote himself to the study of the life and teachings of saints and sufis. And later, he made the purpose larger by actually practising these teachings.

As the Head of the Gudri Shahi Order of sufis for over twenty-five years, Zahur Miyan affected the lives of thousands of people, who came to him from all over the world. Regardless of their caste, creed, country, religion, age or social status, Zahur Miyan helped each person in the way that was appropriate for them.

This book constitutes an important milestone as it attempts to put in one place, the lives and teachings of major sufi saints of the subcontinent. However, the real magic of the book is that it is an account of the lives of saints by one amongst them.

May you be the recipient of the blessings of saints!

INAM HASAN
Gudri Shah Baba V

Sharib House, Ajmer
October, 2005

Preface

The second century of the Hijra (AD 719-816) saw the emergence of a class of persons wearing garments of coarse undyed wool or *sūf* and came to be known as "sufis" or the purified. The sufis sought not to be involved in wrong-doing, to nurture a righteous spirit, and prayed for a clean heart and the renewal of the right spirit within.

The origin of sufism was humble, its rise phenomenal, its development rapid, its influence widespread and its impact profound.

Sufism, born in Arabia, was in course of time reborn in other countries of the world. It conquered nations inturn and nations conquered it.

The sufi saints, belonging to various Orders, in particular the Qadiri, the Chishti, the Suhrawardi, and the Naqshbandi, came to the Indian subcontinent by way of Multan and Sind to preach and to propagate the Gospel of Truth.

By their personal example as well as their precepts and preaching, they transformed and transfigured society, endowing it with new concepts, new values, renewed vigour, and a new lease of life.

A new type of society came into being which had no invidious distinctions of caste, class, creed, or colour, and had, as its foundation, a deep routed humanism, a belief in social equality, universal brotherhood, equality of opportunity, an insistence on women's rights, protection of orphans and the handicapped, the right use of money, a sense of contentment, trust in God, emphasis on inner purification, hope, belief, and faith, tolerance, a reliance on meditation, self-introspection, self-realisation, self-effacement, a belief in an ascetic life, self-help, mutual-help, selfless service, the dignity of individual and, above all, on love, which alone can transform an individual in a way nothing else can.

In the following pages an attempt has been made to describe and discuss in some detail the lives of the sufi saints who have worked, preached, practised, and died on the Indian subcontinent. Attention has been given to their antecedents, rituals, ascetic practices, initiation in the sufi Order, teachings, sayings, and supernatural powers.

I wish in conclusion to acknowledge with love and joy the interest evinced by Khurshid Hasan and Mohammad Siraj in the life and teachings of the sufi saints. I am only too well aware of the labour that Mohammad Siraj put into typing the manuscript at personal inconvenience.

May the saints reward them suitably and provide them amply for their labour and for their sustained interest in the life and teachings of the sufi saints. Amen!

INAM HASAN SHARIB

Sharib House, Ajmer

1

Hazrat Khwaja Moin-ud-din Hasan Chishti

Hazrat Khwaja Moin-ud-din Hasan Chishti is one of the most outstanding saints of the Indian subcontinent, and indeed an international spiritual inspiration. In his personality, there is a complete blending of greatness and grace, meditation and action, precept and practice, the indifference of the mystic and the idealism of a saint.

The sources of his power may be traced to his own exceptional endowments. Throughout his life, he exhibited the noble traits of character which are so peculiar to the august house of Prophet Mohammed, to which he belonged. On the paternal side, he traced his descent from Hazrat Imam Husain and is thus a Husaini, but from the maternal side, he was related to Hazrat Imam Hasan which makes him a Hasani. He is also closely related to Hazrat Shaikh Mohi-ud-din Abd-ul-Qadir of Jilan, better known as Ghous-ul-Azam, Piran-e-Pir.

His great grandfather, Khwaja Syed Ahmad Husain, migrated from Sarman Rai, i.e., Samraa or Uskar in Iraq and eventually settled in Sanjar (in Seistan).

His father, Khwaja Ghiyas-ud-din Hasan, an accomplished man, was well-educated and trained, and a great sufi of his time. His piety and scholarship won him widespread respect and regard, and was held in high esteem by the sufis of Khorasan. His mother, Bibi Mah Nur, alias Umm-ul-Warah, was the daughter of Dawood, son of Abdullah-al-Hambali. It is also said that he had two brothers.[1] He was born in Isfahan,[2] in AH 530.[3]

Names and titles

His name is Moin-ud-din Hasan. Some assert that his full name is Moin-ud-din, but his parents, affectionately, addressed him only as "Hasan."

He is invoked and addressed by various titles, chief amongst which are:

Qutb-ul-Mashaikh Barro Behr (Lord of the land and the sea)
Habib Allah (Beloved of God)
Ata-e-Rasul (Gift of the Prophet)
Khwaja-e-Ajmer (Khwaja of Ajmer)
Khwaja-e-Buzurg (Great Khwaja)
Hind-ul-Wali (Saint of India)
Gharib Nawaz (Patron of the Poor)
Sultan-ul-Hind (Spiritual Sovereign of India)
Naib-e-Rasul-fil-Hind (Deputy of the Prophet in India)
Aftab-e-Jahan (Sun of the World)
Panah-e-Bekasan (Shelter of the Helpless)
Daleel-ul-Arefeen (Argument of the Enlightened)

The Chishti Order does not owe its origin to Hazrat Khwaja Gharib Nawaz, but to Hazrat Khwaja Abu Ishaque of Syria. Once, Hazrat Khwaja Abu Ishaque approached Hazrat Khwaja Mumshad Ali Denoorie in Baghdad with the intention of becoming his spiritual disciple. After the initiation, Hazrat Khwaja Mumshad Ali Denoorie asked him his name. He replied: "This humble being is called Abu Ishaque Shami." Thereupon, Hazrat Khwaja Mumshad Ali Denoorie said: "From today onwards, we will call thee Abu Ishaque Chishti and whosoever enters thy fold till the Day of Resurrection, will be likewise called Chishti."

Subsequently, Hazrat Khwaja Abu Ishaque, on the instructions of his spiritual guide and teacher, moved on to Chisht. The other saints of the Order, namely, Hazrat Khwaja Abu Ahmad Chishti, Hazrat Khwaja Mohammed Chishti, Hazrat Khwaja Abu Yusuf Chishti, and Hazrat Khwaja Qutb-ud-din Maudood Chishti lived, worked, died, and were buried in Chisht, and that was why the spiritual Order came to be known as Chishti. These saints are the spiritual teachers, guides, and precursors of Hazrat Khwaja Gharib Nawaz, which is why Khwaja Gharib Nawaz also came to be called Chishti.[4]

Early life

During his childhood he showed promise of a marvellous

personality, which he was to subsequently attain. In his infancy, whenever any woman came to his house with her child and the child cried for milk, he would signal to his mother that his milk should be given to the child. His mother, understanding this, would give her milk to the child. He was delighted by this spectacle which caused him to laugh out of joy.

On the occasion of a certain Eid, when he was still a child, Hazrat Khwaja Gharib Nawaz, richly attired, was going to Idgah to offer his prayers. On the way, he saw a blind child dressed in torn clothing. Deeply moved, in compassion, he gave the child his own clothes and took him with himself to the Idgah.

When only three or four years old, he would invite children of his age and feed them, but never played with the children of his age.

Khwaja Gharib Nawaz was brought up in Khorasan and received his early education at home. When he was nine years old, he committed the Holy *Quran* to memory. Subsequently, he was admitted to a *maktab* (school) in Sanjar, where he concentrated primarily on the *hadis* and *fiqh* (jurisprudence), and completed his education very early.

On the fifteenth of Shaban in AH 544, his father died. Hazrat Khwaja Gharib Nawaz was then barely fifteen years old.

The turning point

One day, when he was watering his garden between the months of Shaban and Zilhijja in the year AH 544/AD 1150, a mystic named Ibrahim Qandoozi unexpectedly entered. Hazrat Khwaja Gharib Nawaz extended to him the utmost courtesy and a hearty welcome, and offered him a bunch of grapes. The mystic was greatly pleased by the hospitality and the respect accorded to him and wanted to repay Khwaja Sahab. He took out a piece of oil cake and upon chewing a portion of it, gave the rest to Khwaja Gharib Nawaz to eat. As soon as Khwaja Sahab had eaten it up, he underwent a strange transformation. He felt a repugnance for mundane matters and sought to pursue the higher virtues and seek out the truth.

After the death of his father, he had inherited a grindstone and a garden, which constituted his source of income.[5] Now he sold his grindstone and the garden and distributed the proceeds of these amongst the needy, the indigent, and the poor.

In pursuit of knowledge he first visited Khorasan. In those days, Baghdad, Samarqand, and Bukhara were celebrated centres of Islamic learning. From Khorasan he proceeded to Samarqand and then to Bukhara, where he pursued higher studies.[6] He stayed there for about five years, i.e., from AH 544/AD 1150 upto AH 550/AD 1155, continuing his education upto the age of twenty. He counted among his teachers the two outstanding scholars of his time, namely, Maulana Husam-ud-din of Bukhara and Shara'-ul-Islam Maulana Sharf-ud-din.[7]

After completing his education, he set out in search of truth. He reached Iraq in AH 551/AD 1156, where he met the renowned saint Hazrat Shaikh Mohi-ud-din Abdul Qadir of Jilan, better known as Ghous-ul-Azam, in Baghdad for the first time.[8] On meeting Khwaja Gharib Nawaz, Ghous-ul-Azam's forecast for him was:

> This young man will be a great figure of his time. He will be a source of inspiration and a centre of devotion and the focus of affection to myriads of people.

The prophecy proved exact.

Subsequently, Khwaja Gharib Nawaz left Iraq for Arabia, and from there he proceeded to Haroon. In Haroon, he had the unique privilege of meeting the famous saint Hazrat Khwaja Usman of Haroon, who accepted him as his spiritual disciple.

He spent two and a half years in the company and service of Hazrat Khwaja Usman of Haroon, acquiring spiritual attainments and undertaking ascetic practices, and eventually won the approval of his spiritual guide and teacher. He was given the permission to enlist and accept disciples himself and was appointed a spiritual caliph.[9]

He left Haroon for Baghdad, where he met Shaikh Abu Najeeb Suhrawardi. In AH 555/AD 1160, he travelled to Syria where he met a saint called Ohad Mahmud Al-Wahidi Ghuznavi. He then proceeded to Kirman and from there he returned to Baghdad, and then proceeded to Hamadan.

On his way to India, he visited Tabriz, Astrabad, Bukhara, Kharqan, Samarqand, Memna, and Herat. He finally reached Multan on the tenth of Muharram of AH 561/AD 1165. He then left Multan for Lahore where he spent two weeks at the tomb of Hazrat Shaikh Pir Ali Hujwiri better known as Data Ganj Bakhsh.

On his return journey, he visited Ghazni, Balkh, Astrabad, and Ray. On reaching Baghdad, he offered his respect to his spiritual guide and teacher Hazrat Khwaja Usman of Haroon, who was then in Baghdad.

Initiation as a disciple a second time

Hazrat Khwaja Gharib Nawaz himself describes the details of his being initiated as a spiritual disciple a second time in the following words:[10]

> I, Moin-ud-din Hasan of Sanjar, well-wisher of all the faithful, had the honour of meeting His Holiness Hazrat Khwaja Usman of Haroon in the mosque of Khwaja Junaid in Baghdad. His Holiness was surrounded by inspired dervishes.
>
> When this humble being bowed low in due deference, my spiritual guide and teacher Hazrat Khwaja Usman of Haroon asked me to offer two genuflections. I did.
>
> Then His Holiness asked me to sit with my face towards the Ka'ba. He asked me, next, to recite Sura Baqara (Sura Heifer). I did as I was asked to do.
>
> Further, His Holiness commanded me to recite benedictions to the Holy Prophet Mohammed twenty-one times. I obeyed.
>
> Then His Holiness stood up and, holding my hand in his, lifted his face towards the sky and said to me: 'Come, let me cause thee to reach God.'
>
> Subsequently, taking out a *miqraz*, turned it around on the head of this humble being and placed on my head the four-edged cap and bestowed on me the robe. Then he asked me to sit. I sat.
>
> He addressed me thus: 'It is the custom with us, that a new entrant has to go through asceticism for one day and one night. Thou shouldst complete it in this one day and night.' I obeyed.
>
> Next day, when I attended upon him, His Holiness asked me to sit down and recite Sura Ikhlas (Purity of Faith) four thousand times. I did that.
>
> He asked me, next, to look towards the sky. I did.
>
> His Holiness asked me: 'How far dost thou see?'
>
> I replied: 'Up to the Great Throne.'
>
> Next, he asked me to look towards the ground. I did, He asked me 'How far dost thou see?'
>
> I replied: 'Up to the Antipodes.'
>
> Next, he asked me to recite Sura Ikhlas (Purity of Faith), again, a thousand times. I did. He asked me to look towards the sky again. I did. He asked me: 'How far dost thou see now?'
>
> I replied: 'Up to the Great Hidden.'
>
> He asked me next to close my eyes. I did. He asked me to open my

eyes. I did.
Then, showing his two fingers, he asked me: 'What dost thou see therein?'
I replied: 'Eighteen thousand worlds.'
Later, pointing towards a brick ahead, he asked me to pick it up. When I did, I found a handful of *dinars* therein. He said to me: 'Go and distribute them amongst the needy and the poor.' I complied. When I went to him subsequently, he said to me: 'Live in our company for sometime.'
I replied: 'I am at your service, Sir.'

Khwaja Gharib Nawaz accompanied his spiritual guide and teacher wherever he went. They left Baghdad for Mecca, and on their way, they stayed for sometime in Falooja.

About the visit to Mecca, Khwaja Gharib Nawaz himself says:[11]

Having reached Mecca, we were honoured by the glorious vision of the Ka'ba and by going around it. My spiritual guide and teacher here, too, took my hand in his and entrusted it to God Almighty. He prayed for my humble self in Ka'ba.
A voice was heard to the effect that: 'We have accepted Moin-ud-din.'
Then we reached Medina. We offered our respects at the Court of the Holy Prophet Mohammed. My spiritual guide and teacher said to me: 'Make thy respectful *salaams*.'
I offered my reverential *salaams*.
A voice came out saying: 'Peace be on you also, O Head of the Pious of the Earth and the Sea.'
On hearing this, my spiritual guide said to me: 'Now indeed thou hast reached perfection.'

Leaving Medina, they stopped in Oosh, Badakhshan, and Bukhara on their way to Baghdad. After staying in Baghdad for sometime, Hazrat Khwaja Gharib Nawaz once again accompanied his spiritual guide and teacher on his tours and travels, visiting Oosh, Sewistan, and Damascus.

Hazrat Khwaja Gharib Nawaz met Hazrat Moin-ud-din Abdul Qadir of Jilan in Gail a second time in AH 581/AD 1185 and stayed with him for fifty-seven days.

After having served his spiritual guide teacher on tours and travels for twenty years, Khwaja Gharib Nawaz was separated from him in Baghdad, when he was fifty-two years of age.

On this occasion, Hazrat Khwaja Usman of Haroon appointed him as his *sajjadanashin*, his spiritual successor, and conveyed to him the holy relics of the Holy Prophet Mohammed.

Of this Khwaja Gharib Nawaz himself says:

> My spiritual guide and teacher gave me the stick that was placed before him and then honoured me by confiding to me the robe, sandals, stick and the prayer carpet. Then addressing me said thus: 'These holy relics are the sacred possessions of our spiritual ancestors, which we have received from the Holy Prophet Mohammed and I have given them to thee. Thou should'st keep them with thee, as we have done. Whomsoever thou may'st find a real seeker, entrust them to him. Do not hold any hope from the people. Live far from the people and aloof from the public and do not demand or ask anything from anybody.'[12]
>
> Having said these words, my spiritual guide and teacher embraced me[13] and kissed my head and eyes[14] and said:
>
> 'I have entrusted thee to God.' Then he went into trance and I departed.[15]

Khwaja Gharib Nawaz, after receiving the robe of caliphate from his spiritual guide and teacher, left on tours and travels again. He first reached Oosh and then moved on to Isfahan where he met Shaikh Mahmud of Isfahan. He gave the clothes that he was wearing to Hazrat Khwaja Qutb-ud-din Bakhtyar Kaki, implying that he had accepted him as his spiritual disciple. Thereafter, Hazrat Khwaja Qutb-ud-din Bakhtyar Kaki accompanied him on tours and travels in the year AH 583/ AD 1187. Khwaja Gharib Nawaz left Isfahan for Mecca the same year . One day when he was absorbed in prayers in the Ka'ba, he heard a voice saying:

> O, Moin-ud-din! We are greatly pleased with thee.
>
> Thou art given salvation. Ask for anything thou may'st like, so that we may grant that to thee.
>
> He respectfully responded:
>
> O, Great God! Grant salvation to the followers and disciples of Moin-ud-din.

He received the reply:

> O, Moin-ud-din! Thou art our accepted one. I will give salvation to thy followers and disciples and also to those who may enter thy fold till the Day of Resurrection.

After paying respects to the Ka'ba and performing the *hajj* he reached Medina and devoted himself to prayers in the Ka'ba mosque. During his stay, he received a mandate from the Court of the Holy Prophet Mohammed to the effect:

> O, Moin-ud-din! Thou art a helper of my religion. I entrust to thee the country of Hindustan. There prevails darkness. Proceed to Ajmer and spread there the Gospel of Truth.

He was immensely pleased with this mandate but wondered where Ajmer was situated. In the meanwhile, he was consumed with drowsiness. He was blessed by seeing the Holy Prophet Mohammed in a dream, who showed him the city, the fort, and the situation of Ajmer. He was bid farewell and was given a pomegranate from heaven.

Khwaja Gharib Nawaz reached Baghdad and moved on to Chisht on his way to Herat. From Herat, he proceeded to Subzawar in Afghanistan, which was ruled by Yadgar Mohammed, who also became his spiritual disciple.

He left Subzawar and reached Shadman fort, and then left for Lahore via Multan. He then proceeded to Delhi and stopped on the way at Samana (near Patiala), and from there, reached Ajmer for the first time in AH 587/ AD 1191. He had forty followers with him.

In Ajmer, he wanted to stay at the site where the Auliya mosque is now situated but the servants of Raja Prithvi Raj did not allow him to do so on the pretext that the camels of Raja Prithvi Raj usually sat there. Khwaja Gharib Nawaz, thereupon countered: "If the camels sit there, let them sit."

He then shifted to Ana Sagar and occupied the site now known as his Chilla. The camels returned to their usual place and sat there as usual, but once they sat, they were unable to stand up again. The Raja was informed. All the camel-drivers tendered an unconditional apology. Khwaja Gharib Nawaz, accepting the apology said: "Well, go. The camels now stand." When they returned, they actually saw that the camels were standing.

Khwaja Gharib Nawaz left Ajmer for sometime and returned again to Ajmer in AH 588/AD 1191. He left for Baghdad in AH 598/AD 1200 and on reaching Balkh, he accepted Maulana Zia-ud-din as his spiritual disciple. He visited Ajmer a third time in AH 602/AD 1206 and once again in AH 610/AD 1213.

He visited Delhi twice during the reign of Sultan Shams-ud-din Iltutmish. He reached Delhi in AH 611/AD 1214 and stayed in the *khanqah* of Hazrat Khwaja Qutb-ud-din Bakhtyar Kaki, and during his stay, he conferred a robe on Hazrat Baba Farid-ud-din Ganj-e-Shakar.

When his spiritual guide and teacher, Hazrat Khwaja Usman of Haroon, paid a visit to Delhi, Khwaja Gharib Nawaz requested that "some calm, quiet and secluded place may be chosen for his permanent abode and stay," to which His Holiness responded: "O, Moin-ud-din! Live in my company for sometime once again so that thou may'st acquire spiritual powers through the constancy of my training and preaching and after that permanently settle in Ajmer." The renowned poet of Shiraz, Shaikh Sa'di came to Delhi at that time and had the privilege of meeting both the saints.

Khwaja Gharib Nawaz once again visited Delhi in AH 621/AD 1224 at the request of a certain farmer, who implored him to ask the king to set aside the order of confiscation of the produce of his land passed by a certain officer.

He wanted to take Hazrat Khwaja Qutb-ud-din Bakhtyar Kaki with him to Ajmer as Shaikh Najm-ud-din Sughra had complained to him that the presence of Qutb Sahab in Delhi eclipsed his importance and prestige, but when implored by the high and the low of Delhi not to do so, permitted him to remain in Delhi and entrusted the city to his care. He himself returned to Ajmer.

Khwaja Gharib Nawaz married twice. He married Bibi Ummat-ul-lah in AH 590/AD 1194 during his stay in Ajmer. The children born out of this union are Khwaja Fakhr-ud-din, Khwaja Husam-ud-din, and Bibi Hafiz Jamal.[16]

The second marriage with Bibi Asmat-ul-lah, daughter of Syed Wajih-ud-din Mashhadi resulted in the birth of Hazrat Khwaja Zia-ud-din Abu Sa'id.

Death

On Monday, the sixth of Rajab in AH 627 (AD 21 May 1229) he closed the door of his tenement, and throughout the night the people outside heard a mystic sound emerge from it. At the approach of dawn, all was silent.

When the door remained closed at the time of morning-prayers, his devotees and disciples thought this strange. The door was opened, and there he lay, dead, and on his forehead were inscribed the words, which translated, run: "He was a beloved of God and he died in the love of God." His shrine, situated in Ajmer, is a centre of hope to myriads of people.

Caliphs

Hazrat Khwaja Qutb-ud-din Bakhtyar Kaki of Oosh is his premier spiritual caliph and *sajjadanashin* (spiritual successor).

Amongst his prominent caliphs, one may mention the following: Hazrat Khwaja Fakhr-ud-din Abul Khair, Sufi Hamid-ud-din of Nagore, Shaikh Moin-ud-din, Shaikh Wajih-ud-din, Shaikh Burhan-ud-din alias Buddu, Shaikh Ahmad, Shaikh Shams-ud-din Faqari, Abdullah Biyabani, Shaikh Nizam-ud-din of Nagore, Shaikh Mujadd-ud-din of Sanjar, and Shaikh Ali of Sanjar.

Traits of character

Khwaja Gharib Nawaz was very fond of music and fell unconscious in a state of rapture when listening to it. He always appeared to be solemn and sad, and had the utmost respect and regard for his spiritual guide and teacher. Very absorbed, he kept his eyes closed when lost in contemplation, but opened them at prayer time. He followed the precepts of the Holy Prophet in everyday life. Fear of God would cause him to tremble and weep and the dread of the last resting place, the grave, also dominated his thoughts. Sometimes he felt in an elevated mood and was then so much absorbed and lost in meditation that he was quite unmindful of what was going on around him. At other times, he was consumed by a pensive mood, and then he would close the door of his tenement in order to devote himself to contemplation.

He had a forgiving nature and showed love, regard, and respect to all, irrespective of caste, creed, or religion. He was cosmopolitan in outlook, and a man of generous disposition, taking pleasure in helping the poor and the needy.

He was renowned for his hospitality and entertained the people. Myriads of people of the city, with no ostensible means of subsistence, depended upon his *langar* (free distribution of food). He himself ate very little, fasting throughout the year, and wore patched clothes. Very fond of prayers, he would read the *Quran* twice a day. He took no rest or respite for seventy long years and was very particular about his ablutions.

He showed utmost concern for the well-being of his spiritual disciples, and was greatly loved by his spiritual guide and teacher Hazrat Khwaja Usman of Haroon who said of him: "Our Moin-ud-din is a beloved of God and I feel proud of the fact that he is my disciple."

He took to renunciation and self-abnegation.

Literary pursuits

Khwaja Gharib Nawaz was a great mystic poet and has left a collection of poems in Persian. Among his other books, all written in Persian, traced so far, are:

1. *Anis-ul-Arwah*
2. *Hadis-ul-Ma'arif*
3. *Risala Maujudia*
4. *Kanj-ul-Israr*
5. *Kashf-ul-Israr*
6. *Afaq-o-Anfas*

Teachings

Khwaja Gharib Nawaz was himself an institution. His company was a source of inspiration and illumination and his discourses reveal great spiritual insight. They are contained in a book entitled *Daleel-ul-Arefeen* written by his premier caliph and *sajjadanashin* Hazrat Khwaja Qutb-ud-din Bakhtyar Kaki of Oosh.

Mysticism and mystics: He says that "Mysticism is a name and not a custom." By merely being conversant with and studying mysticism, one does not become a sufi. It is the inner life, that marks one out as a mystic. A mystic must have an exact understanding of divine knowledge. He should surrender his will to the Will of God. He should be kind, hospitable, and courteous, devoid of any trace of haughtiness or arrogance or superiority. He should be content, meek and gentle, reposing his utmost trust in God.

The ambition to win disciples and to win applause or fame is foolish and vain. On the contrary, the essential ambition should be to be nearer to the Friend and to be accepted by the Friend.[17]

Discipleship: He says that a disciple must submit his whole self and will to his spiritual guide and teacher. "The spiritual disciple should," observes Khwaja Gharib Nawaz, "by earnestly following and obeying his spiritual guide, try to reach the place where the spiritual guide himself becomes the comb of his disciple."

A spiritual disciple then, should have as his motto, service, love of, obedience to, and faith in his spiritual guide and teacher in order to attain perfection.

Spiritual guide: As regards the spiritual guide, he says that he, indeed, is a guide, friend, and philosopher to his disciple, for his moral, spiritual, and ethical development.

Love: He says: "The path of love is such, that he who treads on it, loses his name and identity." According to him, "Love is all-embracing and all-pervading: the lover's heart is a fireplace of love. Whatever comes in it is burnt and becomes annihilated. There is no fire greater in intensity than the fire of love." The sign of true love is manifested in obedience to and the fear of the Friend.

As regards the repentance of lovers, he says that this is of three kinds. Firstly, it is due to shame; secondly to avoid sin; and thirdly to purify themselves by purging cruelty and enmity from within themselves. Genuine love rules out the idea of treating the Friend with a reserve. The springs of love are in God and not in us. Hence, love is divine.

Prayer: He emphasises the importance of prayer and says that it is a great necessity for the development of the soul.

He does not restrict prayer in its implications, expressions, and meaning, giving a broad connotation to the word "prayer." According to him, prayer consists in selfless service, sympathy, and fellow-feeling. Thus, helping the weak, the aggrieved, the needy, to feed the hungry, and to have the captive freed all constitute prayers.

He says that to see six things constitutes prayer for the mystic. Thus, to see one's own parents in the morning and *salaam* them; to see one's own children with love and affection; to see the Holy *Quran;* to see the face of the learned with respect; to see the gate of Ka'ba; to look towards the face of one's own spiritual guide and teacher and to devote oneself to his service together constitute prayer.

The enlightened: According to him, fear, respect, and shyness are the three things that go to make one enlightened.

The perfection of the enlightened depends upon the loss of the self. An enlightened being is said to be perfect only when all barriers separating him and the Friend are dismantled. Either he must live (in case, he does not to give up himself) or the Friend (when all barriers are removed and there is no separate self anymore).

Renunciation: He lays great emphasis on renunciation, holding that the object should be to have no objective. To lose an objective is to gain the objective.

A perfect dervish should remove from his heart the stain, stress and the burden of anything and everything. He should not give place in his heart to anything and anyone except God Almighty alone. He should not pursue any other object. He should desire nothing except God.

Fast: According to him, the real fast is the renunciation of all religious and worldly desires.

Music: He says that there are three conditions attached to *sama'* (music); these relating to time, place, and community of interest.

It is through *sama'* that the nearness of God is achieved. It confers love on the heart, it gives sincerity to the head, unity to the soul, service to the body, and vision to the eye.

Below are some of his sayings:

- The noise of the lover lasts only so long as he has not seen his beloved. Once he sees the beloved, he becomes calm and quiet, just as the rivers are boisterous before they join the ocean, but when they do so, they are becalmed forever.
- To acknowledge and to claim do not go together.
- Whatsoever he wishes comes before the enlightened and to whomsoever he talks, he gets a reply.
- The enlightened (*arif*) is ever steeped in the love of the Friend. If he stands, it is out of God's love; if he sits, he is busy in prayer; when he sleeps, his thoughts are fixed on Him, and when he awakes, His memory is fresh in his mind.
- He, indeed, is constant and firm in love who, voluntarily and with delight, accepts all troubles and pain inflicted by the Friend.
- The enlightened is he whose heart is a stranger to all save God.
- The enlightened is one who, if he may receive a hundred thousand visions, should not disclose any of them.
- To produce in him the attributes of God is, indeed the humblest thing that the enlightened can do. The greatest thing that the enlightened can do is to make the one guilty and to make him confess, who comes before him with claim, by his own spiritual powers. (The greatest thing that the *arif* can do, is to make the one, who comes before him with a claim, guilty by his own spiritual powers, i.e., he makes the claimant feel guilty because

he comes to realise that he was not, in fact trying to acquire the attributes of Allah.)

- The enlightened is one, who acquires all knowledge, gives myriads of meanings, and everytime dips in the ocean of meaning, so that he may take out from it the jewel of the secret of divine light; he may show such a jewel to the expert jewellers, so that they may like him and may come to know of him, as also one amongst the enlightened.
- The enlightened is one who is indifferent to both the worlds: this world and the world hereafter.
- The enlightened does not repose his trust in anybody except God. Accordingly, he does not pay attention to anyone else besides God.
- The trust reposed by the enlightened in God is such that it would appear that he is bewildered.
- It is characteristic of the enlightened that he is ever smiling. When he smiles, the angels come before him and he, seeing the angels, continues smiling.
- The contented one is one, who does not complain to anybody of any grievous wrong, pain, or sorrow caused by the people.
- The enlightened showers, like the sun, his rays of light on all the world. The entire world is brightened by his light.
- The eyes of the perfect enlightened one (can) see all that is in one's fate.
- The enlightened is distinguished by his outlook towards life. He keeps dear to his heart death, renounces the pleasures of life, and derives comfort and solace by remembrance of God alone.
- There are three things which go to make one an enlightened being, namely, fear, respect, and shyness.

  Fear to him means and implies that he is ever and again ashamed of his shortcomings.

  Respect to him means and implies, that he devotes himself exclusively to prayers.

  Shyness to him means and implies that he does not cast his looks on anybody else except God, the all-pervading.
- The last thing that the enlightened does, is to disdain wealth and splendour.
- The enlightened is an enemy of the world and a friend of God. Hence, he renounces the world and is above the trifles of life.
- The enlightened is one who does not implore any help from

anybody except God.

- The enlightened does not keep in his heart anything except remembrance of God. If he who realises God does not shun the people of the world, then he, indeed, is not blessed.
- A spiritual disciple should follow his spiritual guide and teacher faithfully and devotedly. He should carry out the behests of his spiritual guide and teacher, so that he may attain perfection.
- A dervish should be so close to God, that God may give him whatever he may want. If not, then he has no entitlement to be called a dervish.
- He who wants to be safe from the fire of hell and the fear of the Day of Resurrection should obey God. He should obey Him in every detail, for this is superior to any prayer, namely, to do justice to the aggrieved, to help the helpless, and to feed the hungry.
- Whosoever received a blessing, got it through generosity.
- The repentance of lovers is of three kinds. Firstly, shame; secondly, avoidance of sin; and thirdly, to purify themselves by purging cruelty and enmity from within themselves.
- The pious one is ever lost in the love of God. If he stands, it is out of God's love and if he sits, he is preoccupied with prayer. When he sleeps, his thoughts are fixed on him and when he awakes, His remembrance is fresh in his mind.
- Those verily are the lovers of God, who, if they offer morning prayers, are continually absorbed in the thought of the Friend till the next morning's prayer.
- The enlightened is one who does not keep anything dear to his heart, except remembrance of God.
- There is a time in the life of the contented, when they are enamoured of love, and if then they are torn asunder, they are quite unaware of it.
- There are such lovers of God, whom the love of God has so withdrawn that they are quite unaware of the existence of anything else in the world.
- He whose heart is enamoured of the love of God does not look in any direction in either of the worlds, and should he do so he forfeits his claim to be a true lover.
- He, indeed, is the true lover of God, who renounces from his heart the idea of both the worlds.
- He, alone, is the true lover of God, who severs his bond of love from his parents, brothers, and sons, and devotes himself

exclusively to God and His Prophet.

- He is a true lover, indeed, who welcomes with delight his sorrows and pain, received from his friend.
- The spiritual disciple deserves to be called a dervish only when he lives in the world of non-existence.
- When he comes on the path of love of the Friend, he becomes non-existent.
- There is nothing better in the world than the society of the mystics and the respect shown to the saints.
- The lovers of God directly hear the discourse of the Friend.
- The heart of the enlightened should be such that it may efface everything and may be exclusively devoted to the glorious vision of the Friend.
- It is through prayer, that the service of God is acquired.
- He, indeed, is in a prison house who claims to be pious.
- Be ever prepared for death.
- He who has love in his heart does not feel the least troubled by poverty, hunger, or asceticism.
- There are ten things necessary for a dervish, namely, the quest for God, search for a spiritual guide and teacher, respect, surrender, love, piety, constancy, perseverance, to eat less, to sleep less, seclusion, and last of all, prayer and fasting.
- Likewise, for the mystic also, there are ten things necessary, which are:

1. To acquire perfection in divine knowledge.
2. To be neither sorry and sad himself, nor to make others sorry and sad, nor to think evil of anybody.
3. To point the way towards God and to lead and guide the people towards the Ultimate Good.
4. To be hospitable.
5. To seek seclusion.
6. To pay respect and regard to everyone and to count himself as the humblest and the lowest.
7. To surrender his will to the Will of God.
8. To be patient and persevering in every grief and woe.
9. To be humble and meek.
10. To be contented and to repose trust in God.

Supernatural powers
The ruler of Subzawar, in Afghanistan, called Yadgar Mohammed was a profligate and a tyrant. He owned a garden with a beautiful fountain on the outskirts of the city. Khwaja Gharib Nawaz, on reaching Subzawar, entered the garden and offered prayers there. After praying he began reading the Holy *Quran*.

Yadgar Mohammed was to visit the garden and his servants requested Khwaja Gharib Nawaz to move on. He smiled and said to the servants: "If you are really afraid, go and sit under yonder tree and see what God Almighty does."

In the meanwhile, Yadgar Mohammed entered the garden. Seeing Khwaja Gharib Nawaz sitting there, he scolded his servants for having allowed him to sit there. Khwaja Gharib Nawaz lifted his face high. As soon as Yadgar Mohammed's gaze met Khwaja Sahab's eyes, Yadgar trembled and fainted.

His companions fell at the feet of Khwaja Gharib Nawaz, who, reciting the introductory words (in the Name of God, Most Gracious, Most Merciful) on water, sprinkled it over the face of Yadgar Mohammed. Having recovered his senses, Yadgar tended a respectful apology and, alongwith the members of his staff, became Khwaja Sahab's spiritual disciple.

Khwaja Gharib Nawaz conveyed a message of hope and victory to Sultan Shahab-ud-din Ghori. One night, Ghori saw in a dream that he was standing near Khwaja Gharib Nawaz, who said: "It has been ordained by God, that thou shalt be king of India. Direct thy attention soon." He emerged victorious in the battle that ensued.

Maulana Zia-ud-din of Balkh had no faith in saints. When in Balkh, Khwaja Gharib Nawaz happened to pass by the garden owned by him, uttering the introductory words (in the Name of God, Most Gracious, Most Merciful), Khwaja Gharib Nawaz offered one thigh of a roasted chicken to the Maulana. As soon as he ate it, he became unconscious. When he recovered his senses, he found himself a changed man. He, alongwith his pupils, became a spiritual disciple of Khwaja Gharib Nawaz.

Once, the mother of a person who had been hanged came to Khwaja Gharib Nawaz and sought his assistance. He, with a stick in his hand, reached the gallows alongwith the mother of the deceased and pointing the stick towards the dead body, said: "If thou art innocent come to life by the command of God Almighty and come down from the gallows." He, instantaneously, came to life. Coming down from the gallows, he put his head upon his feet.

After the death of Khwaja Gharib Nawaz, the supernatural and the mystical powers have not ceased to manifest themselves. Once Hazrat Baba Farid-ud-din Mas'ud Ganj-e-Shakar came to the *mazar* (holy shrine) of Khwaja Gharib Nawaz and began to recite the Holy *Quran*. He forgot to recite one word in Sura Kahf and Sura Maryam. Suddenly he heard a voice emanating from the grave, pointing out to him that he had omitted one word and that he should read correctly.

After a lapse of centuries, his tomb is visited every year by thousands of people from all over the world.

What Bethlehem is to the Christians, what Varanasi (Benares) is to the Hindus, what Gaya is to the Buddhists, that or more Ajmer is to the Mussalmans (Muslims) inhabiting the Indo-Pakistan subcontinent and Bangladesh and is rightfully known as the "Medina of Indo-Pakistan."

Why, this is so, is obvious. It is the last resting place of Khwaja Gharib Nawaz.

References

1. *Masalek-us-Salekeen*, vol. II, p. 271.
2. *Siyar-ul-Aqtab*, p. 101; *Khazinat-ul-Asfia*, vol. I, p. 232.
3. Mirat-ul-Israr (MS.); *Iqtibas-ul-Anwar*, p. 144; *Mirat-ul-Ansab*, p. 160.
4. *Masalek-us-Salekeen*, vol. II, p. 196; *Ahsan-us-Siyar*, pp. 3, 133.
5. *Siyar-ul-Arefeen*, p. 5.
6. Ibid., p. 5; *Siyar-ul-Aqtab*, pp. 101-2; *Masalek-us-Salekeen*, vol. II, p. 273.
7. *Ahsan-us-Siyar*, p. 134; *Daleel-ul-Arefeen*, p. 74; *Khazinat-ul-Asfia*, vol. II, p. 257.
8. *Siyar-ul-Aqtab*, p. 106; *Ahsan-us-Siyar*, p. 134.
9. *Siyar-ul-Aqtab*, p. 106.
10. *Anis-ul-Arwah*, pp. 2-3.
11. Ibid., p. 3.
12. *Masalek-us-Salekeen*, vol. II, p. 275.
13. *Anis-ul-Arwah*, p. 34.
14. *Masalek-us-Salekeen*, vol. II, p. 275.
15. *Anis-ul-Arwah*, p. 34.
16. *Ahsan-us-Siyar*, p. 159; *Waqia'a-e-Shah Moin-ud-din*, p. 53.
17. *The Mystical Philosophy of Khwaja Moin-ud-din Hasan Chishti.*

2

Hazrat Khwaja Qutb-ud-din Bakhtyar Kaki

Hazrat Khwaja Qutb-ud-din Bakhtyar Kakí was a gem amongst the saints of the Indian subcontinent. He is the spiritual disciple, premier caliph, and spiritual successor of Hazrat Khwaja Moin-ud-din Hasan Chishti. He is the spiritual guide and teacher of Hazrat Baba Farid-ud-din Mas'ud Ganj-e-Shakar.

He traces his descent from Syedna Hazrat Imam Husain, son of Hazrat Ali (son-in-law of the holy Prophet Mohammed), and is, therefore, a Husaini.

His paternal genealogy is as follows:

> Khwaja Qutb-ud-din son of Syed Moosa son of Kamal-ud-din son of Syed Ahmad son of Syed Mohammed son of Syed Ahmed son of Ishaq Hasan son of Syed Maroof son of Syed Ahmed son of Syed Razi-ud-din son of Syed Hisam-ud-din son of Syed Rashid-ud-din son of Syed Abdullah Jaffer Maroof Ali-al-Naqi son of Syedna Naqi-al-Javvad Abu Jaffer son of Syedna Ali Raza son of Syedna Musa Kazim son of Syedna Jaffer Sadiq son of Syedna Abu Jaffer son of Syedna Mohammed Baqar son of Syedna Imam Zain-ul-Abedeen son of Syedna Imam Husain, son of Syedna Imam-ul-Auliya Hazrat Ali.

Hazrat Qutb Sahab was born in Oosh in AH 569. This birthplace has been traced by some to the vicinity of Baghdad.[1] Some have traced it to trans-Jordan[2] and others situate it near Farghana.[3]

He was born in the middle of the night, a brightness lighting up the whole house and a strange light being caste all around. After his birth he prostrated himself in adoration and uttered the words "Allah, Allah." After sometime he raised his head. The light disappeared.

His name is Qutb-ud-din, although some believe that his name is

Bakhtyar and that Qutb-ud-din is the title conferred upon him by God. Actually the real reason why he is called Bakhtyar is that his spiritual guide and teacher Hazrat Khwaja Moin-ud-din Hasan Chishti used to call him by that name and he became known by it.

There are several reasons for calling him "Kaki," which means "man of bread." When he settled in Delhi, he had no ostensible means of subsistence. His wife used to borrow from the wife of a certain person named Sharf-ud-din and repay it when she was able to do so. Once Sharf-ud-din's wife commented that should she refuse to grant a loan, she and her husband would be reduced to penury. His wife was offended by the tone and temper of Sharf-ud-din's wife and stopped borrowing money from her. When this was mentioned to Hazrat Qutb Sahab, he emphatically told his wife not to borrow any money in future. He suggested that in time of need, on uttering the words "in the Name of God, Most Gracious, Most Merciful," bread could be had from the niche of the tenement. His wife did so, but when she informed Sharf-ud-din's wife of this, bread was no longer forthcoming.

There is another reason for his being called "Kaki." Once Hazrat Nizam-ud-din Auliya explained it to Hazrat Amir Khusrau:

> One day Hazrat Qutb Sahab was sitting by the Hauz-e-Shamsi surrounded by his devotees. It was blowing very cold. The devotees submitted that it would be very nice indeed to have hot bread. Hazrat Qutb Sahab, on hearing this, got into the water, brought out hot bread and gave it to the devotees. Since that day he began to be called "Kaki."

Early life and education

He lost his father when he was a year and an half old. The entire responsibility of his education and training now fell upon his mother's shoulders.

Hazrat Khwaja Moin-ud-din Hasan Chishti, during the course of tours and travels, reached Oosh. Qutb Sahab's mother sent him to Hazrat Khwaja Sahab for the *Bismillah* ceremony. At that time, he was four years, four months, and four days old. Hazrat Khwaja Gharib Nawaz was about to write the slate of Hazrat Qutb Sahab when, suddenly he received inspiration and said: "O Khwaja, wait a little, Qazi Hamid-ud-din of Nagore is reaching soon and he will write the slate of our Qutb and impart education to him."

Khwaja Gharib Nawaz acted accordingly. In the meanwhile,

Hazrat Qazi Hamid-ud-din of Nagore reached thereby the dint of his spiritual powers and performed the Bismillah ceremony.

Hazrat Qutb Sahab, it is said, had learned the fifteen parts of the Holy *Quran* by inspiration and Hazrat Qazi Hamid-ud-din of Nagore taught him the remaining portion, and he was therefore able to learn the entire Holy *Quran* within four days.

At the age of five, his mother sent him alongwith a servant to the *maktab* (school) of the locality. On the way, a certain person met them and suggested: "This boy should be taken to Maulana Aba Hafs for education as he is an experienced, highly educated and trained teacher. He alone is fit to impart education to him."

When he reached there, he requested Maulana Aba Hafs "to educate the child properly as very many things await his attention," and having left him in his care the stranger left. The Maulana then asked the servant whether he knew the stranger, to which the servant replied in the negative. Thereupon, Maulana Aba Hafs said: "He was Hazrat Khwaja Khizr."[4]

Hazrat Qutb Sahab left Oosh in search of Truth. He reached a city where he stayed for sometime. He wanted to meet Hazrat Khwaja Khizr, and so he visited a mosque some distance from the city. At the mosque, he met someone who inquired from him why he had come there. He replied that the inward urge to meet Khwaja Khizr had brought him there. The person asked: "Do you want the world?" Hazrat Qutb Sahab replied in the negative. "Then are you in debt?" Again a negative answer.

During the course of the conversation, a person came out of the mosque and, catching hold of the hands of Hazrat Qutb Sahab, he addressed the person engaged in conversation, saying:

"Neither does he want the world, nor is he in debt. He only wants to meet you." Hearing this, Hazrat Qutb Sahab was immensely pleased. He now realised that the person with whom he was engaged in conversation was Hazrat Khizr himself. All of a sudden, the two persons disappeared.

Initiation into the Sufi order AH *582/*AD *1186*

He wanted to be a spiritual disciple of Shaikh Mahmud of Isfahan but God willed otherwise. During the course of his tours and travels, Hazrat Khwaja Moin-ud-din Hasan Chishti reached Isfahan. When Qutb Sahab went to see him, he was so fascinated, that he became his disciple. Hazrat Khwaja Gharib Nawaz gave him the clothes he was wearing.[5]

Hazrat Khwaja Gharib Nawaz honoured him by appointing him as his spiritual successor and caliph in the mosque of Abul Lais of Samarqand in AH 585. The ceremony was witnessed by such eminent saints and sufis as Hazrat Shaikh Shahab-ud-din Suhrawardy, Shaikh Daud of Kirman, Shaikh Burhan-ud-din Mohammed Chishti, and Shaikh Taj-ud-din Mohammed of Isfahan.

In the company of his spiritual guide, he undertook tours and travels, going to Mecca, Medina, and Baghdad. Alongwith his spiritual guide and teacher Hazrat Khwaja Gharib Nawaz, he left Baghdad in AH 586/AD 1190, visiting Chisht, Herat, Sabzawar, Lahore, Samana, and Delhi. From Delhi, he reached Ajmer in AH 587.

After staying in Ajmer for sometime, he went to Oosh to see his mother. On hearing the news of the arrival of Khwaja Gharib Nawaz in Ajmer a second time, he left Oosh for India.

On the way to Delhi, he stopped in Multan in AH 590/AD 1194. During his stay in Multan, Hazrat Baba Farid-ud-din Ganj-e-Shakar became his spiritual disciple.

In Delhi, his spiritual guide and teacher Hazrat Khwaja Gharib Nawaz came to see him, showering his blessings on him and on his spiritual disciples; particularly on Hazrat Baba Farid-ud-din Ganj-e-Shakar, who was in Delhi at that time. Subsequently, Hazrat Baba Farid-ud-din Ganj-e-Shakar, with the permission of his spiritual guide and teacher Hazrat Qutb Sahab, left for Hansi. Hazrat Qutb Sahab reached Oosh in AH 602 to see his ageing mother.[6] He left for Baghdad, where he met with Hazrat Shaikh Shahab-ud-din Umar Suhrawardi, Shaikh Uhad-ud-din of Kirman, and other saints.[7] He learnt from Hazrat Jalal-ud-din of Tabriz, that Hazrat Khwaja Moin-ud-din Hasan Chishti had left Khorasan for India and that he was staying in Delhi, whereupon he left for India to offer his respects to his spiritual guide and teacher. Hazrat Shaikh Jalal-ud-din of Tabriz accompanied him. They eventually reached Multan during the reign of Sultan Iltutmish in AH 611/AD 1214. The officer-in-charge of Multan, Qubacha Beg, requested him to stay there permanently, which he refused saying that it was a place meant for the activities of Hazrat Shaikh Baha-ud-din Zakariya and, moreover, it was for his spiritual guide and teacher to decide his future permanent place of residence.[8]

He reached Delhi in AH 611/AD 1214 and stayed in Kilokri. Sultan Shams-ud-din Iltutmish requested him to stay in Mehrauli instead of Kilokri, which was quite distant, and this he was pleased to do.

He came to Mehrauli and stayed with a cook who was a devotee of his. Subsequently, Hazrat Qazi Hamid-ud-din of Nagore prevailed and brought him to his house. After staying there a while, he moved his residence to the neighbourhood of E'zaz-ud-din mosque.

After the death of Hazrat Jamal-ud-din Mohammed Bustami of Delhi, the post of Shaikh-ul-Islam fell vacant. Sultan Iltutmish requested Hazrat Qutb Sahab to accept the post, but he declined, whereupon the Sultan appointed Shaikh Najm-ud-din Sughra to the post.[9]

On one occasion he wrote to his spiritual guide and teacher Hazrat Khwaja Gharib Nawaz seeking permission to see him, to which the former responded: "Apparently you are at a distance from me, but inwardly you are close to me. Remain where you are."[10]

Hazrat Khwaja Gharib Nawaz himself went to Delhi in AH 611/ AD 1214 and stayed at the monastery of Khwaja Qutb Sahab, and then again went to Delhi a second time during the reign of Sultan Iltutmish in AH 621/AD 1224. On the second occasion, Khwaja Gharib Nawaz wanted to bring Qutb Sahab to Ajmer, but on the representation of the people of Delhi desisted. Having lived Delhi for sometime, Qutb Sahab got restless and wanted to pay his respects to Hazrat Khwaja Gharib Nawaz. He wrote to him accordingly and this time his request was granted. Reaching Ajmer, he devoted himself to the service of his spiritual guide and teacher. Describing the details of their last meeting, he says: "Saying this, Hazrat Khwaja began to weep." He said to me "O dervish, the reason why I am planted here on the face of this earth is this, that my grave will be raised here. In a few days, I shall be passing away."

As regards the holy relics, Hazrat Qutub Sahab says:[11]

> Shaikh Ali of Sanjar was present. He was ordered to write the *farman* and hand it over to our Shaikh Qutb-ud-din Bakhtyar Kaki, so that he may proceed to Delhi. I confer upon him the caliphate and suggest Delhi as a place for his residence.
>
> When the *farman* was completed, it was handed over to me. I bowed. I was ordered to come near. I went nearer to him. He placed with his own hand the turban and the cap on my head. He gave me the Holy *Quran* and the praying carpet. Then, addressing me said: 'This is the sacred trust of the Holy Prophet, which has reached us through the Chishti Khwajas. I am entrusting it to you. It is incumbent upon you to keep these things in a way as we have kept them, so that

on the Day of Resurrection I may not feel ashamed before the Khwajas.'
I offered respects again and offered two genuflexions. Then he said: 'Go, I have entrusted thee to God and have caused thee to reach the place of honour and respect.'

Hazrat Khwaja Gharib Nawaz, asked him to act upon five things, which are a source of blessing:

The first thing is to become such a type of dervish, who may pose to be rich.
The second thing is to feed the hungry.
The third thing is to express joy in time of grief.
The fourth thing is to repay friendship in spite of enmity.
The fifth thing is to hear the complaints of the distressed and to stand by them.

He returned to Delhi and passed his remaining days there. Twenty days after his return from Ajmer, his spiritual guide and teacher Hazrat Khwaja Gharib Nawaz passed away. He saw him in a dream, and asking how he was, was told: "God has been Merciful enough as to shower His Blessings upon me. He has allotted me a place near the angels and the inhabitants of the throne. I live here."

Marriage and children
He married twice. He married first in Oosh, but divorced his wife three days after marriage because it prevented him from reciting benedictions to the Holy Prophet Mohammed as he had hitherto done three thousand times every night when going to bed.

He married a second time in Delhi. Two sons were born, one named Khwaja Ahmed and the other Shaikh Mohammed who died at the age of seven.

He breathed his last when attending a music concert on the fourteenth of Rabi-ul-Awwal in AH 633 corresponding to the twenty-seventh of November 1235. The funeral prayers were led by Sultan Shams-ud-din Iltutmish. His tomb in Mehrauli near New Delhi is a site of veneration and devotion.

Some of his caliphs
Hazrat Baba Farid-ud-din Ganj-e-Shakar was his premier caliph

and spiritual successor. Some of his other spiritual caliphs are: Shaikh Badr-ud-din of Ghazni; Shaikh Burhan-ud-din of Balkh; Maulana Fakhr-ud-din Halwai; Shaikh Husain; Shaikh Firoz; Shaikh Badr-ud-din Mootab; Shah Khizr Qalandar, and Shaikh Sa'd-ud-din.

Traits of character

He occupies a position of pre-eminence among the saints of the Indian subcontinent, next only to that of his spiritual guide and teacher Hazrat Khwaja Moin-ud-din Hasan Chishti. Hazrat Shaikh Abdul Haq Muhaddis of Delhi writes of him:[12] "He is one of the eminent saints and outstanding sufis."

All the saints and the sufis of his time held him in deep respect and reposed faith in him. His prayers were accepted. It is said that whatever he foretold actually happened. Whoever had the privilege of his company became a saint.[13]

He was deeply devoted to prayer, and prayed regularly five times a day. Having committed the Holy *Quran* to memory, he recited the whole of it everyday. Besides this, he undertook three hundred genuflexions daily,[14] and before going to bed, he offered benedictions to the Holy Prophet Mohammed three thousand times.

He was a man of retiring habits. He ate and talked little and slept little. He did not mix much with the people. Hazrat Mohammed Gesoo Daraz says, that he was always withdrawn, sombre, spending much time in tears. He kept awake all night long in the latter part of his life.[15] He passed his days in poverty. Sometimes, he and members of his family did not have anything eat but he did not reveal this to anyone.[16] In the early part of his life, he had no dining carpet, dish, or cup.

He would not accept offerings made to him. Once, Sultan Shams-ud-din Iltutmish sent him some silver and gold coins, but he refused to accept them.[17]

He followed the tenets of his spiritual guides and teachers and spiritual ancestors very strictly. Once, a minister of Sultan Iltutmish waited upon him and offered him a *farman* granting six villages and a trayful of gold coins on behalf of his master. He smiled and said:

> My Spiritual Guide and spiritual ancestors have not accepted such things. I, too cannot accept them. If I do not follow them today and in contravention of their practice, accept the villages and the gold coins, then how shall I show my face to them

tomorrow (on the Day of Resurrection) and how shall I join them in their fold....

He was deeply absorbed in meditation much of the time.[18]

His trust in God was unique. He had nothing to do with anybody, and for the expenses of his kitchen, he would point in some direction and money would become available according to the need. For the expenses of the sufis, he would take out some gold coins from beneath the praying carpet and spend them all. He did not make his prayers and asceticism public and enjoined this on his spiritual disciples.

He was very fond of music. Sometimes, in a state of rapture, he would remain unconscious for several days.

Hazrat Qutb Sahab was a man of literary taste and was also a poet. He has written the following books in Persian:

(1) *Daleel-ul-Arefeen,* a collection of the discourses of his spiritual guide and teacher Hazrat Khwaja Gharib Nawaz; (2) *Zibdat-ul-Haqa'iq;* and (3) *Risala.*

Among his poetic works are: (1) *Masnavi* and (2) *Diwan,* a collection of his poems.

Some of his teachings are given below:

- The spiritual guide and teacher should possess so much power, that when a seeker comes to him for acceptance as a spiritual disciple, he may eradicate all the lust of the world from his heart and may so purify his heart that any lust, rust, and attachment to the world does not remain. Subsequently, by enlisting him as his disciple he may unite him with God. If the spiritual guide does not possess such power then it should be understood that the spiritual guide and the spiritual disciple are both in the vortex of darkness.[19]
- According to the enlightened, an individual attains perfection by four things, namely, sleeping less, talking less, eating less, and mixing less with the people.

  Turning to Baba Farid-ud-din Ganj-e-Shakar he said: "O dervish, unless you eat little, sleep little, talk little, and mix less with the people, you will never acquire the essence of spiritualism. The class of dervishes is such a class, who have not allowed themselves sleep and who take the society of people as worse than snakes and serpents."

- When the non-believer placed a knife at the throat of Prophet Yahya and began to pierce it, he was about to cry out of sheer agony. At that instant angel Gabriel came to him and conveyed to him the message of God to the effect that if he did so, his name would be wiped off from the list of prophets. On hearing the command of God, he was perfectly calm and with the utmost calm handed over his life to the Creator.[20]
- It was the habit of Hazrat Rabia of Basra that when some misfortune befell her, she was happy and would say that the Friend had remembered her; otherwise she felt defected and sad wondering why the Friend had not remembered her.[21]
- In Baghdad, a dervish was brought before the Qazi on some charge and was sentenced to death. The executioner took him to the place of execution and as usual, made him to sit with his face towards the *qibla*. The dervish turned his face from the direction of the *qibla* and sat with his face towards the direction of the tomb of his spiritual guide and teacher. The executioner said to him that at the time of death, his face should be turned towards the *qibla*, to which the dervish responded: "You busy yourself with your own work. I have turned my face towards my *qibla*. This controversy was still raging when in the meanwhile the order of the caliph was conveyed by a messenger, that the dervish had been pardoned and should be let off."
  Commenting on this episode, Hazrat Qutb Sahab said: "Look, his strength of faith saved him from the gallows."[22]

Some of his sayings are:

- The enlightened is one who may experience strange conditions every moment and every hour, and he may be so absorbed that if at that moment the earth and every other thing enters his breast, he may be quite unmindful of their so entering therein.
- For the enlightened, no curtain is greater than the world itself. The path of enlightenment requires courage of a very high order, so that the secrets may gain ground and may not be exposed, for the secret is the mystery of the Friend.
- The claimant of love who complains in time of trouble is not sincere in love, but on the contrary, is a pretender and a liar.
- He, who is perfect does not expose the secret of the Friend.

- When the dervish becomes perfect, whatever he wills that happens.
- The dervish will never attain the position of nearness, unless and until, he becomes a stranger to all his friends and relatives and takes to renunciation and frees himself from the attachment of the world.
- The dervish who eats to his heart's content, out of desire of self, is a worshipper of the self and not a dervish at all.
- Sainthood is not a pleasure, but implies embroilment in the troubles of the world.
- The spiritual guide and teacher should possess so much power, that he is able to clean the darkness within the heart of his disciple by the dint of his inward power and may cause him to reach God.
- The spiritual disciple must remain the same in the presence and absence of his spiritual guide and teacher, and after his passing away may show him greater respect.
- Whatever pleasure there is in music, is not contained in any other thing and that such a condition cannot be attained without music.
- The manifestation of supernatural powers will deprive one of the remaining stages of life.[23]

Supernatural powers

During his stay in Multan, the officer-in-charge of Multan, Nasir-ud-din Kubacha Beg, came to him and submitted: "The Moghuls are near Multan. They want to take over the city. It is difficult for me to face them. For God's sake, help me." Hazrat Qutb Sahab then gave him an arrow and directed him to shoot it with a bow towards the marauding Moghul hordes, from the tower, after the evening prayers.

Kubacha Beg did so and the Moghuls dispersed and went their way.

One day, a music concert was being held at the residence of Hazrat Qazi Hamid-ud-din of Nagore at which Qazi Sahab was in a state of rapture. Qazi Sadiq and Qazi Imad, who enjoyed a position of pre-eminence in the social and literary circles of Delhi then, reached the residence of Hazrat Qazi Hamid-ud-din of Nagore. At the time, Hazrat Qutb Sahab was about eighteen years old and his beard had not then grown.

The two incumbents in office, Qazi Sadiq and Qazi Imad, said to him: "Is it not according to the sufis, that a woman is not allowed to participate in a music concert?" In response to this, uttering the words, "In the Name of God, Most Gracious, Most Merciful," Qutb Sahab rubbed both his hands over his face.

As he did so, a beard became visible.

Addressing them, he said: "I am not a woman, but a man." They were greatly surprised on seeing such a manifestation of the supernatural powers.

References

1. *Solat-e-Afghan.*
2. *Siyar-ul-Arefeen.*
3. *Masalek-us-Salekeen.*
4. *Firishta,* vol. 2: chapter on Qutb Sahab.
5. *Siyar-ul-Arefeen,* p. 7.
6. *Masalek-us-Salekeen,* vol. 2.
7. Ibid.
8. *Firishta,* vol. 2.
9. *Masalek-us-Salekeen.*
10. *Safinat-ul-Auliya,* p. 95; *Masalek-us-Salekeen,* vol. 2, p. 299; *Khazinat-ul-Asfia,* vol. I, p. 268.
11. *Daleel-ul-Arefeen,* p. 56.
12. *Akhbar-ul-Akhyar.*
13. *Siyar-ul-Aqtab,* p. 142.
14. *Mirat-ul-Isrart.*
15. *Jawame-ul-Kalm.*
16. *Siyar-ul-Auliya.*
17. *Rahat-ul-Qulub.*
18. *Tazkarat-ul-Asfiya.*
19. *Israr-ul-Arefeen.*
20. *Fawaid-us-Salekeen.*
21. Ibid.
22. Ibid.
23. Ibid.

3

Hazrat Khwaja Fakhr-ud-din Abul-Khair

Hazrat Khwaja Fakhr-ud-din Abul-Khair was the eldest son of Hazrat Khwaja Moin-ud-din Hasan Chishti.[1] He was born in AH 591 and his father chose to settle in a village, known as Mandal, situated three miles from Ajmer. When his reverend father, Khwaja Gharib Nawaz was leaving for Delhi a second time, during the reign of Sultan Iltutmish, he implored him to plead on his behalf for the free grant of the village and this was granted.

He had five sons,[2] and he was a perfect dervish, well-versed in temporal and spiritual knowledge.[3]

Hazrat Khwaja Fakhr-ud-din Abul-Khair passed away on the fifth of Sha'ban in AH 661.[4] At the time of his death, he was seventy years old and was buried in Sarwar.[5]

References

1. *Ahsan-us-Siyar,* pp. 159-60.
2. *Tazkara Auliya-e-Hind,* p. 19; *Moin-ul-Auliya,* p. 126.
3. *Khazeenat-ul-Asfiya,* vol. I, p. 284; *Ahsan-us-Siyar,* p. 159.
4. *Marat-un-Nisab,* p.162.
5. *Masalek-us-Saleekeen,* vol. II, p. 196.

4

Hazrat Qazi Hamid-ud-din of Nagore

Hazrat Qazi Hamid-ud-din of Nagore was a renowned saint and sage of the Indian subcontinent and had the unique privilege and honour of being the teacher of Hazrat Khwaja Qutb-ud-din Bakhtyar Kaki. He belonged to the royal family of Bukhara, his father, Ataullah Mahmud, being its ruler. He was born in the year AH 463 and was named Mohammed.

Once, when in Medina, from the court of the Holy Prophet Mohammed, he received the title "Qazi Hamid-ud-din Nagori," and it was under this title that he won widespread fame.

He was brought up under the vigilant care of the sultan, his father. His father took great interest in his education and training. Partly due to love and partly on account of old age, the Sultan abdicated in his son's favour, and the latter began performing his duties of office with ability, grace, and charm. Hazrat Qazi Sahab was fifty-two years old then.

His wife, Bibi Mahroo, died to his deep grief, and this untimely bereavement brought about a change in Qazi Sahab, endowing him with a philosophical turn of mind. Meditating in solitude, he would ponder about the mysteries of life and death. He realised that the world is not lasting; everything is mortal. Such being the nature of creation, it is best to concentrate on the Creator. As an escape from the brittle realities of life, he was advised to go out to hunt and shoot, and did so. Once he wounded a deer. The deer, to his amazement began to speak: "O dear one. Thou art the creation of God. Why hast thou wounded me who is innocent. How wilt thou account for it to thy Creator." These words were sufficient. He returned to his palace, abdicated the throne, and went out in search of Truth.

Together with his father, he left Bukhara for Kirman. There he stayed with Khwaja Abu Bakr of Kirman, and married his daughter

Bibi Hamira. Then he left his dependents in Kirman and went out with his father in search of Truth.

Hazrat Khwaja Khizr was ordained by God Almighty to impart divine knowledge to him. He, Hazrat Khwaja Khizr, accordingly kept him for twelve long years and imparted the knowledge ordained. Having so completed his education, he was asked by Hazrat Khizr to proceed to Baghdad.

Reaching Baghdad, he became a spiritual disciple of a famous sufi saint of his time, Hazrat Shahab-ud-din Umar Suhrawardi. His spiritual guide and teacher honoured him by confiding to him the holy cloak of the Holy Prophet Mohammed and he was subsequently elevated to the rank of a caliph.

He left Baghdad for Mecca. After having made the pilgrimage, he proceeded to Medina where he stayed for a year, two months, and seven days. During his stay there, the title "Qazi Hamid-ud-din Nagori" was conferred upon him. He did not know where Nagore was situated, but once he learnt that Nagore was in India, he determined to go there.

From Medina he reached Mecca where he performed *hajj* and stayed for three years. He left Mecca for Baghdad and there offered his respects to his spiritual guide and teacher, and then proceeded to India, taking the holy cloak with him, and was accompanied by his father, his wife and children. On the way, he stayed in Kirman and then for sometime in Pashoor, leaving his father and the rest of his family there, and eventually reached India alongwith Hazrat Khwaja Moin-ud-din Hasan Chishti.

He reached Nagore in AH 561, and stayed there with an old woman, an oil seller. Here, his doctrine of truth was universally accepted. One day, when in Nagore, he received the following inspiration: "Reach Oosh and educate Our Qutb." Reaching Oosh, he performed the *Bismillah* ceremony of Hazrat Qutb Sahab. Together with his father, wife and children, he left for Delhi. There, he purchased the house of a washerman and began living there. His father died in Delhi.

Music concerts in Delhi

Hazrat Khwaja Qutb-ud-din Bakhtyar Kaki and Hazrat Qazi Sahab held music concerts in Delhi. Qazi Sa'd and Qazi Imad raised objections to this. After discussions, it was decided that Hazrat Qazi Sahab should go to Baghdad and introduce music concerts first, and then there would be no ground for any objection as regards music in Delhi.

The latter therefore left for Baghdad and stayed with one of his spiritual disciples but music concerts were strictly prohibited there. Eventually, it was decided that music concerts were allowed to those who were deserving of them, and such people could be recognised only by those with requisite merit. After the acceptance of his assertion concerning music concerts in Baghdad, he began to hear music concerts in Delhi, in spite of opposition. He was appointed as Qazi of Nagore by Sultan Shamsud-din Iltutmish and remained in office for three years, laying the foundations of the town of "Rohal." Subsequently, he entrusted his office to his second son, Maulana Zahir-ud-din.

After performing the pilgrimage in Mecca and after visiting Medina, he passed the rest of his life in Delhi. He breathed his last on the ninth of Ramazan in AH 643 at the ripe age of a hundred and eighty years. He was buried in Mehrauli, New Delhi.

His caliphs: Shaikh Ahmed Neharwaley, Shaikh Ain-ud-din Qassab, Shaikh Shahi Mooetab, and Shaikh Mahmud Moenna Dooz.

Traits of character

Besides being an eminent saint, he was one of the most learned men of his time, endowed with the knowledge of both outward and the inward life. He was very fond of music.[1] He is the author of seventy-two books, chief amongst which are: *Tawaileh-us-shamoos Sharh; Asma-e-Husna; Laa Meh; Lawaney; Mataley Sharh Chehal Hadis; Kitab Haft Ahbab*, and his *Risala*. Some of his teachings are the followings:[2]

- He who has no relation with God, does not impress people with his word.
- There are four *qiblas*. Firstly, there is the *qibla* binding upon all the Muslims, towards which they face and offer their prayers. Secondly, there is the *qibla* of the heart, in which the mystics are engaged. Thirdly, there is the *qibla* of the *pir* (spiritual guide), which implies that spiritual disciples should pay attention to their spiritual guide. Fourthly, there is the *qibla* of the face of God, the most important among the *qiblas*. The Prophets and all the eminent saints pay attention to this.

Some of his sayings are:

- Forgetfulness of self is the remembrance of God. The heart imbibing this quality does not die. He who does not engage himself in the remembrance of God dies.[3]
- Utmost love and fondness constitute the state of the dervishes. When love prevails, the dervishes are so lost in the vision of the Friend that at that time they are unmindful of anyone else.
- The outward fast implies abstinence from eating and drinking. The real fast implies engagement in prayer at all times, whether in sleep or wakefulness, standing or sitting.

Supernatural powers

When coming from Baghdad to Delhi, he met a yogi on the way who offered him the root of some grass used in alchemy. He threw it into the river. The yogi lamented the loss, whereupon Qazi Sahab took it out of the river and asked the yogi to close his eyes. When he opened them he could see from the throne up to the antipodes. In every direction there appeared to be gold. The yogi was so deeply moved by the result that he became his spiritual disciple.

Once, as there was no rain in Delhi, the king requested the saints to pray for it. Hazrat Qazi Sahab asked for a music concert, so the king arranged food and music. As soon as the music concert began, after the food had been consumed, the rain began to fall in torrents.[4]

References

1. *Fawaid-ul-Fu'ad*, p. 195.
2. *Risala* (Qazi Hamid-ud-din of Nagore).
3. *Anwar-ul-Auliya*.
4. *Khair-ul-Majalis*, p. 30.

5

Hazrat Sufi Hamid-ud-din of Nagore

Hazrat Sufi Hamid-ud-din was a spiritual disciple and caliph of Hazrat Khwaja Moin-ud-din Hasan Chishti. He traced his descent from Hazrat Sa'd, son of Zaid, a companion of the Holy Prophet Mohammed. He was born in AH 568/AD 1172.

His name is Hamid-ud-din, Abu Mohammed his nickname. His spiritual guide and teacher, Hazrat Khwaja Moin-ud-din Hasan Chishti, conferred upon him the title of "Sultan-ut-Tarekeen" or the king of those who have taken to renunciation.

Hazrat Hamid-ud-din used to live in a village called Sawali, now known as Phagli.[1] He owned a plot of land in the village which he cultivated to maintain his dependents. He died in AH 673/AD 1273 and was buried in Nagore.[2]

Traits of character

Hazrat Sufi Hamid-ud-din belongs to a galaxy of ancient saints and was a very learned man of his time, possessing all the mystic qualities. He was a poet and wrote a number of books, the most famous one entitled *Usul-ut-Tariqa*.

According to him, the first requisite of the spiritual path is knowledge, the second practice. The other requisites are intention, sincerity, love, attention, enlightenment, and lastly the opening of the gate, so that the object may appear.

References

1 *Akhbar-ul-Akhyar.*

2 *Khazinat-ul-Asfiya,* vol. I, p. 309; *Siyar-ul-Arefeen,* p. 13.

6

Hazrat Shaikh Badr-ud-din Ghaznavi

Hazrat Shaikh Badr-ud-din Ghaznavi was the spiritual disciple and caliph of Qutb-ul-Aqtab Hazrat Khwaja Qutb-ud-din Bakhtyar Kaki.

His dream

He once dreamt that the Holy Prophet Mohammed, surrounded by his companions and eminent saints, was sitting at a certain place. The Holy Prophet took his hand and entrusted it to a dervish, saying: "O Badr-ud-din, be a disciple of this dervish." The dervish was young, his beard was just sprouting, and was named Khwaja Qutb-ud-din. When he awoke, he made a firm resolve that he would search out that dervish and would enlist himself as his spiritual disciple. He left home and roamed from city to city in search of the person he had seen in his dream.

He himself once related the details of the journey to Hazrat Nizam-ud-din Auliya:[1]

> When I reached Lahore from Ghazni, I found Lahore a populated city. I stayed there for sometime. Then I thought of leaving. I was not sure which way to take. Sometimes I wished to proceed to Delhi and sometimes I thought of returning to Ghazni. I was in a flux.
>
> My heart was greatly attracted to Ghazni, because there my mother, father, brother and other relatives resided. In contrast, there was nobody in Delhi except my son-in-law.
>
> In short, I decided to consult the Holy *Quran*. I approached a saintly man. When I opened the Holy *Quran* with the idea of going back to Ghazni, there was an *ayat* pertaining to torture. But when I opened the Holy Book with the idea of proceeding to Delhi, the *ayat* pertaining to the rivers of heaven and the grandeur

> of heaven decided finally my future journey. Although I personally wanted to go to Ghazni, I made my way towards Delhi and reached there at last.
> When I reached the city, I was informed, that my son-in-law was in confinement. I reached the gates of the palace of the king to convey information about him. . . . I met him on the way. He had some money in his hand. He embraced me. He was exceedingly glad. He took me to his house and placed some money before me. I felt satisfied.[2]

Hazrat Badr-ud-din made anxious enquiries about Hazrat Khwaja Qutb-ud-din. His joy knew no bounds when he found that the dervish of his dream stayed with Hazrat Qazi Hamid-ud-din of Nagore in the city.

He inquired about his age and he was told that Hazrat Qazi Hamid-ud-din was an old man, aged about one hundred and thirty years, but Hazrat Khwaja Qutb-ud-din was in the prime of his youth, aged about seventeen. His beard was just sprouting. Hearing this he was certain that the person was the same individual, he had dreamt of.

The dream realised

Restless to meet him, he saw Hazrat Qutb Sahab participating in a music concert when he reached the monastery.[3]

When the concert was over, he approached him and, placing his head on the ground, disclosed his affection and longing. Thereafter, he, with the utmost respect and humility, said: "This humble being Badr-ud-din wants to be accepted as the disciple of your Holiness." To this Hazrat Qutb Sahab thereupon responded:[4]

> O Badr-ud-din! Thou became my spiritual disciple the very night thou saw in a dream the Holy Prophet Mohammed, who entrusted thee to me and who had said, 'Enlist him as your disciple.'
> I had accepted thee as my disciple the very night before God and had prayed to God Almighty: 'Be gracious enough as to accept Badr-ud-din Ghaznavi and have him included among our friends. . . .'

He was immensely pleased by this but insisted that the ceremony, as was the norm in the Chishti Order, should be performed and that, besides being accepted as a spiritual disciple in the world of dream, the same honour be conferred upon him in this world too and the four cornered cap be placed upon his head.

His request was accepted by Hazrat Qutb Sahab who said: "O Badr-ud-din! Look towards the sky." He obeyed. When asked what he saw, he replied: "I have seen the Throne and the Chair." Hazrat Qutb Sahab asked him: "Whose spiritual disciple art thou? Look towards the sky and read the divine decree." He looked towards the sky and said: "There, I have seen it written, that I am your spiritual disciple."

He asked him to look towards the earth. When he saw thereto he found that he could see up to the antipodes.

At the time of his initiation, he was seventy years old. Subsequently, the robe of the *khalifa* (caliph) was conferred upon him by his spiritual guide and teacher—Hazrat Khwaja Qutb-ud-din Bakhtyar Kaki.

Prior to his passing away, he informed him:[5] "O Badr-ud-din! The blessing, that we have obtained from our spiritual guide and teacher, I have given the same to thee and I have prayed to God, that thou may'st become my beloved." Badr-ud-din was full of devotion for his spiritual guide,[6] Hazrat Qutb Sahab, who entrusted to him the office of *imamat*, and appointed him the priest at the monastery.

Commandments

Hazrat Qutb Sahab asked him to strictly adhere to the following:

- Follow our spiritual anscestors.
- Take to renunciation and poverty.
- Pay respect to the dervishes and the poor.
- Have no social intercourse with the people of the world.
- Abstain from the world.
- Wear *gudri* (patched clothes).
- Be ever engaged in the remembrance of God.
- Love the Friends of God.
- Pay greater respect to the dervishes than to the rich.
- Use your own hands to wash the hands of the dervishes.

Death

Before Hazrat Badr-ud-din died, he appointed Shaikh Iman-ud-din Abdal as his spiritual successor and caliph.[7]

Hazrat Shaikh Badr-ud-din Ghaznavi used to offer a certain prayer every year for the prolongation of his own life, but the year he passed away he did not offer that prayer. When asked the reason for this he replied: "No more span of life remains."[8] The "Red Lion" as he was called in jest by Qazi Minhaj-ud-din[9] was over a hundred years old at the time of his death. He lies buried in the compound of the tomb of Hazrat Qutb Sahab in Mehrauli, New Delhi.

Traits of character

He was very pious and gentle. He had committed the Holy *Quran* to memory and used recite the whole of it once during the day and once during the night.[10]

He was a man of vast knowledge and erudition, and also a poet.[11] One of his sayings runs as follows: "What has the lover of the Beauty of God to do with the ladies of heaven."[12]

Supernatural powers

He used to meet Hazrat Khizr. Once his father expressed his desire to meet Hazrat Khizr and Shaikh Badr-ud-din promised that he would help to arrange such a meeting. One day, he was preaching when his father was also present. At a certain high place, inaccessible to ordinary men, someone was sitting. He pointed out to his father that it was Hazrat Khizr. His father thought it would only be proper to meet him after the sermon was over, but by then that high inaccessible place was vacant.[13]

Once there was a scarcity of rain in Delhi. Sultan Shams-ud-din Iltutmish requested him to pray. The reply was: "So long as Badr-ud-din is alive, there will never be famine in Delhi, nor there will ever be scarcity of rain." As soon as he uttered the words, rain began to fall. It is also said that, by dint of his spiritual powers, he would manage to reach Mecca and Medina every Thursday.[14]

References

1. *Fawaid-ul-Fu'ad*, p. 60.
2. Ibid.
3. *Siyar-ul-Arefeen*, p. 157.
4. Ibid.
5. Ibid., p. 160.
6. *Fawaid-ul-Fu'ad*, p. 152.
7. *Siyar-ul-Arefeen*, p. 160.

8. Ibid., p. 162; *Lataif-e-Ashrafi fi Bayan-e-Tasawwuf-e-Sufi*, p. 368.
9. *Fawaid-ul-Fu'ad*, p. 18.
10. Ibid., p. 156.
11. *Siyar-ul-Arefeen*, p. 159.
12. *Fawaid-ul-Fu'ad*, p. 155; *Siyar-ul-Arefeen*, p. 163.
13. *Siyar-ul-Auliya*, pp.165-66.
14. *Siyar-ul-Arefeen*, p. 160.

7

Hazrat Shaikh Najib-ud-din Mutawakkil

Hazrat Shaikh Najib-ud-din Mutawakkil was the younger brother, spiritual disciple, and caliph of Hazrat Baba Farid-ud-din Mas'ud Ganj-e-Shakar. He has an assured position amongst the sufis.

He belonged to the family of Farrukh Shah, king of Kabul. With the rise of the Ghazni dynasty, Farrukh Shah lost the throne, but continued to live in Kabul. When Chingiz Khan's marauding hordes destroyed Ghazni, one of the ancestors of Hazrat Shaikh Najib-ud-din lost his life in the Battle of Kabul.[1]

His father, Shaikh Jamal-ud-din Sulaiman, traces his descent from caliph Hazrat Umar Faruq. His mother, Bibi Qulsum Khatun, was the daughter of Maulana Wajih-ud-din Khagandi.[2] A very pious and gentle person, she exhibited supernatural powers. He had two elder brothers, the eldest was E'zaz-ud-din Mahmud, while Hazrat Baba Farid-ud-din Ganj-e-Shakar was the next.

Konithval is where Hazrat Shaikh Najib-ud-din Mutawakkil was born. Together with his brother Hazrat Baba Farid, he arrived in Delhi and at the former's behest settled there.

He received the title "Mutawakkil." Notwithstanding the fact that he had a wife and children, he showed a remarkable, indeed exemplary, faith in God.

A person by the name of Atim had built a mosque in Delhi, and he appointed Hazrat Shaikh Najib-ud-din Mutawakkil as its priest. Once it so happened that Atim spent a lot of money on the marriage of his daughter, and was criticised by Hazrat Shaikh Najib-ud-din for this on the ground that had he spent that money in the cause of God, it would have been far better. This annoyed Atim who dismissed him.[3] Going to Ajoodhan, he informed his brother Baba Farid, who remarked: "If Atim went, Aitkar will come." Later a Turk called Aitkar did come and he cared for the family of Shaikh Najib-ud-din Mutawakkil. Aitkar did yeoman service to the family.

Service rendered by Bibi Fatima Sam

Bibi Fatima Sam is a woman saint who has been mentioned in the discourses of Nizam-ud-din Auliya (who is the subject-matter of the next chapter). Baba-Farid-ud-din Ganj-e-Shakar, the brother of Shaikh Najib-ud-din Mutawakkil, used to say about her: "Fatima Sam is a male sent in the guise of a woman." Nizam-ud-din Auliya once said this: "When the lion comes from the forest, nobody asks whether the lion is a male or female. The people should aspire for piety and sanctity, whether they be man or woman." Bibi Fatima Sam treated Baba Farid-ud-din Ganj-e-Shakar and his younger brother Najib-ud-din Mutawakkil as her own brothers. When there was nothing in the house of Shaikh Najib-ud-din Mutawakkil to eat she used to send some bread. Once she sent only one loaf of bread, and he jokingly remarked, "O Great God! Make the king of this city acquainted with our condition, so that he may send us something substantial." Then he smiled and remarked, "Alas! The kings do not possess that inward cleanliness, by which they may be acquainted."[4]

An incident

After he had settled in Ajoodhan, Hazrat Baba Farid-ud-din Ganj-e-Shakar sent him to fetch their mother. On the way, they rested under the shade of some trees. He went to fetch some water for his mother and himself, but when he returned, he found his mother missing. All search proved to be in vain. When he had lost all hope of finding her, he proceeded and narrated all that had happened to Baba Sahab. He, on hearing the account, said that food should be cooked and charity should be given.

After a considerable lapse of time he happened to pass through that jungle again. Near the same tree he found the bones of some human being. Thinking that perhaps they might be the bones of their mother, he collected them all and put them into a bag. Hazrat Baba Sahab met him, and on hearing all the facts asked him to open the bag. When it was opened there was nothing inside.[5]

Meeting Khwaja Khizr

Once, it so happened that on the occasion of a certain 'Id celebration, certain dervishes came to his house and demanded something to eat. He asked his wife to cook something for them but there was nothing in the house; then he asked for his wife's shawl in order to sell it, but when he saw that it was torn at many places and had been patched he realised that nobody would buy it. He then thought of selling his praying carpet, but that too was patched. That obliged him to entertain the dervishes only with water. After they had left, he went to his tenement in the upper storey, sad and dismayed. Even on the occasion of 'Id, his children had to go without food and he was unable to entertain visitors.

Lost in thought, he saw a man entering. The visitor recited a couplet. He understood that this was Khwaja Khizr. Leaving his seat, he paid him respect. Hazrat Khwaja Khizr asked him what he was complaining about. After hearing his explanation Khwaja Khizr asked him to bring something to eat. He expressed his inability to do so, but Hazrat Khwaja Khizr insisted. When he went inside the house, he saw to his great surprise a trayful of food. His wife told him, that someone had brought it. Returning with some food to his tenement, he found that there was nobody there.[6] He said to himself: "This blessing, that I have been given is due to poverty and my straitened circumstances."

Hazrat Shaikh Najib-ud-din Mutawakkil had three sons, Shaikh Ismail, Shaikh Ahmad, and Shaikh Mohammed.

Death

He visited his brother Hazrat Baba Farid-ud-din Ganj-e-Shakar nineteen times during his lifetime. On every occasion, at the time of departure, he would seek his blessings and request him to pray for his future visit. The last time that he visited him, he again made the same request, but this time Hazrat Baba Sahab kept quiet. He returned to Delhi and passed away on the seventh of Ramazan. He lies buried in Delhi near the tomb of Bibi Zulekha, his tomb famous as that of "Shaikh Najib-ud-din the rider of the lion."[7]

Traits of character

He was an outstanding dervish and an embodiment of trust in God. Hazrat Nizam-ud-din Auliya wanted to become his spiritual disciple, but he expressed his inability to accept him as his disciple. Instead, he suggested that he approach Hazrat Shaikh Baha-ud-din Zakariya of Multan and Hazrat Baba Farid-ud-din Ganj-e-Shakar. Hazrat Nizam-ud-din Auliya had once requested him to pray for him so that he might become a Qazi, at which he made this prophetic remark:

> 'You will not become a Qazi, but you will become something else.'

He tended to be so absorbed and lost in contemplation that he was often unmindful of what was happening around him. Hazrat Nizam-ud-din Auliya says:[8] "I did not see a man of his type in the city. He did not know the day, the month, the rate at which grain was sold or meat was sold. In short, he was unmindful of all and everything. He was only devoted to the remembrance of God."

Once Hazrat Baba Sahab said to him:[9]

'Thou art also among the Abdals.'

He wrote *Jame-ul-Hikayat* using as scribe a person called Hamid.[10]

Some of his sayings:

- The perfect Faithful is one, who prefers the friendship of God to the love of his children.[11]
- Do no worry over the loss of the world as it is not lasting.

Supernatural power

Once Shaikh Najib-ud-din visited Budaun. He and his brother went to see a certain rich person called Shaikh Ali. He took off his shoes a few steps from a carpet and then, touching the ground with his feet, sat down on the carpet. Shaikh Ali was annoyed and said, that it was a praying carpet upon which both the brothers were sitting. Shaikh Ali had a book placed before him. Shaikh Najib-ud-din asked for the name of the book but Shaikh Ali did not reply. Taking his permission to open the book he at once read: "In the last days, there will be such saints, who will commit sins in solitude and if the foot of any visitor may fall upon their carpet, they will create hell for him." He gave the book to Shaikh Ali, who, reading that portion, was ashamed and implored his forgiveness.

References

1. *Siyar-ul-Auliya*, p. 59.
2. *Jawahar-e-Faridi*, p. 191.
3. *Siyar-ul-Auliya*, p. 78.
4. *Khair-ul-Majalis*, pp. 52-53.
5. *Fawaid-ul-Fu'ad*, p. 100.
6. *Khair-ul-Majalis*, pp. 52-53.
7. *Jawahar-e-Faridi*, p. 349.
8. *Fawaid-ul-Fu'ad*, p. 103.
9. Ibid., p. 99.
10. Ibid., pp. 21-22.
11. *Siyar-ul-Auliya*, p. 78.

8

Hazrat Khwaja Nizam-ud-din Auliya

Hazrat Khwaja Nizam-ud-din Auliya is an outstanding saint of the Indian subcontinent and the spiritual disciple of Hazrat Baba Farid-ud-din Ganj-e-Shakar.

Family antecedents

Hazrat Khwaja Nizam-ud-din Auliya belonged to a respectable family of Bukhara. His grandfather Syed Ali and his mother's father migrated to India with their family and after staying in Lahore for a short period, moved on to Budaun, U.P. and permanently settled there. Budaun was then a centre of knowledge and learning, and an important city, where many saints, sufis, and learned men lived.

His father Khwaja Syed Ahmad was one such, he was the spiritual disciple of his father (Hazrat Khwaja Nizam-ud-din Auliya's grandfather) Khwaja Syed Ali, and the recipient of the caliphate. After performing the duties of a Qazi for sometime, he took to renunciation and seclusion.

Hazrat Khwaja Nizam-ud-din Auliya was born on the twenty-seventh of Safar in AH 636. His mother, Hazrat Bibi Zulekha, was the daughter of Khwaja Syed Arab. She was an accomplished woman, with great qualities of patience, gratitude, and submission to the Will of God, and was celebrated for her piety, knowledge, and forbearance.

Hazrat Nizam-ud-din Auliya traces his descent, both from the paternal and maternal side, from Hazrat Imam Husain, the son of Hazrat Ali, who was the son-in-law of the Holy Prophet Mohammed.

The title by which he is addressed and invoked is *Mahboob-e-Ilahi* which means "Beloved of God."

Early life and education

His father had died when he was five years old. The responsibility for his education and training now fell on the shoulders of his mother.

She sent him to a *maktab* (school), and there Maulana Shadi Muqrai taught him one part of the Holy *Quran* and he later learnt the whole of the Holy Book.

He finished writing the celebrated book *Qudoori* at the feet of Maulana Ala-ud-din Oosooli. The Maulana,then, in the presence of the saints and learned men, took his turban in his hands and unfolding it, asked him to tie it on his head, which he did.

He committed to memory a book entitled *Muqamat-e-Hareri* under the guidance of Maulana Shams-ud-din, who was famous by the title of "Shams-ul-Malik." The Maulana had no equal in literature and grammar in his days and counted many learned men of the city amongst his pupils.

He achieved distinction in some branches of knowledge like Jurisprudence, the *Hadis*, Commentaries on the Holy *Quran*, logic, philosophy, arithmetic, literature, and grammar. He learned to read the Holy *Quran* by all the seven rhythmic modes. On reaching Delhi, he obtained a certificate of proficiency in "Mashariq-ul-Anwar" from Maulana Kamal-ud-din Muhaddis.

In the company of his spiritual guide and teacher, he finished six parts of the Holy *Quran*, and when he was in Ajoodhan, he devoted himself exclusively to the service of the former, Hazrat Baba Farid-ud-din Ganj-e-Shakar. There he also studied the six chapters of *Awarif* and also some other books.

Alongwith his mother and sister, he left Budaun and came to Delhi which subsequently became his place of permanent residence. There he was greatly benefited by the company of Maulana Amin-ud-din Muhaddis. In Delhi, he took a house on rent and began to live in pursuit of divine life and knowledge in the neighbourhood of Shaikh Najib-ud-din Mutawakkil.

He suffered an irreparable loss in the death of his mother and thereafter derived solace and comfort in the company of Shaikh Najib-ud-din Mutawakkil.

The forecast

One day, he happened to go to the tomb of Hazrat Khwaja Qutb-ud-din Bakhtyar Kaki and there he met a saint who was deeply absorbed. He requested the saint to pray that he might become a Qazi.

The saint replied: "O, Nizam-ud-din! You want to become a Qazi and I see that you are a spiritual sovereign. You will reach such heights, that the whole world will be benefited by you."

The urge to become a Qazi was so great, that he one day requested Hazrat Shaikh Najib-ud-din Mutawakkil to pray for this to happen. He replied: "God Willing, you will never become a Qazi, but instead you will become something else, which I know."

Once, when in Badaun, he was engaged in the study of literature and grammar, a man named Abu Bakr Kharrat, coming from Multan, wanted to offer his respects to his teacher Maulana Ala-ud-din Oosooli. The Maulana inquired about the Shaikhs, saints and sufis of that region. Abu Bakr Kharrat had deep respects and high praise for Hazrat Shaikh Baha-ud-din Zakariya of Multan and had the honour and unique privilege of reciting *qawwali* before him. His prayers and devotion were beyond description. He had illuminated that region by his grace and charm and even his maidservants were engaged in remembrance and recitation of the name of God even while working. Hazrat Nizam-ud-din Auliya, hearing this praise of Hazrat Shaikh Baha-ud-din Zakariya of Multan, was not moved at all.

Coming to the condition of Ajoodhan, he said that there lived Hazrat Shaikh Farid-ud-din Mas'ud Ganj-e-Shakar who had illumined the dark hearts by his inward light and who was a saint of high attainments. He acted as a perfect moon, shedding light and lustre all around. He had captured the hearts of many people there and myriads of them had entered his fold. On hearing these words of praise a wave of fondness, love, and curiosity was born in Hazrat Nizam-ud-din Auliya's heart. He wanted to meet Baba Sahab and derive spiritual ecstasy from his inspiring company. He was at that time just twelve years old. The fondness, love, and devotion continued to increase by the day. He was now so engrossed in thought and so great captivated by his love, that he began to recite his name after every prayer: "Shaikh Farid" ten times and "Maulana Farid" ten times. This devotion was further strengthened by subsequent events. When he left for Delhi to take up permanent residence there, he was accompanied by a certain person named Ewaz. On the way, when he felt any danger, he would cry aloud: "O *pir*! Be present, as we are travelling under thy protection." Hazrat Nizam-ud-din Auliya asked Ewaz: "Who is your *pir* whose protection and help you seek? and where does he live?" The man replied: "My spiritual guide is the same who has attracted your heart towards him and made you his devotee. In other words, he is none other than Hazrat Shaikh Farid-ud-din Mas'ud Ganj-e-Shakar." When living in Delhi, he used to hear a great deal about the spiritual powers of Hazrat Baba Farid. In the Central Mosque of Delhi, Hazrat Nizam-ud-din Auliya sometimes offered prayers at night. Once, after being engaged in a whole night of prayer, at dawn he heard the *mu'azzin* recite the following from the top of the tower: "Has not the time come for the Faithful, that their hearts should bend for the remembrance of God." Hearing this Hazrat Nizam-ud-din Auliya underwent a strange transformation. All charm for this world was lost to him and he became enamoured of a higher life. He became totally a changed man.

The desire to be initiated in the Sufi Order was so great that without the necessary resources he left for Ajoodhan. After a stop in Hansi he accompanied a caravan. On the way, the leader of the caravan, when sensing any danger would cry: "O, our spiritual Guide and Helper! be ever with us to protect us." Hazrat Nizam-ud-din Auliya was told that Hazrat Baba Farid was being invoked.

He stayed three days in Sirsaand, from there one route led to Multan where the famous saint Hazrat Baha-ud-din Zakariya lived and the other way to Ajoodhan where Hazrat Baba Farid lived. Initially unsure of which way to proceed, in a dream, he saw the Holy Prophet Mohammed directing him to go to Ajoodhan. Now, uttering the words "Farid, Farid," he proceeded to Ajoodhan, where he reached on Wednesday, the eleventh of Rajab in AH 655.

Initiation in the Sufi Order

That day, after the noon-prayers, the meeting took place. On seeing him, Baba Sahab recited: "O! the fire of thy separation has made the hearts like roasted meat. The flood of thy fondness has made the lives morose." Hazrat Nizam-ud-din Auliya was so greatly overawed in the presence of Hazrat Baba Farid that he could say no more than how eager and desirous of meeting him he had been. Hazrat Baba Sahab extended him a warm welcome and said that God Willing, he would be benefited by the good things of this world and the world hereafter.

Hazrat Baba Sahab was most kind to him. He gave the cap which he was wearing at that time and presented him some other sacred relics, a robe, sandals, praying-carpet, and stick. Then, addressing him, Baba Sahab said: "O, Nizam-ud-din! I wanted to entrust the domain of India to somebody else. When you were on the way, I heard a voice to the effect that I should wait, Nizam-ud-din comes. He is fit for this domain. It should be entrusted to him."

At the time of his initiation into the Sufi Order, he was twenty years old.

His *pir* did not allow him to leave. One day he asked: "What is your order for me. If you may so approve, I may give up studies and may devote myself exclusively to prayers and asceticism." Hazrat Baba Farid replied: "I do not forbid anyone to devote himself to studies. Do this and do that also. Some knowledge is necessary for a dervish." After staying in Ajoodhan for about seven months he was allowed to leave for Delhi. At the time of departure, Hazrat Baba Sahab conferred on him the special robe handed down to him from the Khwajas of the Chishti Order. On the same day, i.e., second Rabi-ul-Awwal AH 656, he honoured him by giving him the caliphate deed and prayed for his welfare. He directed that he should assiduously pursue ascetic practices, and, bidding him farewell announced: "By the command of God Almighty, I have entrusted the domain of India to his care and I have left this country in his shelter and have appointed him as my spiritual successor." He further directed, that he should show the caliphate deed to Maulana Jamal-ud-din in Hansi and to Qazi Muntakhib in Delhi. He accordingly left for Hansi and showed his caliphate deed to the Maulana, who was happy that it had been given to a deserving person.

Returning to Delhi, he began to preach the Gospel of Truth. Hazrat Nizam-ud-din Auliya shunned worldly pursuits, overcame temptation, and fasted throughout the year.

He went to Ajoodhan to offer his respects three times during the lifetime of Hazrat Baba Sahab and after he died, visited his tomb seven times to derive spiritual blessings.

Change in residence

He was averse to huge crowds of people who, he feared, might prove a source of disturbance. He wanted to live in a desolate and secluded place where he might concentrate on prayer. One day he stayed near Rani tank. After offering prayers in the garden he asked: "O God! I do not want to live anywhere out of my own free will. Keep me where it may be best in my interest to live." He had not even concluded his prayers when he heard a voice to the effect: "Ghiyaspur is the fittest place for you." He, accordingly, began to live in Ghiyaspur which was then a small village. After sometime the population increased and the frequent incursions of noblemen and the courtiers disturbed him and he wanted to move away from there. In the meanwhile, he happened to meet a beautiful young man who sat near him and recited a couplet. This young man said to him, "What is this power and what is this ambition that you want to be separated from the people and seek a secluded place." Hearing these words, he changed his mind, resolving not to move away and passed the remaining part of his life in Ghiyaspur. Subsequently, Zia-ud-din erected a palatial building there, which served as his *khanqah* (monastery).

Last days

In the last days of his life, he devoted himself so completely to prayer that he would pray several times and yet be unaware of this. He would inquire from the people whether he had offered them. He would genuflect, he would weep, he would eat very little, and continually repeat, "we go and we go and we go."

He did not allow anything to be kept or retained in the house. He ordered his devoted *khadim* Iqbal to distribute all the grain amongst the needy, the poor, and the destitute. On a particular occasion, he gave one praying carpet, turban, and a set of clothes to Maulana Burhan-ud-din Gharib and ordered him to proceed to the Deccan. He gave one turban, one set of clothes, and a praying-carpet to Shaikh Ya'qub and allowed him to proceed to Gujarat, and did the same for Maulana Shams-ud-din Yahya. Hazrat Nasir-ud-din Chiragh of Delhi was present then but he did not give him anything that day. Those present were surprised.

On Wednesday, after the noon prayers, he summoned Hazrat Nasir-ud-din Chiragh of Delhi and confided to him the holy stick, the sandals, the praying carpet, the rosary, the special robe, and other sacred relics of Hazrat Baba Farid-ud-din Ganj-e-Shakar and said to him: "You should live in Delhi and bear the tyranny and the harsh treatment of the people."

For four months and a few days he was continually ill. On Wednesday, the eighteenth of Rabi-us-Sani in AH 725, he breathed his last after sunrise. His passing away brought to close an important epoch of spiritual attainments and literary achievements.

Caliphs

Hazrat Nasir-ud-din Chiragh of Delhi was his spiritual successor and premier caliph.

The other eminent caliphs are: Hazrat Amir Khusrau; Maulana Shams-ud-din Mohammed Yahya; Shaikh Qutb-ud-din Munawwar; Maulana Fakhr-ud-din Zarrayi; Maulana Husam-ud-din of Multan; Khwaja Abu Bakr Manda; Maulana Shahab-ud-din Imam; Amir

Hasan, son of Ala of Sanjar; Maulana Burhan-ud-din Gharib; Maulana Wajih-ud-din Yusuf Kala Khari *alias* Chanderi; Qazi Mohi-ud-din of Kashan; Maulana Ala-ud-din Neli; Maulana Fakhr-ud-din Marozi; Maulana Fasih-ud-din; Maulana Karim-ud-din of Samarqand; Khwaja Moin-ud-din; and Maulana Zia-ud-din Barni.

Traits of character

He was a bachelor and devoted all his life to the pursuit of truth. He greatly loved his spiritual guide and teacher and became very close to him winning his confidence by the virtue of his sincerity obedience, and implicit faith. Hazrat Baba Sahab used to say:[1] "Since the time this poor Maulana Nizam-ud-din has come to me and has become my disciple, there has not been any change in his sincerity and faith." Once his spiritual guide, addressing the people, said:[2] "A spiritual disciple should be firm and unshaken in his belief like Nizam."

He passed the various spiritual stages and had eventually reached the stage where he was accepted as being the Beloved of God. In early life he faced the most acute poverty and had no money even to buy a few pieces of bread.[3]

Fatuhat or unsought gift

On a particular day some barley was being boiled in his house. Suddenly, a *faqir*, wearing a *gudri* came to his house and asked for something to eat. He brought the half-cooked barley and placed it before the *faqir*. After eating the barley, the *faqir* threw the earthen cooking vessel on the ground shattering it to pieces, and told him: "O, Maulana Nizam-ud-din! You have been honoured and elevated by the inward blessings of Hazrat Baba Farid-ud-din and I have broken the earthen vessel of your outward poverty." Since that day he received so much *fatuhat* (unsought gift), that he would feed many people everyday.

Langar – free kitchen

His kitchen was open to all. Once, his spiritual guide and teacher Hazrat Baba Farid prayed for him as follows: "May seventy maunds of salt be consumed everyday in your kitchen." This actually happened. Besides this, seventy camel loads of onion skin and vegetable wastes were carried out from his kitchen everyday.

Generosity

His generosity was boundless. Whatever he received during the day was exhausted by the evening. Many people lived on his charity, and to some he granted monthly allowances.

Once a fire broke out in Ghiyaspur in which many houses were destroyed. He was greatly moved by this devastation and he asked Khwaja Iqbal to give two trays full of food, two pitchers of water, and two guineas each to those whose houses had been burnt. Khwaja Iqbal did so and even kings envied his generosity.

Music

He was very fond of music, deriving great spiritual pleasure and inward happiness from music concerts.

High position and status

He occupied a very high status. Once some difficulty experienced by Maulana Wajih-ud-din Paili was solved by Khwaja Khizr. The Maulana asked him where he would find him in future in the event of some other difficulty. Khwaja Khizr replied: "You will find me in the kitchen of Hazrat Mahboob-e-Ilahi Khwaja Nizam-ud-din Auliya."

Once Hazrat Khwaja Moin-ud-din Chishti met some Abdals. One of them said to Hazrat Khwaja Gharib Nawaz: "You have created sensation in the cities of the world." Surprised, Hazrat Khwaja Gharib Nawaz enquired: "Have I done?" The Abdal replied: "No you have not." Khwaja Gharib Nawaz then inquired: "Qutb-ud-din, has he done it?" The Abdal replied in the negative. Khwaja Gharib Nawab then asked whether Farid-ud-din had done so; again to a negative response. Then he inquired, "Whether Nizam-ud-din has done it?"

"Yes," replied the Abdal, "he has done it." Thereupon Khwaja Gharib Nawaz said: "He is in the fourth degree to me?" The Abdal then remarked: "The fact is that whatever is done by your sons will be attributed to you."

Renunciation: prayers

He was detached from the world, the people of the world, and worldly activities. He did not care for kings and other dignitaries. He would pass the night in his tenement all alone, and nobody was permitted to enter. He would keep awake all night devoted to prayers. In the morning, his red eyes would betoken the state of the night.

Literary taste

Hazrat Nizam-ud-din was a very learned man. It is said that he was one of the most learned of his time. His book entitled *Rahat-ul-Quloob* contains the discourses and teachings of his *pir*, Hazrat Baba Farid-ud-din Ganj-e-Shakar. He was also a poet, bearing the poetic nickname "Nizam." His poem in honour of the Holy Prophet is a consummate piece of work.

Teachings

- Courage should be maintained (in renunciation) and one should not entangle oneself in the web of the world. Greed and avarice should be shunned.[4]
- When reading the Holy *Quran*, if one gets a particular joy and solace from some *ayat*, it should be read over and over again. The blessings obtained during the recitation of the Holy *Quran* and music are of three kinds, namely, Light, State and Manifestation.
- Even when one fasts during the day, keeps awake at night, and performs *hajj*, the essential principle is that there should not be the love of the world in the heart.[5]
- When five conditions are fulfilled then, of course, charity is accepted. Of these, two are conditions precedent, two are conditions present, and one is a condition subsequent.

  The two conditions precedent are that whatever is given should be a part of legitimate income and it should be given to some good man who will not spend it on some debased object.

  The two conditions present are that whatever is given should be given with courtesy and kindness, and voluntarily, and it should be given confidentially.

  The condition subsequent is that no mention should be made of whatever is given. In fact, it should be absolutely forgotten.
- Patience means and implies that one should not complain of anything that may be against his will. Submission implies that one should not be bothered about facing any kind of trouble, and act as if nothing has happened.
- *Tawakkul* or trust in God has three stages. The first stage implies, that there is trust, but at the same time there is demand. If a certain person engages a lawyer to argue his case and that lawyer is his

personal friend and also well-versed in his profession, then the client will feel quite satisfied. This implies trust in God and demand as well.

The second stage of *tawakkul* is like that of the infant child who lives on his mother's milk. He has the fullest confidence of maternal love.

The third stage of trust in God is that the dead body is in the hands of those who give bath. The dead body does not move and does not demand anything. Those giving the bath may move, turn, or wash it in anyway they like. This stage of *tawakkul* is, indeed, very high and sublime.

- Prayer is of two kinds. One is compulsory and the other is social. The first type consists of *namaz*, fast, *hajj*, and benedictions to the Holy Prophet Mohammed, where only the one offering it is benefited.

  A social prayer is that by which others are benefited. Unity, kindness, love, etc., constitute this type of prayer. Its reward is great and beyond calculation. Compulsory prayer requires sincerity to be accepted, but the social type of prayer gets its own reward, of whatever kind that may be.
- Hazrat Nizam-ud-din Auliya suggests the following mode of offering prayer:[6] At the time of offering prayer, neither should one think of the sins committed, nor of the prayers and worship offered. If this is done it will be a matter of surprise if the prayer is not granted. Thinking of the sins committed at that time makes the process of acceptance slow. It is therefore, better to focus on the Mercy of God at the time of offering prayer. One should have the fullest faith and confidence, that ones prayer will be accepted. At the time of offering prayers, both the hands should be kept open near the breast. It is also said that both the hands should be kept joined above the breast. Such a form should be assumed as if one is likely to receive something then.
- One should repose ones implicit faith in God and God alone, expect nothing from anyone else except God. Ones faith is not perfect so long as the people of the world do not appear to one to be worse than the mosquito.[7]
- Remembrance of God is the real thing, all else is the preventive of it.[8]
- About perseverance he says:[9] "The treatment meted out to others is of three kinds. Firstly, there are people by whom others are

neither benefited nor troubled. Such people are like minerals. Secondly, there are people by whom others are benefited and not troubled. Thirdly, there are people who are better than the two aforesaid types. They are the people by whom others are benefited and if they are troubled by others they do not seek revenge. On the contrary, they bear it with patience, which is the wont of the truthful."

- One should listen to music only when certain things are available. These things are: *masma'* or the singer; *masmoo'* or whatever is sung; *mustama'* or the person listening; *aalate sama'* or the instruments of music.

  Masma', the person singing, should be an adult and male, *masmoo'* or whatever is sung should not be obscene or frivolous. *Mustama'* or the person listening should be absorbed in the remembrance of God. There should at the time be no vain thought in his heart. The *chang* (harp) and *rubab* (a fours-tringed instrument in the form of a short-necked *guitar*) are not allowed in the musical assembly of the sufis. The harmonium and the *dholak* (a barrel-shaped double-headed wooden drum) are permissible when hearing music. Music is, in fact, a suitable voice. It cannot be illegitimate. In it the heart moves. If the movement is on account of the remembrance of God, it is commendable and if it be on account of evil thoughts, it is illegitimate.

Some of the sayings of Hazrat Nizam-ud-din Auliya:

- Real wisdom lies in the renunciation of the world.
- The dervish should be unmindful of joy and sorrow.
- Once the stomach is full, nothing should be eaten again. Two persons are exempted from the rule. He who receives guests may for their sake eat again with them. The other person is he who fasts and apprehends that he may not get anything to eat before the break of dawn.
- When a person acquires knowledge he is honoured and when he prays his work acquires felicity. On such occasions a spiritual guide is needed who may break both. In other words, he may cause knowledge and deed to be lowered in his eyes, so that he may not take to the worship of self.
- The blessings of God are showered on three occasions. Firstly at the time of hearing music; secondly at the time of food taken

with the object of gaining strength to pray; and thirdly at the time of describing the details of the lives of dervishes.

- One should bear the tyranny of others and should not think of taking revenge.
- He, alone, is fit to be the caliph (spiritual successor) of saints, who is endowed with knowledge, wisdom and love.
- The love of saints overpowers their wisdom.

Supernatural powers

Hazrat Nizam-ud-din Auliya exhibited very many supernatural powers during his lifetime. Some of these are related below:

- Once Hazrat Qazi Mohi-ud-din of Kashan fell seriously ill, with no hope of recovery. Hazrat Mahboob-e-Ilahi honoured him by a visit. Qazi Sahab stood up and received him, fully recovered. After he had left, Qazi Sahab said that apparently he had come to see him, but inwardly he had absorbed his illness.
- The water of the tank dug in his *khanqah* was salty. One day he was present at a music concert. He called Khwaja Iqbal and asked him to fetch a pen, an inkpot, and paper. He wrote something on the piece of paper and asked Khwaja Iqbal to throw it into the tank. The water then became sweet.
- One of his disciples called Badr-ud-din saw one night that a camel was standing just outside his *khanqah*. He rode on the camel. The camel flew into the air and became invisible. At the dead night, the camel returned and Hazrat Mahboob-e-Ilahi got down from it and went into the *khanqah*.
- Sultan Ghiyas-ud-din Tughlaq was jealous of his reputation and prestige, and in consequence bore rancour against him. Once when returning from Bengal to Delhi, the Sultan sent him a message that Hazrat Nizam-ud-din Auliya should leave Delhi. Hazrat Nizam-ud-din Auliya was somewhat saddened by this insolent and impertinent message. He replied: "*Hanooz Dilli dur ast,*" i.e., Delhi is still far away. As it so happened, the Sultan was unable to reach Delhi. The palace at Tughlaqabad, where he had stayed, collapsed and he died. The sentence "*Hanooz Dilli dur ast*" has become a proverb.

References

1. *Fawaid-ul-Fu'ad.*
2. *Rahat-ul-Qulub.*
3. *Rauzat-ul-Aqtab.*
4. *Fawaid-ul-Fu'ad,* Urdu trans., p. 8.
5. *Fawaid-ul-Fu'ad,* p. 69.
6. Ibid., p. 74.
7. Ibid., p. 193.
8. Ibid., p. 200.
9. *Tarikh-e-Firishta,* p. 398.

9

Hazrat Syed Ala-ud-din Ahmad Sabir

Hazrat Syed Ala-ud-din Ahmad Sabir was one of the most outstanding saints of the Indian subcontinent. The Sabiri Order of the sufis owes its origin to him. He traces his descent from Hazrat Imam Jaffer Sadiq,[1] and is related to Hazrat Baba Farid-ud-din Ganj-e-Shakar, whose sister's son he is. According to some, he was born in Khotwali (Khetwal), but there are others who hold that he was born in Herat.

His father's name was Syed Abdullah, his mother, Bibi Hajra, traced her relationship to Hazrat Ibrahim Adham of Balkh. When he was in his mother's womb, the tenement in which she lived was shrouded by clouds of graceful light and there was a sweet and inviting smell all around.[2] He was born before dawn on the nineteenth of Rabi-ul-Awwal in AH 592. When the midwife, Basri, attending upon his mother, wanted to bathe him without having given him ablutions, she felt a strange type of fire seizing her. When this was brought to the attention of his mother, she suggested that he should be given ablutions first and a bath afterwards. That is exactly what the midwife did.

Name

Long before his birth, an indication of this was made by the Holy Prophet Mohammed. Hazrat Imam Jaffer Sadiq says that he once saw the Holy Prophet in his dream, pointing out to him that the soul sitting on his left would appear in the world and his name will be Ali Ahmad.[3]

When he was in his mother's womb, she saw Hazrat Ali in a dream saying to her: "The child that may be born should be named Ali." The following day his mother saw the Holy Prophet in dream ordering her to name the child "Ahmad." After his birth he was given both the names and by the conjunction of the two he came to be known as Ali Ahmad.

When he was born, a dervish resembling Hazrat Khizr visited the house, called him, took him in his lap, kissed his forehead, and made a prophecy to the effect that "This child will be called Alā-ud-ḍin."

Titles

When his father died, his mother brought him to her brother, Hazrat Baba Farid-ud-din Ganj-e-Shakar, and requested him to look after her child Ali Ahmad. Hazrat Baba Sahab gladly agreed. After staying three years with her brother she left for Herat.

Hazrat Baba Sahab appointed him as superintendent of his kitchen. After a passage of time, when his mother saw her son again while visiting Pak Pattan, she was surprised to see Hazrat Ali Ahmad looking very weak, lean, and thin. She complained of this to her brother Hazrat Baba Sahab, who replied:

> You must know that I love your son very much. I have tried my utmost to look after his comfort and health; so much so, that I have appointed him the superintendent of the kitchen. He is in-charge of everything. He manages the kitchen as he likes and distributes as much food as he wishes and to whomsoever he wishes. Under the circumstances there is no justification for your making a complaint to me about his becoming weak. His state of health cannot be ascribed to my so-called indifference towards him. I myself do not know why he has become so pale, weak, lean, and thin.

Hazrat Ali Ahmad was there and intervened, saying: "O, my reverend mother! The service entrusted to me by my uncle related only to the management and distribution of the *langar* (free food). There was no express permission for me to eat out of the *langar*. How, then could I eat anything out of it."

Hearing, this Hazrat Baba Sahab was greatly surprised and extremely happy. He embraced him and immediately conferred upon him very many spiritual blessings and uttered these memorable words "Ali Ahmad is Sabir." Since that day he began to be known, addressed, and invoked as "Sabir," which means patient.[4] He is also known as "Makhdoom" a title conferred upon him by God Almighty.[5]

Early life

His early years were characterised by his ascetic temperament and indifference towards the pleasures of the world. He would consume milk on alternate days. He showed marvellous patience.

When he was two years old, he himself gave up drinking milk. At the age of seven, he would consume coarse food on the fourth or fifth day. His food, generally, consisted of barley bread soaked in water. He slept very little.

Hazrat Ali Ahmad was mostly in an absorbed state and would offer pre-dawn prayers when he was only seven years old. He slept on the floor and fasted. His father died on the seventeenth of Rabi-ul-Awwal in AH 597, when he was only five years old.[6] His mother died on the second of Muharram in AH 614.

It is said that after his mother's death, he was so deeply absorbed, that he didn't emerge from the tenement in which he was living for the next nine years. He was wholly devoted to rigours and ascetic practices and lost in meditation.

Hazrat Baba Farid-ud-din Ganj-e-Shakar did not initially feel it proper to interfere with his routine and rituals but, receiving inspiration, entered his tenement on the eleventh of Muharram in AH 623. He was so deeply absorbed that he was quite unaware of his arrival. Hazrat Baba Sahab recited the Kalima-e-Shahadat seven times in his left ear. He opened his eyes and was surprised to see Hazrat Baba Sahab there and offered him his respects.

Hazrat Baba Farid took Hazrat Ali Ahmad with him and asked him to sit in his company. He put on his head his own cap and caused him to wear his own covering cloth. Since that day he would live during the day with Hazrat Baba Sahab and would retire to his tenement at night and there would be seized by the state of absorption and unconsciousness.

Initiation into the Sufi Order

He was accepted as a spiritual disciple by Hazrat Baba Farid-ud-din Ganj-e-Shakar. Subsequently, he honoured him by accepting him as his caliph and gave him his own cap. He preached to him the Great Mysterious Name handed down to him from his spiritual forefathers and entrusted to his care the domain of Delhi and told him: "Initially get the seal affixed on the caliphate deed by Shaikh Jamal-ud-din of Hansi and then proceed to Delhi."

Hazrat Ala-ud-din Ali Ahmad Sabir accordingly went to Hansi and met Shaikh Jamal-ud-din. After offering the sunset prayers, they both sat together and talked. Hazrat Makhdoom Sabir availed of this opportunity and took out the caliphate deed. It had become dark and no light was available, so they had to wait for sometime. Then, light was provided and the caliphate deed was opened, but the wind blew so hard that the lamp was extinguished and darkness fell again. Hazrat Sabir became impatient and could not wait any longer. He just blew hard and rapidly and there was light. Hazrat Shaikh Jamal-ud-din of Hansi did not like this exhibition of supernatural powers so he took the caliphate deed and tore it to pieces and said to him: "How will Delhi bear one blow from you? You will burn Delhi by one blow."

Hazrat Makhdoom Sabir lost his temper, saying: "You have torn my caliphate deed and I have torn to pieces your spiritual genealogy." Hazrat Shaikh Jamal-ud-din, hearing this, was seized with apprehensions. He inquired: "From the beginning or from the end?" to which he replied: "From the beginning."

Instead of proceeding to Delhi, he returned to Pak Pattan and acquainted his spiritual guide and teacher with all that had transpired. Hazrat Baba Farid-ud-din said to him:

"The thing torn by Jamal cannot be sewn by Farid, but rest assured that by the decree of God, you are appointed in Kalyar." Subsequently, Hazrat Baba Sahab gave him the caliphate deed duly signed.

Hazrat Baba Farid was also informed about the incident of the spiritual genealogy of Shaikh Jamal-ud-din having been torn from the beginning. In reference to this Hazrat Baba Sahab said thus: "The arrow of men is not missed. But it is all to the good that you said that you had torn off his genealogy from the beginning and thus kept the end safe. The disciple of your disciple will pray for Shaikh Jamal of Hansi and by the blessings of his prayer, his genealogy will start again. I have seen it so written on the Safe state. But, you also repeat it with your tongue." He obeyed the order of his spiritual guide, and teacher and said in a low voice: "His genealogy will start again." This actually happened.[7]

Arrival in Kalyar

He arrived in Kalyar in AH 650 (some say AH 652). Hazrat Makhdoom Sabir stayed with Hazrat Baha-ud-din, son of Haroon. As soon as Hazrat Shaikh Baha-ud-din and Shaikh Jamal Mohammed saw him, they were greatly impressed by his personality and spiritual powers. They thought his arrival to be a source of blessings. It was, however, otherwise with other people. Kalyar, then, was not a deserted place, and had an importance of its own. Many learned men and saints and sufis lived there, and they had their own superiority complex, and paid no attention to Hazrat Makhdoom Sabir. When he went to the mosque to offer his Friday prayers, he was not able to find a place and would therefore stay outside. He was greatly upset by the attitude of the people and in a letter he complained about it. This letter to his *pir* ended with the words: "I cannot do anything without the consent and permission of your Holiness. I shall be bound by your orders." Hazrat Baba Sahab replied: "The domain of Kalyar is entrusted to you by the command of God. You are fully empowered to do as you wish."

One Friday it so happened that nobody allowed him to sit and offer prayers in the first rank and was asked to vacate the place that he had occupied. When he and his devotees left, the mosque collapsed and all those present in it were instantaneously killed. Subsequently, the town was gripped by plague which took a very heavy toll of life. The whole city was thus deserted.

Absorption

Hazrat Makhdoom Sabir was so wholly lost in absorption, that for twelve whole years he stood motionless, catching the bough of the *gular* tree. Nobody had the courage to approach to him.

When his *pir*, Hazrat Baba Sahab, learnt of this he was concerned about him. He asked if anybody could go and induce him to sit down. Hazrat Shams-ud-din Turk of Panipat left for Kalyar, volunteering his service.

Reaching Kalyar, he saw that the whole town presented a deserted appearance. He had not the courage to go near Hazrat Makhdoom Sabir straightaway, fearing his wrath. The best thing, he thought, would be to win him over. So, standing at some distance from him, he began to recite the Holy *Quran* in a very melodious tone.

Hazrat Sabir Sahab heard the voice of a human being after all those long years and was moved. He opened his eyes and saw Hazrat Shams-ud-din. He made a sign to him to approach and inquired who he was and why he was there, and then asked him to continue the recitation.

Hazrat Shams-ud-din Turk of Panipat obeyed implicitly. After sometime he expressed his inability to continue reciting because he was tired. He was permitted to sit down but reacted by saying: "How can I be so impertinent as to sit, when your holiness is standing?" Finally, after twelve whole years, Hazrat Makhdoom Sabir let go his hold of the bough of the tree and sat down. He permitted Hazrat Shams-ud-din Turk to live with him which he did for sometime and then left to join the forces of the Sultan.

Hazrat Sabir Sahab bade him farewell and said, that they might not meet again. He should however bear in mind that when he performed any supernatural act he should interpret it to mean that he, Sabir Sahab, was dead. He should then wait no longer, but hasten to Kalyar.

Visit of Hazrat Amir Khusrau

Once, Hazrat Amir Khusrau came and offered him his respects and also conveyed the greetings of his master, Hazrat Nizam-ud-din Auliya. Some *gulars* were taken by Hazrat Amir Khusrau as a present from Baba Sahab to Hazrat Nizam-ud-din Auliya. Hazrat Nizam-ud-din was greatly pleased by this gesture of goodwill and good relations and distributed them among his devotees and disciples to be treated as a holy relic.

Marriage

Some hold the view that he did not marry, remaining a bachelor all his life. There are others who assert that he did marry. It is said that his reverend mother was anxious about his marriage and requested her brother, Hazrat Baba Farid-ud-din Ganj-e-Shakar, to give his daughter in marriage to her son.

Hazrat Baba Farid knew that Sabir Sahab did not want to marry and if force was brought to bear upon him, such a marriage would result in failure. He refused but his sister insisted. Eventually, he agreed because he did not want to hurt her feelings.

The marriage was thus solemnised. It grew dark and the bride was taken to the tenement of Hazrat Sabir Sahab. When in the night he entered it for prayers and meditation, to his great surprise he found a woman sitting there. Seeing her, he inquired who she was. She replied, that she was his wife. Hearing this he spontaneously said: "O, no! God has no wife." That very instant, the tenement caught fire and the flames enveloped and burnt the bride to ashes.

Death

Hazrat Sabir Sahab breathed his last on the thirteenth of Rabi-ul-Awwal in AH 690. His tomb, situated in Kalyar, draws myriads of people, who come season in and season out to seek his spiritual blessings. His *'urs* (death anniversary) is celebrated annually.

Supernatural powers

Hazrat Shams-ud-din Turk was in the pay of the Sultan. He was discovered by the Sultan and was asked to pray that a particular fort could be conquered. Since he did not want to disclose his identity he said that he was like other men in the army and advised that he approach another saint. The Sultan however insisted and so perforce he prayed. There was great joy and jubilation in the royal army, but it was otherwise with him. He felt depressed and sad. His exhibition of this supernatural power reminded him that it should be interpreted as marking the end of the life of Hazrat Sabir Sahab. He immediately resigned his job and left for Kalyar. There he found Hazrat Sabir Sahab dead with a strange type of light surrounding the dead body and a lion was protecting it. Seeing him approaching, the lion moved away. He bathed the dead body and put it in a coffin. But how was he to conduct the funeral prayers? There was nobody. He was relieved of this anxiety when he saw many men coming that way, one of them with a black veil covering his face. He requested this man to perform the funeral prayers.

After having buried Hazrat Sabir Sahab, he was anxious to know the identity of the person wearing the black veil, and asked him to show his face. When the veil was removed, he was greatly surprised to find that the man was Hazrat Sabir Sahab himself. Hazrat Sabir Sahab then pointed towards the dead body and said: "Look, there is *fana* (extinction)" and pointing towards himself, he said: "and here is *baqa* (immortality)."

Spiritual successor

Hazrat Shams-ud-din Turk of Panipat is his only caliph and spiritual successor.

Traits of character

Hazrat Sabir Sahab was a man of very high spiritual attainments and had totally freed himself from base human instincts and imbibed the divine qualities. He was ever lost in contemplation and meditation. He was a man of ascetic habits and had nothing to do with the world, passing his days in penances and rigours. He had utmost *jalal* (wrath).

He had no ostensible means of subsistence. Sharf-ud-din, the *qawwal* who used to recite before Hazrat Baba Farid Ganj-e-Shakar, came to him in the hope of receiving fairly generous bounty from him.

He was utterly disappointed, finding him living in the thatched hut, the roof of which had holes in it.

He was the embodiment of *sabr* (patience). For a considerable period of time, he was in-charge of the kitchen of Hazrat Baba Sahab, but ate nothing himself. This too exemplifies his marvellous self-control. Whatever he prophesied actually occurred.

He had surrendered himself to the Will of God and had no desire, save to be united with God. Hazrat Sabir Sahab was a poet and has written a *ghazal*.

Supernatural powers

Hazrat Sabir Sahab exhibited very many supernatural powers. Let us took at some of them here.

Since he was fond of silence, solitude, and seclusion, and wanted to live in a deserted place, Kalyar (which was a very populous town when he arrived there) became a deserted town after he had taken up his residence there.

When annoyed or angry with his spiritual caliph or successor Hazrat Shams-ud-din Turk of Panipat he would say: "Art thou lame?" And he would instantaneously become so. Then he would pray for him, enabling him to revert to his former condition. When in anger he would say to him: "Art thou blind?" He would straightaway become blind, and then, he would pray: "O, God Almighty, I have only one Shams. Restore his eyesight" and his eyesight would be immediately restored. Hazrat Shams-ud-din Turk of Panipat was obliged to undergo such varying conditions many times everyday and night.

After he passed away, a strange light in the shape of sword circulated around the tomb extending up to twenty-four miles. Nobody could go there. Hazrat Abdul Quddus of Gangah left for Kalyar, and as he approached the tomb of the light appeared as if to prevent him from proceeding further.

On seeing the light, Hazrat Abdul Quddus of Gangah so addressed the soul of Hazrat Sabir Sahab: "I am one of your humble devotees. I am desirous of paying respects." As soon as he uttered these words, the light disappeared. He heard a voice to the effect that: "The attack of men cannot be avoided. Give your sleeve." He obeyed and his sleeve was cut by that sword of light.

Reaching the tomb, Hazrat Abdul Quddus offered his respects. It is said that the soul of Hazrat Sabir Sahab embraced him and said to him that since he belonged to his Order, he was permitted to come to pay his respects.

Hazrat Abdul Quddus submitted that people greatly feared of his wrath. Since they wanted to offer their respects they should be permitted to do so. His supplication was accepted and since that day people were able to approach his tomb, offer their respects, and derive spiritual ecstasy.

References

1. *Mir'at-ul-Ansaab,* pp. 149-59.
2. *Kashf-ul-Ghayyub.*
3. *Anwar-ul-Quds.*
4. *Masalek-us-Salekeen,* vol. II, pp. 340-41.
5. *Siyar-ul-Aqtab.*
6. *Kanj-ul-Ma'arif.*
7. *Siyar-ul-Aqtab,* pp. 180-81.

10

Hazrat Shaikh Sharf-ud-din Ahmad of Munir

Hazrat Shaikh Sharf-ud-din Ahmad of Munir was an eminent saint and an erudite scholar, and was the son of Yahya of Munir. He came to Delhi with the object of becoming a spiritual disciple of Hazrat Nizam-ud-din Auliya, but before he reached Delhi Hazrat Nizam-ud-din Auliya had passed away. He then went to offer his respects to Hazrat Shaikh Najib-ud-din Firdausi, who seeing him said at once:[1] "O, Sharf, come. I have been waiting for you for the last so many years. I have been anxious to meet you for a long time past and I have been waiting." Hazrat Shaikh Najib-ud-din Firdausi accepted him as his spiritual disciple and confided to him the holy relics of his spiritual forefathers. He then permitted him to leave straightaway, saying:[2] "My life depended upon your initiation as a spiritual disciple. I entrust thee to God. If you receive the news of my death you should return to this place without delay." He had not yet gone very far when he heard the sound of weeping coming from the house of Hazrat Shaikh Najib-ud-din Firdausi. When he returned he was informed that the Shaikh had passed away.

The present

It is said that one day Shaikh Sharf-ud-din Ahmad of Munir offered some alchemy to Hazrat Najib-ud-din Firdausi, who threw some water upon it.[3] Instead of mourning the apparent loss, Shaikh Sharf-ud-din was elated. He said that though the touch of dust could change everything into gold, yet it brought heaviness in his heart, and today, thank God, he was freed from these bare ambitions.

When he heard this, Hazrat Shaikh Najib-ud-din Firdausi was extremely pleased with him and wanting to requite him, wrote some words on a piece of paper and gave it to him. When he placed that slip of paper on his head, everything that was beneath the earth was disclosed to him.

Shaikh Sharf-ud-din kissed the paper and placed it before his spiritual guide and teacher. It also constituted a source of heaviness in his heart. He did not desire it. It should be given to the one who longed for it. Hazrat Shaikh Najib-ud-din Firdausi, surprised at the indifference, prayed for him and gave him his blessings.

Death

After staying in a forest for sometime on his way to Agra, he reached his home town, Munir, and died there.

Caliph

Shaikh Muzaffar of Balkh is his most prominent spiritual disciple and caliph.

Traits of character

Shaikh Sharf-ud-din was a perfect dervish and the author of a number of books. His letters are famous for their exposition of mysticism. It is also said that he wrote a commentary on *Adab-ul-Mureeden.*

Teachings

In one of his letters, addressed to Shaikh Muzaffar, he says that he should ever be engaged in his work like men. The various preoccupations, the very many troubles and hardships, and various kinds of trials that beset one treading the spiritual path of perfection should not deter, disturb, or bring about any change of outlook.

He adds that the ways of God are inscrutable and beyond human understanding. It cannot be said by which path God Almighty will confer good luck, comfort, and pleasure on an individual, whether by way of blessing or by way of industry, or by way of gift, or by way of misfortune.

Proceeding, he says that the secrets of God are unknown. If all the states are disclosed to an individual in one way, then the knowledge of an individual will surround the Godhood, and God with His qualities cannot be surrounded.

References

1. *Rozat-ul-Aqtab*, p. 85.
2. Ibid.
3. *Kalimat-us-Sadeqeen.*

11

Hazrat Shaikh Sharf-ud-din Bu Ali Qalandar

Hazrat Shaikh Sharf-ud-din Bu Ali Qalandar is considered to be one of the leading saints. He is related to the great law-giver Abu Hanifa.[1] His father, Salar Fakhr-ud-din, belonged to the Chishti Order, and his mother was named Bibi Hafiza Jamal. He was born in Panipat. He acquired knowledge and learning and took to renunciation and ascetic practices. On his becoming an absorbed one, he threw all his books into a river.

His initiation into the Sufi Order is a matter of controversy. There are some who hold that he was a spiritual disciple and caliph of Hazrat Khwaja Qutb-ud-din Bakhtyar Kaki, but that he received his spiritual training from Hazrat Shaikh Shahab-ud-din Ashiq.[2] It is also said that he was a spiritual disciple of Hazrat Najm-ud-din Qalandar. There are some who believe that he was a spiritual disciple of Shaikh Shahab-ud-din Ashiq, who was a disciple of Shaikh Amad-ud-din Abdal, who was a disciple of Shaikh Badr-ud-din of Ghazni, who was a spiritual disciple and caliph of Hazrat Khwaja Qutb-ud-din Bakhtyar Kaki.[3] Others hold that he was a spiritual disciple of Hazrat Nizam-ud-din Auliya.

He breathed his last on the ninth of Ramazan in the year AH 724 and was buried in Karnal.

Traits of character

He was profoundly absorbed in mystical thought, was a poet and the author of several books on mysticism. His letters to Ikhtiyar-ud-din reveal a deep insight into spiritual matters.[4]

Teachings

In one of his letters, he says that when an individual is shown the Grace of God and the proper mood is conferred upon him, and he is separated from the self, then and only then will love make its own way and show its own manifestation of beauty, and only then will be recognise the beloved.

He goes on to say that an individual should understand his "self" well. Then alone will he be able to understand the world. If an individual recognises the soul, then he will be able to understand the world hereafter.

He emphasises, that an individual should ever be engaged in his quest and should recognise himself. When an individual recognises his self then he will be able to understand love. He goes on to say that the beauty of the manifestation of the world makes the lovers of the world so unmindful in their love that they are not aware of the world, which is their beloved; that it is passing on and strange things are happening; neither are they aware of the world hereafter. That is the problem that confronts us.

Supernatural power

Once a certain devotee of Hazrat Shams-ud-din Turk of Panipat saw him sitting in the shape of a lion. On receiving the message from the former, he left the city and went to live in a deserted place, which came to be known as Yaghooti. He later moved to Bhudda Khera near Karnal.[5]

References

1. *Khazinat-ul-Asfiya*, vol. I, pp. 326-27.
2. *Ma'arif-ul-Vilayat.*
3. *Manaqib-e-Faridi.*
4. *Khazinat-ul-Asfiya*, vol. I, p. 326.
5. Ibid., vol. I, pp. 327-28.

12

Hazrat Khwaja Husam-ud-din Soqta

Hazrat Khwaja Husam-ud-din Soqta was the son of Hazrat Khwaja Fakhr-ud-din Abul Khair and hence the grandson of Hazrat Khwaja Moin-ud-din Hasan Chishti. His father named him after his brother, whose whereabouts were not known.[1]

He was ever absorbed in the remembrance of God. The pangs of love of the Friend made him restless, and caused his eyes to shed tears. He enjoyed the company of Hazrat Nizam-ud-din Auliya.

Hazrat Khwaja Husam-ud-din Soqta was a perfect dervish.

He had two sons and passed away in AH 741 and lies buried in Sambhar.[2]

References

1. *Gulzar-e-Abrar,* p. 23.
2. *Akhbar-ul-Akhiar,* p. 116; *Gulzar-e-Abrar,* p. 33; *Tazkara Auliya-e-Hind,* p. 147.

13

Hazrat Nasir-ud-din Mahmud Chiragh of Delhi

Hazrat Nasir-ud-din Mahmud Chiragh of Delhi was the spiritual successor of Hazrat Nizam-ud-din Auliya. His forefathers belonged to Khorasan. One of them, Shaikh Abdul Latif Nirvi, came to Lahore and settled there. His son, Shaikh Yahya, migrated from Lahore to Oudh. His father, Shaikh Yahya, settled permanently in Oudh. He was a sufi, who was *pashmina* trader, and quite well- off, maintaining slaves.[1] His mother was very pious passed much of her time in prayer, and was known as the Rabia of her time.

Nasir-ud-din was born in Oudh, Mahmud is his title. He is known as "Chiragh Delhi" or Lamp of Delhi. There are certain reasons for this nickname: Hazrat Makhdoom Jahanian-e-Jahan Gasht went to Mecca and there met Hazrat Imam Yafai. During the course of conversation, Hazrat Imam Yafai said that formerly there were many saints in Delhi who all had died. He went on to say: "Now there remains Shaikh Nasir-ud-din of Oudh, who is the *chiragh* (lamp) of Delhi.[2]" The second reason is this that once certain dervishes came to Delhi and met Hazrat Nizam-ud-din Auliya. They were sitting there, when by chance Hazrat Nasir-ud-din Chiragh of Delhi also arrived there. Hazrat Nizam-ud-din Auliya asked him to sit down, but he respectfully submitted: "My back will be turned towards the dervishes." Thereupon Hazrat Mahboob-e-Ilahi said: "The back is not turned towards the lamp." Thereupon he sat down. His front and back were the same. As he used to see from the front, so he began to see from the back too. From that day, he became famous as "Chiragh Delhi" or the Lamp of Delhi. A third reason assigned to this, that once the king, who was jealous of the prestige and honour accorded to Hazrat Nizam-ud-din Auliya, ordered that oil being provided to his monastery be stopped on the day of a certain *'urs* (annual death anniversary). Hazrat Nasir-ud-din informed Hazrat Nizam-ud-din Auliya of this who then asked: "Is there any water in the tank, that is being dug?" He replied in the affirmative. Hazrat Nizam-ud-din Auliya then ordered: "Fill the water in the lamps and burn them." He did so and all the lamps began to shed light. The lamps were thus burnt not on oil, but on water.

Education

After his father's death, when he was nine years old, his mother took great pains in getting him properly educated. He was put in-charge of Maulana Abdul Karim Sherwani, an erudite scholar of his time. After the latter's death he was sent to Maulana Iftikhar-ud-din of Gilan, who was well-versed in the various branches of knowledge. He completed his education at the age of twenty.

Mysticism

From the outset, he had a mystic turn of mind. He took pleasure in renunciation and began to live in the company of a dervish who resided in a desolate place far from the city. He had nothing to do with the world, living on grass and leaves.

From Oudh, he came to Delhi. At that time he was forty-three years old. Some say that he was then only forty. In Delhi, he derived spiritual joy from the company of Hazrat Nizam-ud-din Auliya, who honoured him by accepting him as his spiritual disciple. Subsequently, Hazrat Nizam-ud-din Auliya conferred upon him the robe of caliph, appointing him as his *sajjada-nashin* (spiritual successor). He confided to him all the holy relics which he had received from his spiritual guide and teacher Hazrat Baba Farid-ud-din Ganj-e-Shakar, directing him to keep those holy relics with him with all respect and care as he himself had done.

Once Khwaja Mohammed Gazarooni, the spiritual disciple of Hazrat Baha-ud-din Zakariya of Multan, came to Delhi to see Hazrat Nizam-ud-din Auliya, he stayed in his monastery that night, did his ablutions for the pre-dawn prayer and took off his cotton covering. This covering got lost and he began to abuse Khwaja Mahommed the devotee in-charge of the monastery. Hazrat Nasir-ud-din Chiragh of Delhi was at that time present in the monastery, engaged in prayer. On hearing the exchange of words, he got up and offered his own cotton covering to Khwaja Mohammed Gazarooni, thus ending the matter. The news of this was conveyed to Hazrat Nizam-ud-din Auliya who called Hazrat Nasir-ud-din Chiragh of Delhi and gave him his own cotton covering and prayed for his well-being and honoured him by conferring upon him his temporal and the spiritual blessings.

One day, he conveyed through Hazrat Amir Khusrau his request to Hazrat Nizam-ud-din Auliya that he might be permitted to live in some mountain or forest in order to devote himself exclusively to prayers and asceticism. His spiritual guide replied: "Tell him that he should live in the city and should bear patiently the tyranny and maltreatment meted out to him by the people and in return should undergo sacrifice for their sake and should be generous and kind to them."

Asceticism

Hazrat Nasir-ud-din Chiragh of Delhi underwent the severest type of rigours and asceticism. Once he lived mostly on lemons, with the result that he fell ill. At another time, he didn't eat anything for ten days continuously. When Hazrat Nizam-ud-din Auliya was informed about this, he called him in his presence and asked him to eat bread and pudding. In obedience to the command of his spiritual guide and teacher he did so.

Death

He made a will to Shaikh Zain-ud-din and Shaikh Kamal-ud-din to the effect that after his death, they should place the robe of caliph conferred upon him by his spiritual guide on his breast in the grave, the cap in the direction of his head, the rosary in his finger, and the stick and the shoes beside him.[2] He passed away on the eighteenth of Ramazan in AH 757 and lies buried in Delhi.[3]

His caliphs

Prominent among his caliphs are: Hazrat Khwaja Banda Nawaz; Syed Mohammed Gesoo Daraz; Hazrat Shaikh Kamal-ud-din; Makhdoom Jahanian-e-Jahan Gasht; Maulana Ala-ud-din Sandilla; Maulana Khwajgi; Qazi Mohammed Shadi; Shaikh Sulaiman Rudaulavi; and Shaikh Mohammed Mutawakkil.

Traits of character

Hazrat Nasir-ud-din Chiragh of Delhi had a captivating personality. He was an embodiment of knowledge, wisdom, love and unparalleled patience and perseverance. He had a sacrificing nature and bore with patience and fortitude the tyranny of the people. He rewarded evil with good and strictly adhered to the tenets of his spiritual guide and teacher. He was very fond of music.

He had a forgiving nature. Once a *qalandar* entered his tenement and inflicted eighteen wounds on his face but, he would not allow the assailant to be punished. Instead, he gave him a horse and fifty gold coins and asked him to leave the city as soon as possible so that the people might not harass him. The *qalandar* did so.

Hazrat Nasir-ud-din Chiragh of Delhi also had poetic qualities.

Teachings

He says: "O dervish! In the path of enlightenment he is called the spiritual guide, who has full control over the inward state of his spiritual disciple and who, knowing the outward and the inward difficulties of his spiritual disciple, solves them every moment. Besides, he should cleanse the inward mirror."

He says thus in regard to the obligations of the spiritual disciple:

> The true disciple is one who acts according to the dictates of his spiritual teacher and guide. He sees that only, which may be shown to him by his spiritual guide. He takes his spiritual guide as omnipresent. He brings to the notice of his spiritual guide and teacher all his good and bad ideas that may arise in his mind. He cannot be called a true spiritual disciple who disobeys his spiritual guide even in the slightest degree.[4]

He says: "Asceticism constitutes the capital of a dervish, but that asceticism should be purely for God and not with the object of winning the public applause or that people may take him to be a saintly man. The sincerity with which asceticism is conducted is the key thing, and then alone will it be affective. Thereby, God will cause him to reach the coveted goal."[5]

He says: "The real work is the protection of the self. In meditation, a sufi should keep an eye on his self, i.e., may stop breath so that inner satisfaction may be acquired. The breath will disturb his inner state and cause disturbance."[6]

Sayings

- Sincerity of intention is required in all things.
- The morsel of trade is a good morsel indeed.
- The more the enlightened gets the gnosis of God, the more the relations are severed.
- A dervish should not disclose his need to anyone even though

he may face starvation.

- If the intention be based on good in search of worldly pursuit, then in fact that search constitutes the search for the world hereafter.
- Music for the distressed constitutes almost a cure. As there is a cure for outward pain; in the same way, there is no other cure for inward pain save music.

Supernatural powers

Once he wrote something on a piece of paper and gave it to Aziz-ud-din to present it at the tomb of Hazrat Nizam-ud-din Auliya. Aziz-ud-din wanted to read its contents, but he thought it better to present it first and read it later. He did so but after presenting it to the tomb there was nothing to be read any longer, merely a blank sheet of paper.

One day it so happened that Sultan Mohammed Bin Tughlaq left Delhi for Thatta and took some saints and sufis with him. He also invited Hazrat Nasir-ud-din Chiragh of Delhi, but he conveyed a message to the Sultan saying: "It is not proper for the Sultan to take me with him, because he will not return." This prediction actually proved to be true.[7]

References

1. *Siyar-ul-Auliya*, p. 238.
2. Firishta, p. 399; *Siyar-ul-Arefeen*.
3. *Mirat-ul-Israr*.
4. *Siyar-ul-Auliya*, p. 242.
5. *Muftah-ul-Ashiqeen*, Urdu trans., p. 2.
6. *Khair-ul-Majalis*, p. 99.
7. *Siyar-ul-Auliya*, p. 243.

14

Hazrat Shams-ud-din Turk of Panipat

Hazrat Shams-ud-din Turk of Panipat was the spiritual caliph and successor of Hazrat Ala-ud-din Ahmad Sabir. He belonged to Turkestan where he was brought up and received his education.

His paternal genealogy is as follows: Shaikh Shams-ud-din Turk son of Syed Ahmad Turk son of Syed Abdul Momin son of Hazrat Khwaja Biswi, who had an affiliation with Hazrat Hanifa the son of Hazrat Ali.

Initiation in Sufi Order

After completing his education he took the mystic path of life. He left his home and hearth in search of a spiritual guide. He wandered around Turkestan but failed to achieve his object there.[1] From Turkestan he travelled to Trans-Jordan and then made his way towards India. In India, he wandered from place to place in search of a spiritual guide. His arrival in Kalyar marked the termination of his quest because he was accepted as a spiritual disciple by Hazrat Sabir Sahab. Hazrat Sabir Sahab said to him: "O, Shams-ud-din! know that thou art my spiritual son. I had prayed to God and my prayer has been accepted, that my Order shall spread through thee." He served Hazrat Sabir Sahab for sometime and received his spiritual education and training there. After undergoing rigours and hardships, he underwent inner purification and illumination. Subsequently, he was appointed a spiritual caliph.

The will

Hazrat Sabir Sahab made a will to the effect, that after he died Hazrat Shams-ud-din should not stay in Kalyar for more than three days but move on to Panipat and settle there permanently as that was the domain entrusted to his care.

Hazrat Shams-ud-din Turk was not sure whether he could get on well with Hazrat Shah Bu Ali Qalandar who already lived in Panipat. Hazrat Sabir Sahab however assured him that wherever he might be, he would be spiritually with him, ever helping, assisting, and guiding him. He forecasted that when he went to Panipat he would face no difficulty. Hazrat Shah Bu Ali Qalandar would give up his residence and retire to the outskirts of the city and then, would eventually pass away.

Service

With the permission of his spiritual guide he left Kalyar and joined the service of Sultan Ghiyas-ud-din Balban.

Once it happened, that the Sultan at the head of his army, went out to conquer a certain fort. One night it blew very hard. The light went off and there was darkness all around. The royal water-carrier wanted to fetch some fire in order to boil some water for the Sultan's ablutions. There was light only in one tent and entering it he saw Hazrat Shams-ud-din Turk of Panipat reading the Holy *Quran*. Next day, when Hazrat Shams-ud-din was undertaking his ablutions, the water-carrier found to his surprise that the water in that tank was quite hot. Later, when the water-carrier was alone at the tank, the water was cold again. He then realised that it was the spiritual power of Hazrat Shams-ud-din that had worked behind the burning of the lamp and the temperature of the water.

Later, both the Sultan and the water-carrier, respectfully entered his tent. He was asked to pray for the conquest of the fort, but was reluctant to do so because he did not want to lay any claim on being a spiritual man. Eventually, he prayed for the conquest of the and the fort was conquered.

He resigned and left for Kalyar, and when he reached there he found his spiritual guide and teacher dead. He buried him and performed the funeral rites.

In accordance with his teacher's will he did not stay for more than three days in Kalyar and permanently settled in Panipat. One day, one of his devotees passed through the locality where Hazrat Qalandar Sahab lived. He was extremely surprised to find him sitting in the shape of a lion. Thereupon, Hazrat Shams-ud-din Turk sent him a message that the fittest place for lions to live in is the jungle, so he should go out and settle in a jungle. Hazrat Qalandar Sahab, on receiving the message, shifted to a lonely and deserted place, thus leaving Panipat to his exclusive control.

Death

Hazrat Shams-ud-din Turk of Panipat breathed his last on the fifteenth of Jamadi-us-Sani, AH 716. According to others, he died on the tenth of Sha'ban (some say the nineteenth) of AH 716. He is buried in Panipat.

Caliph

Hazrat Shaikh Jalal-ud-din Kabir Auliya of Panipat is his spiritual caliph and successor.

Supernatural powers

Hazrat Shams-ud-din Turk of Panipat exhibited very many supernatural powers. Once he was asked to prove that he really was a Syed. He then reacted by saying that it is told that fire cannot burn the one belonging to the august family of the holy Prophet Mohammed, and that he willing to demonstrate this immediately, and so he entered the fire. It is said that a fountain appeared within the fire and that he offered his prayers therein. He invited his chief critic, who made the pretence of being a Syed, to come in. The man refused. Suddenly a flame leapt out and his clothes caught fire and he was in great pain. Hazrat Shams-ud-din immediately came out and extinguished the fire. His chief critic, the pretender, was greatly embarrassed. Hazrat Shams-ud-din himself was not in the least harmed by the fire.[2]

REFERENCES.

1. *Siyar-ul-Aqtab*
2. Ibid.

15

Hazrat Amir Khusrau

Hazrat Amir Khusrau was the poet laureate of the Indian sub-continent and the spiritual disciple and caliph of Hazrat Nizam-ud-din Auliya. He belonged to an eminent family of Hazara (Balkh) which was the custodian of knowledge and wealth. His father, Amir Saif-ud-din Mahmud, was amongst the noblemen of Hazara. During the time of Chingiz Khan, he left Afghanistan and came to India, and soon his merit was duly recognised and he was assigned an important post.

Hazrat Amir Khusrau was born in Mominabad, which is now known as Patiale, and was named Abul Hasan. His title is Yamin-ud-din. His two brothers are named Aizaz-ud-din Ali Shah and Husam-ud-din.[1] Brought up in the family tradition, his father took great interest in his education and training. At the age of nine he lost his father. After becoming an orphan a certain relation of his mother who had already expired at an earlier date than his father paid particular attention to his education and training.

Initiation in to the Sufi Order

When he was eight years old his father took him to Hazrat Nizam-ud-din Auliya. He told his father that he wanted to choose a spiritual guide himself, so his father did not insist any further. Hazrat Amir Khusrau waited outside the tenement of Hazrat Nizam-ud-din Auliya, while his father entered it. He then wrote a couplet and told himself that if Hazrat Nizam-ud-din Auliya was a perfect dervish he would call him inside.

This actually happened: Hazrat Nizam-ud-din Auliya asked a devotee to recite some verses that he had composed, which implied permission to enter. The former honoured him by accepting him as his disciple. In course of time he was appointed caliph. Thus, his sincerity, devotion, and love for his spiritual guide secured for him the crown of immortality.

Relations with Khwaja Hasan

His love for Khwaja Hasan was intense and proverbial. When this love assumed major dimensions and became the topic of the city, Prince Sultan Khan had Khwaja Hasan, whipped as punishment. The prince directed him not to meet Hazrat Amir Khusrau, but to everyone's great surprise Khwaja Hasan, after being whipped and in spite of the royal mandate, again went to Hazrat Amir Khusrau. The prince was infuriated and summoned the latter and inquired from him about the relations with Khwaja Hasan. Hazrat Amir Khusrau replied: "Duality no more subsists between us." As proof, he uncovered his arm on which the welts of the whip were visible just where they had been inflicted Khwaja Hasan.

Relations with kings

Hazrat Amir Khusrau and Khwaja Hasan were in the pay of Prince Sultan Khan, the favourite son of Sultan Ghiyas-ud-din Balban, whose headquarters were in Multan. He wanted to resign, but the prince did not allow him to do so.

When Prince Sultan was killed in Multan, he came to Delhi and was soon in the pay of Amir Ali. After the accession to the throne, Hazrat Amir Khusrau became a favourite of Sultan Jalal-ud-din Khalji. He was a favourite of all the kings, who ascended the throne during his lifetime and had very cordial relations with Sultan Qutb-ud-din Mubarak Shah. He was a great favourite of Sultan Ghiyas-ud-din Tughlaq, after whose name he wrote the book entitled *Tughlaqnama.*[2]

Qalandar Sahab

Once he went to Panipat as the personal envoy and representative of Sultan Ala-ud-din Khalji to offer some presents to the renowned saint Hazrat Qalandar Sahab. He was received with due regard. Hazrat Qalandar Sahab was greatly moved on hearing his poetry, and then he recited his own. On hearing them Hazrat Amir Khusrau began to weep. On seeing this Qalandar Sahab said: "O, Khusrau! Thou weepest only. Hast thou understood something?" Hazrat Khusrau promptly replied: "I weep for this reason that I have not understood anything." Hazrat Qalandar Sahab was greatly pleased with reply and the result was that he accepted the presents sent by Sultan Ala-ud-din Khalji.[3]

Future title

One day he thought to himself that his poetic nickname "Khusrau" was like worldly people and how nice it would have been had like those of dervishes. He told this to his spiritual guide and teacher. Hazrat Nizam-ud-din Auliya, after some contemplation said: "On the Day of Judgment thou shalt be called by the title 'Mohammed Kasa-e-Lais' (Mohammed, increasingly greedy for blessings)."[4]

Will

He has made a talisman of the paper on which he had written all the words and phrases of love and affection concerning him, which his spiritual guide and teacher, Hazrat Nizam-ud-din Auliya had said about him. He made a Will to the effect that the sheet of paper containing these words and phrases should be buried with him in his grave, so as to be a possible source of his salvation.

Death

At the time Hazrat Nizam-ud-din Auliya died, he was in Lakhnauti with Sultan Ghiyas-ud-din Tughlaq.[5] Hearing the news of his death, he came down to Delhi and resigned his post. He distributed all that he had amongst the poor and the needy persons and severed all connections with the world. He wore the clothes of mourning and began to spend most of his time at the grave of his spiritual guide and teacher. He lived in this way for about six months and could bear no further separation. He breathed his last on the eighteenth of Shawwal in AH 725. He was buried at a small distance from the eternal place of rest of Hazrat Nizam-ud-din Auliya.

Traits of character

Hazrat Amir Khusrau was not only a great poet, a scholar of vast learning and erudition, an eminent writer, but at the same time he was a saint, a sufi, and a sage. He used to wake up regularly in the dead of night and offer prayers and recite seven parts of the Holy *Quran*. Notwithstanding the fact that he was in service, he took to an ascetic life and fasted throughout the year for forty years.[6] It is also said, that by the dint of his spiritual powers, he alongwith Hazrat Nizam-ud-din Auliya performed the pilgrimage to Mecca.

Devotion to his spiritual guide

Hazrat Amir Khusrau had greatest love for and intense devotion to his spiritual guide and teacher. When in Delhi, he used to pass most of the time in the company of Hazrat Nizam-ud-din Auliya. He had in fact attained the position of being absorbed and lost in the personality of his spiritual guide.

Once, a certain person came to Hazrat Nizam-ud-din Auliya, to seek financial help from him. This man had seven daughters, but was unable to finance their marriages. It happened that there was nothing in the monastery that day apart from a pair of sandals. Hazrat Nizam-ud-din Auliya therefore gave him the sandals, which did not greatly please him. He left Delhi and stayed in a tavern for the night and as happened, Hazrat Amir Khusrau also stayed there. He sensed the smell of his spiritual guide and made a round of the tavern in search of any person who had come from Delhi. When he met him, he was informed about the presentation of the sandals. Then Hazrat Amir Khusrau took the sandals and gave in return all the money and all the precious articles that he had with him wrapping the sandals in his turban he tied them on his head and went to his spiritual guide and teacher Hazrat Nizam-ud-din Auliya.[7]

The love of the spiritual guide

Hazrat Nizam-ud-din had great love and affection for him.[8] Once he said: "I feel tired of all; so much so that I am tired of my own self, but I never feel tired of thee."

On another occasion, he said: "I will not enter paradise without him. Had it been permissible for two persons being buried in the same grave, I would have made a will, that he should be buried in my grave."[9]

Out of love, his spiritual guide would refer to him as the "Turk of Allah." Once he prayed: "May God grant me salvation for the sake of the pangs of sorrow of the breast of this Turk."[10]

He also said once: "On the day of Judgment, it would be inquired from everyone as to what he had brought." When that will be inquired from me I will say: "The pangs of sorrow of the breast of this Turk of Allah."

Poetic taste

Hazrat Amir Khusrau has written a great deal of poetry. It is estimated that the number of the verses he wrote is less than five hundred thousand, out over than four hundred thousand.[11]

It is said, that the renowned poet and mystic, Hazrat Shaikh Sa'di, of Shiraz, came to India to meet him.[12]

Once, he met Hazrat Khizr. He asked him to be so kind as to give him the liquid of his mouth. Hazrat Khizr replied, that it had already been given to Shaikh Sa'di of Shiraz. Thereafter, he made the same request to Hazrat Nizam-ud-din Auliya. By the blessing of that liquid his poetry received universal recognition.

Literary output

Hazrat Amir Khusrau has written about ninety-two books. His famous book entitled *Rahat-ul-Mohibbeen* encompasses the discourses of his Hazrat Nizam-ud-din Auliya. Amongst his other books the most famous are: *Tuhfat-us-Saghir; Wasf-ul-Hayat; Ghurrat-ul-Kamal; Nihayat-ul-Kamal; Quran-us-Sa'dain; Matla'e Anwar; Sheerien Khusrau; Laila Majnoon; Aina-e-Sikandari; Hasht Bihisht; Taj-ul-Fatooh; Nuh Sipihr; Ei'jaz-e-Khusravi, Tughlaqnama; Khazaen-ul-Futuh;* and *Manaqib-e-Hind.*

Supernatural power

When Shaikh Rukn-ud-din Abul Fatah of Multan raised his hands at his funeral and wanted to pray, he got up and recited the verse which, translated runs: "We have been so much absorbed in the love of our spiritual guide and teacher / that we do not require the beneficence of the benefactor."

References

1. *Nafahat-ul-uns.*
2. Firishta, p. 402.
3. *Sharf-ul-Manaqib.*
4. *Nafahat-ul-uns,* p. 548.
5. Firishta, pp. 402-3.
6. Firishta, p. 403; *Safinat-ul-Auliya,* p. 99.
7. *Safinat-ul-Auliya,* p. 100.
8. *Lataif-e-Ashrafi fi Bayan-e-Tasawwuf-e-Sufi,* p. 360.
9. Firishta, p. 403.
10. Ibid.
11. *Safinat-ul-Auliya,* p. 99.
12. *Nafahat-ul-uns,* p. 548.

16

Hazrat Maulana Fakhr-ud-din Marozi

Hazrat Maulana Fakhr-ud-din Marozi combined in himself the qualities of saint and a scholar. He concentrated first on the acquisition of knowledge and learning, and acquired a profound knowledge of commentaries on the Holy *Quran*, the *Hadis*, and jurisprudence, committing the Holy *Quran* to memory.

After completing his education, he was attracted towards the inner life and was accepted as a spiritual disciple by Hazrat Nizam-ud-din Auliya. He loved his spiritual guide deeply and shifted to Ghiaspur in order to be close to him, passing the rest of his life there.

Advice

Hazrat Nizam-ud-din Auliya wrote to him regarding the secret of the love of God. He wrote:

> The mystics and those leading the inner life are unanimous in this respect, that the important aim and the great object of the people is in fact the love of God Almighty. It is of two kinds, namely, love of person and love of qualities. The love of person is among the gifts and the love of qualities is among the acquired things. What pertains to the gifted things has nothing to do with acquisition and action. What is among the acquired things is acquired after all.
>
> The way of acquiring love is the constant remembrance of God with the heart, devoted and unmindful of all. This requires leisure. There are four things that are detrimental and opposed to leisure. They are the people, the world, the self and Satan. The way of removing the people is taking to seclusion and it is a near and efficacious way, and the way of escaping from the world is taking to contentment, and the way of getting rid of the self and Satan is to pray to God.[1]

Traits of character

Hazrat Maulana Fakhr-ud-din Marozi had a forbearing nature, his outlook towards life characterised by trust in God and contentment. He took pleasure in abstinence and renunciation. He was a pious man and lived on what he earned by copying the Holy *Quran*. He used to meet unseen men.

Death

He died in AH 736 and was buried in Delhi near the tomb of his master.

Supernatural powers

Once he was thirsty and there was no one who could fetch water for him. To his great surprise, he saw a cup full of water. He broke that cup and said that he would not imbibe such water. When he brought this to the notice of his spiritual guide and teacher, he suggested that the water should have been drunk.[2]

On the another occasion, he required a comb but had none with him who could fetch one. Suddenly a comb appeared from the wall, which took in his hand and used.[3]

REFERENCES

1. *Siyar-ul-Auliya,* pp. 454-55.
2. Ibid., pp. 298-99.
3. Ibid., p. 299.

17

Hazrat Maulana Ala-ud-din Nili

Hazrat Maulana Ala-ud-din Nili is a celebrated saint, completed his education at an early age. He was well-versed in jurisprudence, *Hadis*, logic, commentaries on the Holy *Quran*, and mysticism. He committed the Holy *Quran* to memory. He became a spiritual disciple of Hazrat Nizam-ud-din Auliya and was subsequently elevated to be the caliph.

Gift of his spiritual guide

One day, Hazrat Nizam-ud-din Auliya was as usual sitting in the upper storey of his monastery. Hazrat Maulana Ala-ud-din Nili came there and began to offer prayers in the courtyard of the prayer hall. Those who had not yet prayed, began to offer their prayers behind him.[1] He recited sections of the Holy *Quran* in a very melodious tone. Hazrat Nizam-ud-din Auliya, hearing this was greatly moved and seized by a state of rapture. He ordered a devotee of his called Iqbal to present his special prayer carpet to Hazrat Maulana Ala-ud-din Nili.[2] The latter took the praying carpet, kissed it, rubbed his eyes with it, placed it on his head, and counted it as his greatest treasure on earth.

Respect for the spiritual guide

Once it happened that he together with Maulana Shams-ud-din Yahya and some other devotees came to Delhi from Oudh. As was to be expected, they lost no time in paying their respects to Hazrat Nizam-ud-din Auliya. According to custom, he asked them all to go to the tomb of Hazrat Qutb-ud-din Bakhtyar Kaki and pay their respects.

After a short stay Hazrat Nizam-ud-din Auliya asked them to leave Delhi. They were surprised and a bit sad about this. They both left for Oudh, but on reaching Tal Pattan, Hazrat Maulana Ala-ud-din Nili fell ill with high fever.

A letter was sent to Hazrat Nizam-ud-din Auliya informing him of his illness and seeking further instructions. On being informed, he sent him some money and ordered him to return to Delhi, sending his special palanquin to bring him.

He was extremely pleased to receive the order to return to Delhi, but flatly refused to ride in the palanquin. He said that he had not the courage, the boldness, and the impertinence to ride the special palanquin of his master. He left for Delhi in a hired conveyance and ordered that the palanquin should precede it, so that he might be able to see it all the way, and by the blessing of seeing it he might recover.[3]

On reaching Delhi, he narrated the details of his illness to his spiritual guide. Hazrat Nizam-ud-din Auliya then asked Khwaja Iqbal to bring a portion of the morning meal, and Hazrat Maulana Ala-ud-din Nili ate it all and the fever subsided and he fully recovered. He was asked why he did not ride the palanquin. He submitted: "If your Holiness may show regard and love to this humble being it is indeed very kind of your Holiness. But this humble being should be ever aware of his own conditions and should not forget it." Later, whenever he saw the palanquin, he paid it the utmost respect and reverence and would derive spiritual blessings from it.

Meeting Maulana Hisam-ud-din

Once he and Maulana Shams-ud-din Yahya went to see Maulana Husam-ud-din. He was not at home, so they waited for him. After a while he came, carrying some rice and some dried wood. They wanted to help him, but he did not allow them to do so, saying: "It is my duty to carry my load."

He gave the rice to be cooked and they all sat on a mat. Maulana Shams-ud-din placed a pair of trousers before him and Maulana Ala-ud-din Nili placed a silver coin. He entertained them both. When they were leaving he placed the silver coin, presented by Maulana Ala-ud-din Nili before Maulana Shams-ud-din Yahya, whose pair of trousers he placed before Maulana Ala-ud-din Nili, apologising for not accepting them.[4]

Traits of character

Maulana Ala-ud-din Nili was a very learned man combining piety with learning. He, wore the dress of the *ulamas* (the learned men) though at heart he was a dervish. He was a fluent and charismatic speaker. He recited the Holy *Quran* with such a sweet and melodious voice, that the audience was spellbound.

He paid the utmost respect to his spiritual guide and teacher. Hazrat Maulana Ala-ud-din Nili was a man of simple habits, unassuming, and unattached to the world, and took to renunciation.

Last days

In his last days, he gave up the study of books, except one; and also stopped ritual practices except one. The one book to which he confined himself was entitled *Afzal-ul-Fawaid,* which contained the discourses and directions of his spiritual guide and teacher Hazrat Nizam-ud-din Auliya, deriving spiritual ecstasy and inspiration from it. He read it over and over again, copied it with his own hand, and never allowed it to be lost sight of.[5]

Someone asked him why this was so, to which he replied: "It is true, that there are very many books on mysticism and enlightenment, but for me the inspiring discourses of my spiritual guide and teacher constitute the source of salvation."

Death

Hazrat Maulana Ala-ud-din Nili died in AH 762 and lies buried in Delhi, near the tomb of his spiritual guide and teacher.

References

1. *Lataif-e-Ashrafi fi Bayan-e-Tasawwuf-e-Sufi,* p. 357.
2. *Siyar-ul-Auliya,* p. 276.
3. Ibid., p. 277.
4. Ibid., p. 250.
5. Ibid., p. 278.

18

Hazrat Shaikh Burhan-ud-din Gharib

Hazrat Shaikh Burhan-ud-din Gharib was a spiritual disciple and caliph of Hazrat Nizam-ud-din Auliya.

The caliphate
Some of the old devotees of Hazrat Nizam-ud-din Auliya, namely, Khwaja Mubashshir, Syed Husain, and Syed Khamoosh consulted among themselves and decided that Shaikh Burhan-ud-din Gharib was an old and devoted disciple who deserved promotion and was, otherwise, fit for appointment as a caliph.[1]

They took him to Hazrat Nizam-ud-din Auliya and submitted that his old spiritual disciple had come to pay his respects to him and expected favours from him. The Shaikh thereafter, kissed the ground underneath the feet of his master. Khwaja Iqbal then brought the cap and the robe, given on behalf of Hazrat Nizam-ud-din Auliya, and having the hand of his holiness placed on them, caused them to be worn by Hazrat Burhan-ud-din Gharib in the presence of his master, declaring him also a caliph.

Displeasure of the spiritual guide
When he was about seventy years old he had become very weak and it was difficult for him to sit on the ground. He used to wrap up his blanket fourfold and used to sit on it in the monastery.

Ali Zumbeli and Malik Nusrat, who were related to Sultan Ala-ud-din and had become spiritual disciples of Hazrat Nizam-ud-din Auliya, complained to their master that he sat on *gaddi* and posed to be a *sajjada* (spiritual successor). Hazrat Nizam-ud-din Auliya was displeased with him and did not talk to him, when he came. Mixed feelings of sorrow and surprise overtook him and quietly he went to the prayer hall and sat there. Later, Khwaja Iqbal came to him and told him that Hazrat Nizam-ud-din Auliya had given the order, that he should leave the monastery immediately. Unaware of the reason for the displeasure of his guide, he was extremely confused. He went to the house of his old friend Maulana Ibrahim, who however was afraid that he would also incur the displeasure of Hazrat Nizam-ud-din Auliya did not help, therefore, he went to his own house and passed his days in tears. His friends, acquaintances, and admirers used to come to his house and consoled him.

After sometime, his old friend Hazrat Amir Khusrau pleaded on his behalf. He went to Hazrat Nizam-ud-din Auliya with the turban round his neck and stood before him respectfully. Seeing him thus, his holiness asked: "What is this, O Turk?" He promptly replied: "I want Maulana Burhan-ud-din to be forgiven." Hazrat Nizam-ud-din Auliya smiled and asked: "Where is he? Call him here." Maulana Burhan-ud-din Gharib and Hazrat Amir Khusrau both went before him with the turban wrapped round their necks. The Maulana placed his head on the ground beneath his feet. His holiness forgave him and he was honoured by reinstatement as a spiritual disciple and was accepted as a caliph.

Traits of character

Hazrat Shaikh Burhan-ud-din Gharib was very fond of music and was a very popular figure. Hazrat Amir Khusrau and Hazrat Amir Hasan were personal friends of his Hazrat Nasir-ud-din Chiragh of Delhi used to stay with him.

He had utmost respect for his spiritual guide and teacher Hazrat Nizam-ud-din Auliya. He never sat with his back towards Ghiyaspur, where his spiritual guide lived.[2]

Death

He died in Devagir and lies buried there. The city Burhanpur is named after him.

REFERENCES

1. *Siyar-ul-Auliya.*
2. *Akhbar-ul-Akhyar,* Urdu trans., p. 203.

19

Hazrat Maulana Shams-ud-din Mohammed Yahya

Hazrat Maulana Shams-ud-din Mohammed Yahya was a pious and pure man, the son of Mohammed Yahya.

He acquired advanced education and was well-versed in jurisprudence, the commentaries, and the *Hadis*. He had been taught by Maulana Zahir-ud-din, from whom he learned the *Bazoodi*.

The access

Hazrat Maulana Shams-ud-din Mohammed Yahya was an intimate friend of Maulana Sadr-ud-din Nauli. They lived together. Both of them used to hear a great deal about the spiritual greatness of Hazrat Nizam-ud-din Auliya, but had never met him.

One day, when they came to Ghiaspur to wash their clothes, they decided that they should go to Hazrat Nizam-ud-din Auliya and see what kind of dervish he was and find out the extent of his learning and knowledge.

They however resolved that they would not touch his feet, nor kiss his hands, nor touch the ground beneath his feet. They would only say *salaams* according to the Islamic practice and then sit down.

However, as soon as Hazrat Nizam-ud-din Auliya looked towards them, they were both disarmed and indeed so overpowered by his personality, the contrary to their firm resolve and determination they bowed down in reverence.[1] He asked them to sit down. He, then, asked them about their education and they replied that they studied the *Bazoodi* with Maulana Zahir-ud-din. He smiled and asked a searching question from the portion of *Bazoodi* that they had studied. Even their teacher Maulana Zahir-ud-din could not satisfactorily resolve this difficult question. Then Hazrat Nizam-ud-din Auliya discussed the problem at length to their complete satisfaction, greatly impressing them with his learning. He gave Maulana Shams-ud-din a pair of trousers and to Maulana Sadr-ud-din he gave a turban.[2]

The following day, when the former went to Maulana Zahir-ud-din, he had that pair of trousers tied over his head.

Initiation in the Sufi Order

The next time Maulana Shams-ud-din went to Hazrat Nizam-ud-din Auliya, he asked to be initiated as his spiritual disciple. He was accepted and began to live in the company of his spiritual guide. Subsequently, he was honoured with the robe of caliphate.

His spiritual guide gave him the following piece of advice: Abstain from the world and its concomitants. Do not be inclined towards the people of the world. Be perfectly absorbed in God.

Pupils

Hazrat Maulana Shams-ud-din Mohammed Yahya had many pupils. Hazrat Nasir-ud-din Chiragh of Delhi was one of the eminent ones to whom he taught the *Bazoodi* and received great respect from him.[3]

Last days

His last days were clouded with anxiety and worry. He was asked by Sultan Mohammed Bin Tughlaq to proceed to Kashmir. Receiving the order, he returned home and began to make preparations for the journey. Sultan Mohammed bin Tughlaq had appointed some men to take him there.

One day, he said to those present: "What do these people say? I have seen my spiritual guide and teacher in a dream and he called me to him. I go to my spiritual guide. Where do those people send me?"

The next day, a growth appeared on his chest and was operated upon. When Sultan Mohammed bin Tughlaq learnt of his illness, he would not believe it, thinking it was a pretext. Here therefore called him into his presence. He went there lying in a palanquin, and on his return he felt acute pain.

Death

Hazrat Maulana Shams-ud-din Mohammed Yahya passed away in AH 747 and was buried in Delhi near the tomb of his spiritual guide.

Traits of character

He never married, preferring to remain a bachelor. He spent all his life engaged in prayer, ascetic practices, penances, and fasts. He took delight in service. He had inner illumination and outward purification. He was very informal but did not like to meet people engrossed in the world. Whatever unasked for gifts were expended by his devotee, Fatuh, under his instructions. Nothing was saved. Among the learned men, he had an assured position. He accepted only a few people as his spiritual disciple, accepting them only under compulsion and then too only if he found them sincere seekers of truth. He was very fond of music which would sometimes send him into a state of rapture.

Supernatural powers

Once, Maulana Sulaiman, who was a spiritual disciple of Hazrat Nasir-ud-din Chiragh of Delhi, visited him after Friday prayers. To his surprise, he saw, that Maulana Shams-ud-din was writing a book. He thought to himself that the Shaikhs, saints and sufis generally devote themselves to absorption after the Friday congregational prayers and wondered what kind of dervish he was who took to writing a book. Hazrat Maulana Shams-ud-din Mohammed Yahya could read his thoughts. He raised his head and said to him thus: "O, Sulaiman! I am not devoid of that."[4]

REFERENCES

1. *Siyar-ul-Auliya*, p. 223.
2. Ibid., p. 225.
3. Ibid., p. 224.
4. Ibid., pp. 226-27.

20

Hazrat Qazi Mohi-ud-din of Kashan

Hazrat Qazi Mohi-ud-din of Kashan was a prominent saint, sage, and scholar. He traced his relationship from Hazrat Imam Hasan, the eldest son of Hazrat Ali who was the son-in-law of the Holy Prophet Mohammed. His forefathers belonged to Tabristan, where they ruled for a long period. The massacres and plunder of Chingiz Khan forced his grandfather, Qazi Qutb-ud-din, to migrate. He came to India during the reign of Sultan Shams-ud-din Iltutmish, and settled in Multan where he established his own school. He was celebrated for knowledge, learning, honesty, and integrity.

Hazrat Shaikh Baha-ud-din Zakariya used to come from far off and offer his prayers there. One day, Qazi Sahab asked him why. He replied: "I act upon the *Hadis* that whosoever offered his prayers behind a pious learned man, he, in fact offered prayers behind the Messenger of God."[1]

After living in Multan for sometime, he came to Delhi. Once the Sultan summoned him when he was in his private apartment, while outside Syed Nur-ud-din was sitting on the right and Qazi Fakhr-ul-Aimma was sitting on the left side. When he reached there, they inquired as to where he would sit. He replied: "Under the shade of the fountain of knowledge." On reaching the Sultan, he did *salaam* to him. The Sultan stood up in order to pay him respects. He caught hold of his hand and led him inside the private apartment and caused him to sit near him.[2] The Sultan appointed him Qazi of Oudh, whose duties he discharged with ease, grace, and distinction.

Education and training

He received his early education under the vigilant care of his father, Qazi Jalal-ud-din of Kashan, who brought him up in the family traditions.

He completed his education at a comparatively early age. After his father died, he succeeded him as the Qazi of Oudh.

Initiation in the Sufi Order

After performing his duties as Qazi of Oudh for sometime, he thought of resigning the post. His outlook towards life and his way of thinking and his approach towards life underwent a change. He got disenchanted with the world and lost interest in mundane affairs.

He wanted to be initiated into the Sufi Order and therefore went to Hazrat Nizam-ud-din Auliya and requested him to accept him as his humble spiritual disciple. His request was granted and not only he was accepted as a spiritual disciple, but subsequently the robe of caliph was conferred upon him.

The gift of the spiritual guide

His spiritual guide, Hazrat Nizam-ud-din Auliya, gave him a blanket, which with all respect and deference, he brought to his house and placed it in a box. After a lapse of time he opened the box, took out the blanket, kissed it and rubbed his eyes with it. He found the blanket profusely perfumed and scented. He would periodically open the box and see the blanket and then put it back. Several years passed, but there was no decrease in the aroma of the blanket, and this greatly surprised him. One day, he took the blanket and washed it thoroughly. The more he washed, the greater was the aroma.

He narrated all this to his spiritual guide and teacher who, with tears in his eyes, said thus: "Qazi Sahab, this is my courage which is placed in the person of the lovers of God."

Advice

The deed of caliphate which he received from his spiritual guide contained the following piece of advice:[3] You must renounce the world. Do not feel attracted towards the world and its people. Do not accept a *jagir*. Do not accept the reward of kings. If travellers come to you as guests and you have nothing (with which to entertain them) take such an occasion as blessed and as a grace of God.

Hazrat Nizam-ud-din Auliya also vouchsafed the following caution: "If you did the same and I am sure you will do the same, then you are my caliph and if you failed to do so, then God is the caliph over Mussulmans."

Renunciation

After being initiated in the Sufi Order and having been honoured by the robe of caliph, he wholly retired from the world. He resigned his post, bringing the certificate of the post of Qazi and tearing it in the presence of his spiritual guide and teacher.

After resigning his post, he found himself without any ostensible means of subsistence and began to face financial difficulties. One of his devotees informed Sultan Ala-ud-din Khalji about his financial difficulties without his permission and knowledge. The Sultan ordered that the post of Qazi of Oudh should again be assigned to him and his pay of the period, that he had not worked be advanced to him.[4]

The *farman* was prepared accordingly and the Sultan persuaded him to accept the post. He went to his spiritual guide and teacher for consultation, instruction, and guidance.

Hazrat Nizam-ud-din Auliya did not like it, saying: "Because such a thought occurred to your mind, such a thing happened."[5] He himself was distressed at his action and refused to accept the covetous office of Qazi of Oudh and passed his days in poverty, taking poverty as his pride.

Love of his spiritual guide

Once he fell seriously ill with no hope of recovery. When Hazrat Nizam-ud-din learnt of his illness he went to see him, and Qazi Mohi-ud-din stood up to pay his respects. From that instant he began to recover. When his spiritual guide left, he said that apparently Hazrat Mahboob-e-Ilahi had come to see him, but inwardly had absorbed his malady.[6]

His pupils

Hazrat Qazi Mohi-ud-din of Kashan had many pupils. At the behest of Hazrat Nizam-ud-din Auliya the son of Bibi Mastoora, the daughter of Hazrat Baba Farid-ud-din Ganj-e-Shakar, became his pupil. Hazrat Shaikh Aziz-ud-din also received his education from him,[7] and the famous saint and sage Hazrat Nasir-ud-din Chiragh of Delhi was also one of his prominent pupils.[8]

Death

He breathed his last on the fifteenth of Rabi-ul-Awwal in AH 719 and was buried in Delhi.

Traits of character

Hazrat Qazi Mohi-ud-din of Kashan was one of the most outstanding and profound scholars of his time. He had a very large number of pupils and was, so to say, the teacher of the city. He was also a man of generous disposition and nurtured no superiority complex. He renounced his comfort, pleasure, his important post, and took to the service of God and a life of poverty. It was a genuine inward urge, that forced him to resign his post as Qazi of Oudh and he later dedicated himself to prayer, penance, ascetic practices, and rigours. He was in search of inner happiness, mental peace, and spiritual pleasure, which he found in this new phase of life.

Hazrat Qazi Mohi-ud-din of Kashan was a patient, persevering, polite, and pious man. His spiritual guide and teacher, Hazrat Nizam-ud-din Auliya, paid him great respect, and whenever he came to him would stand to express this. In short, Qazi Mohiy-ud-din of Kashan was an embodiment of service, sharing, and sacrifice.

References

1. *Fawaid-ul-Fu'ad,* p. 191.
2. Ibid., p. 192.
3. *Siyar-ul-Auliya,* p. 295.
4. Ibid.
5. Ibid.
6. *Khair-ul-Majalis,* Urdu trans., p. 109.
7. *Siyar-ul-Auliya,* p. 202.
8. *Khair-ul-Majalis,* Urdu trans., p. 109.

21

Hazrat Khwaja Amir Hasan

Hazrat Khwaja Amir Hasan was not only an eminent poet of Persian, but was also a saint belonging to the Chishti-Nizami Order. He was the son of Ala of Sanjar.

Initiation into the Sufi Order

Once, Hazrat Nizam-ud-din Auliya went to Hauz-e-Shamsi with his devotees. Amir Hasan was sitting there and was engaged in merry-making. He was on intimate terms with Hazrat Nizam-ud-din Auliya and used to frequently visit him in Budaun. Seeing him, he recited two couplets. Hazrat Nizam-ud-din Auliya in reply said: "Yes, it is true that society has its own effect." Hearing these words, he was so moved that he vowed to be pious and to become his spiritual disciple.

Death

Hazrat Khwaja Amir Hasan died in AH 736 and was buried in Daulatabad.

Traits of character

He had an assured position among the learned men of his time. He was endowed with all the mystic qualities. He was a very good poet and has written some verses in praise of Sultan Ghiyas-ud-din Balban. His famous book *Fawaid-ul-Fu'ad* contains the discourses of his spiritual guide Hazrat Nizam-ud-din Auliya. Hazrat Amir Khusrau used to of it, that he would have been pleased had all his books been ascribed to Amir Hasan and this one book of himself.

Hazrat Khwaja Amir Hasan remained a bachelor throughout his life.[1] He dearly loved his spiritual guide. Once, when they were together, it was blowing hard and the door would open and shut. He caught hold of the door with one hand, so that disturbance might not be caused. After an hour, Hazrat Nizam-ud-din Auliya looked in his direction and found him clasping the door. He asked "Why do you not leave it?" He, placing his head upon the floor, submitted: "I have caught hold of this one door." His holiness smiled and said: "You have caught hold of this door and held it strongly."[2]

References

1. *Akhbar-ul-Akhyar,* Urdu trans., p. 225.
2. *Fawaid-ul-Fu'ad.*

22

Hazrat Shaikh Sadr-ud-din Tabib-e-Dilha

Hazrat Shaikh Sadr-ud-din Tabib-e-Dilha was the spiritual disciple of Hazrat Shaikh Nasir-ud-din Mahmud Chiragh of Delhi. His father, Shaikh Shahab, was a merchant and requested Hazrat Nizam-ud-din Auliya to pray that he might have a child. Hazrat Mahboob-e-Ilahi asked him to come at the time when music was played.[1] He did so.

The former, in a state of rapture, rubbed his back with his back and conveyed to him the good news that a son would be born to him. His wife, by the quite old, became pregnant that very night. When Shaikh Sadr-ud-din was born, his father brought him to Hazrat Mahboob-e-Ilahi, who took him in his lap and caused him to wear a shirt sewn by him. He was named Shaikh Sadr-ud-din Ahmad.

Education and training

Hazrat Mahboob-e-Ilahi entrusted him to the care of Hazrat Nasir-ud-din Mahmud Chiragh of Delhi, directing him to look after his education and training, saying that he was his son. He was thus brought up under the vigilant care of Hazrat Nasir-ud-din Chiragh of Delhi who imparted to him external and inward knowledge. He attained perfection.

Death

He breathed his last in AH 759 and was buried in Delhi.

Caliphs

Hazrat Shaikh Fath-ul-lah of Oudh and Hazrat Shaikh Ahmad Chishti are his two spiritual caliphs.[2]

Traits of character

Hazrat Shaikh Sadr-ud-din Tabib-e-Dilha is the author of two famous books on medicine entitled *Fasih* and *Mateen*.[3] He was a man of very generous disposition. Once the fairies took him for the treatment and he recovered. The fairies gave him a letter with the instruction that he should show it to a dog with such and such a features living ina such and such locality. He searched out the dog and showed the letter. The dog took him to a place outside the city and dug up some earth as if pointing to something. He dug the ground and found some treasure which he distributed among the poor and the indigent.

References

1. *Masalek-us-Salekeen*, vol. II, p. 423.
2. Ibid., p. 424.
3. Ibid., p. 423.

23

Hazrat Khwaja Zia-ud-din Nakhshabi

Hazrat Khwaja Zia-ud-din Nakhshabi was an eminent saint and a prominent sufi who lived in Budaun. He was a spiritual disciple of Hazrat Shaikh Farid, the grandson and spiritual caliph of Hazrat Sufi Hamid-ud-din of Nagore.[1] He died in AH 751.

Traits of character

Hazrat Khwaja Zia-ud-din Nakhshabi led a retired life and devoted himself to the remembrance of God and the reading and writing books. He is the author of several books, the most famous among them being *Salak-us-Saluk, Ashara Mubashshara, Kulliyat, Guziyat,* and *Tootinama.*

Teachings

- He says that once a person purchased a slave girl. During the night he asked the slave girl to stretch out his bedding so that he might sleep. The slave girl submitted: "O, Khwaja! have you also got some Master? "The person replied in the positive. She thereupon asked: "Does he sleep or not?" He replied in the negative. The slave girl then said: " Then do you not feel ashamed that your Master keeps awake and you go to bed."[2]
- According to those enforcing the mandates of *tariqat,* he who is governed by his cat is better than one who is governed by his self.
- Once Shaikh-ul-Masha'ikh Abdullah Khafif fell ill, a physician came to him and inquired from him the illness he suffered from. The Shaikh replied: "Existence, sure and simple. When existence will be annihilated, the illness will also be eradicated."

  Once someone asked from a dervish, "To what does the world resemble most." The dervish replied: "The world is not so fit that someone may resemble it."

- Once a person went to a dervish and told him that he wanted to live with him for sometime. The dervish asked him: "With whom will you live after me?" He replied: "With God then." The dervish thereupon said that he should think that he did not exist and that he should live with God from that the time onward.
- Once a worldly man asked for water from a dervish who gave him very bad and hot water. The man said: "The water is very hot and bad." The dervish replied: "O, Khwaja! we are in a prison house and the prisoners do not drink good water."
- According to him, one should be at war with one's self. He says: "O, dervish! wage war with thy self one day from morning till evening. They are indeed men, who wage such a war with their self, that no reconciliation is ever affected. O, my dear friends! whoever scrutinises his self, thereby removes all claims and only the meaning remains."
- A person said: "I am given to understand, that the whole world is deserted. Had it been populated, at least someone would have prevented me from doing the work that I do and would have called me to account. The population of the world is due to the men of religion. When the number of the men of religion is decreased the world becomes sinful on that account."

Saying

- Rich men get four things from their wealth, namely, physical pain, disturbance of the heart, loss of religion, and the account of the Day of Resurrection. The dervishes get four things from their sainthood, namely, physical comfort, peace of heart, safety of religion, and freedom from the account on the Day of Resurrection.

References

1. *Akhbar-ul-Akhyar*, Urdu trans., pp. 231-32.
2. *Salek-us-Saluk*.

24

Hazrat Shaikh Kamal-ud-din

Hazrat Shaikh Kamal-ud-din was an embodiment of spiritual perfection. His family lived in Oudh, where he was born. He is related to Hazrat Nasir-ud-din Chiragh of Delhi, being his sister's son. He traces his descent from Hazrat Imam Hasan,[1] the eldest son of Hazrat Ali, son-in-law of the Holy Prophet. His father was called Abd-ur-Rahman[2] and his mother was very pious and was known as the Rabia of her time.[3] He had one brother, Zain-ud-din Ali. He was a caliph of Hazrat Nasir-ud-din Chiragh of Delhi.[4] On account of his vast erudition and knowledge he was known as "Allama" – the great learned man.

Initiation into the Sufi Order

He left for Delhi and became a spiritual disciple of Hazrat Nizam-ud-din Auliya and was subsequently honoured with the title of caliph, and received the robe from Hazrat Nasir-ud-din Chiragh of Delhi.[5] After being elevated as a caliph, he went to Ahmedabad. There, he propagated the doctrine of truth and many people joined his fold.

Pilgrimage

Hazrat Shaikh Kamal-ud-din went on seven pilgrimages to Mecca, and also went to Medina to pay his respects to the holy shrine of the Holy Prophet Mohammed. He visited Jerusalem also. While returning to Delhi via Khorasan, on many kings and noblemen came into contact with him.

Gifts

He received very many unasked for gifts. When he returned to Delhi, he had with him thirty camels laden with precious articles and thirty thousand gold and silver coins.[6] Seeing all this, Hazrat Nasir-ud-din Chiragh of Delhi said: "Shaikh Kamal-ud-din! why have you brought so much world with you?"

He submitted:[7] "On the way, I was informed that Hazrat Nizam-ud-din Auliya had passed away and that you have succeeded him. If I go empty handed, what will the people of the world say. That is way I have brought with me these outward things. Now, I will distribute them among the learned, the pious, and the needy." He did that.

Once he sought the advice of Hazrat Nasir-ud-din Chiragh of Delhi about a gift. Tatar Khan wanted to offer him eighty rupees a day, wrote this down, and presented the document to him. Hazrat Nasir-ud-din Chiragh of Delhi advised him: "As you have received the allowance without your asking and intention, it thus amounts to an unasked for gift. You accept it."

Wife and children

At the command of Hazrat Nasir-ud-din Chiragh of Delhi, he entered into a marriage contract.[8] He had three sons and one daughter.[9] His eldest son, Shaikh Nizam-ud-din, died in the prime of his youth. His two other sons were Shaikh Nasir-ud-din and Shaikh Siraj-ud-din. His daughter was given in marriage to Shaikh Burhan-ud-din.

Death

Hazrat Shaikh Kamal-ud-din died on the twenty-seventh of Ziq'ada in AH 756 and lies buried in Delhi.

Traits of character

Hazrat Kamal-ud-din was a man endowed with supernatural powers, was an accomplished dervish and also a very learned man. Hazrat Nasir-ud-din Chiragh of Delhi used to pay him great respect.[10] Hazrat Makhdoom Jahanian-e-Jahan Gasht learnt the commentary, *Mashareq-ul-Anwar* from him. Hazrat Banda Nawaz Syed Mohammed Gesoo Daraz had respect, praise, and admiration for him.

Among his prominent caliphs the following may be mentioned.[11] Maulana Ahmad of Thanesar; Maulana 'Alam of Panipat; Tatar Khan; and Maulana Sangrayza of Multan. The deed of caliphate, granted by Hazrat Nasir-ud-din Chiragh of Delhi to Hazrat Makhdoom Jahanian-e-Jahan Gasht, was written by him.[12] Sultan Firoz Shah, his noblemen, the ministers, and the high and the low alike reposed utmost faith in his spiritual greatness and powers.

References

1. *Anwar-ul-Arefeen*, p. 313.
2. Ibid.
3. *Siyar-ul-Arefeen*.
4. *Akhbar-ul-Akhyar*.
5. *Majalis-e-Hasania*.
6. *Takmila-Siyar-ul-Auliya*, p. 15.
7. Ibid., pp. 15-16.
8. *Anwar-ul-Arefeen*.
9. *Majalis-e-Hasania*.
10. Ibid.
11. Ibid.
12. *Takmila-Siyar-ul-Auliya*, p. 16.

25

Hazrat Shaikh Jalal-ud-din of Panipat

Hazrat Shaikh Jalal-ud-din of Panipat was the spiritual caliph and successor of Hazrat Shams-ud-din Turk of Panipat. He traced his descent from the third caliph of Islam, Hazrat Usman. His father, Shaikh Mohammed, was a rich man. He received the name Khwaja Mohammed; he is addressed and invoked as "Jalal-ud-din."

He was a born saint. During his childhood, he appeared to be absorbed in thought and would sometimes go to deserted places and jungles and engage himself in the remembrance of God. He was averse to public haunts.

Initiation into the Sufi Order

Hazrat Sharf-ud-din Shaikh Bu Ali Qalandar loved him greatly and visit him daily at his house. On his attaining majority, he implored Hazrat Bu Ali Qalandar to accept him as his spiritual disciple. He refused, saying that his spiritual guide and teacher would be arriving soon. Hazrat Shams-ud-din Turk reached Panipat and permanently settled there. Once he saw Hazrat Jalal-ud-din, sitting on horseback, and said to his companions: "I see my blessing shining in the forehead of this boy." As soon as he uttered the words, Hazrat Jalal-ud-din saw him, dismounting from the horse and, placing his head on his feet thus became his spiritual disciple. Towards the closing years of his life, appointed him as his caliph and conferred upon him the robe and entrusted to him the holy relics of his spiritual forefathers.

Renaming a village

Once, during the course of his tours and travels, he happened to pass through a village. He saw that the villagers were greatly disturbed and confused and were leaving it hurriedly at night with all their belongings. He was told that heavy snow had fallen and had damaged the crop so that they were unable to pay the land revenue. They were afraid that they would be harassed and tortured if they did not pay it in time and that is why they were leaving. He, addressing the villagers, said, that if they agreed to sell the village to him and rename it "Jalalabad" after him, he was prepared to pay them even more than was needed.

The villagers agreed. He asked them to bring iron and all articles of iron available and also to collect wood. Then he directed them to throw all the iron in the wood, set fire to it all and see what happened the following morning.

He himself left the village that night. The villagers found the following morning that the articles of iron had turned into gold. They were immensely pleased; paying the land revenue and keeping the remaining amount to themselves. They renamed the village as "Jalalabad."

The royal visit

Sultan Firoz-ud-din Tughlaq came to Panipat, offered him his respects, and implored his blessings.

Marriage and children

Hazrat Shaikh Jalal-ud-din had five sons: Khwaja Abd-ul-Qadir, Khwaja Ibrahim, Khwaja Shibli, Khwaja Karim-ud-din, and Khwaja Abd-ul-Wahid.

Death

He breathed his last on the thirteenth of Rabi-ul-Awwal in AH 765 and was buried in Panipat.

Caliphs

He had over forty spiritual caliphs, Hazrat Shaikh Ahmad 'Abd-ul-Haq of Rudoli the most outstanding among them.

Traits of character

It is said that the spiritual earnings of Hazrat Ala-ud-din Ahmad Sabir were squandered by Hazrat Jalal-ud-din of Panipat. His spiritual blessings extended to all. Upon whomsoever he cast a look or a glance became a saint. Whatever he predicted actually happened. He received spiritual blessings from and the good wishes of many saints, which further contributed to his spiritual greatness.

Hazrat Shaikh Jalal-ud-din of Panipat was a very generous man and used to feed a thousand people a day and a thousand people every night. If by chance a thousand people could not come, he would invite people from the market and entertain them. He was fond of hunting and shooting. In his last days, he was so much absorbed in thought, that he was unaware of what was going on around him. His devotees and disciples would whisper in his ears the words *Haq, Haq*—"God, God" and then, he would regain consciousness and offer prayers. He occasionally attended music concerts and was deeply devoted to prayers.

In youth, he had been a man of very fastidious tastes, living in luxury, ease, and comfort, wearing expensive clothes and spending a great deal on himself. He was a man of great character with a magnetic personality and was quite well-off.[1]

Supernatural powers

Once when walking, he met a very old woman on the way, who was going with a pitcher in her hand to fetch water. She was very weak and walked with great difficulty. Out of pity, he took her pitcher, went to the well, filled it, and brought it to her house saying: "Here is the pitcher full of water. Keep it with you. May God Almighty bless the water." Since that day, the water in the pitcher, notwithstanding use never fell short.

One day he went to the riverside and there he found a yogi, sitting with his eyes closed. After a while the yogi opened his eyes and said that he had a Philosophers Stone with him and that he had made up his mind that whosoever came to him first when he opened his eyes would receive that invaluable stone. He therefore entrusted the Philosophers Stone to Hazrat Shaikh Jalal-ud-din who took it and then threw it into the river. This saddened and angered the yogi. He advised the yogi to enter the river and fetch his stone and he, while doing so, saw thousands of such stones lying in the river. He took his own stone and one more from the countless lying there, emerging from the water with two stones. Shaikh Jalal-ud-din chided the yogi for having taken a stone not belonging to him. The yogi threw both his stones at his feet and became his devotee and disciple.[2]

An alchemist suggested to one of his sons, that he should learn from him the way of preparing alchemy, and thereby escape starvation. When this was brought to, Shaikh Jalal-ud-din's notice, he spat on the wall of the tenement, transforming it all into pure gold. Then he said to his son that this was the real alchemy.

Hazrat Makhdoom Jahanian-e-Jahan Gasht reached Delhi and fell ill and all hope of recovery was lost. When Hazrat Shaikh Jalal-ud-din learnt of it, he went to Delhi by dint of his spiritual powers. After *salaams* he asked him to spread out both his hands and said: "I give you ten years of my life." Hazrat Makhdoom accepted this generous offer and later returned to Panipat fully recovered.

The spiritual genealogy of Hazrat Jamal-ud-din was cut off from the beginning by Hazrat Sabir Sahab. Through Hazrat Jalal-ud-din's grace and kindness the genealogy started through Shaikh Burhan-ud-din, Qutb-ud-din Munawwar, and Shaikh Nur-ud-din Anwar — all of Hansi.

REFERENCES

1. *Anwar-ul-Arefeen; Siyar-ul-Aqtab.*
2. *Siyar-ul-Aqtab.*

26

Hazrat Shaikh Nur-ul-Haq Wad-din

Hazrat Shaikh Nur-ul-Haq Wad-din is one of the leading saints of the Indian subcontinent and is better known as Shaikh Nur Qutub-e-'Alam. He is the son, spiritual disciple, and caliph of Hazrat Ala-ul-Haq. His elder brother was named Azam Khan. He used to afford facilities to the inmates of his father's monastery and to render service to them. Shaikh Nur Qutb-e-'Alam was lost in the love of God and was a very humble and unassuming person. His letters discuss various aspects of mysticism.

Death
Shaikh Nur Qutb-e-'Alam died in AH 813 and was buried in Pindwa.

Caliph
Shaikh Husam-ud-din is his spiritual caliph.

Teachings
He says, that the saints of yore prescribed ninety-nine stations according to the names of God to recover the path of spiritual perfection. His spiritual forefathers prescribed fifteen stations for the purpose, but he prescribes three stations only. According to him, the first station appertains to rendering accounts before an individual is called upon to render accounts. The second station relates to the place where it may be said that an individual who has his two days equal is at a loss (as these days did not bring spiritual progress). The third station is that where it may be said that the prayer of the *faqir* serves to eradicate hazards.[1]

Sayings

- The utmost limit of prayer is this, that an individual, whenever he may search his heart, may find it with God under all conditions, just as a child when he sleeps in love with something, on waking up, demands the same thing.

- In generosity be like the sun, in hospitality be like water, in forbearance be like the earth and bear the tyranny of the people.
- The world is a place of pride, the self is partially blind, and God is self-respecting.
- The *sajjada,* who sits on the *gaddi* should not look to his right or left.

Reference

1. *Rafiq-ul-Arefeen.*

27

Hazrat Shaikh Fath-ul-lah

Hazrat Shaikh Fath-ul-lah was one of the *ulamas* of Delhi and was engaged in teaching. He became a spiritual disciple of Hazrat Shaikh Sadr-ud-din Tabib-e-Dilha. He underwent many ascetic practices, but to no avail. He brought this to the notice of his spiritual guide and teacher who suggested that he give up teaching and distribute his books amongst the students. He retained some costly and rare books and distributed the rest among the students. In spite of that there was no noticeable effect. Again he approached his spiritual teacher who directed him to distribute the books that he still had. He did so and eventually reached spiritual perfection.[1]

Death

Hazrat Shaikh Fath-ul-lah breathed his last in the year AH 821. He lies buried in Oudh.

Caliphs

Hazrat Shaikh Qasim of Oudh and Hazrat Shaikh Mohammed 'Isa of Jaunpur are his two caliphs.[2]

Traits of character

He was a very learned man of his time and greatly absorbed in contemplation. Very fond of music, once for three days and nights he was absorbed in it. At the time of prayer, five times a day, he would regain consciousness and offer prayers.

REFERENCES

1. *Masalek-us-Salekeen,* vol. II, p. 424.
2. Ibid., p. 425.

28

Hazrat Khwaja Syed Mohammed Gesoo Daraz

Hazrat Khwaja Syed Mohammed Gesoo Daraz was a famous saint known and respected throughout the Indian subcontinent and was a disciple and spiritual caliph of Hazrat Nasir-ud-din Chiragh of Delhi. He was born on the fourth of Rajab in AH 721 in Delhi and named Mohammed. His nickname is Abul Fatah and he is addressed and invoked as "Sadr-ud-din," "Wali-ul-Akbar-us-Sadiq," and "Gesoo Daraz." He was related to Hazrat Imam Zain-ul-Abedeen, son of Hazrat Imam Hussain, son of Hazrat Ali, who is the fourth caliph of Islam and son-in-law of the Holy Prophet Mohammed. He traced his descent from the Holy Prophet, being related to him in twenty-two degrees. Syed Yusuf Husaini was his father, who was a spiritual disciple of Hazrat Nizam-ud-din Auliya. His father, whose nickname was Syed Raja, and also benefited from the spiritual blessings of Hazrat Nasir-ud-din Chiragh of Delhi. In the Deccan came to be known as "Raju Qattal" because he had waged a war against his own self.

Sultan Mohammed bin Tughlaq wanted to shift the seat of government from Delhi to Daulatabad and ordered the residents of Delhi to migrate to Daulatabad and settle there. His father, Syed Yusuf Husaini, left Delhi alongwith his family on the twentieth of Ramazan in AH 728. Reaching Daulatabad on the seventeenth of Muharram in AH 729, he settled there at a place known as Roza Khuldabad. His mother was an accomplished woman whose father was a spiritual disciple of Hazrat Nizam-ud-din Auliya. Aggrieved by her brother Malik-ul-Umra Syed Ibrahim Mustofi, who was Governor of Daulatabad, she left for Delhi alongwith her two sons and reaching Daulatabad on the fourth of Rajab in AH 736 began to live there. His elder brother was named Syed Husain.

Reasons – nickname Gesoo Daraz

There are several reasons for calling him Gesoo Daraz. He had very long hair and which was why he came to be called "Gesoo Daraz" or one who with long locks of hair.

Another reason assigned, is that once he was carrying on his shoulders the palanquin in which his spiritual guide and teacher, Hazrat Nasir-ud-din Chiragh of Delhi, was sitting. Suddenly his locks of hair, extending to his knees, were entangled in the wheel of the palanquin. Out of respect for his spiritual guide and teacher, he chose not to stop the palanquin to disentangle his hair from the wheel. His spiritual guide was greatly pleased with him and recited a couplet, conferring upon him the title of "Gesoo Daraz."[1]

Early education and training

Hazrat Gesoo Daraz received his early education and training at home from his father and his maternal grandfather. During his stay in Khuldabad, he committed the Holy *Quran* to memory. He was deprived of paternal care when he was ten years, three months, and one day old. His father passed away in Khuldabad on the fifth of Shawwal in AH 731.

Initiation in the Sufi Order

When he was in Khuldabad he would hear a great deal about Hazrat Nizam-ud-din Auliya and Hazrat Nasir-ud-din Chiragh of Delhi and of developed a great sense, love and fondness for Hazrat Nasir-ud-din Chiragh of Delhi. When he saw him in the mosque of Sultan Qutb-ud-din Aibak on the occasion of the Friday prayers, his joy and fondness knew no bounds. Taking his brother with him he paid his respects to Hazrat Nasir-ud-din Chiragh of Delhi, who honoured him by accepting him as his spiritual disciple. He was subsequently appointed as a spiritual caliph.

Hazrat Gesoo Daraz continued his education even after his being initiated as a spiritual disciple, acquiring external knowledge and counted among his teachers such learned people as Maulana Sharf-ud-din Katheli, Maulana Taj-ud-din Bahadur, and Qazi Abd-ul-Muqtadar. He completed his education when he was nineteen.

Instructions of spiritual guide

After completing his education, he devoted himself exclusively to prayer, ascetic practices, rituals, inner purification, and illumination.

His spiritual guide directed him to undertake regular ablutions as far as possible and to maintain fasts in the month of Sha'ban.[2]

Marriage and children

At the age of forty he married Bibi Raza Khatoon, the daughter of Maulana Syed Ahmad, son of Maulana Jamal-ud-din Maghrabi. He had two sons and three daughters. His eldest son, Syed Husain alias Syed Mohammed Akbar Husaini, died during his lifetime on the fifteenth of Rabi-us-Sani in AH 812. His second son, Syed Mohammed Yusuf alias Syed Mohammed Asghar Husaini, succeeded him as *sajjada* (spiritual successor). His eldest daughter was Bibi Fatima and was nicknamed Sati Bibi. His second daughter was named Bibi Batul, and his third Bibi Umm-ud-din.

Departure from Delhi

On the eve of Tamerlane's invasion he left Delhi alongwith his family. On the seventh of Rabi-us-Sani in AH 801 they started for Daulatabad. On the way he stayed, together with one of his spiritual disciples, Maulana Ala-ud-din, in Gwalior. He honoured him by appointing him as one of his spiritual caliphs. After staying in Gwalior for sometime, he resumed his journey. He then stopped in Chanderi and then reached Baroda from where he went to Khambayat and after staying therefor sometime, returned to Baroda. From Baroda he left for Daulatabad via Sultanpur, eventually reaching Khuldabad.

Relations with Bahmani kings

Sultan Firoz Shah Bahmani, on receiving the information of his arrival in Khuldabad, directed the Governor of Daulatabad, to go to him, make an offering, and request him to visit Gulbarga. He accepted the invitation.

When he reached Gulbarga, Sultan Firoz Shah Bahmani received him at the head of his family, noblemen, courtiers, and the army and accorded him a very warm welcome.

He stayed in Gulbarga for some years in a monastery behind the fort. Subsequently, he decided to settle there permanently and lived there for about twenty-two years.

Sultan Firoz Shah Bahmani held him in high esteem and reposed great faith in his spiritual powers. A few days before his death Feroz Shah abdicated the throne in favour of his younger brother, Sultan Ahmad who, like his elder brother was a devotee and admirer of his.

He believed in his spiritual greatness and reposed his utmost faith in his spirituality. After the demise of Hazrat Syed Mohammed Gesoo Daraz, he erected a dome over his tomb which is said to be the highest ever erected on the tomb of any saint in the Indian subcontinent.

Death

Hazrat Syed Mohammed Gesoo Daraz breathed his last on the sixteenth of Ziq'ada in AH 825 at the ripe age of one hundred and four years, four months, and twelve days. His tomb, situated in Gulbarga is an object of veneration and draws myriads of people to itself.

Caliphs

Some of the prominent among his spiritual caliphs are: Qazi Nur-ud-din Ajoodhi, Maulana Moin-ud-din Tohanvi, Hazrat Syed Husain alias Syed Akbar Husaini, Hazrat Syed Abul -Ma'ali son of Syed Ahmad, Maulana Shaikh Ala-ud-din of Gwalior, Qazi 'Alim-ud-din son of Sharf-ud-din, Hazrat Syed Yusuf alias Syed Mohammed Asghar Husaini, and Malikzada Usman son of Jaffer.

Trait of character

Hazrat Gesoo Daraz was very pious and strictly adhered to the *sunnah* of the Holy Prophet, offering prayers regularly. He served his spiritual guide and teacher very faithfully and would wake up in the middle of the night to devote himself to rituals, remembrance of God, and prayer. After the Ishraq prayer, he used to dine with his sons and teach them commentaries on the Holy *Quran* and the *hadis*. At noon he would rest a little and after Zuhr prayers, would regularly recite the Holy *Quran*. At night about fifty people dined with him daily.

When accepting anyone as his spiritual disciple, he used to place his right hand on the hand of the new entrant and say:

> Know, that you have promised to this humble being and to the spiritual guide of this humble being and to his spiritual guide and to all the saints of the Order, that you will ever and anon protect your looks and your tongue and will firmly hold to the way of the *shari'at*. Do you accept it?

The spiritual disciple would then say: "Yes sir, I have accepted." After the offer and acceptance, he would say: "Praise be to God of the worlds." Then, taking a pair of scissors, he would recite aloud the *takbir*,

God is great, and then cutting some hair near the right and left ears he would recite the *takbir*. He would then place the four-edged cap on his head and direct him to offer two genuflexions and then issue certain instructions.

Initially, he listened to music accompanied by musical instruments, and later without the latter.

Literary accomplishments

Hazrat Syed Mohammed Gesoo Daraz was an eminent poet and has left a large collection of poems. During his span of life, which extended to about a hundred and five years, he wrote about one hundred and five books. This means, that he wrote one book each year. Famous among them are *Tafsir-ul-Quran* (commentaries on Holy *Quran*) related to commentaries on the first five parts of the Holy *Quran; Sharah Mashariq-ul-Anwar; Ma'arif Sharh Awarif; Targoma Awarif; Sharh Taaruf; Sharh Adab-ul-Mureeden; Khatma; Sharh Fasoos-ul-Hukm; Isma-ul-Israr; Hadaiq-ul-uns; Hawas-e-Quwwat-ul-Quloob;* and *Istiqamat-us-Shari'at ba Tariq-ul-Haqiqat.*

Teachings

He says that the advantage of being a spiritual disciple is that on the Day of Judgement, the spiritual guide and teacher will plead his case and will help and assist him and thus save him from hell fire.

- A spiritual disciple of his spiritual guide died. The disciple had not faithfully followed the tenets and precepts of his guide, so the angels of torture descended but, seeing the four-edged cap on his head, stood aside. They inquired about the cap. The deceased replied that it was that of Hazrat Nasir-ud-din Chiragh of Delhi. Under the circumstances how could they subject him to torture?

  Proceeding further, he says that unless the dervish enjoyed so much honour and prestige in the court of God Almighty, that merely being connected with him, an individual may escape hell fire, it is not proper for him to accept anyone as his spiritual disciple.
- Discussing prayer and its efficacy, he says that prayer offered in conformity with the conditions attached to it is certain to be accepted. If an individual nurtures any doubts about its being accepted or has not observed the conditions precedent, then

it is no use of complaining of its non-acceptance.

- About repentance, he says that the best repentance is that once offered, one does not sin again. According to the laws of *shari'at*, if repentance is not offered in this way, it will not be a correct type of prayer.

  The mystic treats repentance otherwise. According to it, if repentance is offered, then if he may pick up dust in his hand and it may be instantaneously transformed into gold.

  He says, that there is no difference of opinion, that to feed the poor and the hungry is considered praiseworthy in every religion. There is in fact nothing better than to feed the hungry, to give them rest and respite, and to console them.

  According to him, if one does not even receive one, basic needs then this constitutes privation. He who is happy under such circumstances and does not wish for more than his needs, is known in the terminology of *tariqat* as pious; and if he neither decries nor wishes to get more than it is case of submission. If one does not desire more, but may wish for more than it constitutes contentment. If one desires more, but finding difficult to achieve, abandons the quest then it is called greed. If one is overpowered by necessities and those necessities are not to be fulfilled, then the individual concerned is confused indeed.

- Discussing human nature, he says that the condition of human beings is strange. When an individual is seized by any calamity, he makes a hue and cry and complains to the people, not realising, that the commiseration of the people cannot be of any use to him and that their enmity can likewise do him no harm.

  Complaining to the people means and implies, that the person concerned has put his trust in them and taken them to form a part of divine powers. There is no doubt that one will have to pay heavily for such idolatry and the individual concerned will find himself detached from God.

- God has not created human beings for greed or lust nor for pastime or play, nor for eating or drinking, nor for sleeping and marriage, but the principal object is this and this alone, that they may worship God.

- The world, is like a prostitute, who at first gives individual access to her body and when she finds that the individual loves her and is under her grip and cannot elude her net, then she surrounds the individual on all sides and confines him like a fly in a casket, eventually slaughtering him. At that time he is awake, but in vain.

Sayings

- There is nothing better than to renounce the world.
- The spiritual guide and teacher is well-acquainted with the ups and downs of the spiritual path. Without his help and guidance the way cannot be traversed. The goal cannot be reached by mere rigours and ascetic practices without the assistance of the spiritual guide.
- It is wrong to suppose that trust in God means and implies abandoning ones means.
- He who is doing good should not be proud and neither should he imagine that those engrossed in evil deeds are deprived of the Mercy of God.
- To the saints and the enlightened, service and respect of the spiritual guide and teacher are obligatory.
- The wise should keep an eye on the end. He should pray, that his external enemies should be shown the light of guidance.
- The *faqir* should sit in a secluded place and devote himself to his work.
- The world is an embodiment of trials, tribulations, and hardships.
- The faithful is not afraid of anyone except God.
- A sound heart results in a sound vision. That vision becomes such that it turns dust into alchemy.
- Piety is the cure of all the spiritual ills.
- A spiritual disciple should do his utmost to achieve and acquire moral culture.

References

1. *Akhbar-ul-Akhyar.*
2. *Jawami'-ul-Kalam.*

29

Hazrat Shaikh Ahmad Abd-ul-Haq

Hazrat Shaikh Ahmad Abd-ul-Haq traced his descent from the second caliph of Islam, Amir-ul-Momeneen Hazrat Umar.[1] His family belonged to Balkh. His grandfather, Shaikh Dawood, disgusted with the ravage and plunder perpetrated by Halaku Khan, migrated to India with some members of his family.

An accomplished man, he was posted by Sultan Ala-ud-din Khalji in Oudh. He died in Rudoli and was buried there. His father was named Umar and he had one elder brother, Shaikh Taqi-ud-din, a very learned man who lived in Delhi.

Early life and education

At the age of seven, he would wake up in the middle of the night and offer pre-dawn prayers in a separate corner. His mother, who did the same, thought that it might be unhealthy for him to get up in the middle of the night prohibited him from doing so. At the age of twelve years he left home and reached Delhi. In Delhi, his elder brother cared for him and imparted to him external knowledge, laying stress on his education, morals, and training. Shaikh Ahmad Abd-ul-Haq repeatedly told his elder brother that he wanted to imbibe divine knowledge and spiritual science, not being satisfied with merely learning the alphabet and grammar. His elder brother found him adamant and eventually took him to a philosopher for advice to whom he said: "I want the knowledge of God. I am not interested in anything. I only seek the pleasure of God."

In quest of truth

He left Delhi in search of truth and went to Bihar. In a certain city he found two dervishes who were deeply absorbed in contemplation. One of them was called Shaikh Ala-ud-din, the other as "Neem Langoti" because he did not wear, any clothes barring a wrapper around his waist. They failed to quench his spiritual thirst, so Hazrat Shaikh Ahmad Abd-ul-Haq proceeded to Rooda and there met a dervish called Shaikh Fath-ul-lah. They did not however get on well because there was a conflict of ideology. The dervish pursued a way of life that did not admit or any restriction whereas Hazrat Shaikh Ahmad Abd-ul-Haq chose the path of love and affection.

Dissatisfied there too he thought to himself that as the living beings had been unable to satisfy him, he should live in the company of the dead. This idea acted as a spur and he began to wander in desolated places, jungles, and graveyards, uttering the words *O, Hadi, O, Hadi,* "O, Guide! O, Guide!" repeatedly.

Subsequently, he dug a grave for himself and sat in it continuously for six months lost in meditation and exclusively devoted to remembrance of God. Here too, he failed to achieve his goal and in his quest reached Panipat.

The test

Hazrat Shaikh Jalal-ud-din, through his spiritual powers aware of his coming, ordered his devotees and disciples to lay many delicious dishes on the dining carpet, and also required them to have several horses laden with costly goods, standing in front of the gate of his monastery. His purpose was to test Shaikh Ahmed Haq's faith, belief and devotion. When Hazrat Shaikh Ahmad Abd-ul-Haq arrived he was greatly surprised and said to himself that a man living in such regal splendour could not be a real dervish. He, therefore, left the monastery and wandered around the whole day. In the evening, he reached a certain place, and when he inquired its name, he was told that it was Panipat. He stayed there that night and left the following morning. In the evening, he again found himself in Panipat and once again went on his way the following morning. He reached a thick forest and did not know in which direction to go suddenly he saw a man sitting upon a tree and inquired from him the way to the city. The reply was that the route to the city lay before the gate of Shaikh Jalal-ud-din of Panipat, and if he was in any doubt, he should inquire from the two men approaching.

He went on and actually saw two men approaching and, inquiring about the direction they replied that he had lost his way. The straight route lay across the gate of Shaikh Jalal-ud-din's monastery. He wanted to be sure of this and repeated the question three times and received the same reply.

Initiation in the Sufi Order

Now, all doubts dispelled, truth dawned upon him. He now began to think that it had all been ordained by God, and that he should go to Hazrat Shaikh Jalal-ud-din of Panipat and enlist himself as his spiritual disciple. On his way, he had two thoughts. He would greatly like it if Shaikh Jalal-ud-din would place a cap on his head, that had been rubbed on the grave of Hazrat Shams-ud-din Turk of Panipat.

Secondly, he would be delighted if he received *halwa* (sweetmeat) and bread. Lost in thought, he reached the monastery in the evening. He was told that the Shaikh had gone to the grave of his spiritual guide and teacher, Hazrat Shams-ud-din Turk of Panipat. He went there too and offered him his respects and placed his head at his feet.

The Shaikh could read his thoughts. He took off his cap, rubbed it over the tomb of Hazrat Shams-ud-din Turk, and placed it on his head. In the meanwhile, a certain person arrived and offered bread and *halwa* to Hazrat Shaikh Jalal-ud-din which was accepted and some of it given to Hazrat Shaikh Ahmad Abd-ul-Haq. Then the Shaikh smiled and, said, "This is your desire. Your desire is fulfilled." Hazrat Abd-ul-Haq uttered the words *Haq, Haq*, "God, God" three times. Then Hazrat Jalal-ud-din took his hand in his hand and accepted him as his spiritual disciple. He subsequently attained spiritual perfection and his spiritual guide and teacher conferred upon him the robe of caliph.

Public entertainment

Once he told his devotees and disciples that a lamp had been burning in the monastery of Shaikh Abu Ishaq and it would continue to shed its light and lustre till the Day of Resurrection.

He expressed the wish that food be cooked in a cauldron and people at large should eat it and that it should not be exhausted so long as the world existed. In pursuance of his desire, he had food cooked in a cauldron and declared it open to all free of cost. This public entertainment lasted for three days and the food remained undiminished. On the fourth day, he told himself that God alone gives sustenance to whomsoever He likes, without limits. He alone is the cherisher of the world, in providing sustenance, he alone knows his work well. So why should we be concerned with it all. Acting on the tenets of his inner voice, he took away the cauldron and thus stopped public entertainment.[2]

Marriage and children

His first son, Abd-ul-Aziz, died at a very early age.[3] As did his three other sons. His fifth son, Shaikh Mohammed Arif, survived him.

Death

He passed away on the fifteenth of Jamade-us-Sani in AH 837 and was buried in Rudoli, U.P.

Caliphs

His spiritual guide and teacher had prayed to God that he should be the torchbearer of his message, and this is what actually happened. He carried the message of his spiritual guide and teacher to all those who came into contact with him. He trained some people who cared the message further after his death. Among his caliphs may be mentioned the following:

> His son, Mohammed Arif was his premier caliph and *sajjadanashin* (spiritual successor), the other caliph was Shaikh Mohammed, son of Mohammed Arif.

Traits of character

Hazrat Shaikh Ahmad Abd-ul-Haq was a man of very simple habits. It is said of him that he would reach the mosque a little before prayers and himself sweep the mosque. He was absorbed in contemplation for most of the time and so deeply that he was quite unaware of what was going on around him. He was unmindful of the weather, did not remember which day, month, or year it was. For about fifty years, he went to the central mosque, but in spite of this, he did not know the way there. He would forever recite the words *Haq, Haq,* which is why his spiritual guide began to call him "Abd-ul-Haq."

He underwent many ascetic practices, penances, and rigours. Once to mark his repentance over what he had said in a state of absorption, he, irrespective of the biting cold, be entered a river in the middle of the night and there stood on one leg. This ascetic practice continued for six months.

On another occasion, tired of the world and the people of the world, he thought of retiring to a secluded place. The best place he thought, would be a grave. He dug a grave himself, entered it, and closed it. He remained there for six months, and when he was taken out he was found to be very weak.

He reposed his utmost trust in God, was kind-hearted, gentle, and generous.

Teachings

He used to say that Allah is without name and nomenclature. If he was to coin a name it would not be better and greater than the name "Allah" whose meaning has a deeper implication and significance, than any other, connoting perfection and proof of existence.[4]

Saying

Once he said that Mansur was a child because he could not control himself and because he had disclosed the secrets. There are some men who drink the water of an entire river and do not make a fuss about it. He would say that whosoever entered his fold would be saved from the fire of hell.

References

1. *Ma'arej-ul-Vilayat.*
2. *Siyar-ul-Aqtab.*
3. Ibid.
4. *Akhbar-ul-Akhyar.*

30

Hazrat Syed Badi-ud-din Qutb-e-Madar

Hazrat Syed Badi-ud-din Qutb-e-Madar was an important saint, a Hashemite.[1] On the maternal side, he traced his descent from Hazrat Syedna Imam Hasan, son of Hazrat Ali, son-in-law of the Holy Prophet Mohammed. His father, Syed Ali of Halb, was the son of Syed Baha-ud-din. Fatima was the name of his mother, who was the daughter of Syed Abdullah, the son of Syed Zahid. He was born in Halb on the first of Shawwal in AH 442.[2] He is addressed and invoked as "Qutb-e-Madar."

Education and training

After the *Bismillah* ceremony his father entrusted him to the care of one of the leading men of his time, Maulana Hazifa of Syria who first taught him grammar and the Holy *Quran*. After completing the Holy *Quran*, he pursued other branches of knowledge. At the age of twelve, he acquired proficiency in various branches of law. Subsequently, he concentrated on the commentaries on the Holy *Quran*, the *hadis* and jurisprudence and came to be known as "Muhaddis." At the age of fourteen, he was considered as one of the leading learned men of his time.

Initiation in to the Sufi Order

Hazrat Syed Badi-ud-din Qutb-e-Madar became a spiritual disciple of Hazrat Taifoor of Syria.

Tours and travels

He went to Mecca and performed the pilgrimage. He, then, went to Medina to offer his respects to the tomb of the Holy Prophet. He received the mandate from the court of the Holy Prophet to proceed to India. Coming to India, he stayed in Gujarat for sometime and visited some other parts of India. He went on another pilgrimage to Mecca and later visited Medina, Kazmen, Baghdad, and Najaf.

Back in India, he arrived in Ajmer and stayed on a hillock called "Kokela Pahari." He met Hazrat Khwaja Moin-ud-din Hasan Chishti in Ajmer, and then leaving it visited other parts of the country. He again travelled to Mecca to perform the pilgrimage, then visiting Medina, Najaf, and Halb. Subsequently, he went yet again to Medina and received the mandate from the court of the Holy Prophet to go to India and settle there near Kannauj.

After visiting Arabia and Khorasan, he reached India. He visited Ajmer, Kalpi, Jaunpur, and then reached Makanpur, and also visited Kanpur, Ghatampur, and Surat.

Again he went to Mecca and performed the pilgrimage for the last time, also going on to Medina. Hazrat Syed Badi-ud-din Qutb-e-Madar again returned to India and began to live in Makanpur. On his way to Jaunpur, he stayed in Lucknow. When he reached Jaunpur, he was accorded a rousing reception by Sultan Ibrahim Sharqi,[3] and stayed there for some years and then, at eventually, left for Makanpur.

Death

Hazrat Syed Badi-ud-din Qutb-e-Madar made a will to the effect that he had appointed Syed Mohammed Arghoon, Syed Abu Turab Fansur, and Syed Abul Hasan Taifur as his spiritual successors. He also directed, that his funeral prayers should be led by Maulana Husam-ud-din Salamti. He breathed his last on the seventeenth of Jamade-ul-Awwal in AH 838 and lies buried in Makanpur.

Successors, disciples and caliphs

Within his lifetime he had appointed Syed Mohammed Arghoon, Syed Abu Turab Mansur, and Syed Abul Hasan Taifur as his spiritual successors.

Among his prominent disciples were: Qazi Syed Sadr-ud-din Mohammed, Shaikh Mohammed of Lahore, Maulana Shaikh Folad, Shaikh Ilyas, and Mir Syed Sadr-e-Jahan.

Among his caliphs were: Hazrat Qazi Mahmud, Syed Ajmal of Jaunpur, Syed Jamal-ud-din, better known as Mir Syed Jaman Jannati, and Qazi Mathey.

Traits of character

He was an Owaisi, had travelled widely, and was very well read, and a great saint.

Teachings

In a letter,[4] he says that the saints pay particular attention to those whose hearts can bear the secret and the light of God. By knowledge is meant enlightenment.

Inner knowledge is that in which all the secrets are disclosed. This knowledge confers belief and satisfaction and does not admit of discussion. Indeed, the knowledge that is acquired by discussion acts as a curtain between an individual and God Almighty.

Sayings

- Upon the enlightened the secret of God are disclosed.
- Protect your heart.
- A *qalandar* is one, who moulds his habits according to the habits and attributes of God.

Supernatural powers

Qazi Mahmud, who lived in Kantoor, had no son. When Hazrat Qutb-e-Madar was staying in Kantoor, Qazi Sahab requested him to pray for the birth of a son to him. He assured him, that it would happen and asked him to name the child Meethey Madar. When the son was born, Qazi Sahab did that.

In Surat, he saw a blind man and he pitied him. He undertook ablutions and sprinkled the used water on the eyes of the blind man, and then he prayed for the restoration of his eyesight. The prayer was accepted and the man was able to see once again.

References

1. *Safinat-ul-Auliya; Tazkarat-ul-Karam.*
2. *Madar-e-'Azam.*
3. Ibid., p. 83.
4. Addressed to Qazi Shahab-ud-din.

31
Hazrat Qutb-e-'Alam

Hazrat Qutb-e-'Alam was the grandson of Hazrat Syed Jalal of Bukhara. He settled in Gujarat.

Name
His name is Syed Burhan-ud-din.

Title
He is invoked and addressed as "Qutb-e-'Alam."[1]

Death
Hazrat Qutb-e-'Alam died in AH 857 and lies buried in Tabooh, about six miles from Ahmedabad, Gujarat.

REFERENCE

1. *Akhbar-ul-Akhyar.*

32

Hazrat Shaikh Abul-Fatah of Jaunpur

Hazrat Shaikh Abul-Fatah of Jaunpur was born on the fourteenth of Muharram in AH 772. He was a spiritual disciple and pupil of his grandfather Qazi Abd-ul-Muqtadar.

Hazrat Shaikh Abul-Fatah of Jaunpur was engaged in teaching and lived in Delhi, but subsequently went to Jaunpur where he settled permanently.

Death

He died on the thirteenth of Rabi-ul-Awwal in AH 858.

Traits of character

Hazrat Shaikh Abul-Fatah of Jaunpur was a very pious and learned man and led a very simple life. He adhered strictly to the tenets of his spiritual guide. He conducted long discussions with Qazi Shahab-ud-din concerning jurisprudence and other subjects and was also a poet. He wrote some panegyrics in Arabic and some poetry in Persian.

33

Hazrat Shaikh Mohammed Arif

Hazrat Shaikh Mohammed Arif was the son, spiritual caliph, and successor of his father Hazrat Shaikh Ahmad Abd-ul-Haq.

The prophecy
All the children born before him died. Hazrat Shaikh Abd-ul-Haq's wife complained to her husband that no child of their's survived. His reply was that there was no cause for anxiety for a son would be born and he would by the Grace of God survive and carry his message. When he was born, his father named him Arif.

Paternal love
His father loved him deeply and brought him up under his vigilant care. His education and training was his father's principal concern. His father was anxious that he should attain majority during his lifetime. Once he said to his wife that the angels of mercy and grace came to him several times and asked him to submit his life and be united with God Almighty, but everytime he refused, saying that he would not depart from this world until he had solemnised his son's marriage.

Marriage
Hazrat Shaikh Ahmad Abd-ul-Haq asked Hazrat Shaikh Nur-ud-din, who was a spiritual caliph of Syed Musa, to give his daughter in marriage to his son Shaikh Mohammed Arif, and the proposal was accepted. On the appointed day the marriage party reached the bride's father's house. This news reached Qazi Shams-ud-din, the father-in-law of Shaikh Nur-ud-din. He opposed the marriage on the ground that the way of life of two families was very much different.

Hazrat Shaikh Abd-ul-Haq learnt of the opposition and was very annoyed in anger shot an arrow at Qazi Shams-ud-din and blood began to flow from his stomach. When his condition became critical, he was brought to Hazrat Shaikh Abd-ul-Haq, who prayed for his recovery.

The betrothal ceremony was performed and it was decided, that the marriage would be solemnised after six months, and this was done.

Death

Hazrat Shaikh Mohammed Arif died on the fifteenth of Safar in AH 859.[1]

Caliph

His son, Shaikh Mohammed, is his premier spiritual caliph and successor.

Traits of character

Hazrat Shaikh Mohammed Arif was a very kind and courteous, man who followed the precepts and practices of his reverend father, and would not annoy or anger anyone by word or deed. He passed most of his time in prayer and nurtured no superiority complex, identifying himself with the common man. All who came to him were captivating by his good manners. He took each to be of one of his own and anyone who spent time in his company felt that he had received his greatest courtesy and kindness.[2]

Supernatural power

Qazi Shams-ud-din, who opposed his marriage, died after the marriage was performed.

References

1. *Mir'at-ul-Israr; Khazinat-ul-Asfiya.*
2. *Anwar-ul-Aun.*

34

Hazrat Shaikh Mohammed

Hazrat Shaikh Mohammed was the son, spiritual caliph, and successor of his father Hazrat Shaikh Mohammed Arif. At the time of his death, his eldest son, Budh, was in Shahabad with Hazrat Abd-ul-Quddus of Gangoh.[1] He called his son, who reached there just before his death.

Death

Hazrat Shaikh Mohammed made a will to Hazrat Abd-ul-Quddus of Gangoh to the effect, that he should look after his son, Hazrat Budh, and impart to him good education and training. He breathed his last on the twenty-first of Sha'ban. The year of his death is not definitely known.

Caliph

Hazrat Abd-ul-Quddus of Gangoh is his most outstanding spiritual caliph.

Traits of character

Hazrat Sheikh Mohammed possessed all the mystic qualities that go into the making of a perfect saint. His unflinching loyalty to the mystic creed won for him the respect and regard of the people. He believed in service before self and completely surrendered himself to the Will of God.

Reference

1. *Anwar-ul-Arefeen.*

35

Hazrat Syed Abd-ul-Malik

Hazrat Qazi Syed Abd-ul-Malik belonged to the Qadiri, Chishti, Jehanian, and Suhrawardi Orders. He was the spiritual disciple and caliph of Hazrat Syed Jalal-ud-din of Bukhara, better known as Makhdoom Jahanian-e-Jahan Gasht,[1] and also received the robe of caliph from Hazrat Qazi Shaikh Qayam-ud-din of Delhi, who was a spiritual disciple and caliph of Hazrat Nasir-ud-din Mahmud Chiragh of Delhi.[2] He is known as "Shah Ajmal."

Death

Hazrat Syed Abd-ul-Malik passed away on the twenty-fifth of Ramazan in AH 864 and was buried in Bahraich,U.P.

References

1. *Masalek-us-Salekeen,* vol. II.
2. Ibid.

36

Hazrat Shaikh Sarang

Hazrat Shaikh Sarang, a nobleman of Sultan Firoz Shah, was an eminent saint.

Initiation into the Sufi Order

He became a spiritual disciple of Hazrat Shaikh Qawam-ud-din, who showed him the way of inner illumination and inner remembrance of God.[1] He went on a pilgrimage and met Shaikh Yusuf Eirgi and received spiritual blessings from him.

The unsought gift

Hazrat Shaikh Raju Qattal sent to him the robe and other holy relics, that he had received from his spiritual forefathers. Since he had not asked for them, he returned them all. They were sent to him again. Shaikh Husam-ud-din, who belonged to the Suhrawardi Order was present there this time and persuaded him to accept the holy relics.[2] Which he eventually did and benefited from the blessings they brought.

Caliph

Hazrat Shah Meena is his spiritual caliph.

Traits of character

Hazrat Shaikh Sarang is the founder of the famous city Sarangpur.[3] He renounced his wealth, position, and pleasures for after his beliefs and after being initiated as a spiritual disciple, underwent ascetic practices rigorously.

Teachings

Hazrat Shaikh Sarang took the pleasures of the world to be debased and transient and believed it to be dangerous to be engrossed in the world. Spiritual values are higher than the material gains.

References

1. *Anwar-ul-Arefeen*, p. 457; *Akhbar-ul-Akhyar*.
2. *Anwar-ul-Arefeen*, p. 458.
3. Ibid., p. 457.

37

Hazrat Shah Meena

Hazrat Shah Meena is counted among the great saints of the Indian subcontinent and was born, a saint.

His uncle, Hazrat Shaikh Qawam-ud-din prophesied his birth, saying that a son would be born to his brother Shaikh Qutb-ud-din, a dervish who would be a source of pride to their family.

When he was born, he would not drink milk during the day in the month of Ramazan. He was named Mohammed and is addressed and invoked as Shaikh Meena.

Reasons for calling him "Meena"

Meena is a word that is used out of respect and reverence, as the word "Meena" is used. It is said that when the news of his birth was conveyed to Hazrat Shaikh Qawam-ud-din, he said, thus: "Come, O my Meena," which is why came to be known as "Shaikh Meena."

There is another reason: Hazrat Shaikh Qawam-ud-din had a son, Shaikh Meena, with whom he got annoyed because of his visits to the king without his permission. When the disobedient son was on his way to his father to implore pardon, people informed Hazrat Shaikh Qawam-ud-din of this. He said that he did not want to see his son, and that very day Shaikh Meena died. Then Hazrat Shaikh Qawam-ud-din expressed to Shaikh Qutb-ud-din his desire that a son should be born to him who should be known as Mohammed Meena in memory of his own son. When a son was born to Shaikh Qutb-ud-din, he was named Mohammed and was called "Shaikh Meena."[1]

Childhood

When he was two or three years old, he saw some birds flying. His father, understanding his gestures and his language, said, to the birds: "O, birds! you are being called by Shaikh Meena." The birds came down and sat in a row besides him and did not fly away until he allowed, them to do so.

Education and training

On attaining the age of five he was admitted in a *maktab* (school). The teacher asked him to say the first letter of the alphabet, so he said: "Alif." Then he was asked the second letter, but he did not comply, speaking instead of the existence and nature of duality and to describe the implications and the inner meaning of the word "Alif." The teacher in-charge was greatly surprised to hear him and he was left to himself.

He received his early training from Hazrat Shaikh Qawam-ud-din and lived under his care up to the age of ten and later approached Hazrat Raju Qattal and learnt from him knowledge of the self and spiritual training.

Appointment as a Qutb

At the age of twelve, he was appointed a Qutb. Qazi Shahab-ud-din, who was one of the spiritual disciples of Hazrat Badi-ud-din Shah Madar, disclosed that his spiritual guide and teacher had informed him that Shaikh Meena had been appointed a Qutb. Hazrat Shah Madar gave Qazi Shahab-ud-din a praying carpet made of pashmina to be presented to Hazrat Shaikh Meena. The Qazi, accordingly, offered him the praying carpet, which he accepted.

Initiation in Sufi Order

At the age of fifteen, he became a spiritual disciple of Hazrat Shaikh Sarang and lived in the company of his spiritual guide and teacher for twenty years. His devotion and service secured for him the robe of caliph from his spiritual guide and teacher and he was allowed to leave.

Ascetic practices

Notwithstanding the fact that he was born a saint and was appointed as a Qutb at an early age, he underwent very many ascetic practices. When offering prayers he felt drowsy and in winter he would drench his clothes in cold water during winter nights and would not sleep at all during the night. Whenever the desire to undertake ablutions with hot water seized him in winter, he would instead, bathe in cold water. Sometimes, he would sit on a wall and offer prayers there so that the fear of falling down would bolster his concentration and keep him alert and prevent him from falling asleep.

Death

Hazrat Shaikh Meena breathed his last on the twenty-third of Safar in AH 884 and lies buried in Lucknow.

Caliphs

Shaikh Qutb-ud-din was appointed by him as his *sajjadanashin* during his lifetime and he conferred the robe of caliph on Shaikh Sa'd.

Traits of character

Hazrat Shah Meena undertook ablutions every two hours. He had a forgiving nature and prayed for those who cursed him, conferring his blessings upon those who hated him. He loathed publicity, and never disclosed his fasts and penances. The *ulama* (the learned people) of his time, felt themselves inspired by his company and were greatly benefited by his profound study of *Awarif-ul-Ma'arif*. He would say, that the love of his spiritual guide and teacher was all that he sought.

Teachings

He says that a sufi who acts according to his desire is not a sufi. He is, in fact, a dacoit of the way of religion of the Holy Prophet Mohammed.

He says, that food taken after undertaking ablutions, praises God Almighty and a lightness runs through the veins.

According to him, the real companionship of an individual is with water and dust, hence by their use the fire of the search of the world is extinguished and it is hoped, that the fire of the world hereafter will also be extinguished. It means that by using water and if this is not available, then dust, in one's ritual ablutions for the prayers, then the longing for this world and for the world hereafter will leave and one will only be interested in God.

Supernatural powers

Hazrat Sa'd says that once journeying from a town named Anam to his native town Mohani. When crossing the river, turbulence caused him to fall from the horse in a desperate situation, he invoked the help of his spiritual guide and teacher Hazrat Shaikh Meena and found him there catching him by the hand and helping him out of the water.

- He was running a high temperature when he went to him. At that time, he was eating at the *'urs* of Hazrat Nasir-ud-din Chiragh of Delhi. His guide gave him a piece of bread and asked him to eat it, and as soon as he had done so he slept. When Hazrat Sa'd woke up, he found himself perfectly well.

- A person died, but even after death, his head was continually moving and in spite of strenuous efforts could not be stopped. Eventually, he was brought to Shaikh Meena, who at once said that the person could not become a spiritual disciple of anyone. Shaikh Meena asked for his cap and spiritual genealogy, placing the cap on the head and the genealogy on the chest of the dead man and then head stopped moving.

Reference

1. *Akhbar-ul-Akhyar,* Urdu trans., pp. 328-29.

38

Hazrat Shaikh Ahmad Khatto

Hazrat Shaikh Ahmad Khatto preached and practised the Gospel of Truth in Gujarat. His forefathers lived in Delhi where he himself had been brought up.

Initiation into the Sufi Order

Once, when playing with the children of his age, a windstorm swept him far away from his home town. He was found by Baba Ishaq Maghrabi, a perfect dervish who lived in Khatto and brought up by him.[1]

He became a spiritual disciple and caliph of Baba Ishaq Maghrabi.

Ascetic practices

After completing his education, he undertook very many ascetic practices in the mosque of Khane Jahan in Delhi. He used to break his fast with a little custard. After the death of his teacher Baba Ishaq, he sat in a secluded place, where he ate only forty dates in forty days.

Pilgrimage

Hazrat Shaikh Ahmad Khatto went to Mecca and performed the pilgrimage and then went to Medina where he received the spiritual blessings of the Holy Prophet. Returning to India, he went to Gujarat at the instance of Sultan Muzaffar and settled in a town named Sarkhag.

Death

He died and was buried in Sarkhag.

Traits of character

In Gujarat, he won unique popularity and to entertained, a large number of people everyday.

Teachings

He said that wearing expensive clothes would be a hindrance to him. His knowledge, coupled with his good clothes, would induce himself to become powerful. He therefore preferred to hide himself in coarse garments.[2]

He said, that it is easy to come to the dervishes, but very difficult to get away safely.

Supernatural power

Long before the invasion of Tamerlane, he had learnt it was impending. Fifteen days before the invasion, he had acquainted his disciples and devotees. According to his direction some of them went to Jaunpur, but he himself preferred to stay on.

The Moghuls imprisoned him. Tamerlane, on being informed of his moral and spiritual qualities, released him and showed him great respect.

He says that he was imprisoned along with forty companions, devotees, and disciples. Everyday, he used to receive forty pieces of bread from the Unseen, which were sufficient to feed for him and forty companions.

REFERENCES

1. *Tohfat-ul-Majalis.*
2. Ibid.

39

Hazrat Mir Syed Ashraf Jahangir Simnani

Hazrat Mir Syed Ashraf Jahangir has an assured position among the perfect dervishes. He is named Syed Ashraf and his title is "Jehangir" or the holder of the world.

He travelled extensively with Amir Syed Ali of Hamadan. Coming to India, he became a spiritual disciple of Shaikh Ala-ul-Haq, son of Asad of Lahore. After his initiation, he traversed the path of spiritual perfection with speed, grace, and distinction. He was a contemporary of Qazi Shahab-ud-din of Daulatabad.

Death

Hazrat Mir Syed Ashraf Jahangir Simnani lies buried in a small town named Kichhauchha Sharif, U.P.

Traits of character

He was a very learned man; a perfect dervish. He was endowed with supernatural powers and could combat the *jinns*, and his name is still invoked for this. His letters discuss various points and illuminate many aspects of mysticism.

Teachings

He says that *tauhid*, i.e., knowing God as one, means and implies that the lover may merge himself in the qualities of the beloved. Attention of an individual should be solely and entirely towards God under all circumstances, whether it be joy or grief, pain or pleasure. Everything should be considered to emanate from God, as the pen in the hand of the writer.[1] Everything should be considered as a useless and every person should be considered as a non-entity before God.

According to him, it is necessary for the sufis to be acquainted with the knowledge of the unity of God, for *tariqat* and *haqiqat* depend upon this very knowledge.[2]

Defining a saint, he says that he is one who has the love of God in his heart, and cares for no one else but God. He should be pure for it is necessary for prophets to be innocent. A saint should be immune from committing even minor sins.[3]

Sayings

- So long as one is not disinterested in the affiliations and attractions of the world, one Will not be benefited by frequent prayer and desirable ascetic practices.
- He who does not take to rigours and ascetic practices will not acquire the wealth of vision.
- Sainthood means that an individual continues to exist after annihilation and is endowed with purity and serenity.
- Do not view anyone with contempt, for the friends of God are often hidden.
- The enlightened should see manifestation of the Glory of God in all creation.
- The censured one is he who neither discloses the good, nor hides the evil.

Supernatural power

One day he called the cat of Kamal Pandit and narrated to her the implications of inner knowledge. After hearing him for sometime, the cat remained unconscious for an hour. When she regained consciousness, she kissed his feet.

Since that day, the cat was always with his devotees and would listen with rapt attention to the religious and spiritual discourses and would notify the arrival of guests by mewing as many times as the number of guests that had arrived.

After his passing away, the cat lived on for sometime. During the lifetime of Hazrat Syed Abd-ur-Razzaq, a special dish was being prepared in a cauldron. A black snake fell to the cauldron. The cat repeatedly pointed out this through gesture, but nobody took any notice. She eventually leapt into the cauldron and died, and only then was the black snake was discovered.

Thereupon the *sajjadanashin* (spiritual successor) Hazrat Abd-ur-Razzaq said that the cat laid down her life for the sake of *faqirs*, and she was accordingly buried.[4]

References

1. *Lataif-e-Ashrafi*, vol. I, p. 6.
2. Ibid., p. 18.
3. Ibid., p. 26.
4. Ibid., p. 26.

40
Hazrat Syed Shah Buddhan

Hazrat Syed Shah Buddhan was the spiritual caliph of Hazrat Qazi Syed Abd-ul-Malik, better known as Shah Ajmal of Bahraich.

Early life and education

His father had lost several sons. When Hazrat Syed Shah was six years old, his father took him to Hazrat Husam-ud-din for his blessings and he requested him to pray that he have a long life.[1] He replied: "God Willing, he will be a great saint." His father then asked him to pray that he might be endowed with some knowledge. He replied: "He will be a great learned man." His father next sought that he should have some divine knowledge. Thereupon he replied: "By the Grace of God, he will be an enlightened individual and will live long."

He was brought up under the vigilant care of Maulana Husam-ud-din of Fatehpur and attained external and the inward perfection.[2]

Initiation into the Sufi Order

He became a disciple of Hazrat Syed Abd-ul-Malik, better known as Shah Ajmal of Bahraich; he also received the robe of caliph from him. He is also the spiritual disciple and caliph of Hazrat Husam-ud-din of Fatehpur, the spiritual caliph of Qazi Abd-ul-Muqtadar.

Death

Hazrat Syed Shah Buddhan passed away on the eight of Shawwal in AH 880 and was buried in Bahraich, U.P.

References

1. *Masalek-us-Salekeen*, vol. II.
2. *Khazinat-ul-Asfiya; Ma'arej-ul-Vilayat.*

41

Hazrat Shaikh Abdullah Shattari

Hazrat Shaikh Abdullah Shattari traced his descent from Hazrat Shaikh Shahab-ud-din Suhrawardi. He was an outstanding saint, belonging to the Shattariya Order, and was considered an authority on rituals, practices, usages, customs, and manners, relating to the Shattariya Order. He traced his spiritual genealogy to Shaikh Najm-ud-din Kubra in the fifth degree.

Hazrat Shaikh Abdullah Shattari used to beat the drum and cry out: "Is there any seeker, whom I can show the way of God?" He would keep an eye on everyone and would refer to those nurturing doubts and bereft of faith and belief as blackboards.

He would say, that there should not be any blackboard, so that something might be said about divine matters. It is said that whenever any seeker came to him, he would test his wisdom, intelligence, and common sense.

He was a perfect dervish with outward charm and inner graces. He is also the author of a book that, deals with the rituals, practices, and meditation relating to the Shattariya Order. He died in AH 890 and lies buried in Mandu.

42

Hazrat Shaikh Darvesh Mohammed

Hazrat Shaikh Darvesh Mohammed was the spiritual caliph of Hazrat Shaikh Fath-ul-lah of Oudh. He is said to be the spiritual guide and teacher of Hazrat Shaikh Abd-ul-Quddus of Ganh.[1] His father's name was Shaikh Qasim.

Initiation into the Sufi Order

Hazrat Shaikh Darvesh Mohammed became a spiritual disciple of Hazrat Shaikh Fath-ul-lah of Oudh, received the robe of caliph, pertaining to the Chishti-Nizami Orders, from him.[2] He was also the spiritual disciple of Hazrat Syed Buddhan of Bahraich, and from him, he received the robe of caliph pertaining to the Qadiri, Chishti, Suhrawardi, and Jahanian Orders.[3]

Death

Hazrat Shaikh Darvesh Mohammed breathed his last on the sixteenth of Muharram in AH 896 and lies buried in Faizabad, U.P.

References

1. *Masalek-us-Salekeen*, vol. II, p. 425.
2. *Lata'if-e-Qudsi*.
3. *Masalek-us-Salekeen*, vol. II, p. 425. See also *Tazkarat-ul-Abedeen* and *Iqtibas-ul-Anwar*.

43

Hazrat Shaikh Husam-ud-din of Manakpur

Hazrat Shaikh Husam-ud-din of Manakpur was a prominent saint. His grandfather Maulana Jalal-ud-din of Manakpur was a spiritual disciple of Hazrat Shaikh Mohammed, who was a caliph of Hazrat Nizam-ud-din Auliya and a very pious and learned man. His father was called Maulana Khwaja.

Initiation into the Sufi Order

He was a spiritual disciple and caliph of Hazrat Shaikh Nur-ul-Haq, better known as Shaikh Nur Qutb-e-'Alam.

Teachings

Hazrat Shaikh Husam-ud-din of Manakpur was well versed in the *shari'at* and *tariqat*. According to him, spiritual disciples resemble their spiritual guides inasmuch as do the patches on clothes. The sincere disciple, who obeys his spiritual guide resembles a white patch on white cloth. It is washed with the cloth and the patch also becomes white. In the same way, whatever spiritual blessings are derived by the spiritual guide are also shared by him and he also attains perfection. He who does not obey his spiritual guide is like a black patch on white cloth. He, also, derives spiritual blessings from his spiritual guide, but not to that the same degree enjoyed by the former.... However that may be, there should be a spiritual guide.[1]

Sayings

- He who treads the spiritual path, by remembrance becomes a lover and by meditation becomes enlightened.
- One should not give up reading the Holy *Quran*, even if one has attained the position of a Qutb. One should at least read one part everyday.

- A dervish should have four things, two in sound condition and two broken. Religion and belief should be sound, but the legs and heart should be broken.
- Greed is a malady, to ask is agony, and to refuse is death.

Supernatural power

After becoming a caliph, he would subject himself to starvation for days together. One day, one of his children was hungry and came to him and began to weep. He could not control himself and prayed. Then a certain person sent him a trayful of food. Another sent him dal weighing forty seers. Subsequently, he was sad that he had asked for trifles.

Reference

1. *Rafiq-ul-Arefeen.*

44

Hazrat Khwaja Husain of Nagore

Hazrat Khwaja Husain of Nagore traced his decent from Shaikh Wahid,[1] and is also related to Hazrat Sufi Hamid-ud-din of Nagore. He became a spiritual disciple of Shaikh Kabir. He lived in the company of his spiritual guide and teacher for a long time. He acquiring the inner and exterior knowledge and after attaining perfection, he was allowed to leave Gujarat.

He went to Nagore and then to Ajmer and devoted himself to the service of Hazrat Khwaja Moin-ud-din Hasan Chishti at his tomb. Receiving a spiritual indication from Hazrat Khwaja Gharib Nawaz, he went to Nagore and began to preach the Gospel of Truth.

Invitation accepted

Sultan Ghiyas-ud-din Khalji of Mandu invited him a number of times,[2] but he did not accept the invitation. Once, he received the sacred hair of the Holy Prophet. His courtiers told him that Khwaja Husain would surely accept an invitation to be blessed by the sacred hair. The Sultan acted accordingly and Hazrat Khwaja Husain left at once for Mandu where the Sultan accorded him a warm welcome. It is said, that as soon as he saw the sacred hair, it flew into his hand.

Then the Sultan offered him presents and made an offering in cash which Khwaja Husain refused to accept. Finding his son somewhat inclined towards the gifts, he advised him to take a part of the amount to be spent on constructing the tombs of Hazrat Khwaja Moin-ud-din Hasan Chishti and Sufi Hamid-ud-din of Nagore. The amount was accepted and accordingly spent.

Traits of character

There is a consensus of opinion that he was a perfect dervish and an accomplished saint. He was endowed with knowledge, learning, fondness, love, hope, belief, and faith.

He had a bullock-cart and drove it himself and also cared for the bullocks on his own. He wore coarse clothes.

He was a man of literary taste and wrote several books, one of which is a commentary on the Holy *Quran* entitled *Nur-un-Nabi*. Hazrat Khwaja Husain of Nagore had the utmost respect and love for the Holy Prophet. His worldly possessions consisted of a house, a well, and a garden, all of which he dedicated to the Holy Prophet in whose name he put the property in trust.

References

1. *Akbhar-ul-Akhyar,* Urdu trans., p. 375.
2. *Moin-ul-Auliya,* pp. 273-74; *Ahsan-us-Siyar,* pp. 34-37.

45

Hazrat Shaikh Sa'd-ud-din of Khairabad

Hazrat Shaikh Sa'd-ud-din of Khairabad was a spiritual disciple and caliph of Hazrat Shah Meena and a pupil of Maulana A'zam from whom he acquired the external knowledge. He was well-versed in the external and the inner knowledge, was very fond of music, and is an author of several books. His book entitled *Magma'-us-Saluk* encapsulates the life and discourses of his spiritual guide and teacher Hazrat Shah Meena.

Hazrat Shaikh Sa'd-ud-din of Khairabad had many spiritual disciples, some prominent among them include, Shaikh Safe, Shaikh Mubarak, and Shaikh-ul-lah.

46

Hazrat Sama-ud-din Suhrawardi

Hazrat Sama-ud-din Suhrawardi, born in Multan in AH 808,[1] was an outstanding saint of the Suhrawardi Order. He traced his descent from Hazrat Musa'ab son of Hazrat Zubair, companion of the Holy Prophet Mohammed.[2] His father, Fakhr-ud-din, was the spiritual disciple of Syed Sadr-ud-din Mohammed, alias Raju Qattal.[3] His elder brother was named Shaikh Ishaq.[4]

Education and training

Maulana Sama-ud-din, the famous pupil of Mir Syed Sharif Girgani, was his teacher, and under him he completed his education. He acquired proficiency in jurisprudence, the *Hadis*, and the commentaries. Inward knowledge he acquired from his reverend father. When he was twelve years old, his father used to call him to his private chamber and would guide him, offer him advice, and acquaint him with the divine philosophy and the implications of mysticism. He used to pray for him with all humility: "O, Great God! From Thy Bounty and Abundance, give to Sama-ud-din the eternal graces and everlasting wealth."

Initiation into the Sufi Order

His father acted as his spiritual guide, but he was in fact a disciple of Hazrat Shaikh Kabir-ud-din Ismail. He went to Hazrat Shaikh Kabir and requested him to accept him as one of his humble disciples. The latter thereupon told him, that he would secure for him the robe of caliph from his brother Shaikh Fazlullah. Everytime he requested this, he received the same reply.

One day, picking up courage, he submitted that initiation in the Sufi Order is purely a matter of personal faith and devotion. It is a state of heart, he said, and that he found himself inclined towards him and him alone in point of faith, dedication, and devotion. He recited a couplet which, translated, runs: "If you confer kindness or may not confer/I will not leave [your] door;/ I have taken hold of your door, I have no other place."

Hearing the couplet, Hazrat Shaikh Kabir was immensely pleased and embraced him. Taking him to his special tenement, he honoured him by accepting him as his disciple and prescribed the gospel. After his performing the thanksgiving prayer, the special robe of caliph was conferred upon him.

Advice

After being appointed caliph, he thought, he should discontinue the acquisition of worldly knowledge, concentrating instead on inner purification and illumination. His spiritual guide and teacher reading his thoughts, said:[5]

> The foundation of *shari'ah* and the strength of religion depend upon knowledge. Do not give it up. I have prayed to God, that the people of the inner and outer life may both alike derive benefit from you and in the manner and to the extent our spiritual forefathers have been endowed with spiritual and worldly wealth, I hope you will similarly achieve the same.

Access to kings

Hazrat Sama-ud-din Suhrawardi left Multan for Delhi, and on the way stayed in Ranthambore and Bayana for sometime. He reached Delhi during the reign of Sultan Bahlul Lodi and settled there permanently.

When Sultan Bahlul Lodi came to him to offer his respects, he gave him this piece of advice:[6]

> Oh, Sultan! Thou hast become Sultan in old age. Fear God and abstain from falsehood and sin. Offer thanks to God. Offering thanks to God increases blessings. God says: 'If you offer thanks, I will give you more. . . if you are unthankful, know that my wrath is great.' Last you should be involved in it.

He gave him his special praying-carpet. The Sultan, placing it over his head, sought leave of him.

On receipt of the news of the demise of Sultan Bahlul Lodi, his son, Nizam, went to him to pay his respects and submitted, that he wanted to be taught "Mizana-us-Sarf." Under the pretext of the lesson, he inquired from him the meaning of the phrase: "May God make thee blessed in both the worlds." When he provided the meaning, Nizam requested him to repeat the phrase, and caused him to repeat it three times. He, then, kissed his hands and humbly remarked: "I have gained my object. I wished the aforesaid words to emanate from your blessed tongue."

Hazrat Sama-ud-din Suhrawardi was delighted at his polite way of expressing his implied object. He went into trance and then said: "Nizam, I have prayed to God, that thou may'st become the Alexander of thy time and many people may be benefited by thee." Nizam Khan ascended the throne and became as famous as Sultan Sikander Lodi.

Last days

Hazrat Sama-ud-din Suhrawardi has two sons: Hazrat Shaikh Abdullah Biabani and Hazrat Nasir-ud-din, who succeeded him. Hazrat Shaikh Abdullah Biabani left home to wander in forests and deserted places so his whereabouts were not known. The pangs of separation made greatly saddened his father. His chief spiritual disciple and caliph, Hazrat Maulana Jamali, on returning home from pilgrimage, expressed his desire to find and to bring home his son. He was pleased with about this, embraced him, gave him his special clothes, and handed over to him a letter addressed to his son. The next day, however, he called Shaikh Jamali to him and said: "God knows whether you may be able to meet my son or not. I do not want you to be separated from me. Be present here for my funeral prayers."

Death

A week later, i.e., on the seventeenth of Jamade-ul-Awwal in AH 901, he breathed his last. He lies buried in Mehrauli, New Delhi.

Caliphs

His eminent caliphs are: Hazrat Nasir-ud-din, Maulana Shaikh Jamali, and Shaikh Udhan.

Traits of character

He was well-versed in the knowledge of the *shari'at* and *tariqat*. His generosity knew no bounds. Thousands of rupees were received as unsought gifts, but he would save nothing and spend all, sometimes borrowing money in order to meet the needs and requirements of others. He had all the finer qualities. Hazrat Shaikh Abd-ul-Haq thus says of him:[7]

> Shaikh Sama-ud-din was an embodiment of piety, purity, and of ceremonial and real knowledge. He had a perfect concentration of attention. If he cast a glance of grace and kindness towards any spiritually depraved, his chest was cleared of spiritual malady and if he cast a smiling look, the skirt of his hope was filled up with the flowers of his object.

Hazrat Sama-ud-din Suhrawardi was a man with literary taste. He wrote a commentary on the *Lamyat* of Shaikh Fakhr-ud-din of Iraq and has also written a book entitled *Miftah-ul-Israr*.[8]

Teachings

He says:[9]

> There are three people, who will remain deprived of the blessings and mercy of God. Firstly, the old men engrossed in sin. Secondly, the young, who on account of the hope of repentance do not cease to commit sins. Thirdly, there is the king who lies.
> The meaning of introspection is this, that if one is not able to adopt and adhere to the present state of the dervishes, he may at least follow their actions, sayings, and deeds, so that the effect of the outward condition of the dervishes may remove the stain and the rust of the inward malice and impurity.

Rituals and practices

He used to wake up in the middle of the night and offer prayers, genuflecting for an hour at a time, and then would meditate till sunrise. In addition, he offered all the other prayers of the day. Following the afternoon prayer, he would meditate again. After the night prayer, he would go to his house and devote himself to prayers, and again meditate after the sunset prayer.

Supernatural powers

His devoted disciple and caliph had reached Gujarat after his return from pilgrimage. He was unaware of this. One day, however, he said: "Thank God, Jamali has returned." After a few days, a certain person came from Gujarat and informed him of the arrival of Hazrat Jamali there.

Hazrat Jamali says that he met with many hazards during the journey. Sometimes he lost all hope of life, and on such occasions he saw him clearly joyfully offering him a betel leaf and encouraging him and assuring him of safety. Hazrat Jamali says, that on account of his guidance, help, and assistance the confusion and anxiety was immediately transformed into comfort, solace, and satisfaction.

References

1. *Al-Mashahir,* p. 29.
2. *Misbah-ul-Arefeen; Shams-ut-Tawarikh,* vol. 2, p. 2.
3. *Al-Mashahir,* p. 49.
4. Ibid., p. 44.
5. *Siyar-ul-Arefeen.*
6. *Al-Mashahir,* p. 42.
7. *Akhbar-ul-Akhyar.*
8. *Al-Mashahir,* p. 46.
9. Ibid., p. 42.

47

Hazrat Shaikh Ahmad Mujad Shebani

Shaikh Ahmad Mujad Shebani was born in Narnaul, brought up in Ajmer and buried in Nagore. He traces his descent from Imam Abu Hanifa. His father, Qazi Mujad-ud-din, was the son of Qazi Tajul- Afzal bin Shams-ud-din Shebani, Imam Mohammed Shebani. He had six brothers and was himself the eldest.

Education and training
He completed his education when he was eighteen years old. Even when a student, he used to hold discussions with the *ulama* and make speeches in Arabic and Persian.

Initiation into the Sufi Order
He was a spiritual disciple and caliph of Hazrat Khwaja Husain of Nagore.[1]

Death
He left Narnaul and settled in Ajmer when he was eighteen years old and left Ajmer when he was ninety. He went to Narnaul, where he stayed for about four years. He died on the twenty-fifth of Safar in AH 927 and was buried in Nagore.

Traits of character
He did not pay any attention to the world or the people of the world. He made no distinction between the rich and the poor and a relation and a stranger so far as the do's and don'ts of Islamic law were concerned.

He was very pious and ever devoted to the remembrance of God. He greatly enjoyed music. He generally dressed in ordinary, clean and well-washed clothes. He had a couple of sets of fine clothes and a long turban which he always kept with him to be worn on special occasions such as Eid and Friday prayers.

Shaikh Ahmed Mujad Shebani was very bold and had the courage to speak the truth and to act according to *shari'at* and the dictates of his conscience. It was a custom at the court of the kings of Mandu for people to offer the rulers *salaams* by bowing down very low and by placing their finger of evidence on the ground. He and Qazi Idris of Delhi did not do so, holding it to be contrary to Islamic precept practice. He said, *salaam aleikum,* "Peace be on you" and sat down beside the king. The king was not displeased. He appointed Qazi Idris, the Qazi of Ajmer and gave him four villages. The forefathers of Hazrat Ahmad Shebani had performed the work of issuing *fatwas*. This was now entrusted to Hazrat Shaikh Ahmad Shebani.

Teachings

He would say to his spiritual disciples, that the religious people should not disgrace themselves before the people of the world, for they are the people who see only the outward condition.

Reference

1. *Akhbar-ul-Akhyar,* Urdu trans., p. 378.

48

Hazrat Khwaja Khanu

Hazrat Khwaja Khanu was a prominent spiritual figure of his time and a spiritual disciple of Hazrat Khwaja Husain of Nagore.[1] He also received the robe of caliph from Shaikh Isma'il son of Shaikh Husain Sarmast, who lived in Chanderi. He received spiritual blessings from Hazrat Khwaja Moin-ud-din Hasan Chishti.

Among his prominent spiritual disciples and caliphs, the following may be mentioned: Shaikh Nizam-ud-din of Narnaul, his brother Shaikh Isma'il, and Shaikh Munawwar, who lived in Agra.

Death

Hazrat Khwaja Khanu died in AH 940 and lies buried in Gwalior.

Traits of character

He was a saint endowed with great spiritual powers. He did not stand to receive any visitor due to a physical infirmity and old age. When questioned about it, he replied: "I have grown old and I have become weak, I cannot stand for each and every visitor. To stand for some visitors specially and not to stand for others will imply a distinction, which is opposed and contrary to the way of life of dervishes. I should therefore be excused."

Reference

1. *Akhbar-ul-Akhyar,* Urdu trans., p. 456.

49

Hazrat Maulana Shah Jamali

Hazrat Maulana Shah Jamali was a prominent mystic poet and saint belonging to the Suhrawardi Order of the sufis. His father Fazl-ul-lah was an accomplished man who died when he was a minor. He was hard-working and intelligent and took great pains to acquire knowledge and learning and achieved distinction in customary knowledge.

His name is Hamid. His spiritual guide Hazrat Maulana Sama-ud-din named him Jamali.[1] It is also said that formerly he was named Jalal Khan but at the instance of his spiritual guide and teacher he called himself Jamal Khan.[2] His former poetic pseudonym "Jalali" was changed into "Jamali," and it was under the latter that he became famous.

Initiation into the Sufi Order

After completing his education, he thought of being initiated in the Sufi Order and was accepted as a disciple by Hazrat Sama-ud-din Suhrawardi. He was subsequently raised to the dignified position of caliph. Living in the company of his spiritual guide and teacher, he concentrated on the acquisition of the grace of inner life, devoting himself to prayers, rituals, fasts, abstinence, ascetic practices, and penances. He was ever engaged in the service of his spiritual guide and teacher, voluntarily performing the duty of helping his teacher in his ablutions. He would hold the handkerchief, the washing basin and the jug with him and go outside the city to fetch the pieces of earth for his master's ablutions in a basket which he carried on his head.

The love of his spiritual guide

His teacher loved him greatly. He says: "Hazrat Makhdoom loved this humble being very much." When I went to perform the pilgrimage, he used to pray for me at the time of the pre-dawn prayer: "O God! Cause Jamali to reach me safe and sound and enable me to see his face and lighten my eyes by the light of his vision with thy grace and kindness,

O the Most Merciful of all the Merciful.' About the reunion he says:[3] "When I returned home from pilgrimage and went to him to pay my respects, he embraced me and kissed me and said: 'At last my prayer, that I used to offer before dawn has been accepted'."

Tours and travels

Hazrat Maulana Shah Jamali was very fond of tours and travels. He performed a pilgrimage to Mecca and then went on to Medina and derived spiritual blessings from the holy tomb of the Holy Prophet Mohammed. He also visited Multan and met Shaikh Sadr-ud-din and went to the tomb of Hazrat Shaikh Baha-ud-din Zakariya of Multan to offer his respects. He went to Herat and there he met Shaikh Sufi, Hazrat Shaikh Abd-ul-Aziz Jami, Maulana Nur-ud-din Jami, Hazrat Maulana Mas'ud Sherwani, and Maulana Husain. Reaching Baghdad, he derived spiritual blessings from the tomb of Hazrat Shaikh Abd-ul-Qadir of Jilan, better known as Ghous-ul-A'zam, and from the tomb of Hazrat Shaikh Shahab-ud-din Suhrawardi.

He also visited Yemen, Egypt, Jerusalem, Syria, Iraq, Arabia, Azerbaijan, Gilan, and Khorasan and came in contact with a number of saints, sages, sufis, and poets.[4]

Relations with kings

Sultan Sikander Lodi was a devotee of his and reposed faith in him. He himself was a poet; his poetic pseudonym being "Gul Rukhi," he would get his poetry edited by Hazrat Jamali. He was in Sambhal, when returned to Delhi from Iraq, Syria, and Arabia. When he came to Hazrat Jamali learnt of his arrival, he sent him a letter, written in verse, inviting him to Sambhal.

Emperor Babur and Humayun also believed in his spiritual greatness, paying him utmost respect and reverence. They visited his house more than once to pay their homage and respect.[5]

Children

He had two sons: Shaikh Abd-ul-Hai and Abd-us-Samad alias Shaikh Gadai.

Death

Hazrat Maulana Shah Jamali breathed his last on the tenth of Ziq'ada in AH 942. He lies buried in Mehrauli, New Delhi.

Traits of character

Hazrat Jamali was a very pious and saintly man. He was forever lost in meditation and in the remembrance of God. He was humble and gentle, and very generous extending kindness, courtesy and hospitality to all. He was deeply attached to his spiritual guide and teacher and saw service as the path to salvation.

Like the mystics and the sufis, he travelled widely. Among the sufis, he was accepted as an enlightened one and among the learned men, he occupied a position of prestige, honour, and distinction. He was endowed with all the requisite spiritual and moral qualities for him to be called an outstanding saint.

Literary taste

Hazrat Maulana Shah Jamali was a great scholar and the author of a number of books, the most famous of which are *Siyar-ul-Arefeen* and *Mir'at-ul-Ma'ani.*

He was an inspired poet. It is said, that Shaikh Jamali was counted among the leading poets of the time of Sikander Lodi.[5] He has left a *divan,* which contains about nine thousand Persian verses. His *masnavi* entitled *Mehr-o-Mah* has been characterised as a unique piece of poetry.

Supernatural power

Sultan Ibrahim Lodi, the last king of the Lodi dynasty, was weak-willed and self-seeking. Sultan Ibrahim was against him and he too bore some ill-will against the Sultan. He says that the ill-will subsequently turned into cordial relations, but the effects of it endured. Babur invaded India and defeated Sultan Ibrahim's large army. The First Battle of Panipat, fought in AD 1526 decided the fate of India. Sultan Ibrahim Lodi was not only deprived of the crown and the throne, but was killed.

References

1. *Al-Mashahir,* p. 204.
2. *Rauzat-ul-Aqtab,* p. 92.
3. *Al-Mashahir,* p. 209.
4. Ibid., p. 215.
5. *Darbar-e-Akbari.*

50

Hazrat Shaikh Abd-ul-Quddus

Hazrat Shaikh Abd-ul-Quddus of Gangoh was an eminent saint, sage, and philosopher of the Sabiri Order that is spread throughout the Indian subcontinent. He was born in AH 861. His father's name was Safi-ud-din, and Shaikh Rukn-ud-din and Shaikh Abd-ul-Kabir were his two famous sons.

Initiation into the Sufi Order

He became a spiritual disciple of Hazrat Shaikh Mohammed, the grandson of Hazrat Shaikh Abd-ul-Haq. Besides this, it is said that he enjoyed inner affiliation with Hazrat Shaikh Abd-ul-Haq of Rudoli. He had besides also received the robe of caliph from Hazrat Darvesh Qasim of Oudh of the Suhrawardi and Chishti Orders.

Domicile

One of his devotees, Umar Khan Kashi, a nobleman enjoying the confidence of the king, requested and persuaded him to leave Rudoli and settle in Shahabad, Delhi, which he did. He stayed for over thirty years in Shahabad.

The First Battle of Panipat in AD 1526 decided the fate of the subcontinent. Babur emerged victorious, routing the forces of Sultan Ibrahim Lodi, who was himself slain. The establishment of the Moghul empire in India dissipated the Afghans and led to the decay and decline of their influence.

Shahabad, a stronghold of the Afghans, had to pay a heavy price and was destroyed, the Moghuls were not wishing to have an Afghan stronghold there.

Under the circumstances, Hazrat Abd-ul-Quddus was forced to leave the town and settle elsewhere. He preferred Gangoh, a small town in Saharanpur, U.P.

Death

Hazrat Abd-ul-Quddus breathed his last on the fifteenth of Jamade-ul-Akhir in AH 945.[1] At that time, he was eighty-four years old and was buried in Gangoh, U.P. It is also said that he died while listening to music.

Caliphs

His prominent caliphs are: Shaikh Phooru, Shaikh Abd-ul-Ghafoor, Shaikh Rukn-ud-din, Shaikh Abd-ul-Kabir, and Shaikh Jalal-ud-din Mahmud.

Traits of character

Hazrat Abd-ul-Quddus was one of the most learned men of his time, deeply absorbed in contemplation and adhering strictly to the tenets of the Holy Prophet Mohammed. Observance of the *sunnah* of the Holy Prophet was to him an article of faith. He was born a saint,[2] and signs of his spiritual greatness were visible even when he was a child. During his childhood, whatever he prophesied actually occurred.

He was engaged in agriculture which was his source of livelihood. When the crop was ripe, he would first of all give a portion of it to the dervishes and then appropriate the balance for his own use. He was a very generous man and would never allow a beggar to return from his door empty handed. After passing through all the stages of learning and devotion he achieved spiritual perfection.

He is the author of a number of books, the most celebrated of which *Anwar-ul-Aun*. His letters disclose his deep insight and vast knowledge and learning. He was a poet too and very fond of music. Sometimes, when listening to music he would enter into a state of rapture, of spiritual ecstasy.

Teachings and sayings

Once a music concert was held in Delhi where he was present. Suddenly, he stood up and said: "Mansur was murdered by foolish people," and repeated these words several times. A member of the audience stood up and named a learned man and enquired "was he also a fool?" The response was that he referred to him also.

Supernatural powers

Hazrat Abd-ul-Quddus exhibited very many supernatural powers.

Once he went to a town named Chachpur, and there was engaged in prayers at the dead of night. Suddenly, he cried aloud, asking the residents of the town to come out of their houses with all their goods and cattle. He foretold that fire was soon raze the town to the ground. Nobody took notice of what he said, but shortly the town was engulfed in flames, could not be extinguished, and razed the entire town.

Hazrat Shaikh Rukn-ud-din says that Maulana Chandon (his teacher and a spiritual disciple of his father Shaikh Abd-ul-Quddus) once went to a tank to wash his clothes, and there saw a very beautiful woman. His passions were aroused and it became difficult for him to control himself. To his great surprise, he saw Hazrat Abd-ul-Quddus standing in the water with a stick in his hand. The moment the Maulana saw his spiritual guide and teacher standing there, he was ashamed of his ignoble thought and returned home. Hazrat Abd-ul-Quddus, seeing him, smiled and said: "You need not be afraid. The spiritual guide is in fact the protector and he protects his spiritual disciples." His son, Hazrat Shaikh Rukn-ud-din states, that after he died, when he was given the ritual bath and shrouded in the coffin, he placed his hand on his chest. He found, that his heartbeat and inner remembrance to be the same as it had been during his lifetime.

References

1. *Akhbar-ul-Akhyar; Mir'at-ul-Israr.*
2. *Ma'arij-ul-Vilayat.*

51

Hazrat Shah Abd-ur-Razzaq Jhungana

Hazrat Shah Abd-ur-Razzaq Jhungana belongs to the Qadiri Order of the sufis and was an eminent saint. He was the spiritual disciple and caliph of Hazrat Shaikh Mohammed Hasan. Syed Ali of Ludhiana is one of his prominent spiritual disciples.

Death
He died in AH 949.

Traits of character
Hazrat Shah Abd-ur-Razzaq Jhungana was a perfect dervish and an erudite scholar who exhibited very many spiritual power and underwent very many spiritual practices and rigours. It is said that he derived spiritual blessings from Hazrat Shaikh Abd-ul-Qadir of Jilan better known as Ghous-ul-Azam Piran-e-Pir. A very patient man, he was patient and persevering in times of adversity and hardship. He paid the utmost respect to the Syeds, or the descendants of the House of the Holy Prophet. Once, he saw a Syed in police custody and stood as surety for him. He advised him to abscond and assured him that he would bear the consequences of that. The person absconded and he found himself in deep trouble but bore all the tribulations with fortitude. He is the author of several books.

Teachings
In one of his books he says that the quickest way to reach up to God is that of remembrance and to engage with the face of the spiritual guide; this alone, without any other spiritual practice, is sufficient to enable an individual to reach up to God. For a beginner there is no other path to God except engrossing himself with the face of the spiritual guide, for the divine world is the world of meaning and it is not possible to see it except in the shape of the perfect personality of a perfect man in the form of God who mirrors perfection.

52

Hazrat Shaikh Hamza

Hazrat Shaikh Hamza was among the descendants of Hazrat Shaikh Baha-ud-din Zakariya of Multan. He traces his descent from Hazrat Syed Mohammed Gesoo Daraz. His parents lived in Narhar. Initially, Hazrat Shaikh Hamza was in the employ of the king. One night, when guarding the palace, it struck him that he should serve someone who would look after him and not one whom he had to look after. He resigned his job and left for Ajmer to receive the blessings at the tomb of the great saint Hazrat Khwaja Moin-ud-din Hasan Chishti. In Ajmer, he received spiritual blessings from a contemplative person named Bayan and lived in the company of Shaikh Ahmad Mujad.

After living in Ajmer for sometime, he returned to his home town. He then moved to Dharsoo, which is not very far off from Narnaul and settled there permanently. It is said in Dharsoo, there lived some Syeds living in an abject condition wishing improve their conditions, he settled in Dharsoo, and to educate them appointed two Maulvis, one of Persian and the other of Arabic.

Death

Hazrat Shaikh Hamza breathed his last on the twenty-fifth of Rabi-us-Sani in AH 957.

Traits of character

He was ever engaged in prayer and spent a great deal on students and dervishes.

Teachings

According to him, the world is like fire and it is sufficient that we cook something from it and use it to keep ourselves warm in winter. When the fire increases, it burns and kills.

53

Hazrat Shaikh Aman

Hazrat Shaikh Aman of Panipat was an outstanding saint and scholar, and was named Abd-ul-Malik. He is addressed and invoked as 'Aman-ul-lah, but is better known by a part of his title, i.e., "Aman." He was a pupil of Shaikh Mohammed Maudood Lari and a spiritual disciple of Shaikh Mohammed Hasan. He belonged to several Orders of the sufis, but preferred the Qadiri order to the rest. He traced his descent from Shah Ne'mat-ul-lah Wagi of the Qalandariya Order.

Death
Hazrat Shaikh Aman passed away on the twelfth of Rabi-ul-Akhir in AH 957.[1]

Devotees and pupils
Hazrat Shaikh Aman had a large number of devotees and pupils. Prominent among them are: Shaikh Taj-ud-din, son of Zakariya of Ajoodhan, Shaikh Rukn-ud-din, Shaikh Husain Chishti, Maulana Husain Naqshi, and Shaikh Sarf-ud-din, the father of Shaikh Abd-ul-Haqq, Muhaddis of Delhi.

Traits of character
Hazrat Shaikh Aman holds a position of eminence among the mystics. He adhered to the doctrine of *tauhid* as propounded by Shaikh Ibn-al-Arabi and not permit idle gossip in his presence. He was continually engaged in the remembrance of God and was very fond of reading books on mysticism.

He kept no worldly goods, articles of food and drink, furniture and the like and ate very little and kept awake at night. Sometimes, when offering prayers, he would stop and, repeating the words "Thee do we worship and Thine is the aid we seek," would faint. He was a very learned man, and has written several books on mysticism a *tauhid*, or the unity of God. One of his famous books is entitled *Asbat-ul-Wahdiyat*, and he has also written a commentary on *Lawaih*, by Maulana Abd-ur-Rahman Jami. He was a great lover of books and prior to his death, bidding farewell to his books, he said that he was greatly inspired by them and he had derived a great many blessings from them.

He paid great respect to the Syeds, and it is said that while he was engaged in teaching if the children of the Syeds came that way, he would at once stand up with the book in his lap and so long as the children remained standing he had not the courage to sit down.

Teachings

According to him, a perfect dervish is one with civilized manners and bearing in his heart the love of the family of the Holy Prophet Mohammed. An indication of the pinnacle of the love of God is for an individual to follow the Holy Prophet and the sign of the love of the Holy Prophet is love of the members of his family. He says, that everyone is given something that acts as a source of joy and pleasure; but his pleasure and joy consist in the books written by the sufis.

Reference

1. *Akhbar-ul-Akhyar*, Urdu trans., p. 474.

54

Hazrat Shah Abd-ur-Rahman Janbaz Qalandar

Hazrat Shah Abd-ur-Rahman Janbaz Qalandar was a prominent saint of the Qalandariya Order; a Hashemite. His father Syed Ala-ud-din Abbasi was a Qutb of his time and the son of Syed Nasir-ud-din Ata'ullah Abbasi. His mother Syeda Bibi was a very pious woman. He was born in AH 861 and belonged to a Syed family of Kantoor. He was named Kamal-ud-din, but is better known as Imam Abd-ur-Rahman and he is addressed and invoked as "Janbaz Qalandar."

Education and service

When he was four years, four months, and four days, the ceremony of *Bismillah* was performed. At the age of five, he began to study grammar and the Holy *Quran*. He also studied other branches of knowledge and completed his education when he was fourteen.

After his father's death when he was fifty, he went to Delhi during the reign of Sultan Sikandar Lodi. There he came into contact with Maulana Aladad, the author of the famous book entitled *Badi-ul-Meezan*. The Maulana was so impressed with him, that he appointed him as a teacher in Madrasa Dar-ul-Khilafat. Very soon, he also, like Maulana Aladad, gained fame and became a favourite of the king. Sultan Sikander Lodi appointed him *imam* of a mosque where he conducted prayers. Emperor Humayun appointed him as his *imam* and would offer prayers behind him. He came to be known as Imam Danishmand.

Return from Delhi

After living in Delhi for twelve years, he sought leave of the king to go to his aged mother. The king agreed and presented him with some villages for his maintenance. His mother was not pleased to see him, believing that pursued worldly honour, position, and prestige and wishing him to engage himself a quest for God. She suggested that he refer the matter to the noble soul of his father. His father told him not to waste his time, and that he would become a Qutb for which he should prepare himself. It was imperative that he should proceed to Jaunpur and become a spiritual disciple of Hazrat Shaikh Abd-us-Salam.

Initiation into the Sufi Order

He eventually reached Jaunpur. Seeing him, Hazrat Shaikh Abd-us-Salam said: "Come, O, my Janbaz!" and from that day he became known as "Janbaz." Janbaz embraced him and lived in his company for twenty-five days. After his being initiated as a spiritual disciple, he received spiritual training and soon received the blessings of the fourteen Orders.

From Jaunpur, he went to Laharpur. His mother, on learning that he was coming from Hazrat Abd-us-Salam after being initiated as his spiritual disciple and receiving very many spiritual blessings from him, was greatly pleased. She embraced him and kissed his forehead.

Marriage

He married Bibi Syeda Rai Malik, the daughter of Syed Aladiya Shaheed Samani Tarmozi, who traced her relationship from Hazrat Imam Zain-ul-Abedeen. He had seven sons, namely, Syed Abd-us-Sami Abbasi, Syed Abd-ul-Latif Abbasi, Syed Amin-ud-din Abbasi, Syed Abul-Fazl Abbasi, Syed Abul-Ma'ali Abbasi, and Syed Rafi-ud-din Abbasi.

Death

He died in AH 976 and was buried in Laharpur.

Spiritual disciples

He left a large number of spiritual disciples, prominent among whom are: Shaikh Mahmud Qalandar of Lucknow, Syed Khizr son of Syed Aladiya Shaheed Samani Malik, Chand of Bahriach, and Qazi Aladad of Jaunpur. He imparted spiritual training to Syed Khizr and appointed him as his spiritual caliph.

Traits of character

He was a Qutb. Besides knowledge and learning, he possessed spiritual insight, and is greatly honoured by the Qalandariya Order.

He devoted himself to the propagation of truth.

Supernatural powers
On his way to Jaunpur from Laharpur, he found the river in spate, with no boat available. He asked the cart driver to drive the cart into the river and crossed it in that way.

> Qazi Aladad of Jaunpur was a very learned man but did not believe in mysticism and criticised Hazrat Janbaz Qalandar and call the sufis hypocrites. One day, when holding forth in this vein, a certain disciple of Hazrat Janbaz Qalandar was sitting there and hearing what was being said, narrated it to Hazrat Janbaz Qalandar. Who was then absorbed in contemplation. He, in that state, said: "I have deprived the Qazi of his knowledge." The Qazi was at that time teaching, and Hazrat Janbaz Qalandar standing there and telling him that his knowledge had been taken away from him on account of his pride. The Qazi, suddenly found himself totally bereft of knowledge. He at once left for Laharpur, implored forgiveness and became his disciple and spent the rest of his life in his service.

55

Hazrat Shaikh Salim Chishti

Hazrat Shaikh Salim Chishti was an eminent saint of the Indian subcontinent and in Arabia was known as Shaikh-ul-Hind. He was related to Hazrat Baba Farid-ud-din Mas'ud Ganj-e-Shakar. His father, Shaikh Baha-ud-din Chishti, left Delhi and settled in Sikri (Fatehpur Sikri), becoming a sepoy.[1] Hazrat Shaikh Salim Chishti, it is said, was born in Fatehpur Sikri in AH 897[2] but others say that he was born in Delhi in Sarai Ala-ud-din Zinda Pir. He was brought up by his brother Shaikh Musa, who treated him like a son. When a son was born to Shaikh Musa, he left for Sirhind, where he acquired knowledge and learning. He was fortunate to have Shaikh Mujaddad-ud-din as his teacher, the latter addressing him as "Malak-ul-Ulama." When he was in Sirhind, he would often visit the tomb of Hazrat Shaikh Zain-ud-din Chishti which was situated at some distance from there.

Tours and travels

He went to Mecca and performed several pilgrimages and stayed in Medina for several years, deriving spiritual blessings from the tomb of the Holy Prophet Mohammed. He visited other parts of Arabia and some other adjoining places.

Initiation into Sufi Order

During his tours and travels, he met Qutb-ud-din Shaikh Ibrahim Chishti, who accepted him as his spiritual disciple. Subsequently, he honoured him by conferring upon him the caliph's robe.

Fatehpur Sikri

Returning to Fatehpur Sikri, he devoted himself to ascetic practices, rigours, and prayers. Opposition to him by Hemoon, known as Hemoon Baqqal, forced him to go abroad again. He left for Mecca in AH 962. After many tours and travels he returned to Fatehpur Sikri in AH 976. He married there and had two sons, Shaikh Badr-ud-din and Qutb-ud-din.[3]

Relations with the imperial court

Hazrat Shaikh Salim Chishti was held in great regard and esteem by Sher Shah Suri and Salim Shah Suri, both reposing great faith in his spiritual powers. Emperor Akbar also paid him great respect and would occasionally visit him.[4]

Death

He passed away on the twenty-ninth of Ramazan in AH 979.[5] He was buried in Fatehpur Sikri, and his tomb has been described as an exquisite piece of architecture.

Caliph

His eldest son was his caliph and *sajjadanashin*.

Traits of character

He fasted for most of the year and took a cold water bath everyday. Hazrat Shaikh Salim Chishti was a man of ascetic temperament who led a simple life devoted to service, sharing, and sacrifice.

Supernatural power

Emperor Akbar had no son and approached Shaikh Salim Chishti with the request that he pray for one. The latter did so and Prince Salim (who ascended the throne and assumed the title of "Jahangir") was born. The child was named after him.

REFERENCES

1. *Tarikh-i-Firishta*, p. 403.
2. *Akhbar-ul-Akhyar*, Urdu trans., p. 521.
3. *Tarikh-i-Firishta*, p. 404.
4. Ibid.
5. *Akhbar-ul-Akhyar*, Urdu trans., p. 522.

56

Hazrat Shaikh Jalal-ud-din Mahmud

Hazrat Shaikh Jalal-ud-din Mahmud of Thanesar was the caliph of Hazrat Abd-ul-Quddus of Gangoh and belonged to Balkh. He traced his ancestry both from the paternal and the maternal side to the second caliph of Islam Hazrat Umar Faruq. He committed the Holy *Quran* to memory at the age of seven and completed his education when he was seventeen years old, having acquired proficiency of grammar, logic, the *fiqh*, the *hadis* and commentaries on the Holy *Quran*. He left Balkh and came to India and settled in Thanesar, taking to teaching and preaching.

Initiation into the Sufi Order

Shaikh Jalal-ud-din did not believe in the mystic way of life and had no respect for the sufis, laughing at them and scorning their way of life. The officer-in-charge of Thanesar, a devotee and disciple of Hazrat Shaikh Abd-ul-Quddus of Gangoh, invited his spiritual guide to Thanesar.

One day Shaikh Jalal-ud-din met this officer and told him that he had heard that his guide indulged in music, which was against the tenets of Islam. He wanted to meet his *pir* and discuss this with him and said that he would try to meet him as and when this was convenient. He asked him to convey his *salaams* to the "Dancing Pir."

This done, Hazrat Shaikh Abd-ul-Quddus smiled and told his disciple to return the *salaams* and say that the "Dancing Pir" not only dances himself but causes others also to dance. Once, when Hazrat Shaikh Abd-ul-Quddus of Gangoh was engaged in prayer, he heard a voice to the effect: "We have entrusted Jalal to you. Bring him in your fold and make him acquainted with our glory and manifestation." He interpreted this to be a divine command. Leaving aside all formalities and the notion of false prestige, he himself went to the school where Hazrat Jalal-ud-din Mahmud taught. He quietly sat in a corner and only after classes were over, Hazrat Shaikh Jalal noticed him and asked who he was. He replied, that as an introduction it was sufficient for him to say that he was the Dancing Pir to whom he had conveyed his *salaams*. He gazed into his eyes deeply and that was sufficient to transform Hazrat Jalal-ud-din. The rust, lust, and darkness were eradicated from his heart which was enveloped in glorious light. He was blessed with a vision of God. He wanted to be admitted in the Order, to which Hazrat Abd-ul-Quddus agreed. The latter took off his cap and placed it on his head. His spiritual guide and teacher suggested he undertake *commemoratio cordis*, or remembrance of God by heart and directed him also to take to ascetic practices. He asked him to avoid the people as far as possible and seclude himself. After sometime he experienced a great inner transformation and underwent a state of unconsciousness. He would write about his spiritual progress to his spiritual guide from Thaneswar, and the latter would offer him congratulations and good wishes regarding the progress made. Eventually, finding him fit and deserving, his spiritual guide summoned him and conferred upon him the robe of caliph and appointed him as his spiritual caliph, prayed for him, and gave him his blessings.

The visit of Emperor Akbar

Emperor Akbar, on his way to Punjab to curb down the rebellion of Mirza Mohammed Hakim, halted at Thanesar in AH 980, paid his respects to Shaikh Jalal-ud-din and sought his blessings.

Death

Hazrat Shaikh Jalal-ud-din Mahmud died at the ripe old age of ninety-five years in AH 989 and was buried in Thanesar.

Caliph

Hazrat Shaikh Nizam-ud-din of Balkh is his spiritual caliph and successor.

Traits of character

His spiritual guide and teacher, Hazrat Abd-ul-Quddus, loved him deeply.[1] He was an accomplished man of letters and well-versed in various branches of knowledge. He would issue *fatawas* which were regarded as being the correct approach towards the problems concerned.

After his initiation in the Sufi Order he was gifted with inward knowledge. By studying the book of nature, he identified himself with nature. His ascetic practices, penances, and the spirit of renunciation placed him in a position where self had no place. He was deeply absorbed in contemplation and was frequently found to be in a state of unconsciousness. When the time of prayer approached his spiritual disciples would whisper in his ears the words *Haq, Haq* (God, God) on hearing which he would regain consciousness and offer prayer, thereafter relapsing into his former state.

Supernatural power

One of his disciples, who had kept his company for a long time and had undergone very many ascetic practices did not find himself at all improved spiritually. He deplored the wastage of so many years. One day, he thought to himself that formerly there had lived and flourished saints like Najm-ud-din Kubra who had caused seekers to reach a position of spiritual eminence and enabled them to achieve sainthood, and such saints must be living and guiding people even now.

Hazrat Shaikh Jalal-ud-din Mahmud could read his thoughts. He said to him: "Yes, there are some people even now, who cause the seeker to reach up to God Almighty by a single glance." Saying that, he cast a glance upon him and the latter fell down and remained unconscious for three days. When he came to his senses, he placed his head upon Shaikh Jalal-ud-din's confessed that he had not seen those things for years, which through that one look he had been able to see.

The disciple survived for a week. When the news of his death were conveyed to Shaikh Jalal-ud-din, he felt sorry for him and said: "Everybody is not competent enough to bear this burden."

Reference

1. *Iqtibas-ul-Anwar.*

57

Hazrat Khwaja Baqi Billah

Hazrat Khwaja Baqi Billah was an outstanding saint of the Nakshbandi Order. On his mother's side, he traces his descent from Hazrat Shaikh Umar of Yaghistan the maternal grandfather of Hazrat Khwaja Ahrar. Her mother descended from the family of the Holy Prophet.[1] His father's name was Qazi Abd-us-Salam,[2] and had settled in Kabul. He was counted among the learned and pious, and was well-versed in mysticism, jurisprudence, and the *hadis*. With piety, he combined wealth, honour, and prestige.

Khwaja Baqi Billah was born in Kabul in AH 971, though some believe who assert that he was born in AH 972. He was named Syed Razi-ud-din, but became famous as Khwaja Mohammed Baqi Billah.[3]

Education and training

At the age of five, his father got him admitted in a *maktab*. There he completed learning the Holy *Quran*. After elementary education he was sent to Maulana Sadiq Halwai[4] and accompanied him to Trans-Jordan. He had yet to complete his education, when he found himself being attracted towards mysticism. A learned member of a literary society in Trans-Jordan expressed his regret at this, and when the Khwaja heard of this, he said, let him present the most difficult book and if he be not satisfied with the reply given, then alone will his regret be justified.

He did his utmost to acquire the graces of inward knowledge. In Trans-Jordan he would roam around in search of saints, sufis, sages, and dervishes, and in this quest visited Balkh, Badakhshan, and Samarqand, and also visited Lahore. He derived spiritual ecstasy and blessings from such eminent and outstanding saints as Hazrat Khwaja Abeed, Hazrat Amir Abdullah of Balkh, Hazrat Shaikh of Samarqand, and Hazrat Shaikh Baba-i-Wali.[5]

Meeting with a saint

In Lahore, there lived a saint deeply absorbed. Hazrat Khwaja Baqi Billah did his utmost to meet him and in contemplation was eventually able to do so. The saint called him near him and prayed for him and conferred upon him many spiritual blessings.

Initiation into the Sufi Order

From Lahore he proceeded to Trans-Jordan. One night, he saw Hazrat Khwaja Amkangi in dream saying to him: "O son! we are waiting for you. Come soon and wipe off the pangs of separation." Receiving this mandate, he went to him and was accepted as his spiritual disciple. Hazrat Khwaja Amkangi kept him with him for three days and three nights.[6] There he passed his time in silence and seclusion. This afforded him an opportunity to get acquainted with the state and station of Khwaja Amkangi and received spiritual blessings from him. Subsequently, his teacher honoured him by conferring upon him the robe of caliph. It is also said that he had received too the spiritual blessings of Hazrat Khwaja Baha-ud-din Naqshbandi.

Arrival in India

At the behest of his teacher he came to India. Reaching Lahore a second time, he stayed there for a year and then left for Delhi where he settled permanently.

Wives and children

He had two wives, and from each wife he had one son. Hazrat Khwaja Ubaid-ul-lah was the eldest of the two, and the second was named Khwaja Mohammed Abdullah.

Death

He breathed his last on the twenty-fifth of Jamade-ul-Akhir in AH 1012 at the age of forty and was buried in Delhi.

Caliphs

Among his spiritual caliphs, Hazrat Shaikh Ahmad of Sirhind enjoys pre-eminence. Among his prominent caliphs are: Shaikh Taj-ud-din of Sambhal; Khwaja Husam-ud-din, and Shaikh al-Huddad.

Traits of character

He was kind, gentle, humble, and hospitable. He loved seclusion and observed silence for most of the time. He said very little, ate and slept little. He showed the utmost respect to the dervishes, learned people, and the Syeds. He had a forgiving disposition and his mercy and love extended to all. He showed sympathy to the afflicted, the down-trodden, and the dejected. His piety, patience, perseverance, generosity, and simplicity made him sublime. He devoted most of his time to prayer, contemplation and meditation, and took to renunciation and self-abnegation. He was a man of literary taste and has written a *risala*.[7] His letters are exquisite examples of literature, and he was a poet too.

Teachings
He says:[8] "Renunciation means and implies, that the heart may be freed from the blessings of this world and the world hereafter and may be unmindful of all the conditions and visions and all the attraction and concentration should be towards the eternal being." Also:[9] "This does not constitute *tawakkul* or trust in God, that one may give up the means and may not pay attention to the cause."

Sayings

- Piety implies abstinence from fascinating things.
- Contentment implies the giving up of useless things, living on bare necessity, and abstaining from extravagance in eating, drinking, and living.
- To give up things appealing to the self and to abstain from things liked and cherished, constitutes patience.
- There are three types of spiritual guides, namely, these appertaining to the robe of caliph, to training and education, and to company and society.
- Those who have bowed their heads in submission and willingness do not see trouble and misfortune in the shape and form of trouble and misfortune.
- Permanent meditation is a great blessing, as it is a cause of acceptance in the heart.

Supernatural powers
A few days before his death, he said that it appeared from certain dreams, that some great member of the Naqshbandi Order would expire in the near future.[10]

One day the son of his coachman came to him and said that his father had developed acute pain in his stomach. He replied that he had usurped the rights of his horse and would recover, when he returned it. The father admitted the truth of this, gave some oil and grain to the horse, and then recovered.[11]

There lived in his neighbourhood a person who was being maltreated by a certain officer. He conveyed a message to the officer to the effect that it was not wise to perpetuate tyranny because dervishes lived in the neighbourhood. The tyrant did not care in the least and was warned a second time by Hazrat Khwaja Baqi Billah. It so happened, that after two or three days, the tyrant was involved in a case of theft and was subsequently put to death alongwith his relatives.

References

1. *Hazrat-ul-Quds,* p. 231.
2. Ibid., p. 246.
3. Ibid., pp. 244-45.
4. *Anwar-ul-Arefeen,* p. 368.
5. Ibid.
6. *Hazrat-ul-Quds,* p. 231.
7. Ibid., p. 245.
8. Ibid., pp. 244-45.
9. *Hayat-e-Baqa,* p. 22.
10. *Hazrat-ul-Quds,* p. 254.
11. Ibid., p. 255.

58

Hazrat Ahmad Mujaddid Alif Sani

Hazrat Shaikh Ahmad Mujaddid Alif Sani was a towering spiritual figure of the Indian subcontinent. He traced his descent from the second caliph of Islam, Hazrat Umar Faruq. His ancestors belong to Kabul and migrated from there and settled in Sirhind. His father, Abd-ul-Ahad, was a very learned man, and a spiritual disciple of Hazrat Shaikh Abd-ul-Quddus of Gangoh. Hazrat Shaikh Rukn-ud-din honoured him by accepting him as one of his spiritual caliphs, pertaining to the Qadiri-Chishti and Sabiri Orders of the sufis in AH 979. His father also received the robe of caliph from Hazrat Shah Kamal of Kotal[1] and is the author of several books on mysticism. He died on the seventeenth of Rajab in AH 1007. His mother belonged to a town called Sikandara in Bulandshahr, U.P. He had six brothers, and among his three elder ones Shaikh Shah Mohammed and Shaikh Mas'ud are quite well-known. Among his younger brothers, Shaikh Ghulam Mohammed and Shaikh Dawadoo were prominent.

He was born on Friday night on the fourteenth of Shawwal in AH 971 in Sirhind (East Punjab) and was named Ahmad, with the pseudonym "Abul Barkat." He is addressed and invoked by such titles as "Badr-ud-din" and "Mujaddid Alif Sani."

Why he is known as "Mujaddid Alif Sani"

He is known as Mujaddid Alif Sani, which means that he revived and conferred freshness on religion from the outset, allegedly bringing to life a decaying order. He opposed superstitions and other practices which he thought were at variance with the real spirit of religion. It is also said, that he brought about a healthy transformation in the decaying mystic Order and thereby lent it life and vigour.

Childhood

Unlike other children of his age, he never wept or cried and was always smiling. He was never naked, and neither his clothes or his body were ever polluted.

The prophecy

During his infancy he once fell ill. His father brought Hazrat Shah Kamal of Ketal home in order to bless his infant son. When he saw Hazrat Shaikh Ahmad, he cried out in excitement: "May God give him a long life. He will be a practical learned man and a perfect enlightened individual. Many people, like you and me will be benefited by his company. His name will be remembered till the Day of Resurrection. . . ." Then Hazrat Shah Kamal, from love, put his tongue in his mouth and sucked it with great force. Thereupon, Hazrat Shah Kamal said: "The blessings of our Qadiri Order have been thus conferred upon him."

Early education and training

Hazrat Shaikh Ahmad was brought up under the care of his father and committed the Holy *Quran* to memory. His father taught him some books on outward knowledge. Very soon he acquired fairly sound knowledge. His quest for knowledge took him to Sialkot. Maulana Kamal of Kashmir taught him some books. He then proceeded to Kashmir and obtained the certificate of proficiency in the *hadis* from Shaikh Yaqub Sarfi. He also read *Tafsir-e-Wahidi* and other works by Wahidi, *Tafsir-e-Bezadi* and other books of Qazi Beza, *Sahih Bukhari* with all its implications, *Mishkat* and *Tirmizi*. He was also permitted to read and recite *Qasida-e-Burda*, in addition to the books cited above, by Qazi Behlal of Badakhshan. In this way, he completed his education by the time he was seventeen.

Initiation into the Sufi Order

Initially he became a disciple of his father Hazrat Abd-ul-Ahad and derived spiritual blessings from five spiritual guides and teachers and received the deed of caliph from each of them. He was appointed as a spiritual caliph by Hazrat Shaikh Yaqub Sarfi of Kashmir of the Kibrooya-Suhrawardi Orders. Hazrat Shaikh Ahmad shook hand with Hazrat Haji Abd-ur-Rahman of Badakhshan, better known as Haji Rimzi and he in turn shook hands with his own spiritual guide.

From his father, he received the deed of caliph, pertaining to the fifteen Orders, namely, Farooqiya, Siri Saqtiya, Suhrawardiya-Shahabiya, Suhrawardiya-Bahayiya, Suhrawardiya-Chishtiya-Jalaliya, Qadiriya, Qalandariya, Chishtiya-Sabiriya, Nizamiya-Gesoo Daraziya-Chishtiya-Nizamiya-Sadriya, Chishtiya-Nizamiya-Jalaliya, Qadiriya-Jalaliya-Kubroya-Jalaliya, Suhrawardiya-Jalaliya, and Madariya.

He used to hear a great deal about the Naqshbandi Order. When he reached Delhi in AH 1008, his friend Maulana Hasan of Kashmir asked him to pay his respects to Hazrat Khwaja Baqi Billah. They both went and were invited by the latter to stay in the monastery for some days. He agreed and stayed with him for a month and a half. He requested Hazrat Khwaja Baqi Billah to accept him as one of his humble spiritual disciples. Hazrat Khwaja Baqi Billah, summoning him in privacy, initiated him and suggested to him the inward Remembrance of God. After sometime, Hazrat Khwaja Baqi Billah conferred the robe of caliph upon him thereby allowing him to accept spiritual disciples. His spiritual guide and teacher allowed him to return to his native town, Sirhind.

He received the special robe of Hazrat Shaikh Abd-ul-Qadir of Jilan (better known as Ghous-ul-Azam, Piran-e-Pir) from Hazrat Syed Shah Sikandar and also the deed of caliph from him, pertaining to the Qadiriya-Jaddiya Orders.

Delhi, Sirhind, Lahore, and Ajmer

Arriving in Delhi a second time, he paid his respects to his, spiritual guide and teacher and after receiving further spiritual blessings from him returned to Sirhind. When he come to Delhi a third time Hazrat Khwaja Baqi Billah asked him to devote special spiritual attention to his two minor sons. Having done this, he later gave them special spiritual attention, in their absence. After staying for sometime in Delhi, he returned to Sirhind, where he did not stay long soon leaving for Lahore. He had by then become famous, and many people entered his fold. Maulana Jamal-ud-din Talvi and Maulana Abd-ul-Hakim of Sialkot became his devotees and spiritual disciples.

Subsequently, returning to Delhi, he stayed there for sometime and then returned to Sirhind, where he began to preach and propagate the doctrine of truth.

He went to Ajmer to offer his respects to and to receive blessings from the tomb of Hazrat Khwaja Moin-ud-din Hasan Chishti and stayed there for sometime.

Relations with the imperial court

His growing influence, coupled with his views on religion, politics, and mysticism brought about a storm of opposition. He was involved in an intrigue that obtained at the court of Emperor Jahangir, with the result that he was imprisoned in Gwalior fort and spent two years there. Subsequently relations with the emperor improved. Emperor Shah Jahan, who was heir-apparent then, had great respect and regard for him and Emperor Jahangir regretted that he had imprisoned him.

Marriage and children

He married and had seven sons and three daughters. His eldest son, Khwaja Mohammed Sadiq, died at the age of only eighteen on the ninth of Rabi-ul-Awwal in AH 1018. His other sons were Khwaja Mohammed Sa'id, Khwaja Mohammed Masoom, Khwaja Mohammed Faruq, Khwaja Mohammed 'Isa, Khwaja Mohammed Ashraf, and Khwaja Shaikh Mohammed Yahya. His three daughters were Bibi Ruqya Banoo, Bibi Khadija Banoo, and Bibi Umme Kulsum. They all died young during their father's lifetime.

Death

Hazrat Shaikh Ahmad Mujaddid Alif Sani passed away at the age of sixty-three on the twenty-eighth of Safar in AH 1034. His tomb, situated in Sirhind, is an object of reverence and veneration.

Caliphs

He left a large number of spiritual caliphs. Prominent among whom are: his sons apart from Khwaja Mohammed 'Isa and Khwaja Mohammed Ashraf, Maulana Mir Mohammed Na'man of Akbarabad (Agra), Shaikh Abd-ul-Hai of Hissar, Syed Baqar of Sarangpur, Syed Mohibbullah of Manikpur, Maulana Shaikh Abd-ul-Hadi of Budaun, Maulana Shaikh Tahir of Lahore, Maulana Sadiq of Kabul, Khwaja Mohammed Hashim of Burhanpur, Maulana Hamid-ud-din of Ahmedabad, and Syed Mubarak Shah of Bukhara.

Traits of character

He was a very kind and courteous individual who followed the tenets of the Holy Prophet in his everyday life. He possessed all the mystic qualities, which go to make life noble, beautiful, and true, and was an embodiment of patience, gratitude, forbearance, hospitableness, piety, contentment, trust in God, and submission. He would accompany Muslim funeral processions, visit to the sick and invalids to inquire about their health and to console and encourage them.

Hazrat Shaikh Ahmad loved his spiritual guide intensely, paying him the greatest regard and respect.[2] It is said that among the spiritual disciples and caliphs of Hazrat Khwaja Baqi Billah, no one was as devoted to him as he was. Hazrat Khwaja Baqi Billah felt proud of him.

He was a very accomplished man and strictly observed the laws of *shari'at*. He offered prayers regularly and fasted during the month of Ramazan. He was a man of literary taste, and his letters, numbering a few hundred, which have been published are a treasure-house of knowledge, learning, the laws and regulations of *shari'at*, and of mysticism.

The letters have been published.[3] He is the author of a number of books. Chief among them are: *Isbat-an-Nabuwah; Risalat dar Radd-e Rawafin; Sharh ar-Rubaiyat fil-Khwaja Abd al-Baqi, Talluqat al-Awarif; Risalat Ilm-e-Hadis, Risalat Tahliliyah, Risalat al-Mukashafat al-Ghaybiyah, Risalat Adab al-Muridin, Mabda O Ma'ad;* and *Ma'arif Laduniyah.*

Teachings

It is said that he propounded a new concept of social, moral, spiritual, and religious values. He holds that society is dynamic and not stationary. He emphasises that human nature is capable of change, but that for this a good environment, proper education, and adequate training are required.

He preferred religious education and training to the propagation of the doctrines of those treading on the spiritual path. He took Prophethood to be higher than *wilayat* (sainthood). He did wish saints to live a secluded life, preferring those who passed their days in the sunshine of human society.

He belonged to the Hanafi sect and considered it to be the best. He extolled the Naqshbandi Order and considered it to be higher, better, and nobler than the other Sufi Orders. He did believe that the Remembrance of God should be loudly conducted and saw not point in individuals secluding themselves believing it went against the *sunnah* of the Holy Prophet Mohammed.

He deprecated music and felt that to bow down on graves was un-Islamic. Likewise, he held the celebration of the *'urs*, the death anniversary of a saint, to go against Islamic precept and practice. He was opposed to offerings of sandalpaste and lighting up graves. He thought that Milad-un-nabi (commemoration of the birth of the Holy Prophet, was praiseworthy, but he did not like the way in which it was conducted. He felt, that there was nothing wrong in visiting the graves and tombs of the saints and invoking them for help, but deprecated the practice of bowing down over them and kissing them.

He was a firm believer in *tauhid* or the unity of god.

Sayings

- Despondency is in fact idolatry. Always be hopeful.
- Whatever God does is best.
- One should be patient when involved in some trouble and submit oneself to His Will. One should be steadfast in his worship and one should not be disobedient to him.
- Blessings received from any quarter should be ascribed to one's spiritual guide and teacher.
- The good things and the blessings of this mortal world are beneficial only when they are treated in conformity with the laws of the *shari'at* and are collected for the world hereafter. Otherwise they are akin to fatal poison with a sugar coating.

Supernatural powers

He exhibited very many spiritual powers. Some are related below:

- A certain dervish requested him to show him the way that led to God. He gave him a piece of bread to eat. As soon as he ate it, he found himself a changed man and inward blessings were showered upon him.
- A nobleman who had incurred the displeasure of the king was summoned from Lahore to Delhi to be tied to the feet of an elephant and killed. On his way he reached Sirhind and invoked the Hazrat's help and assistance. The latter prayed for him when he reached the Imperial Court, quite contrary to his expectations, a robe of honour was conferred upon him instead of his being put to death.
- Once one of his spiritual disciples was confronted by a lion in a jungle. He implored and invoked his aid. The Hazrat

appeared there at once with a stick in his hand, drove the lion away and then disappeared. His companions inquired who that was to which he replied that he was his spiritual guide and teacher Hazrat Shaikh Ahmad Mujaddid Alif Sani.

- A certain person sent him a present and requested him to pray for the recovery of a patient. He did not accept the present. After some contemplation he said: "I pray for his salvation," and subsequently, it was learnt that the patient had been dead at the time.

References

1. *Mabd-o-Ma'ad.*
2. *Zibdat-ul-Muqamat.*
3. Shaikh Ahmad Sirhindi, *Maktubat-e-Iman-e Rabbani,* Lucknow, 1889.

59

Hazrat Shaikh Abu Sa'id

Hazrat Shaikh Abu Sa'id was the spiritual caliph of Hazrat Shaikh Nizam-ud-din and was very closely related to Hazrat Shaikh Abd-ul-Quddus of Gangoh. His father's name was Shaikh Nur-ud-din and his mother was the daughter of Hazrat Shaikh Jalal-ud-din Mahmud of Thanesar.

Initiation into the Sufi Order

He became a disciple of Hazrat Shaikh Jalal-ud-din of Thanesar. His spiritual guide entrusted him to Hazrat Shaikh Nizam-ud-din for spiritual education and training. Under his guidance, he attained spiritual perfection and achieved a position of eminence, and subsequently received the robe of caliph from him. Coming from Balkh, where he had gone to receive the blessings of Hazrat Nizam-ud-din, in India he began to preach and propagate the Gospel of Truth.

Inward urge

Hazrat Nizam-ud-din left for Balkh. Hazrat Shaikh Abu Sa'id felt his absence very today and it became difficult for him to bear the pangs of separation. He began to wander about. One day he went to the tomb of Hazrat Shaikh Abd-ul-Haq and wept bitterly, and then heard a voice from the grave said that if he really was a seeker of truth he should go to Nizam-ud-din who was in Balkh as the latter alone possessed his (Hazrat Abd-ul-Quddus) affiliation in ample measure.

On the third day, he saw a man, who he could not recognise, who told him that he was prepared to take him to Balkh. He took his hand, seated him on a horse, and the two together left for Balkh. At some distance from Balkh the man disappeared. It was only then that he realised that the man was no other than Hazrat Abd-ul-Quddus himself.

When he reached Balkh he was received cordially by Hazrat Nizam-ud-din who had already known that he was coming to Balkh through his spiritual powers.

Asceticism

Hazrat Nizam-ud-din, finding him imperfect, suggested a course of spiritual practices and rituals. For twelve long years he engaged in ascetic practices. At the expiry of that time he narrated his spiritual experiences and his spiritual state to his guide, Hazrat Nizam-ud-din. The latter then suggested that he rid himself of the consciousness of self which he said was a hindrance in his way to achieving the ultimate goal, i.e., realisation of God.

The sons of Nizam-ud-din had dogs and he was asked to look after these. He obeyed.

One day, it had rained heavily and there was so much mud, that it was difficult to walk. Hazrat Nizam-ud-din was at the time sitting on the balcony with some of his devotees and admirers. Hazrat Abu Sa'id wanted to take the dogs to the jungle as he usually did. The dogs were tied with a rope that he held in his hand. Some other dogs of the neighbourhood surrounded the dogs he was leading. They leaped, but Hazrat Abu Sa'id did not allow them to fight, and not faltering or failing in his duty, continued to hold the rope. The result was that he fell down on the mud and ruined his clothes. At this time, he told himself: "How fortunate is Hazrat Nizam-ud-din who is sitting comfortably in the balcony and how wretched my condition."

At that instant, he saw a light that circumscribed the whole world and heard a voice saying: "Moses prayed and he got our vision. Mohammed (may peace be upon him) was honoured by ascension, but thou hast got a glimpse of our image without any effort whatsoever."

Hazrat Nizam-ud-din learnt of his being so honoured where he was sitting through his spiritual powers. He told those surrounding him, that Hazrat Shaikh Abu Sa'id had at last been accepted and that God Almighty in his Infinite Mercy and Grace had revealed himself to him. He called Hazrat Abu Sa'id and asked him to rest and relax in order to achieve further nearness to God. Later he found him to be perfect and conferred upon him the robe of caliph and entrusted the holy relics of his spiritual forefathers to him and bade him farewell. Hazrat Shaikh Abu Sa'id went to Gangoh and began to preach the gospel of truth.

Death

He breathed his last on the first of Rabi-us-Sani in AH 1049[1] and was buried in Gangoh.

Caliphs

His prominent caliphs are: Shaikh Mohammed Sadiq, Shaikh Ibrahim of Rampur, Shaikh Mohibbullah of Allahabad, Shaikh Ibrahim of Saharanpur, and Shaikh Khwaja of Panipat.

Traits of character

Hazrat Shaikh Abu Sa'id greatly loved and respected his spiritual guide and teacher. His simple habits and his spirit of renunciation endeared him to all who came in contact with him. He was a man of strong determination and was not daunted by the difficulties besetting the path of spiritual enlightenment. He worked ceaselessly and determinedly to reach the goal of realisation of God. In the process, he underwent very many ascetic practices and penances and detached himself from worldly matters and worldly pleasures. Indeed, his sole pleasure was the steadfast pursuit of truth. His outlook towards life was characterised by indifference pain and pleasure and was richly endowed with hope, belief, and faith.

Supernatural power

A certain person came to him and submitted, that he was a seeker of truth, but had insufficient strength and stamina to undertake the various ascetic practices necessary to achieve the goal. He implored that, by virtue of his blessed look he might be enabled to reach the desired destination. Hazrat Abu Sa'id had at that time a stick in his hand. Pointing towards the stick, he said that by a mere three strokes of the stick he would cause the seeker to reach God. Saying thus, he inflicted a stroke of the stick on his head. The world of Malkut was opened to him. A second stroke disclosed the world of Jabrut, and the third opened the world of Mashhood. The man lay unconscious for three days, and when he regained consciousness, he became his disciple.

REFERENCE

1. *Hadiqat-ul-Auliya.*

60

Hazrat Shah Abd-ul-Haq

Hazrat Shah Abd-ul-Haq of Delhi spread the knowledge of the *hadis*. Besides being a great scholar and a learned man, he was also an eminent saint. He belonged to a respectable family of Bukhara. His grandfather, Agha Mohammed, combined worldly wealth, honour and prestige with knowledge, spiritual insight, and the idealism of a saint. For Central Asia, thirteenth century AD was a period of turmoil and an insecurity of life and property. His grandfather left home and came down to India during the reign of Sultan Ala-ud-din Khalji and was able to gain access to the Royal Court. The Sultan sent him and others to conquer Gujarat where he later settled. His grandfather had one hundred and one sons, a hundred of whom died during his lifetime. He took the remaining one son with him and left Gujarat for Delhi. He died on the seventeenth of Rabi-us-Sani in AH 739.

His father was called Maulana Saif-ud-din, and was a sufi, a man of literary taste, and a good poet. Hazrat Shah Abd-ul-Haq was born in Delhi in AH 958.

Education and training

Hazrat Shah Abd-ul-Haq received his early education at home. He was very intelligent. He completed the Holy *Quran* in a few months and committed it to memory very rapidly. He completed his education when he was eighteen years old.

Pilgrimage

He left Delhi for Mecca to perform the *hajj*. In AH 996 he met Shaikh Abd-ul-Wahab Manqi and received inward knowledge and spiritual education from him. He studied some works on mysticism under him and in accordance with his directions and under his supervision, devoted himself to prayers at the Ka'ba. He visited certain places of veneration and sanctity when he was in Mecca. He himself describes thus:[1]

> This humble being, when he was in Mecca used to go to the residence of the Holy Prophet Mohammed, which is known as 'Bait-e-Khadija' and which is next only to Ka'ba, the house of God, in point of veneration, holiness and sanctity. There I used to stand and cry like a beggar and used to say: 'O, Prophet of God! give something. And O Prophet of God! this humble being and your beggar is present at your door.' Whatever I thought at that time and whatever my tongue allowed me to speak I used to beg and return with the skirt of hope filled up.

Initiation into the Sufi Order

First he became a spiritual disciple of his revered father and later, at his instruction, went to Hazrat Syed Musa Gilani and became his spiritual disciple. He was greatly benefited by his special attention.[2]

On reaching Medina, he became a spiritual disciple of Hazrat Shaikh Abd-ul-Wahab Manqi, who subsequently conferred upon him the robe of caliph pertaining to the Chishti-Qadiri, and Shazliya Orders of the sufis. In this way, Hazrat Abd-ul-Haq was attached to four Sufi Orders, namely, the Chishti, Qadiri, Shazli, and Naqshbandi.

Indication

He says: "I was accepted as a spiritual disciple by Hazrat Ghous-ul-Azam at the instance of the Holy Prophet." After being enlisted as a disciple, the Holy Prophet had foretold in Persian: "Thou shalt be great."

Return to Delhi

Receiving the mandate from Hazrat Shaikh Abd-ul-Wahab Manqi, he returned to Delhi and established a school there where religious education was imparted. He passed the rest of his life in Delhi.

Death

Hazrat Shah Abd-ul-Haq died on the twenty-first of Rabi-ul-Awwal in AH 1051 and was buried in Mehrauli, New Delhi.

Traits of character

A man of profound knowledge and learning, his spiritual eminence was characterised by his practical approach towards life. He led a simple life, ever engaged in prayers and ascetic practices. His son, Shaikh Nur-ul-Haq, was pious and saintly. Hazrat Shah Abd-ul-Haq is known as "Muhaddis" in the Indian subcontinent. Well-versed in the knowledge of the *hadis*, he took great pains in spreading this knowledge in the subcontinent. It is estimated, that he wrote over a hundred books on a variety of topics. His best known are: *Usool-e-Hadis; Marj'ul Bahrain; Lataiful-Haq; Akhbar-ul-Akhyar fi Asrar-ul-Abrar; Isma-ul-Rijal; Madarijun-Naboowat; Jame'-ul Barkat;* and *Takmil-ul-Iman.*

Teachings

He says:[3]

> In the terminology of the body of those well-versed in the knowledge of the Hadith, the Hadith is applied to the saying, practice, and speech of the Holy Prophet. The Hadith, the authenticity of which reaches up to the Holy Prophet, is known as *marfee*; the authenticity of which reaches up to the companion of the Holy Prophet is known as *maqoof* and the authenticity of which reaches up to the follower is known as *maqto.*
>
> Among the kinds of Hadith may be mentioned *shaz, mankir* and *muallil.*[4]
>
> The real kinds of Hadith are three, namely *sahih* [correct], *hasan* [good], and *zaeef* [weak].[5]
>
> If the correct Hadith is stated by one person, then that Hadith is *gharib* [poor]. If it is stated by two persons, then it is *aziz* [popular] and if it is stated by more than two persons, then it is *mashhoor* [famous].[6]
>
> The six books (of Hadith) those are, famous in Islam, are called *Sihah-us-Sittah,* are: *Sahih Bukhari; Sahih Muslim; Jame' Tirmizi; Sunan Abu Dawood; Nasa'i;* and *Ibn-e-Maja.* According to some *Muwatta'* of Imam Malik substitutes *Ibn-e-Maja.*[7]

Pointing out the straight path, he says:[8]

The safe path for the one treading the spiritual path and the means of permanence for the seeker constitute this, that to dive deep into philosophical thought should be treated as unlawful and he may abstain from too many arguments and may keep the door of argument of those engaged in discussion and quarrel closed. . . .

Of the accord between *shari'at* and *tariqat,* he says:[9]

It should not be presumed, that the system of mysticism is against the laws of religion, *shari'at,* and the Holy Book of God and the *sunnah* of the Holy Prophet. There is not the minutes difference or any kind of mutual conflict between the two. The sufis are the purest gems of the *millat.* They are in fact those, who outwardly and inwardly choose the light of *sunnah* and open the curtains of reality. They are unique in their presence on and practice of the path of enlightenment and authentic in their investigation of meaning and certain in sincerity and clear in knowing the deception of self and singular in culture, ethics, and morality. Nobody has exceeded them in outward graces, inward accomplishments, purity of heart and soul. No other group can compete them in deeds, states, and stations, fondness and eagerness, points and indications and in all other accomplish ments.

Sayings

- The sign of good fortune, success and honour and good luck is meeting saintly people.[10]
- Some people live behind the curtain of piety and purity on account of shame and honour.[11]
- It is a bad thing to sit idle and not to use the gift of intelligence. It results in the loss of intelligence.[12]
- Not to be thankful for blessings invites the wrath of God.[13]
- To be concentrated on one thing and to acquire it well results in the annihilation of its opposite.[14]
- The solace of the heart lies in unity, while the disturbance of the heart lies in multiplicity.[15]
- The worst thing of all is the society of the imperfect. To me the imperfect in this respect is one who is not anxious for perfection and who does not regret his condition.[16]

References

1. *Lata'if-ul-Haq* , Urdu trans. of *Nukat-ul-Haq,* p. 8.
2. *Rauzat-ul-Aqtab,* p. 95.
3. *Usool-e-Hadis,* trans., pp. 3-4.
4. Ibid., p. 12.
5. Ibid., p. 14.
6. Ibid., p. 21.
7. Ibid., pp. 28-29.
8. *Marj'ul-Bahrain,* trans., p. 11.
9. Ibid., p. 24.
10. *Lata'if-ul-Haq,* p. 11.
11. Ibid., p. 12.
12. Ibid., p. 15.
13. Ibid., p. 16.
14. Ibid., p. 17.
15. Ibid., p. 27.
16. Ibid., p. 46.

61

Shaikh Mohammed Sadiq

Hazrat Shaikh Mohammed Sadiq was the spiritual caliph and successor of Hazrat Shaikh Abu Sa'id. His father's name was Shaikh Fath-ul-lah. He married and had children. Shaikh Dawood and Shaikh Mohammed were the two of the better known sons.

Initiation into the Sufi Order

Hazrat Shaikh Abu Sa'id came to Gangoh from Balkh and settled there. On the occasion of Eid, Hazrat Shaikh Mohammed Sadiq went to him to offer his respects and greetings. Hazrat Shaikh Abu Sa'id was greatly pleased to see him. He said then and thereto his admirers and devotees: "I see the light of my sainthood in the forehead of this boy."[1]

Hazrat Shaikh Mohammed Sadiq was attracted to him, and sought to be accepted as a spiritual disciple. This actually, happened. His spiritual guide and teacher suggested and he adopt certain rituals and practices, the chief among them being *commemoratio cordis.*

His parents raised a storm of opposition and said: "It appears that Shaikh Abu Sa'id wants to detach our son from worldly affairs and unworthy for them like himself." Hazrat Shaikh Abu Sa'id learnt of this and told him that if his parents had formed such an opinion, what had he to say to this. He respectfully submitted that what he thought best for him was indeed the best of all and that he did not ask for anything from him except his blessed good wishes and kindness. He added: "I will see the vision of God only if and when he appeared in the shape of the spiritual guide and teacher." At the behest of his spiritual guide he sought the consent of his parents.

Reward

Subsequently, he engaged himself in ascetic practices and rigours, and eventually his labour was rewarded in the form of the robe of caliph from his spiritual guide and teacher. It is said, that he was rewarded with a shaft of light by the Holy Prophet Mohammed, Hazrat Ali gave him a sword of light, and the spiritual power of his spiritual guide gave him a mirror of red and white light in which the entire world could be viewed.

Death

Hazrat Shaikh Mohammed Sadiq breathed his last on the eighteenth of Muharram in AD 1627 and was buried in Gangoh.

Caliphs

His eight caliphs are Shaikh Dawood, Shaikh Mohammed, Shaikh Ibrahim of Moradabad, Shaikh Abd-us-Subhan of Saharanpur, Shaikh Abd-ul-Jalil of Allahabad, Shaikh Jamal, Shaikh Mubarak, and Shaikh Yusuf.

Traits of character

Hazrat Shaikh Mohammed Sadiq was very fond of music and was endowed with a great reservoir of love. He underwent very many ascetic practices.

Supernatural power

One day he visited a certain farmer's field and asked the farmer to accompany him. The farmer regretted his inability to do so. He had watered half the field and if he accompanied him the other half would remain unwatered and would yield no harvest.

He insisted and informed the farmer that he should not worry at all. The portion of the field that had not been watered would yield twice as much of the crop as that from the portion he had watered. The farmer thereupon accompanied him leaving half the field unwatered, and when the crop ripped, the Hazrat's words proved prophetic.[2]

REFERENCES

1. *Anwar-ul-Arefeen; Iqtibas-ul-Anwar.*
2. *Anwar-ul-Arefeen; Kashf-ul-Israr.*

62

Hazrat Syed Shah Amir Abul-Ila

Among the saints of the Indian subcontinent, Hazrat Syed Shah Amir Abul-Ila occupies a unique position. His grandfather, Hazrat Amir Abd-us-Salam, migrated from Samarqand to India during the reign of EmperorAkbar. He stayed in Narnaul for sometime and then went to Fatehpur Sikri. After staying there for a while he performed the pilgrimage to Mecca. From Mecca he went on to Medina where he died.[1] His father, Hazrat Amir Abul-Wafa, died of cholic. Syed Shah Amir Abul-Ila was a minor at that time.

He was born in Narpala in AH 990 and was named Amir Abul-Ila. He traced his relationship on his fathers side from Hazrat Imam Husain, son of Hazrat Ali, son-in-law of the Holy Prophet Mohammed, and this makes him a Husaini, but on his mother's side he was an Ahrari Khwaja.

Early life and education

His grandfather, when he left on his pilgrimage entrusted him to the care of Khwaja Mohammed Faiz, better known as Khwaja Faizi, who was his (Hazrat Amir Abul-Ila's) maternal grandfather. Khwaja Faizi, who occupied the post of Nazim, took him to Burdwan and oversaw his education and training. In a short time, he completed his education which, besides outer knowledge, also included inward knowledge. He also received military training and in the course of time became well-versed in the military sciences.

The appointment

His maternal grandfather, Khwaja Faizi, was killed in a battle so Raja Man Singh appointed him to the post so vacated. His appointment as Nazim was subsequently confirmed by the imperial court.

The dream

One night, he dreamt of three persons telling him that he should give up his present state and adopt their state and condition. Later one of them shaved his head with a razor. The second person caused him to wear a coffin, and the third placed a turban on his head.[2]

When he awoke, he found himself a transformed man. He called a barber and got his head shaved and donned the garb of dervishes. He wanted to resign his post and renounce the world but was persuaded by Raja Man Singh not to do so, assuring him of promotion in the near future. This enabled the latter to retain his services till the impending battle. The battle was fought and Usman Afghan was defeated.[3]

The second dream

After the battle was over he returned to Burdwan. That very night he dreamt of the Holy Prophet Mohammed with Hazrat Ali, Hazrat Imam Hasan, and Hazrat Imam Husain, whom he had seen in the previous dream. They asked him to take to his ancestral calling and retire from the world and worldly affairs.

Arrival in Akbarabad

Emperor Akbar died in the meanwhile. Emperor Jahangir, who ascended the throne, issued a *farman* directing all the noblemen and the Nazims posted in various provinces to come to the Imperial Court to undergo a test of fitness. On receipt of the order, he immediately left for Akbarabad (Agra). On his way, he met Hazrat Yahya of Munir, with whom he stayed for sometime. Leaving Munir, he eventually reached Agra.

He was warmly received at the Imperial Court. The emperor one night offered him a goblet of wine. Out of respect he took it, but put it away. The goblet was given a second time. Again he took it and did the same. The emperor was enraged and said: "What! such expression of your obstinacy. Are you not afraid of the royal wrath?" He replied: "I am not in the least afraid of royal wrath. I am afraid of the divine wrath."

The transformation

Coming home he now firmly resolved to sever his connections with the world. He distributed all that he had amongst the poor, the needy, and the indigent. Emperor Jehangir called him again and sent Syed Mir Abd-ul-Hayee to fetch him, but he refused and resigned his position.

Hazrat Ali directed him to proceed to Ajmer for his share of the spiritual blessings of Hazrat Khwaja Moin-ud-din Hasan Chishti.

The next morning, after offering prayers, he came out wearing a sheet of cloth and a white wrapper tied around his waist. Whatever little he still had with him, he distributed to the poor and thus freed himself from the burdens and shackles of ignoble worldly possessions.

He left for Delhi on his way to Ajmer. He stayed in Delhi for sometime deriving spiritual ecstasy and blessings from the tombs of Hazrat Khwaja Qutb-ud-din Bakhtyar Kaki and Hazrat Nizam-ud-din Auliya. He then went on to Ajmer and stayed there. Hazrat Khwaja Gharib Nawaz conferred upon him many spiritual blessings and paid special spiritual attention to him.

One night, when he was going around the tomb of Hazrat Khwaja Gharib Nawaz, he was blessed with a unique manifestation. He saw that Hazrat Khwaja Gharib Nawaz, appearing in human form and, standing with his face towards the *qibla*, gave him with his fist closed, something round, red in colour and as large as bead from a rosary.

As soon as had eaten it he found himself a changed man. The darkness, the rust, the lust, the worldly connections, all that was impure were instantaneously eradicated from his heart. He saw the light, the divine light, the kindly light, kindly leading him on. Hazrat Khwaja Gharib Nawaz instructed him to become a spiritual disciple of his uncle—Amir Abdullah and also to marry his daughter.[4] He was also directed to return to Akbarabad and settle there permanently to preach and propagate the Gospel of Truth.

Return from Ajmer

He followed these instructions and returned to Akbarabad and awaited the arrival of his uncle Amir Abdullah, who was then in Burdwan. He was restless and anxious to meet him at the earliest. This state of restlessness took him to the tomb of Hazrat Amir Jaffer, son of Hazrat Amir Zain-ul-Abedeen, son of Hazrat Amir Taqi-ud-din of Kirman in Chagnora (Agra district). There, in a state of absorption, he received the inspiration that he should not worry at all and that Hazrat Amir Abdullah was due to reach Agra in the very near future. On his return from Chagnora, he found to his great joy and satisfaction, that Hazrat Amir Abdullah had already reached Agra.

Initiation into the Sufi Order

He immediately went to Hazrat Amir Abdullah to offer his respects. He wanted to request him to accept him as his humble spiritual disciple but was so overpowered by his magnetic personality that he found himself unable to express his desire. Khwaja Qasim came to his rescue and submitted on his behalf that Hazrat Amir Abul-Ila wanted to be his spiritual disciple. Hazrat Amir Abdullah promptly honoured him by accepting him as his spiritual disciple and completed the ceremony of initiation into the Sufi Order by taking off a ring from his finger and putting it on the former's.

What then transpired he himself says: "I found myself relieved of a great burden. I felt as if I was sitting in a boat and the boat was sailing smoothly and I was thus traversing and covering all the distance and all the stations and all the states."

His spiritual guide and teacher conferred upon him the robe of caliph and entrusted to him the deed of spiritual genealogy and allowed him to spread the order by accepting spiritual disciples. He also permitted him to listen to music, if he was so inclined. In this way, he got himself initiated in the two prominent Sufi Orders, the Chishti and the Naqshbandi.

Subsequently, appointing him as his spiritual successor (*sajjadanashin*), his spiritual guide and teacher passed away.

Marriage and children

As instructed spiritually by Hazrat Khwaja Gharib Nawaz, he married the daughter of his uncle and spiritual guide Hazrat Amir Abdullah. He had two sons. The eldest son was named Amir Faiz-ul-Illa who became a spiritual disciple and caliph of his father. His second son, Amir Nur-ul-Illa, was his father's spiritual disciple, caliph, and spiritual of his father. It is also said that he had a daughter.[5]

Death

Hazrat Amir Abul-Ila breathed his last on Tuesday, the ninth of Safar in AH 1061 at the age of seventy-one years. His tomb is in Agra.

Caliphs

His prominent spiritual caliphs are: his eldest son, Amir Faiz-ul-Illa, his younger son, Amir Nur-ul-Illa, Mulla Wali Mohammed, Mir Syed Mohammed of Kalpi, and Dost Mohammed of Burhanpur.

Traits of character

He was a saint who had merged his self and took pleasure in the remembrance of god. After he resigned his post, he did not care in the least for worldly position, rank or honour. His hope, belief, contentment, trust in God, piety, ascetic practices, spirit of renunciation, and silent service place him among the outstanding saints of the Indian subcontinent. He was a man of literary taste and the author of a book entitled *Risala Fana wa Baqa.*

Teachings

Fana (extinction) is the goal of the *faqir*. It is the consummation and the attainment of perfection. *Fana* is of three kinds, namely, *fana fil af'aal* (extinction of acts), *fana fis-sifat* (extinction of qualities), and *fana fiz-zat* (extinction of the self).

Fana fil af'aal means, that the *salik* (the one who treads on the path to spiritual perfection) should come out of his authority and the authority of all the world. The object of it is that all those movements, acts, and deeds that he formerly ascribed to himself and to others, he should now ascribe to, and take them as emanating from God Almighty alone. He should ascribe all his acts to God in just the way in which the movement of a key is related to the hand and changing the sides of a dead body is related to the hand of the person giving the bath. He should not ascribe anything or any act to anyone else besides God, for that would constitute idol worship and idolatry.

Fana fis-sifat means that the *salik* should know his qualities as well as the qualities of others as the qualities of God Almighty. He should ascribe all his qualities and of others, such as knowledge, intention, power, hearing, seeing, speech, etc., which he knew as his possession and the possession of others, to God alone and know them to be the qualities of God Almighty. He should not ascribe them to himself and to others, for to do so constitutes idol worship and idolatry.

Fana fiz-zat means that the *salik* should know his self and the self of all the world as the Self of God Almighty. Reaching this station, he should know what he thought his self and the world itself as the world is in fact nothing but God Almighty. He should believe that God Almighty, descending from the absolute position, has manifested himself in different shapes and forms. Whatever he may see, he should believe to be a friend and not a stranger. The Holy Prophet has said that an individual who recognises his reality in such a way that he is not himself, but God who has manifested himself in such, a form, such is an individual who realises God.

- He says that so long as thou art and thy personality exists, thou wilt not be able to find the smell of God. When thou shalt become extinguished, thou wilt see the manifestation of God.
- He suggests the way to approach the subject, firstly the *salik* should treat the whole world as a mirror. He should continue to see the manifestation of the beauty of God in this mirror and should be so concentrated, absorbed, and confined in this affiliation that the thought of it may continue to dominate his heart and eye at all times and at all moments.

Subsequently, the *salik* should successfully traverse this station and achieve a high position and see all the world as God and believe that it is God who has manifested himself in different forms and shapes. He should exert himself strenuously for this. It is the utmost, incessant, continuous, and unceasing labour, that eventually pays. Idle chatter and mere boasting will not lead very far. When the seeker exerts his utmost he will see very many manifestations and will be rewarded in various ways. He should carry on and reach a higher position and keeping himself aloof from the remaining curtains by exerting himself in the negation of his self and in the affirmation of the existence of God. The object of it is that by closing his outward eyes, he should think that what he took to be "I" is in fact not "I." He is indeed God himself who has manifested himself in such a shape and form.

He should acquire such absolute concentration in this that he may forget himself and all the world totally and absolutely, and that only then will he find the quest and the sought to be one and curtains will be removed. This is what is known as the realisation of God; the ultimate aim and goal of all seekers of God. To be united with God constitutes the pinnacle of glory for dervishes. Hence, a real sufi is no one who takes to seclusion or ascetic practices, but, on the contrary, a real sufi is one who takes to extinction.

Sayings

- One who is familiar with the people of the world is a stranger to God.
- One, who has recognised himself, his tongue becomes tied.
- Silence is the crown of the faithful.
- The people of the world are cowards, foolish, and without common sense. Their life is a handkerchief, their rosary is wealth, position, rank and honour. The world is a place where much can be learnt. It is an ignoble world. The world should be hated and condemned. It forms part of the inheritance of Satan. The people of the world are cunning and crafty and are ever engrossed in thoughts of money.
- Nobody knows the value of a saint, apart from the saint himself.
- Man should not prefer his own good to the good of others.

Supernatural powers

- He exhibited very many supernatural powers. Once, Hazrat Mulla Umar, who was one of his devotees, when attending a music concert, underwent a state of rapture. He cried aloud and died. Those present were greatly perturbed and brought him into the presence of Hazrat Syedna. He gazed towards the dead body and it began to move and regained life.[6]
- Once, Hazrat Syedna was eating. A dog came and sat in the courtyard of his house, so he threw a bone towards it. The dog took the bone in his mouth and began to chew it and from that instant it sat down in a secluded nook and did not re-emerge. The dog died there and with its breath, showed the mark of remembrance.[7]
- A *faqir*, Jamal Shah, who belonged to the Madariya Order, came to him and asked for his blessings. Hazrat Syedna suggested that first of all he should consult his wife regarding this as he (the *faqir*) was responsible for her maintenance. Jamal Shah disappointed, returned home.

The following day, armed with bow and arrow, he went to Hazrat Syedna with a malignant motive. Jamal Shah reminded him of what he had said yesterday. Thereupon, Hazrat Syedna said that he remembered all. Hazrat Syedna cast a lingering glance upon him and that was sufficient. Jamal Shah began to run hither and thither, began to cry aloud that Hazrat Syedna had filled his blanket with blessings and it had become difficult for him to lift the blanket. He asked the people to place the blanket upon his shoulders, and when they did so Jamal Shah became an absorbed one.

References

1. *Israr-e-Abul-Ila,* p. 9.
2. Ibid., pp. 11-12.
3. Ibid., p. 19.
4. Ibid., p. 20.
5. *Risala Nigar-e-Qasim,* p. 75.
6. *Israr-e-Abul-Ila,* p. 70.
7. Ibid., p. 72.

63

Hazrat Sarmad

Hazrat Sarmad was not only an outstanding poet, but a great mystic and martyr. Among the saints and sages of the Indian subcontinent he enjoys a privileged position.

It is said that he was an Armenian Christian.[1] Others say that he was a Jew. He came from Kashan, which was then a flourishing trading centre.[2] There is no contradiction in this as there was a fairly substantial Armenian population in Persia. Hazrat Sarmad embraced Islam.

He has been called by his poetic pseudonym "Sarmad." In some books however, he has been referred to as "Sa'id-e-Sarmad," which leads us to believe that a part of his Islamic name must have been "Sa'id" and this, in conjunction with his poetic pseudonym became "Sa'id-e-Sarmad."

His *Ruqqat* and *Rubaiyat* are evidence of his vast knowledge. He was well-versed in Persian and was also acquainted with Arabic.

Turning point

India was famous for her fabulous wealth, and Persian arts and crafts were in great demand in India. That is why Sarmad, a trader, went for India, i.e., to sell Persian arts and with the proceeds purchase the precious stones from India. In those days, Persian traders used to come to India by way of Sindh which provided the shortest route. At Thatta, then a flourishing city, Sarmad became a prey to Goddess Minerva. Sher Khan Lodi says: "When on the way to India to trade, he saw at Thatta a Hindu boy and fell in love with him."[3] Some say that it was at Surat,[4] while Azad Bilgrami speaks about Azamabad (Patna). Sher Khan Lodi, appears, however, to be most reliable source.

Love, as is usual, brought about a transformation in his life. He abandoned his trade and severed all worldly connections and renounced all worldly comforts. He lost his balance and wandered about like a madman. He freed himself from obligations and limitations to such a degree that he eventually "freed himself from the burdens of his clothes," and went about stark naked. He was restless, and constantly travelling.

Arrival in Delhi

Wandering thus, he reached Delhi. Delhi then was the centre of much political intrigue. Emperor Shah Jahan was about to be deposed by his third son Aurangzeb. Sarmad was warmly welcomed at Court. He soon became a great friend and favourite of Dara Shikoh, Emperor Shah Jahan's eldest son and hence heir to the throne. Dara Shikoh was possessed of considerable natural abilities. He had a mystic turn of mind and loved the company of dervishes, irrespective of their religion. This, coupled with his views in religious matters, militated against his political interests. Dara Shikoh reposed great faith in the spiritual powers of Hazrat Sarmad, and extended great love, regard, and esteem to him.

Repercussions

Time passed. The War of Succession (1657-58) decided the fate of Dara Shikoh, who was captured, imprisoned, and eventually beheaded. Having disposed of all his rivals, Aurangzeb ascended the throne in AD 1658.

Dara Shikoh's admirers, associates, friends and well-wishers found themselves under threat in the new political set-up and felt insecure. Many left Delhi, but Hazrat Sarmad stayed on. Now he was in Delhi without his prince patron. Aurangzeb had always thought him to be a heretic, and indeed Sarmad's catholicity and Aurangzeb's orthodoxy were irreconcilable. Besides, on account of his having being a friend, an associate, and a "guide" of Dara Shikoh, Aurangzeb felt that on some pretext or an other Sarmad should be done away with. Aurangzeb felt he could only be politically secure only if nobody connected with Dara Shikoh in any degree whatsoever, remained in or around Delhi. In India, the great game of politics had always been played from behind the curtain of religion.

The charge-sheet

A charge-sheet was framed against Hazrat Sarmad. The first charge levelled against him was that he refuted the physical ascension of the Holy Prophet Mohammed. The second was that he was intimately and closely associated with Dara Shikoh and the third that he preferred to be naked, which was contrary to Islamic canons. The fourth charge was that he did not recite the whole of the *kalimah*.

The ecclesiastical council

Sarmad was always naked from head to foot, irrespective of the weather. The chief of Delhi, Mulla Qazi, at imperial command met Sarmad and asked him why he was naked when he knew that it violated Islamic precept. Sarmad replied: "A too high position to the lowly one like me gave; He is in my bosom and I am in his quest; The thief quite strangely has made me naked."

The Qazi was enraged and reported to the emperor that Sarmad should be punished as an ocular proof of his guilt had at last been found. The emperor suggested that Sarmad should be summoned before a council consisting of the *ulama* and the *maulvis*.

Ali Quli Khan of Daghistan quotes Khalifa Ibrahim of Badakhshan, to the effect that when Sarmad was summoned before the ecclesiastical council and was asked to don some clothes, he flatly refused.[5]

The council held that guilt has been proven but the emperor took a contrary view asserting that as it would be contrary to Islamic law and jurisprudence to put a man to death just because he was naked.

The emperor had heard, that Sarmad did not recite the whole of the *kalimah* (*La ilaha illallah*—There is no deity but God). He suggested, that he should be asked to recite the entire *kalimah*. When asked to do so, Sarmad recited only a part of it, i.e., "There is no deity but God." The council insisted that he recite the full *kalimah*. He replied that so far he had known only the negative aspect of the *kalimah*. He had yet to enter the second stage, when he could imbibe the positive aspect. The council declared that if he did not repent for his sinful omission, he was a heretic and liable to be put to death. Sarmad stuck to his stand.

Judgement

The ecclesiastical council pronounced unanimous judgement declaring him a heretic and awarding him capital punishment.

Martyrdom

The following day (in AD 1659) he was beheaded. When the executioner proceeded towards him with a glittering sword in his hand, Sarmad, seeing him smiled and uttered the following memorable words: "I must sacrifice myself to Thee, Come, Come/In whatever shape Thou may'st come,/I recognize Thee well."

Sher Khan Lodi says, that after uttering these words, Sarmad recited the following verse:

> There arose a noise and from the sleep of non-existence we opened our eyes,
> Seeing that the turbulent night remained still, we went to sleep again.

After this, he smilingly placed his head beneath the executioner's sword. Khalifa Ibrahim of Daghistan says that after he was beheaded, he said the full *kalim* three times, i.e., "*La ilaha illallahu Muhammad-ur-Rasoolullah* – There is no deity, but God and Mohammed is the Apostle of God."

He was buried near the Delhi Central Mosque (Jama'Masjid built by Shad Jahan) and his tomb, even after the lapse of centuries, is the centre of devotion.

Literary taste

He was a man of literary taste. His letters entitled *Letters of Sarmad* are exquisite. He has written many *rubaiyats* in Persian, and these are known as *Rubaiyat of Sarmad.*[6] Two his *rubaiyats*, in translation read:

> Everybody wishes this and the next world to gain,
> My ambition is to be freed from this strain;
> Make me a runner after Thee
> O, come out of the curtain and free me from the pain.
> Pardon my sins with Thy Merciful Light,
> Accept my tears shed in the night;
> We are full of sins, it is strange to say;
> Thy Mercy is the best cure, as it makes us right.

Supernatural Powers

After he was beheaded, he not only recited the full *kalimah* three times, but was also engaged in the adoration of God. Aurangzeb, despite his long span of life had no peace of mind. He spent most of the time far from Delhi in the Deccan and there he died and was buried.

References

1. Sher Khan Lodi, *Mirat-ul-Khiyal.*
2. Ali Quli Khan Daghistani, *Riyaz-ush-Shu'ara.*
3. Ibid.
4. Ibid.
5. Zahurul Hassan Sharib, trans., *Rubaiyat of Sarmad.*
6. Ibid..

64

Hazrat Mir Syed Mohammed

Hazrat Mir Syed Mohammed was the spiritual disciple and caliph of Hazrat Syed Shah Amir Abul-Ila. He belongs to the august house of the Holy Prophet Mohammed and he is thus a Syed. He received his education from Maulana Umar Gagmoi.

Initiation into the Sufi Order

He became a spiritual disciple of Hazrat Jamal of the Chishti Order who subsequently conferred on him the robe of caliph.

One night, he dreamt of Hazrat Ali and Hazrat Naqshband of Bukhara, telling him to go and acquire the spiritual blessings of a saint buried in Akbarabad (Agra).

As directed, he, accompanied by some spiritual disciples, left for Akbarabad (Agra). In Agra, he inquired about the dervishes, who lived there and was told that there lived only two outstanding saints in Agra. One was Mir Noman, the spiritual caliph of Hazrat Shaikh Ahmad of Sirhind, and the other was Hazrat Syed Shah Amir Abul-Ila. He thought of going to Mir Noman, and left in a palanquin for his monastery but the bearers of the palanquin, in error, took him to the monastery of Hazrat Syed Shah Amir Abul- Ila. He did not step down from the palanquin, but instead instructed the bearers to take him to the monastery of Mir Noman. The bearers left, but again they lost their way and brought him to the monastery of Hazrat Syed Shah Amir Abul-Ila. When this happened several times, he thought that it appeared to be a Decree of God that he should go to Hazrat Syed Shah Amir Abul-Ila.[1]

This time, he got down from the palanquin and entered the monastery. Hazrat Syed Amir Abul-Ila was at that time sitting in the monastery with some of his devotees, disciples, and admirers. Seeing him, he cried aloud. Hazrat Mir Mohammed was not alarmed by the cry and kept his composure. Then Hazrat Abul-Ila caught hold of his hand and cried aloud. Hazrat Mir Mohammed could not withstand this, his body was stricken with tremors and his heart beat rapidly, an affiliation with Hazrat Syed Amir Abul-Ila finding a place in his heart.

He began living in his company and acquired the spiritual graces. Ultimately, he attained perfection and was given the robe of caliph of the Naqshbandi-Abul-Ilai Orders. He was then allowed to return to Kalpi from whence he had come, and there, he took to the propagation of the Gospel of Truth. Many people entered his fold.

Marriage

He married, and his son, Syed Ahmad, his eminent spiritual caliph, succeeded him.

Death

He breathed his last on the twenty-sixth of Sha'ban in AH 1071, and was buried in Kalpi, U.P.[2]

Traits of character

Hazrat Mir Syed Mohammed was a man of simple habits and reposed the utmost faith in God. He did not hanker after worldly pleasures or worldly position. He was a great mystic and an accomplished saint.

References

1. *Israr-e-Abul-Ila,* p. 141.
2. Ibid.

65

Hazrat Syed Dost Mohammed

Hazrat Syed Dost Mohammed was the spiritual caliph of Hazrat Syed Amir Abul-Ila. He was born in AH 996, was educated in Delhi, and well-versed in outward knowledge.

In search of truth

Hazrat Syed Dost Mohammed was not satisfied with the mere attainment of outward knowledge, hankering for spiritual perfection. His quest took him to various parts of the country. Eventually, reaching Bengal, he stayed there for sometime and came in contact with many saints, but was still dissatisfied.

One day, a certain person, finding him restless and ever in quest of a perfect dervish told him that one such lived in Akbarabad (Agra) and his name was Hazrat Amir Abul-Ila. Whosoever went to him found his spiritual quest amply rewarded and whosoever lived in his company for sometime found himself illumined and transformed. This information gave him some hope and he left for Akbarabad.

Initiation into the Sufi Order

Once there, he purchased some sugar pills and went to Hazrat Syed Amir Abul-Ila who was then sitting in the courtyard of the mosque surrounded by his devotees, spiritual disciples, and admirers. He presented the sugar pills and himself sat respectfully in a corner. Seeing him, Hazrat Syed Amir Abul-Ila inquired who he was, where he lived and why he had come.

His response was:[1] "My name is Dost Mohammed. I am a wanderer. Hearing the name and fame of your holiness, I have come from Bengal. I am thirsty and want the wine of unity of God to quench my thirst, I request and implore your holiness to show me light."

Hazrat Syedna, hearing this, smiled, took one sugar pill, presented by him and ate it. Then he said:[2] "Dost Mohammed! you have sweetened my mouth. Now it is obligatory upon me to sweeten yours. Come near and sit before me and look towards me." As soon as he gazed at him he experienced such a sense of spiritual exaltation, that it conferred upon him inner peace and tranquillity, totally and instantly freed from the pangs of inner conflict. He went into a trance and was unmindful of the afternoon prayers. Those present wanted to bring him to consciousness in order to enable him to offer the afternoon prayers, but Hazrat Syedna asked them not to do so. After sometime he himself regained consciousness and offered the afternoon and the evening prayers, and after the night-prayers, he spent the night in the mosque.

The following morning, after the morning prayers were over, Hazrat Syed Amir Abul-Ila honoured him by accepting him as his spiritual disciple and raised him up to the exalted position of being his spiritual caliph.

The mandate

After his appointment as a spiritual caliph, he was instructed by his spiritual guide and teacher Hazrat Syed Amir Abul-Ila to go to Burhanpur and settle there permanently. He was sorry to receive the mandate because he did not want to be dismissed so soon from the presence of his spiritual guide and teacher, wishing to stay on and serve him. He requested that he allowed to stay for some more time in his company, and this request was granted. He lived there for a year, acquiring inner knowledge and deriving spiritual blessings. On the expiry of a year he left for Burhanpur where he settled. The pangs of separation, were difficult to bear but he controlled himself.[3] Through his magnetic personality, the prestige of the Order was hugely increased.

Death

He breathed his last on Friday the twenty-sixth of Jamadi-us-Sani in AH 1090 and was buried in Aurangabad.

Caliphs

His prominent caliphs are: Hazrat Musafir Shah, Hazrat Mahmud Shah, and Hazrat Shah Farhad.

Traits of character

He greatly loved his spiritual guide and teacher and was deeply absorbed in contemplation. When overpowered by the state of spiritual exaltation, he would escape to the forests or other desolate places and cry aloud. It is said that the animals and the birds, hearing him crying aloud, would undergo a state of rapture and begin to dance.

Occasionally the sound of his cry would ignite a fire that enveloped the jungle. If, when in such a state, he cast a glance on anyone, or if anyone looked then towards his face, he too underwent a strange transformation, tearing his clothes and running away to the jungles.

He was not in the least interested in worldly gains, honour, position, or status. For him, his affiliation with his spiritual guide and teacher was sufficient.

References

1. *Israr-e-Abul-Ila,* p. 143.
2. Ibid.
3. *Nigar-e-Qasim.*

66

Hazrat Shaikh Dawood

Hazrat Shaikh Dawood was the son, spiritual caliph, and successor of Hazrat Shaikh Mohammed Sadiq.

Spiritual education and training

His spiritual education and training was his father's principle concern. It is said that one day, when offering the morning prayers, his father raised his finger of evidence, a graceful light ensued from it enveloping the entire world and eventually disappeared into the finger. Thereafter, the wall cracked and the blessed soul of the Holy Prophet appeared and addressed him: "This is a light of the sainthood of your son Shaikh Dawood. His Order will spread from the East to the West. Do your utmost to impart him with spiritual education and training."[1] From that day onward, his father took particular interest in his spiritual education and training, and eventually he attained perfection.

Ascetic practices

Hazrat Shaikh Dawood devoted himself exclusively to ascetic practices and prayers and kept himself aloof from worldly affairs.

Death

He breathed his last on the sixth of Sha'ban in AH 1095, though some hold that he died on the sixth of Ramazan in AH 1095.[2] He was buried in Gangoh.

Caliphs

His prominent caliphs are: Shaikh Soonda, Shaikh Bulaqi, Syed Gharib-ul-lah, and Shah Abul-Ma'ale.

Traits of character

He was a man of vast knowledge and erudition, and was considered an authority on mystic knowledge. Any disputed point concerning mysticism was referred to him. His spiritual guide and teacher, Hazrat Mohammed Sadiq, concurred with the opinions expressed by him. He did not believe in ostentation or show, was rational and sober in thought and serenely conducted his everyday life.

References

1. *Iqtibas-ul-Anwar.*
2. *Shajra Manzoom.*

67

Hazrat Shah Abul-Ma'ale

Hazrat Shah Abul-Ma'ale was the spiritual caliph of Hazrat Shaikh Dawood. His father's name was Syed Mohammed Ashraf and he lived in Amethi,U.P. His father died when Hazrat Abdul-Ma'ale was a minor. His mother, anxious that he should receive good education, entrusted him to Hazrat Shaikh Mohammed Sadiq, who imparted him outward and the inward knowledge. Later, as was his wont, he sent him to Hazrat Shaikh Dawood for the completion of his education.

Initiation into the Sufi Order

He was engaged in penances and ascetic practices. Subsequently, Hazrat Shaikh Dawood conferred upon him the robe of caliph.

Death

He breathed his last on the twelfth of Rabi-ul-Awwal in AH 1116 and was buried in Amethi.

Caliph

Syed Mohammed Sa'id Miran Shah Bhika is his prominent caliph.

Traits of character

He was fond of music and deeply devoted to prayer, penances, and ascetic practices, and had a forgiving nature. One of his neighbours would abuse and insult him, but that did not bother him. Some of his devotees thought of punishing his neighbour for his behaviour but Hazrat Abdul-Ma'ale would not permit this. The man died, and when Hazrat Abdul-Ma'ale learnt of this he was extremely upset and would eat nothing for seven days on end. When asked why, he said: "Without such people, the saints and the prophets cannot be freed from the dust of stain. This man was to me like a washerman. Who washed the dirt from the clothes of this humble being. Now, who will wash that dirty patch?" Saying this he cried loudly. In the beginning of his mystic career, he did not eat anything for two or three months on end.

He was initially so deeply absorbed in concentration – that his devotees had to inform of the time for prayers. After praying he would again relapse into his former state. Later, he would trance himself when the time for prayers approached. The devotees asked why this was so, to which he replied that the prayer itself came to him in concrete form therefore did not require the assistance of others to awaken from his trance in time for prayers.

Teachings

He says, that life and death lie in the negative and affirmative aspect of the *kalimah* (there is no deity but God). If anyone whispers the negative aspect of the *kalimah* with sincerity heart in the ear of the living, he will die and, if the opposite occurs and he whispers the positive aspect of the *kalimah* with stet into the ear of the dead, he will come alive.

Those present requested him to demonstrate the truth of this. He stood up and whispered the negative aspect of the *kalimah* into the ear of a cow, and it fell down dead. Then he whispered the positive aspect of the *kalima* into the other ear of the dead cow, which promptly stood up.

Supernatural power

Once, he was sitting on a wall in a certain village. Molasses were being boiled in a very large frying utensil just below the wall. Somebody, in a melodious voice, recited a couplet. Hearing the couplet he underwent a state of ecstasy, cried aloud, and fell down into the utensil. The people sitting there, ran up to him and took him out of the utensil and to their astonishment, there was not a scratch on his body.

68

Hazrat Mohammed Sa'id Miran Shah Bhika

Hazrat Mohammed Sa'id Miran Shah Bhika was the spiritual caliph of Hazrat Shah Abul-Ma'ale. He traces his descent from Hazrat Imam Husain, son of Hazrat Ali, son-in-law of the Holy Prophet Mohammed. His forefathers belongs to Zoroastrians. One of them, Zaid, came to India and settled in Siwana, formerly known as Siyana.

His father was named Syed Yusuf. Hazrat Miran Shah Bhika was born on the seventh of Rajab in AH 1046, and was named Mohammed Sa'id. His pseudonym is "Miran Shah Bhika."

Education and training

His mother brought him up and was wholly preoccupied with his education, his father having died when he was seven years old.

In order to escape the evil designs of members of the family member, she left Siwana and settled in Kohram, which is near Sirhind (East Punjab). There she went and Hazrat Miran Shah Bhika sent to a school where he studied outer knowledge. In school, he became very intimate with one of his class-fellows. The other students, noticing the unusual familiarity, remarked to that it was not proper for him, to cultivate so intimacy the son of a *faqir*. Hazrat Miran Shah Bhika, unable to tolerate such a remark and slapped a student on the face. The principal of the school expelled him from school in consequence.

Readmission

After being expelled from the school he would loiter around and play on the streets with boys of his own age. It so happened that one day Hazrat Shah Jalal, son of Shah Qamees Qadiri, came to Kohram to train his spiritual disciples. When he saw him playing on the street, he enquired who he was and was informed that he was the son of Syed Yusuf.

He showed him kindness and expressed his concern for his future welfare and said: "O, my dear boy! this is not the time to play. Do not waste your time in merry-making. This is a time for study." He replied that he was helpless having been expelled from the school.

Hazrat Shah Jalal evinced great interest in his education. He took him to principal the following morning. The teacher felt adamant, and told Hazrat Shah Jalal that he was prepared to accommodate him in every other respect, but not in the case of Miran Shah Bhika. Thereupon Hazrat Jalal told him that he was impertinent for not obeying his spiritual guide and teacher. The principal was ashamed and tendered an apology and readmitted Hazrat Miran Shah Bhika to his school.

Hazrat Shah Jalal suggested that he should teach him the Holy *Quran* and the two famous works of Shaikh Sa'di entitled *Gulistan* and *Bustan*.

He also appointed four of his spiritual disciples to look after him and to pay for all the expenses incurred.

The prophecy

Hazrat Shah Jalal told the principal that Miran Shah Bhika was an intelligent boy and that he was certain that very soon he would become pupil a teacher. He then whispered softly into the ear of the teacher: "Know; this son of a Syed is the Qutb of his time. You should serve him as best as you can."

The assignment

A resident of Kohram, who was in service, when transferred elsewhere took Hazrat Miran Shah Bhika as a private tutor for his son. There he underwent a state of change and was attracted to the mystic way of life. He would meet dervishes and saints belonging to all denominations, live in their company, and seek their blessings irrespective of their religion or nationality.

When the person who had taken him with him learnt of this he was alarmed. He thought that if he secretly left with anyone of them, his mother would blame him for his negligence, and thought that best thing would be to send him back to Kohram.

Return to Kohram

On his return to Kohram, his quest continued. He was told, that there lived in a village called Maloia a dervish who was an embodiment of spiritual perfection. He went to the dervish, Baynava Shah Qasim, and began to live in his company. There, he would collect wood for fuel. One day, Hazrat Shah Qasim asked twelve of his spiritual disciples to lift a log of wood and place it on the wall in order to form a roof. The log was so heavy that all twelve of them were unable to lift it up jointly. Hazrat Miran Bhika Shah, in one motion, raised it and placed it on the wall. It was initially a little too short but by a mere touch of his hand it covered the entire length. All the onlookers were greatly astonished by this feat of power. The disciples interpreted it otherwise, believing that he had performed the arduous task by dint of the spiritual power with which he was endowed.

This caused jealousy amongst Hazrat Qasim's spiritual disciples and complained to their spiritual guide: "This dervish, who has nothing to do other than to collected wood and draw water, and who is totally unacquainted with the secrets of mysticism, has been shown special favour and grace and has been endowed with absolute spiritual powers whereas they who have passed so long in your service have gained nothing."

Greatness affirmed

Hazrat Qasim, hearing this, smiled and quietly responded: "Know that the real distributor is God Almighty himself. He himself is the son of a Syed. His father and his forefathers were all accomplished men. I can do nothing. I am helpless." At that time Hazrat Qasim's spiritual guide and teacher was also present there and told him in plain language: "You and I are like a small tank and Miran is like a large river. Neither of us can irrigate. Allow him to leave."

The departure

After receiving permission to leave the village, he did not know where to go and what to do and therefore requested Hazrat Qasim to enlighten him. Shah Bhawal, one of Shah Abul-Ma'ale's devotees happened to be there and asked him to accompany him. He promised that he would take him to a perfect dervish who would enable him to reach his goal. He then suggested, "that a spiritual disciple should have the power of recognising the spiritual guide." To this Shah Miran retorted: "The spiritual guide should possess the power of recognising the spiritual disciple." He and Shah Bhawal then left for Amethi where Shah Abul-Ma'ale lived.

Arrival in Amethi

When Miran Shah and Shah Bhawal came near Amethi, Miran Shah stopped in order to smoke and Shah Bhawal proceeded alone. When Shah Bhawal paid his respects to Hazrat Shah Abul-Ma'ale, he was asked as to where he had left his companion. Shah Bhawal went out to fetch him. When Shah Bhawal and Miran Shah reached in the presence of Hazrat Shah Abul-Ma'ale, Shah Bhawal was again asked where his companion was Miran Shah understood the hint and replied that he had given up smoking. And from that day Miran Shah abstained from smoking. Hazrat Shah Abul-Ma'ale suggested to Miran Shah certain rituals and spiritual practices and allowed him to leave.

Return

He reached the village called Maloi and remained in a trance for three days, and when he regained consciousness, he moved on to Kohram. There he spent all his time in ascetic practices. He would soak a piece of bread in water and eat it on every seventh day. On one occasion he learnt through his spiritual powers that a hair of the beard of Hazrat Abul-Ma'ale had fallen on the carpet on which he sat and immediately left for Amethi in order to fetch it when he reached he disclosed his reason for coming. He searched and he found the hair. Hazrat Shah Abul-Ma'ale took little notice of this, and in fact told him that it was not a mark of sainthood. Real sainthood meant something else, and asked Hazrat Miran Shah to stay in his company for three days, and each day gave him a roasted chicken to eat. This diet purified his heart. Then he allowed him to leave and instructed him to be ever engaged in the Remembrance of God. Once back in Kohram he was ever absorbed in prayer penances, and ascetic practices.

The urgent call

After the lapse of sometime, he received a letter from Hazrat Abul-Ma'ale, summoning him to his presence. As he had become weak and was not fit enough to undertake the journey, he expressed his inability to be with him and informed him that he would soon arrive.

After the bearer of the letter had left, he regretted, he had not obeyed the order and eventually left for Amethi, U.P. He covered the long distance quite soon, reaching Amethi late in the evening. Hazrat Shah Abul-Ma'ale inquired: "On which day, did you leave Kohram?" He replied: "I left Kohram this morning." Then he asked: "How did you cross the river?" He replied: "I walked on the water and my feet did not get wet."

After these questions and answers, he asked him to return and said: "Miran, reliance should be placed on outward conditions." This warning was sufficient for him. On his return journey, he crossed the river by boat. At Kohram, he severed all his connections with the world and would pass the night sitting on the embankment of a well engaged in prayer. He wore torn clothes and ate coarse food.

The robe of caliph

Hazrat Shah Abul-Ma'ale had told him that he need not come to him again. He himself would find the time to visit him. After a lapse of time he did this and honoured him by entrusting to him his clothes, cap, and parchment.

Hazrat Miran Shah apologised and submitted that he had not the requisite capacity and the desired ability to wear the garments so kindly entrusted to him. Thereupon, Hazrat Abul-Ma'ale told him that he could not understand why he hesitated in obeying his Order. At last, he put on that dress. On emerging from the tenement, he honoured him by accepting him as his spiritual caliph.

Death

He breathed his last on the fith of Ramazan in AH 1131 at the age of eighty-five years and was buried in Kohram.

Caliphs

Hazrat Miran Shah left forty-two spiritual caliphs. Prominent among are: Shaikh Aman-ul-lah and Syed Mohammed Salim.

Traits of character

He was an accomplished saint who had attained proximity to God. His privations, penances, ascetic practices, and spirit of renunciation marked him out for a great spiritual destiny.

Supernatural powers

Hazrat Miran Shah Bhika exhibited very many supernatural

powers. Once, the roof of the tenement of his spiritual guide needed repair. His devotees and spiritual disciples did their utmost to repair it but were unsuccessful. Hazrat Shah Abul-Ma'ale then said that Miran Shah Bhika would repair it alone, and he was called for the purpose. He removed the grass and began to repair it. It is said that at every knock, he found a station disclosed to him.

The son of one of his spiritual disciples, who lived in Tudhan, died. After about two hours, he happened to reach the village. The father of the boy not wishing to disclose the news of his son's death to him, put dead body in a separate room. The food was prepared, and when it was served, he asked his spiritual disciple, to call his son to partake of it with them. The father evaded the remark. Hazrat Miran Shah then said that he would not eat until the boy came. Finding him adamant, the disciple disclosed that his son had died, the former then told the father that the boy was not dead, and that he should go and see him, and awaken him if he was asleep. When he did so the disciple found his son breathing. He shook him. The boy got up and accompanied his father and when he met Hazrat Miran Shah he paid respects and kissed his feet.[1]

Reference

1. *Hadiqat-ul-Auliya; Samrat-ul-Fawaid.*

69

Hazrat Shah Mohammed Farhad

Hazrat Shah Mohammed Farhad, who was born in Delhi, has many devotees and spiritual disciples in the Indian subcontinent. His father was attached to the Royal Court and was appointed the Subedar of Burhanpur.

In search of truth

Hazrat Mohammed Dost Mohammed, at the command of his spiritual guide and teacher Hazrat Syedna Amir Abul-Ila Ahrari of Akbarabad (Agra) travelled to Burhanpur and settled there. His fame spread far and wide, and people came in large numbers to seek his blessings.

Hazrat Mohammed Farhad's father would occasionally visit him accompanied by his son, then twelve or thirteen years old. He was greatly fascinated by Hazrat Dost Mohammed's personality and began visiting him on his own which his father disapproved of and forbade. This injunction fell on deaf ears so eventually his father thought that he himself should request Hazrat Dost Mohammed not to allow him (Hazrat Farhad) to come. One day he went to him and tald:[1]

> 'I have only one son, sir. If he continues to come to your Holiness, I am certain he will become a useless man.' Hazrat Dost Mohammed replied: 'Let both of us try and forbid him, so that he does not come here again.' This dual attempt to prevent him from visiting Hazrat Dost Mohammed was foiled by fondness. His father had realised the consequences of his son visiting Hazrat Dost Mohammed and was bent upon checking him. He again approached Hazrat Dost Mohammed who this time replied: 'You want him to stand before the king with folded hands, but God

Wills otherwise. It is the Decree of God, that the king should stand before him with folded hands.' This was a foretaste of things to come.

Initiation into the Sufi Order

His father now decided against placing any restrictions on Hazrat Farhad's movements, enabling the latter to visit Hazrat Dost Mohammed without any let or hindrance. After a while he became his spiritual disciple and subsequently won the distinction of being appointed his caliph.

The will

His spiritual guide and teacher, Hazrat Dost Mohammed, a few days before his death made a will that he should not stay in Burhanpur after his death, but instead should go to Delhi and settle there and propagate and preach the Gospel of Truth and guide, teach, and inspire the people.

Hazrat Farhad acted accordingly.

Death

Hazrat Farad breathed his last on the twenty-five days of Jama-di-us-Sani in AH 1135 and was buried in Delhi.

Caliphs

Hazrat Shah Burhan-ud-din Khudanama and Hazrat Shah Asad-ul-lah are two eminent caliphs of him.

Traits of character

He was a *qutb* of his time. He was so greatly absorbed in contemplation that he was unmindful of his clothes, food, or drink. Sometimes he was so engrossed that when sitting on a carpet he was found searching for something. When people asked him what he was searching for he would reply: "Farhad was sitting here. Where has he gone?" In short, he had lost human qualities and instead had imbibed those of an angel. On whomsoever he cast a glance was transformed. He achieved spiritual perfection and was blessed with inner illumination.

Reference

1. *Anwar-ul-Arefeen*, p. 473.

70

Hazrat Syed Nur Mohammed

Hazrat Syed Nur Mohammed belonged to the Naqshbandi Order. He derived spiritual blessings from and was greatly benefited by Shaikh Saif-ud-din, and enjoyed the company of Hafiz Mohammed Mohsin.

Death
He breathed his last on the eleventh of Ziq'ada in AH 1135 and lies buried in Budaun, U.P.[1]

Caliph
Hazrat Mirza Mazhar Jane-Janan was his most outstanding caliph.

Traits of character
He was deeply absorbed in contemplation but would recover consciousness at the time of prayer. He strictly adhered to the tenets of the Holy Prophet and engaged in ascetic practices and meditation.

He ate only to survive. When he felt the pangs of hunger, he would consume whatever was immediately available. He did not accept the invitation of the rich, saying that food of the rich was not above doubt and suspicion. Once he received food from a worldly man but did not eat it on the ground that it contained the dark seeds of impurity. If he ever borrowed a book from any worldly man, he would not read it for three days on the ground that on account of its inglorious association, it contained dark rust. Having retaining the book for three days, when he found that his own association and contact with it had eradicated the darkness from it, he would read it. He was a very learned man, well-versed in inner and outward knowledge.[2]

Hazrat Mirza Mazhar Jane-Janan found him a perfect dervish and an accomplished spiritual figure. To him, he represented the "panorama of God on earth."

References

1. *Anwar-ul-Arefeen.*
2. *Muqamat-e-Mazhari.*

71

Hazrat Shaikh Kalim-ul-lah of Shahjahanabad

Hazrat Shaikh Kalim-ul-lah was one of the greatest spiritual figures of the Indian subcontinent. His forefathers belonged to Khagand (Turkestan). His father was Shaikh Nur-ul-lah was also said to have been a Haji, and was referred by some as "Shaikh Haji Nur-ul-lah." During the reign of Emperor Shahjahan, he was counted amongst successful and able engineers of the time and traced his descent from the first caliph Amir-ul-Momenin Hazrat Abu Bakr Siddique.

Hazrat Kalim-ul-lah was born in Delhi on the twenty-fourth of Jamade-us-Sani in AH 1060.[1]

Education and training

Hazrat Kalim-ul-lah learnt the *hadis*, jurisprudence, and acquired other types of knowledge, including inward knowledge.

He counted among his teachers such learned persons as Shaikh Abur-Raza, Shaikh Abul-Fath Qadari, and Hazrat Shaikh Burhan-ud-din, better known as Shaikh Behlal, son of Kabir Mohammed son of Ali-us-Siddique of Burhanpur.

Search for truth

He met a certain dervish who suggested he practise certain rituals. These did him some good but failed to secure for him his goal. He questioned the dervish regarding the time when he would be able to secure the goal but received no satisfactory answer. He therefore abandoned the rituals.[2]

When he was in the prime of youth, he fell in love with a Hindu boy, a Khatri by caste. The boy did not return his love;[3] indeed paid him scant attention. There lived in the city a saint, who was deeply much absorbed in contemplation. It was said of him that his acceptance of a gift was an indication for the donor that he would succeed in his object. His refusal, on the other hand, indicated the opposite.

Hazrat Kalim-ul-lah visited the saint and presented him some sweets, which the latter accepted. The following day, when he went to the boy he loved and he was surprised to find, that he paid him attention and caused him to sit near him. This had an adverse effect on him and his love vanished, to be replaced by a longing for a higher life. He then began visiting the saint periodically. On one such visit the saint called him near him and placing his head on his thigh, slept. When he awoke, there was a changed in his condition: a state of exaltation and absorption took hold of him. When he went to him next time, the saint could read his thoughts. Asking him to sit by him he said:[4] "If you want fire of this type, I have plenty of it. But Hazrat Shaikh Yahya of Medina has water with him. Go to him."

Initiation into the Sufi Order

Hazrat Kalim-ul-lah performed the pilgrimage to Mecca in AH 1101. From Mecca, he went on to Medina in a caravan. When he reached the outskirts of the city he rested in an oasis. Hazrat Sḫaikh Yahya of Medina, by dint of his spiritual powers, learnt of his arrival and deputed someone to fetch "Kalim-ul-lah," who was with the caravan outside the city.

The person so and called aloud, but nobody responded. Hazrat Kalim-ul-lah heard his name being called out, but remained silent because he was under the impression that someone else with the same name was being hailed. The man returned to Hazrat Shaikh Yahya of Medina and reported the lack of response. He was asked to go again and hail him this time by the name of Kalim-ul-lah of Shahjahaṇabad. Eventually Hazrat Kalim-ul-lah reached Shaikh Yahya of Medina who was awaiting him.[5] He then recited a couplet which the latter was greatly pleased to hear. Hazrat Kalim-ul-lah then requested Hazrat Yahya to accept him as his humble devotee and spiritual disciple. Not only he was accepted as such but he was also honoured by being elevated to the position of a caliph. He remained for some in Hazrat Yahya's company, acquiring and attaining the inner grace of life, and eventually traversed the spiritual stations and states.

Return to India

At the behest of his spiritual guide and teacher, he returned to India. He went to Delhi and began to live between Red Fort and Jama' Masjid (Central Mosque), spending the rest of his life there teaching, guiding, and propagating the doctrine of truth.

He owned a house that brought in a rent of two and a half rupees a month while himself lived in a house rented for half a rupee. The remaining two rupees, he utilised to meet his expenses and those of his dependants.[6]

Death

Hazrat Kalim-ul-lah passed away on the twenty-fourth of Rabi-ul-Awwal in AH 1142. At the age of eighty-one years and nine months. His tomb in Delhi is situated between Red Fort and Jama' Masjid.

Child

His son, Hazrat Mohammed Ghous, was saintly, and the spiritual disciple and caliph of Hazrat Maulana Fakhr-ud-din, Fakhr-e-Jahan.[7]

Caliphs

Notable among his caliphs were: Hazrat Maulana Nizam-ud-din of Aurangabad, Hazrat Mohammed Hashim, Maulana Shah Zia-ud-din, Maulana Shah Jamal, and Khwaja Yusuf.

Traits of character

Hazrat Kalim-ul-lah was a man of very fastidious tastes. He bathed daily and wore very neat and clean clothes. He adhered to the tenets of the Holy Prophet very strictly and offered many genuflexions everyday. A very learned man, he took to renunciation and asceticism, and was very fond of music. "He took great joy in reciting the Holy *Quran*, did not sleep during the night, and was greatly devoted to prayer."

He was a fine speaker, and whenever he spoke, his lucidity and the ease and grace of delivery held the audience spellbound. Emperor Farrukh Siyar, who was an admirer of him and reposed faith in his spiritual powers, tried many times to induce him to accept his offerings, but none of these whether house or *jagir*, were accepted.[8]

His letters are a treasure-house of mystical knowledge and

teachings, and have been published. He is also an author, his best known works are:[9] *Sawa-as-Sabil; Tasneem; Ashra-e-Kamila; Quran-ul-Quran; Muraqqa Sharif; and Kashkole.*

Teachings

His letters, addresses, and books conveyed his message and his teachings. He wrote as follows his caliph, Hazrat Shaikh Nizam-ud-din, about public popularity:[10]

> One should be thankful to God, if crowds of people wait upon him. The greater the increase in the number of people waiting upon an individual the greater the thanks that should be offered to God. It is purely and absolutely the kindness and blessing of God Almighty, that crowds of people may come and wait upon one. One should not be weary of crowds of people, for this reward is not the lot of everyone.

He says:

> All the unasked for gifts received should be spent forthwith. One should be indifferent to the day they are not received, hunger and poverty have their own important effect.
> Union means and implies severing connections from all things and not paying any attention towards anyone or anything. It means, in fact, to be lost and annihilated in the Absolute without colour. The beginning of this state is to be unmindful of all the senses. This state is just like death, the only difference being that there is no consciousness in death, whereas in this state, there is consciousness.[11]
> Spend all your energy and all your time in acquiring the remembrance of God. Do not be engaged, even for a moment, in something that may distract you from acquiring the remembrance of God.[12]

Sayings

- Enlightenment is of two kinds: one pertains to knowledge and the other concerns the state.
- Unity of God has stages, namely, unity of faith, unity of knowledge, unity of state and unity of God.

- To entrust ones all in the hands of forgetfulness constitutes trust in God.
- A fast is the highest and the greatest type of prayers.

Supernatural powers

He exhibited very many supernatural powers:

- When he went to Medina, he stayed at a place at a little from the city. Suddenly, he emerged from the inn where he was staying and asked others to do so too. As soon as the inn had been evacuated its roof collapsed. There was no loss of life.
- One of his disciples owned a garden, and in this two trees dried up. The disciple submitted to him that the garden constituted his only source of livelihood and implored his blessings. He gave water from his ablution to him, with the direction that he should pour it over the roots of the dried trees. When this was done the dried trees became green once again.
- One year there was no rain in Delhi. Some learned peoples went to him and requested him to pray for the coming of rain. He raised his hands and prayed: "O Great God! have mercy upon Thy people." As soon as the prayer was concluded, rain began to fall.

REFERENCES

1. *Anwar-ul-Arefeen*, p. 429.
2. *Takmila-Siyar-ul-Auliya*, pp. 77-78.
3. *Khulasat-ul-Fawaid; Takmila Siyar-ul-Auliya*, p. 79.
4. *Takmila-Siyar-ul-Auliya*, p. 79.
5. Ibid., pp. 79-80.
6. Ibid., p. 85.
7. *Manaqib-e-Fakhriya*, p. 16.
8. *Takmila-Siyar-ul-Auliya*, p. 85.
9. Ibid., pp. 80-81.
10. Ibid.
11. *Maktubat-e-Kalimi*.
12. *Kashkole*, p. 3.

72

Hazrat Shah Nizam-ud-din of Aurangabad

Hazrat Shah Nizam-ud-din of Aurangabad was an important saint; the spiritual disciple and caliph of Hazrat Shaikh Kalim-ul-lah of Shahjahanabad (Delhi) and the father and spiritual guide of Hazrat Maulana Fakhr-ud-din, Fakhr-e-Jahan. He traced his descent from Hazrat Shaikh Shahab-ud-din Umar Suhrawardi[1] and was born in Nigraan (Kakori) in AH 1060.[2]

Initiation into the Sufi Order

He came to Delhi in search of truth. Hearing a great deal about Hazrat Shaikh Kalim-ul-lah of Shahjahanabad (Delhi), he wanted to meet him. When he went to him, a music concert was being held at his monastery and the doors were closed. It was customary in the monastery not to allow a stranger to participate in music concerts. He knocked on the door and was permitted to enter. Those there were greatly surprised that contrary to the general practice, a stranger had been allowed to come in. His Holiness then said to those present: "Know you all, that this person is not a stranger. He is a familiar figure." The reason was that the spiritual guide and teacher of Hazrat Shaikh Kalim-ul-lah of Shahjahanabad had informed him that a person possessing such and such features and named Nizam-ud-din would come to him. Hazrat Shaikh Yahya of Medina had directed him to accept that individual as his spiritual disciple and confer upon him the robe of caliph. Hazrat Shaikh Yahya of Medina had also informed him, that at the time of Hazrat Nizam-ud-din's initiation as a spiritual disciple, he would recite a couplet, which would run:[3] "I have entrusted to thee my wealth/now thou knowest the less or more of the account."

Hazrat Shah Nizam-ud-din began to live in Hazrat Kalim-ul-lah's company acquiring outward knowledge and was later accepted as a spiritual disciple. He then took to renunciation and ascetic practices and eventually was deemed to have attained perfection. The robe of caliph was conferred upon him and the Deccan was entrusted to his care.

He left Delhi and settled permanently in Aurangabad, which became the centre of his moral and spiritual activities. He began to preach the Gospel of Truth and attracted myriads of people into his fold. It is said, that he had one lakh spiritual disciples.

Marriage and children

He married and had five sons, namely, Mohammed Imad-ud-din, Ghulam Moin-ud-din, Ghulam Baha-ud-din, Ghulam Kalim-ul-lah, and Mohammed Fakhr-ud-din, who subsequently became famous as "Fakhr-e-Jahan."

Death

Hazrat Shah Nizam-ud-din of Aurangabad passed away on the twelfth of Ziq'ada in AH 1142. His tomb, situated in Aurangabad, is an object of devotion for thousands of people.

Caliphs

His son, Hazrat Maulana Fakhr-ud-din, was his premier caliph and *sajjadanashin*. Among his prominent caliphs, the following may be mentioned: Khwaja Kamgar Khan, Syed Shah Sharif, Shah Ishaq-ul-lah, Shah Mohammed Ali, Khwaja Nur-ud-din, Ghulam Qadir Khan, Mohammed Yar Beg, Mohammed Jaffer, Sher Mohammed, and Karam Ali Shah.

Traits of character

He showed the utmost courtesy to all, who came contact with him, would offer something to every visitor, and would not hesitate to recommend people for various things. Initially he did not accept presents, but on the direction of his spiritual guide and teacher he began accepting them. He was greatly devoted to the remembrance of God and was often in a state of absorption. He is also the author of several books on mysticism, the most famous among them, entitled *Nizam-ul-Qulub* deals with rituals and spiritual practices.

Teachings

He lays great emphasis on *commemoratio cordis*. According to him, without this, it is difficult to attain spiritual perfection, and therefore one should not neglect it. According to him there is nothing better than the outward remembrance of God, and says that this should be undertaken before eating.

Supernatural powers

- On the occasion of an *'urs* (death anniversary), a music concert was being held in his monastery. A certain person came in and began to discuss with him a certain verse that the *qawwals* were reciting. He politely replied to his query, but when he tried to prolong the discussion, he told him that now it was the time for *qawwali* (music concert) and not for entering into discussion. When he inquired who he was replied that he was Abd-ul-Ghani. To this Hazrat Nizam-ud-din said that one should not lie to the dervishes. Then the man said that he was named Abdullah and left. After some days, the person came to him again. This time he told the man that he was neither called Abdullah nor Abd-ul-Ghani, assaying his real name and domicile. Ashamed, the person became his devotee.
- Nawab Nizam-ul-Mulk Asaf Jah was not yet firmly in control of the Deccan, when Mubariz Khan, at the head of a large army reached Shakar Khera to oppose him. Nawab Nizam-ul-Mulk went to him and asked for his spiritual help and requested him to pray for his victory. After some contemplation, Hazrat Nizam-ud-din said that he would emerge victorious. When he insisted that some sign of this that would provide him solace and satisfaction, he said that there would appear on the tents of Asaf Jah on Thursday, the sandal-mark of a hand. This actually happened on that particular day and he was victorious in the battle.

References

1. *Manaqib-e-Fakhriya,* p. 3.
2. See also *infra,* ch. 76.
3. *Takmila-Siyar-ul-Auliya,* p. 95.

73

Hazrat Mohammed Sallim

Hazrat Mohammed Sallim was the spiritual caliph of Hazrat Miran Shah Bhika. He traces his descent from Hazrat Imam Husain, son of Hazrat Ali, son-in-law of the Holy Prophet Mohammed. His father was Syed Mohammed Raza and he was born in Ropar.

Initiation into the Sufi Order

He was enamoured with the higher life. The inward urge took him to Hazrat Miran Shah Bhika, who accepted him as his spiritual disciple. He was so deeply absorbed in prayer and ascetic practices that for twelve years his whereabouts were not known. This mysterious disappearance was a source of great concern to his parents. Hazrat Miran Shah Bhika learnt of his parents' state through his spiritual powers and summoned him from Andaman Island and sent him straight back to his parents. They had wept so much that they had become blind. Learning that he returned, they were overjoyed and to such a degree that their eyesight recovered. They solemnised his marriage.

Death

Hazrat Mohammed Sallim breathed his last on the twenty-second of Ramazan in AH 1175 and was buried in Ropar.

Supernatural power

Once his nephew and caliph asked him whether a saint was empowered to appear in whatever shape he wished. He replied that this was true. Having done so, he rubbed his hand over his face and appeared as a small boy. He did so again and now looked quite young. When he did it a third time he appeared as an old, white-bearded man.

74

Hazrat Shah Wali-ul-lah

Hazrat Shah Wali-ul-lah was one of the leading scholars and saints of the Indian subcontinent. He traces his relationship from the second caliph of Islam, Amir-ul-Momeneen Hazrat Umar. His father, Hazrat Shah Abd-ur-Rahim, was well versed in outward and inward knowledge, and was a spiritual disciple and caliph of Hazrat Shah Syed Abdullah of Agra.

Hazrat Shah Wali-ul-lah was born on the fourth of Shawwal in AH 1114,[1] and was named Ahmad. He became famous as Wali-ul-lah.[2]

Education and training

His father paid particular attention to his education and training. At the age of five he was sent to a *maktab* by his father. At the age of seven, he completed the Holy *Quran* and began studying other books.

At the age of fifteen he completed his education and turned his attention to the inner graces of life. His father taught him social manners and etiquette, and mysticism[3] and his advice proved an asset Hazrat Wali-ul-lah in later life. He himself says:[4] "And from him I learnt the branches of outward knowledge and the manners of *tariqat* and saw supernatural powers being exhibited by him, had difficulties by him and from him I learnt some of the uses of *tariqat*."

Initiation into the Sufi Order

At the age of fifteen, he became his father's spiritual disciple. The latter had an association with several Orders of mysticism, but essentially belonged to the Naqshbandi. Two years after Hazrat Wali-ul-lah was accepted as a spiritual disciple, his father appointed him caliph and empowered him to accept disciples and ultimately elevated him to be his premier caliph. He also received the robe of caliph from Hazrat Shaikh Abu Tahir of Medina. Before he was seventeen his father passed away. He succeeded him and devoted himself to the diffusion of knowledge and learning, and the propagation of the doctrine of universal truth.

Pilgrimage

He went to Mecca in AH 1143 and performed *hajj*. From Mecca, he went to Medina and found solace at the tomb of the Holy Prophet. This journey afforded him the opportunity of getting into close contact with many saints, sufis, and scholars. During his stay there, he collected *hadis*. He returned to Delhi in AH 1145 and devoted himself to teaching and propagation of truth.

Marriage and children

He was married at the age of fifteen and had four sons: Hazrat Shah Abd-ul-Aziz, Maulana Shah Rafi-ud-din, Maulana Abd-ul-Qadir, and Shah Abd-ul-Ghani.

Death

He died on the nineteenth of Muharram in AH 1176.[5] He lies buried in Delhi.

Traits of character

Hazrat Shah Wali-ul-lah is one of the outstanding literary and spiritual figures of the Indian subcontinent, and was unique in mental and spiritual accomplishments. He was very well-versed in ethics, metaphysics, divine knowledge, and the spiritual sciences.[6] A man of deep faith with the utmost trust in God, he led a very simple life. Author of many books, some of his best known are: *Lamyat; Humyat; Qaule-amil-fi-Bayan-e-Sava-us-Sabeel; Anfas-ul-Arefeen; Tafsir-e-Quran; Taflimat-e-Ilahiya; Makateb-e-Arabi; Khair-e-Kaseer; Fause-ul-Harmen*. He was also a poet, and bore the poetic pseudonym "Amin."

Teachings

He says:[7]

> I will make a will to Seeker of Truth to this effect, that he should not have social intercourse with the rich and the high, the only exception being when it is with the intention of preventing them from perpetuating tyranny or preparing them for the performance of good deeds. And neither, should he keep company of the ignorant sufis nor of those ignorant people devoted to prayers and nor of the jurists who are only devoted to prayers and neither of those

acquainted with *hadis*, who are opposed to *fiqh*. . . .

Prescribing some "Dos" for the Seeker of Truth, he says:[8]

The Seeker of Truth should be a learned sufi. He should have nothing to do with the world. He should be ever absorbed in sublime thought, should be inclined towards, the *sunnah* of the Holy Prophet, pursue the search of *hadis*. . . .

Concerning seclusion he says:[9]

One should be confined to seclusion to the extent that the performance of good deeds does not suffer, e.g., inquiring about the condition of the invalid, offering condolence to the sad and the afflicted, and attending literary societies. . . . Barring the aforesaid occasions, one should prefer seclusion and solitude.

Sayings

- Men are endowed with different types of abilities and everybody attains perfection according to his inherent ability.
- Among the causes of accident, one cause is luck.
- The object of accepting an individual as a spiritual disciple is to make him perfect in mandates and to prevent him from un-Islamic things and to guide him towards inner satisfaction and to free him from ignoble habits and to endow him with commendable qualities.

References

1. *Malfoozat Shah Abdul Aziz*, p. 56.
2. *Faisla-Wahdat-ul-Wajood-was-Shahood*, p. 2.
3. *Anfas-ul-Arefeen*.
4. *Qaule-Jamil-fi-Bayan-e-Sava-us-Sabeel*, pp. 151-52.
5. *Malfoozat Shah Abdul Aziz*, p. 56.
6. *Siyar-ul-Akhyar*.
7. *Quale-Jamil-fi-Bayan-e-Sava-us-Sabeel*, p. 136.
8. Ibid.
9. *Humyat*, Urdu trans., *Qatrat*, p. 18.

75

Hazrat Mirza Jane-Janan Mazhar Shaheed

Hazrat Mirza Jane-Janan Mazhar Shaheed was a perfect dervish and a mystic poet of the Indian subcontinent. He was a Syed, tracing his relationship from Hazrat Ali, the son-in-law of the Holy Prophet Mohammed.

His forefathers migrated from Taif to Turkestan in AH 800. On his return from exile in Iran, Humayun brought with him two brothers named Mahboob Khan and Baba Khan. The two brothers belonged to the family of Hazrat Mazhar Shaheed's forefathers and traced their relationship from Amir Kamal-ud-din. He traced his relationship from Baba Khan.[1]

His mother traced her relationship from Tamerlane.

His father, Yehram Khan, served Aurangzeb. In the last days of his life he had severed his connections with worldly affairs, and had been spiritually benefited by a dervish belonging to the Qadiri Order of sufis.

Forecast about his birth

He was born in AH 1113[2] and was named Shams-ud-din; Maulana Jalal-ud-din Rumi, the famous author of the *Masnavi*, had forecast his birth some five hundred years earlier.[3]

Education and training

He acquired ceremonial knowledge during his father's lifetime. Haji Mohammed Afzal of Sialkot, the pupil of Shaikh Abdullah Ibn-e-Salim of Mecca, taught him the books on *hadis*. Hafiz Abd-ur-Rasool of Delhi, the pupil of Shaikh Abd-ul-Khaliq Shauqi, taught him the Holy *Quran*.

He completed his education when he was twenty years old. Even at this early age he felt no attraction towards the world, and was indeed disenchanted with mundane affairs. He entered a new world of light, emphasising the need for self-purification leading to inner illumination.

Initiation into the Sufi Order

Going to Hazrat Syed Nur Mohammed of Budaun, he begged him to accept him as a humble spiritual disciple, which the holy man did. After sometime Hazrat Nur Mohammed conferred upon him the robe of caliph of the Naqshbandi Order of the sufis. He lived in the company of his spiritual guide and teacher and engaged himself in ascetic practices, rigours, and self-denial, as well as acquiring the graces of the spiritual life.

His search continued. After his spiritual guide and teacher passed away he met many dervishes and saints of the Naqshbandi Order, from whom he received spiritual blessings.[4]

Subsequently, he went to Hazrat Shaikh Mohammed Abid Sunami and stayed with him for sometime and received his spiritual blessings. Ultimately, he was permitted by him to enrol spiritual disciples and was given the robe of caliph of the Qadiri, Suhrawardi, and Chishti Orders of the sufis. He was thus a member of all the four main Sufi Orders, and so equipped, began to preach the Gospel of Truth.

Last days

In the last days of his life, Hazrat Mirza Sahab devoted himself wholly rituals and prayers, deeply absorbed in contemplation. Many disciples entered his fold.

Hazrat Mirza Sahab knew that his end was approaching. Mulla Nasim came to see him and, bidding him farewell, he said with tears in his eyes: "It does not appear, that we shall meet again."

One day, offering thanks to God for the blessings conferred upon him, he said:

> There is no desire in my heart, which may not have been fulfilled. The real benefactor elevated me by real peace, gave me much knowledge, enable me to perform good deeds, conferred upon me the supernatural power of *istiqamat* (permanence), gave me all that was needed in the Order, endowed me with the supernatural and other mystic powers, sent to me the pure to acquire spiritual blessing, and enabled me to cause them to reach high positions and stations.

He expressed a desire for martyrdom, which brings man very close to God.

Death

Hazrat Mirza Sahab made a will expressing the wish that in the matters regarding his coffin and burial, the *sunnah* of the Holy Prophet should be strictly adhered to, as also in the performance of his funeral rites. His followers and devotees he willed should strictly adhere to the *sunnah*. They should not take the real object to be distinct and separate from God Almighty and the matters to be followed to be separate and apart from the Holy Prophet Mohammed. They should remain in touch with the ceremonies and the habits of the dervishes, should avoid the company of people engrossed in the world, and update their religious and spiritual education and knowledge. On Wednesday, the seventh of Muharram, he was fatally attacked by a person belonging to the hordes of Najaf Khan. There was profuse and continual bleeding for three days, and all hope of recovery lost. He expired on the tenth of Muharram in AH 1195 after the sunset prayers, thereby fulfilling his wish to achieve martyrdom. He was buried in Delhi.

Caliph

Hazrat Shah Abdullah, better known as Shah Ghulam Ali Ahmadi, was his prominent caliph.

Traits of character

He was a perfect dervish and an embodiment of truth, integrity and sacrifice. He was a fluent speaker, a good conversationalist, and a man of simple habits. His vast knowledge of men and matters, of spirit and spiritualism, and of the *shari'at* and *tariqat*, combined with his mystic way of life, penances, rigours, and ascetic practices, won for him spiritual greatness.

He was unique in precept and practice, and strictly adhered to the precepts of the Holy Prophet. Hazrat Mirza Sahab was a man of scholarly habits and literary taste. His discourses and letters reveal his deep knowledge and learning, and represent a unique contribution to the mystic knowledge. He was also an outstanding poet.

Teachings

He says:[5]

> Prayer is a combination of conditions, brought about by the recitation of the Holy *Quran*, rosary, benedictions to the Holy Prophet Mohammed, and seeking forgiveness for ones own sins. The correct and the most real conditions are obtained in prayer, provided the conditions attached to it are fulfilled.
>
> During the blessed month of Ramazan, the inner affiliation is immensely improved. It is necessary that when observing a fast one should abstain from backbiting and telling a lie, otherwise the fast is no more than mere hunger.
>
> Whatever trouble, pain and suffering created for us from people is the result of our action. If respect is shown to elders and love and regard to those younger than us, then nobody can do you wrong.

In his system known as the Mazharya system, the first indication that is given to the seeker of Fath-ul-Bab.[6] At that time, the heart, which has become unmindful of its reality, is reminded of its former state and is attracted towards that. Very soon the flame of graceful light, which had begun rising from the heart, now appears from the body. The heart of an individual, by its very nature, is bright and glittering, but generally, because it becomes engrossed with the material world and too many contacts, it has become black and devoid of light, like coal. But a sincere seeker, taking faith and devotion with him, can go to some perfect dervish and a gifted spiritual guide. The spiritual guide will then instruct him to devote himself to the remembrance of God and casts his gaze upon him. By the grace of his attention, the light of remembrance is generated in his heart. The black coal, as it was, now begins to glitter, and when his whole heart is illumined by the light of remembrance, then there arises from it a flame of graceful light.

Hazrat Mirza Sahab gives the following instructions:

- Take to piety and chastity.
- Have patience and trust in God.
- Spend more time in the company of the saints, for the friendship of the friends of God is the means of being near to God.

- Cultivate contentment.
- Eradicate greed and avarice from your heart.
- Repose no hope in friends and strangers, and regard them as being of no consequence.
- Do not look down upon anyone.
- Regard yourself as the lowliest and the humblest.
- Do not take pride in your prayers and worship.
- As far as possible oppose your self, but not to such an extent that it tires you and deprives you of the pleasure of prayer.

Supernatural powers

- The famous saint Hazrat Shah Mohammed Afaq of Delhi was born as a result of his prayer.
- As has been said above, he was fatally attacked and mortally wounded by a person belonging to the horde of Najaf Khan. Najaf Khan reaped disastrous consequences, dying that very year bereft of power.

References

1. *Kalimat-ut-Tayyebat* (*Maktoobat Hazrat Mirza Sahab*), p. 12.
2. *Maktoobat-e-Mirza Sahab*, p. 13.
3. *Miftah-ut-Tawarikh*.
4. *Maktoobat-e-Mirza Sahab*, p. 13.
5. *Kalimat-ut-Tayyebat* (*Malfoozat Mirza Sahab*), p. 84.
6. *Hidayat-ut-Talebeen*, p. 17.

76

Hazrat Maulana Mohammed Fakhr-ud-din

Hazrat Maulana Mohammed Fakhr-ud-din was the pride of the Indian subcontinent. Through Hazrat Shaikh Shahab-ud-din Suhrawardi, he traces his descent from the first caliph of Islam Amir-ul-Momeneen Hazrat Abu Bakr Siddique. He has called himself "Siddique."[1]

His forefathers settled in a town named Nigraan (Kakori) in Oudh. His father, Hazrat Nizam-ud-din, when he came to Delhi first became a spiritual disciple and subsequently caliph of Hazrat Shaikh Kalim-ul-lah of Shahjahanabad (Delhi). He then left for the Deccan and settled in Aurangabad, where he lived, worked and died. His mother belonged to the family of Hazrat Syed Mohammed Gesoo Daraz.[2]

He was born in Aurangabad in AH 1126.[3]

His father conveyed the news of his birth to his spiritual guide and teacher Hazrat Shaikh Kalim-ul-lah of Shahjahanabad (Delhi), who was delighted and sent his own clothes to him. He named him as "Maulana Fakhr-ud-din" and said, "He is my son."[4]

Hazrat Shaikh Kalim-ul-lah of Shahjahanabad prophesied that "This boy will illuminate the city of Shahjahanabad by the light of his preachings." That is exactly what happened.

He had four brothers.[5] Hazrat Mohammed Ism'ail was his elder brother. His three step-brothers were Ghulam Moin-ud-din, Ghulam Baha-ud-din, and Ghulam Kalim-ul-lah, and all of them became his spiritual disciples,[6] as did his sister.

Reasons for calling him "Mohibbun-Nabi"

He is addressed and invoked as "Mohibbun-Nabi," the Beloved of the Holy Prophet. That is because, when he visited the Court of Khwaja Gharib Nawaz in Ajmer, he met a person who had come there to get some serious problem resolved. The person received in a dream an indication from Khwaja Gharib Nawaz that he should know and recognise Hazrat Maulana. He will solve the difficult and his name is "Mohibbun-Nabi." The person searched him out and finding him related the whole dream. Another reason assigned is that once he was present at the tomb of Hazrat Nasir-ud-din Chiragh of Delhi on the occasion of the *'urs*, he saw in a dream, that Hazrat Nasir-ud-din Chiragh of Delhi gave him something from the food meant for free distribution and told him:[7] "You are Mohibbun-Nabi."

Education and training

His father paid special attention to his training and education. His father made him study some books, notable among them being *Sharh Wiqaya, Mashariq-ul-Anwar, Nafahat-ul-Uns,* and a book on medicine and a book on military science. He then went to Miyan Mohammed Jan Giyo who made him study *Fasoos-ul-Hukm* and other books. The thirst for knowledge and learning led him to Maulvi Abd-ul-Hakim, who besides being an erudite scholar, was well-versed in jurisprudence, who taught him *Hidaya*.[8]

Childhood

He did not take pleasure in playing with boys of his age. It was as if he had been selected for the special mission from childhood.

One day, when he was seven years old, he was pressing his father's feet and felt a little drowsy. The Holy Prophet gave him five dried grapes and when he awoke he saw these in his hand. In the meanwhile, his father had also awaken and, clutching his hand told him: "I too have my share in these."[9] Together they ate up all the grapes.

Initiation into the Sufi Order

His father accepted him as his spiritual disciple long before he became a major, and at the age of fifteen conferred upon him the robe of caliph. A year later his father passed away.

Ascetic practices

After his father's death, he took to ascetic practices and rigours, devoting himself to prayers, penances, and fasts, not allowing even those close to him to learn of his condition. One day, an associate and spiritual fellow Kamgar Khan who had also been his father's disciple suggested that he establish a remembrance circle at which devotees should remember God aloud. In response to this he smiled and said that he should pray for him, to enable him to accomplish this. Khwaja Kamgar Khan raised his hands to pray, but to his deep regret, he suddenly found himself deprived of the ability to bestow spiritual blessings and spiritual wealth. He apologised, imploring Hazrat Maulana forgiveness. He pardoned him and conferred upon him not only the spiritual wealth and blessings he had been deprived of but gave him something in addition.[10]

Years of service and subsequently

At his request, Nawab Nizam-ud-Daula Nasir Jung appointed him as Naib Bakhshi or Sipih Salar. After performing his duties for three years, he resigned the post and went to Aurangabad.[11] One day, when he absorbed in prayers, he heard a voice saying: "Break the chains and be free, O son." Hearing this voice, he thought of going to Delhi. He went to his father's tomb and the inspiration that he received there confirmed him in his resolve. He reached Delhi at last by AH 1160.[12]

Six months after his arrival in Delhi, he went to Pak Pattan to be benefited by the spiritual blessings emanating from the tomb of Hazrat Baba Farid-ud-din Mas'ud Ganj-e-Shakar.

On the way to Pak Pattan, he stayed in Panipat for four nights and derived spiritual ecstasy from the tomb of Hazrat Bu Ali Shah Qalandar was benefited from his spiritual graces and blessings.

Marriage

He accepting the advice of physicians, married in Aurangabad. A son was born, who was named Ghulam Qutb-ud-din.[13]

Death

Hazrat Maulana breathed his last on the twenty-seventh of Jamade-us-Sani in AH 1199[14] at the age of seventy-three. His tomb in Mehrauli is an object of veneration.

Caliphs

Some of his prominent caliphs were: Hazrat Khwaja Nur Mohammed Maharwi; Hazrat Maulana Mir Zia-ud-din; Hazrat Maulvi Khuda Bakhsh; Nawab Ghazi-ud-din Khan whose poetic pseudonym is "Nizam;" Shah Fath-ul-lah; Maulvi Mohammed Ghous; Shah Rooh-ul-lah; Shah Qamr-ud-din, and Hazrat

Mohammed Ghous.

Traits of character

Hazrat Maulana Mohammed Fakhr-ud-din combined in himself all the outward and inward graces of life. He was polite, courteous, accommodating, and obliging. He received everyone with a broad smile and extended every respect and regard, irrespective of his position, status, or vocation.[15] Even when ill he would stand to pay respect to anyone who called upon him.

He had a sacrificing nature and was intensely devoted to prayer. He took delight in rigours, ascetic practices, penances, and fasts and derived spiritual joy and solace from meditation and contemplation. His generosity knew no bounds: whatever offerings were received, he would distribute them all, refusing to keep anything for himself. He was so humble, meek, and gentle that when his sweeper, Peera, did not come to his monastery for two continuous days, he inquired about him. On learning that he was ill, he himself went to see Peera, gave him some money, and apologised for not looking after him earlier.[16]

He was a man well versed in knowledge and learning. His letters set out a mystic philosophy of great profundity and have been published as *Ruqqat-e-Murshidi*. He is an author of several books, the best known of which are: *Fakhr-ul-Hasan; Aqa'id-e-Nizamiya; Sirat-e-Muhammadiya;* and *Ain-ul-Yaqeen*.

Teachings

His teachings are the signposts of a high spiritual life. Some of them are:

> He says: Attainment of nearness to God is in fact the real purpose. The ways are different, whether it be by remembrance aloud, or by remembrance secret, or by contemplation, or by meditation, or by concentration.[17]
>
> Unconsciousness is a great blessing. One should be thankful for it. But one treading on the spiritual path should not be content with it. He should in fact treat it as the means to an end; a end being the achievement of the real purpose and the high spiritual stage. Unconsciousness is caused even by intoxicants, such as opium. The difference is that this type of unconsciousness is not commendable, but condemnable. On attaining the state of

unconsciousness, one should be even more devoted to ascetic practices and penances.[18]

As far as possible, one should be devoted to remembrance, but not to such a degree that it has an adverse effect on the person's health.[19]

Sayings

- Remembrance of God is the best of all.
- The world is the crop for the world hereafter.
- He who trades the spiritual path, should not be deceived by himself.
- Man is the manifestation of all the qualities of God.

Supernatural powers

- On his way to Delhi from Aurangabad he met an old blind woman who requested him to restore her eyesight. He rubbed his hand over her eyes and she was immediately able to see.[20]
- One of his disciples, Qazi Anwar Zia, was suffering from consumption and, losing all hope of living, came to see him. He embraced him, and immediately after that Qazi Sahab recovered and felt such a sense of strength and vitality that it appeared as if had never been ill.

References

1. *Takmila-Siyar-ul-Auliya,* p. 94.
2. *Khulasat-ul-Fawaid.*
3. *Manaqib-e-Fakhriya,* p. 4.
4. *Takmila Siyar-ul-Auliya,* p. 105.
5. *Manaqib-e-Fakhriya.*
6. *Takmila Siyar-ul-Auliya,* p. 106; *Manaqib-e-Fakhriya,* p. 5.
7. *Takmila Siyar-ul-Auliya,* p. 114.
8. Ibid., pp. 106-7.
9. Ibid., pp. 105-6; *Manaqib-e-Fakhriya,* p. 5.
10. *Manaqib-e-Fakhriya,* pp. 7-8.
11. Ibid., p. 6.
12. Ibid., p. 11.
13. *Takmila Siyar-ul-Auliya,* p. 120.
14. *Manaqib-e-Fakhriya,* pp. 51-52.
15. Ibid., p. 16.
16. Ibid., p. 18.
17. *Ruqqat-e-Murshidi,* p. 50.
18. Ibid., pp. 62-64.
19. Ibid., pp. 64-65.
20. *Fakhr-ut-Talebeen,* pp. 33-34; *Manaqib-e-Fakhriya,* pp. 9-10.

77

Hazrat Shah Abul-Barkat

Hazrat Shah Abul-Barkat was the spiritual caliph of Hazrat Shah Rukn-ud-din Ashiq and was born in AH 1125.

Initiation into the Sufi Order

He lived in the company of Hazrat Shah Rukn-ud-din Ashiq for three years. During this period he served him so well, that he not only expressed his admiration but made him the recipient of special favours and spiritual graces.

Seeing him so devoted to his service, Hazrat Shah Rukn-ud-din Ashiq asked one of his devotees to persuade him to enlist himself as his spiritual disciple. When the message was conveyed to him, he remained silent. The next day, he was again reminded. This time he replied that there were so many others who should also be persuaded. When the reply was conveyed to Hazrat Shah Rukn-ud-din, he asked the devotee to go to him again and convey that a cow does not give her milk to her calf without reason. Had there been no specific reason for this the cow would not have allowed the calf to suck her blood. There was a secret and it had a deeper significance and implication. He conveyed that his object was not just to enlist him as his spiritual disciple: it was quite likely that he might attain salvation by doing so. He agreed and became his spiritual disciple.

Stay in Azimabad, Gwalior, and Allahabad

After Hazrat Rukn-ud-din Ashiq passed away he stayed in Azimabad (Patna) for sometime, preaching and propagating the Gospel of Truth. At the invitation of the late His Highness Daulat Rao Scindia, he visited Gwalior, and during his stay there, people from all communities and denominations flocked to him. From Gwalior, he went to Allahabad where he stayed for sometime.

Death

Hazrat Shah Abul-Barkat passed away in AH 1225 in Allahabad at the age of one hundred.[1] He was initially buried in Allahabad, and subsequently the corpse was reburied in Azimabad.

Caliph

Hazrat Shah Wajihullah was his prominent spiritual caliph.

Traits of character

He led a simple life dedicated to the steadfast pursuit of truth. He believed in service, sharing, and sacrifice, and reposed the utmost faith in God. His life was suffused with contentment, hope, belief, and faith.

Supernatural power

When his body was disinterred to be taken to Azimabad, it was found to be in exactly the same condition in which it had been buried. Those assembled to see it, were extraordinarily surprised.

REFERENCE

1. *Israr-e-Abul-Ila*, p. 149.

78

Hazrat Syed Mohammed Azam

Hazrat Syed Mohammed Azam, born in Ropar, was the spiritual caliph of Hazrat Syed Mohammed Sallim and the nephew of Hazrat Syed Mohammed Sallim.

Initiation into the Sufi Order

After acquiring external knowledge he was attracted to the mystic way of life. He became a spiritual disciple of his uncle Hazrat Mohammed Sallim, undertook spiritual practices, and attained spiritual perfection. His spiritual guide and teacher conferred upon him the robe of caliph and appointed him as his *sajjadanashin*.

Death

Hazrat Syed Mohammed Azam breathed his last on the twenty-ninth of Rabi-us-Sani in AH 1227.

Caliphs

His prominent spiritual caliphs were: Hafiz Muhammed Musa, Syed Bhika son of Ghulam Mohammed, Khwaja Bakhsh, and his son Mohammed Bakhsh.

Traits of character

He was hospitable and entertaining; very humble and gentle. He did see himself as being a cut above the rest. He served and helped people with all the means at his command. Sometimes he would sit at the door of the mosque. If anyone asked him to fetch salt or any other thing, he would run to the market to do so. He was the least concerned about his status or position.

He would pour water into his food. Someone asked why he did so, to which he replied that it was to stop himself from offering it to others.

He was indifferent to the pleasures of the world. Once he was entertained by one of his spiritual disciples. After he had left, the host discovered that there had been no salt in the food. He went to him and apologised for this, to which he replied that he did not cognise the taste of salt and spices.

79

Hazrat Shah Abd-ul-Aziz

Hazrat Shah Abd-ul-Aziz, born in AH 1159, was the learned son of a learned father, Hazrat Shah Waliullah. He was a saint and the son of a saint. An outstanding scholar, an eminent sufi, a prominent saint, and a great sage, he was one of the most learned men of his time. He has left a lasting legacy that continues to guide people today and will continue to guide future generations. He received his education from his father.

Initiation into the Sufi Order

He was his father's spiritual disciple and caliph and followed his father's lead. About it, his father Hazrat Shah Waliullah said:[1]

> In fact God Almighty has conferred upon me and the people of my time great favour, because he has favoured me with that system of spiritualism which is very close to other systems. . . . Whosoever will think of acquiring the system, God Almighty will surely reward him, for God has given me this information by inspiration to this effect that: 'We have appointed thee the *imam* (head) of this system and have caused thee to reach the heights of the skies and from today onward have closed all the other ways and systems of attaining nearness to God, except this one and that system pertains to thy love and following. So, the person bearing enmity to thee has been deprived of the heavenly and the earthly blessings. In other words, thy enemies have been deprived of all the good and blessings.'

He lost his father when he was about seventeen years old. After to draw his father's death in AH 1176, he succeeded him and continued inspiration from him.

Stay in Delhi

Hazrat Shah Abd-ul-Aziz passed his entire life in Delhi engaged in teaching and propagating the knowledge of the *hadis*. To be counted among his pupils implied social distinction. His testimony concerning outward and inward knowledge was treated as a passport to success. He counted among his pupils some eminent learned men, scholars, sufis, jurists, and those well-versed in the *hadis*. Among them were: Maulana Shah Rafi-ud-din, his brother; Mohammed Ishaq, his maternal grandson; Mufti Sadr-ud-din; Maulana Rashid-ud-din; Hazrat Shah Ghulam Ali; Maulvi Abd-ul-Hai; Maulvi Mohammed Isma'il Shaheed; Maulana Mir Mahboob Ali; and Maulana Hasan Ali.

Children

He had three daughters, who all died during his lifetime, and no son, his eldest daughter was given in marriage to 'Eisa; the second was married to Shaikh Mohammed Afzal son of Shaikh Ahmad, the third to Abd-ul-Hai.

Death

Hazrat Shah Abd-ul-Aziz contracted an aliment that continued to threaten his life. His protracted illness made him very weak, causing him to preach only twice a week. During his illness, on the appointed day he thought of standing, two persons supported him, but as began preaching they left him there alone yet he continued to preach.

He apportioned all his goods. He used to recite the following: "I too present myself with the commentary of the Holy *Quran* in my bosom."

He wore coarse clothes: a long coarse khadi shirt and pyjamas. He made a will to the effect that, "My coffin should be like my dress." About his funeral prayers, he willed that it should be held outside the city and that the king should not be allowed to accompany the funeral procession.[2]

He passed away in AH 1239. His will was scrupulously observed with the high and the low joining his funeral prayers. Such a huge crowd attended, that the funeral prayers were conducted fifty-five times. He was buried near his father outside the Turkman Gate in Delhi.

Traits of character

Hazrat Shah Abd-ul-Aziz's command of outward and inward knowledge was unique. He was well-versed in the knowledge of the *hadis* and was a saint who propagated and preached the Gospel of Truth. He was pious and extremely devoted to prayers. He was generous, kind, and hospitable. He dressed simply and ate frugally.

He wrote a number of books, the chief amongst which are: *Bustan-ul-Muhaddeseen; Ejala Nafai Usool-e-Hadis; Sharh Meezan-ul-Mantiq; Risala Ghana; Risala Wasila-e-Nijat; Risala Tafzil.* His *fatwas* are famous, his letters inspiring, and he wrote some poetry.[3]

Teachings

There are four types of saints. Some are absorbed. Some are devoted to *hadis* such as *qutb, ghous,* etc. Some are innovators and some are those who take to seclusion.[4]

Attention is of four kinds, namely imprinting, inspiring, absorbing, and the fourth type, that all the qualities of the one giving attention should be mirrored in that of the recipient to such a degree that the outward shape may appear to be the same.[5]

The illumined are of four kinds. Firstly, there are the *salik majzoob,* who in the beginning strove for and in the end received enlightenment. They are the best of all. Secondly, there are the *majzoob Salik,* who were at first elevated with absorption and then took to the path of enlightenment, just like Prophet Moses (May peace be upon him) who went out to fetch fire and was blessed with a vision of God. Thirdly, there are the *salik bakht,* who are not elevated to be absorbed. And fourthly, there are the *majzoob*-absorbed, pure and simple, who through a vision of God have lost consciousness.[6]

Undoubtedly, un-Islamic actions do bring about impurity and some un-Islamic actions such as cunning, treachery, fraud, deception, pride, vanity, haughtiness, self-assertion, worldly pursuit, lust for power, etc., have such an adverse effect, that they totally severe the affiliation that the seeker has been able to establish with God. Some actions have only this effect, that if some minor sin is committed by mistake, the heart instead of experiencing light feels itself surrounded with rust and darkness.[7] The perfect learned man is one, who is well-versed in four things, namely, teaching, study of books, reading and writing, and religious discussion.

In reciting the Holy *Quran,* the outward signs of reverence are that one should be respectful and should sit with one's face towards the *qibla* and pronounce every word clearly, distinctly, and correctly and to stop at the places where this is enjoined. The inward signs of reverence are that the beginner should think that as he is reading God Almighty is sitting and listening as a teacher. And he who has reached perfection should think, that he is hearing the Holy Book directly from the mouth of God.

Once a bishop came to him alongwith Mr. Mitciff. It was decided that if in the course of the religious discussion the bishop was vanquished, would pay him a sum of two thousand rupees. If he was defeated, Mr. Mitciff would pay two thousand rupees on his behalf to the bishop. The question put by the bishop was: "Your Prophet is the beloved of God. Your Prophet did not make any representation to God at the time of the assassination of Imam Husain, although the beloved of the beloved is more beloved still. God would have surely paid attention." Hazrat Shah Abd-ul-Aziz's reply was: "When the Holy Prophet went to make the representation, a voice was heard from the curtain invisible saying that 'it is true the people have perpetuated tyranny over your maternal grandson and have assassinated him. But we, at that time, were reminded of the crucifixion of our own son—Christ, and that made our grief fresh.' Hearing this, our Holy Prophet fell silent." This reply silenced the bishop who, having lost paid the amount due.

The *fatwas* of Hazrat Shah Abd-ul-Aziz are admirable and logical. A certain person posed the question: "Is it permissible to offer funeral prayers for prostitutes?" He replied: "When the funeral prayers of those who are on familiar terms with them are offered, why then should not funeral prayers for prostitutes not be offered."[7]

A certain merchant, when leaving Delhi, told his wife: "If you go to your father's home, then it will tantamount to my divorcing you." When the merchant returned he was informed that his wife had been to her father's home. He asked for a *fatwa* from the *ulama*. The *ulama* were unanimous in their *fatwas* that the divorce was complete. The merchant loved his wife very dearly and was deeply saddened and downcast. He approached Hazrat Abd-ul-Aziz for his opinion. After a patient hearing he delivered this *fatwa*:

> The woman went there, when her father was dead. The house then did not belong to her father, but in fact belonged to her then. So, she went to her own house and not to her father's house. Therefore, there could be no divorce. All the *ulama* agreed with

his interpretation.[8]

Sayings

- By the remembrance of God, the heart feels satisfied.
- Love is necessary for ability.
- Absorption is, pure and simple, the blessing of God.
- Every religion ordains the protection of five things, namely, wisdom, of the self, of religion, of genealogy, and of wealth.
- An individual should be sympathetic, and particularly so those near and dear to him.

Supernatural powers

Hazrat Shah Abd-ul-Aziz used to tie his turban up to his eyes when going to the Central Mosque on Friday for prayers. A person called Fasih-ud-din asked why he did so. Instead replying directly, he pulled his turban on his head and fainted. When he recovered consciousness, he revealed that of the five or six thousand people in the Central Mosque, one hundred or so amongst them had human form. Of the rest, some were in the shape of monkeys, some in that of bears, and others were in the form of other animals. He told Fasih-ud-din that this was why he covered his eyes with his turban.[9]

Colonel Iskiz reposed great faith in him and, as he had no child, once requested him to pray for him. He prayed and conveyed the good news to him that his wish would be fulfilled and a son, would be born to him. This son, when born, he said should be named Yusuf (Joseph). This was done.[10]

References

1. *Risala Tafhimat-e-Ilahiya,* trans.
2. *Kamalat-e-Azizi,* p. 191.
3. *Malfoozat-e-Shah Abdul Aziz,* p. 14.
4. Ibid., p. 9.
5. Ibid., p. 18.
6. Ibid., p. 20.
7. Ibid., p. 21.
8. *Kamalat-e-Azizi,* p.176.
9. Ibid; *Fatwa-e-Aziziya,* pp. 390-91.
10. *Kamalat-e-Azizi,* pp. 180-81.

80

Hazrat Hafiz Musa

Hazrat Hafiz Musa was the spiritual caliph of Hazrat Shaikh Mohammed Azam. He completed his education at an early age and committed the Holy *Quran* to memory.

Initiation into the Sufi Order

Hazrat Hafiz Musa was of a mystic turn of mind. After he had completed his education, he devoted himself to prayer. Not satisfied by mere prayers, he set out in search of a spiritual guide and teacher. His inner urge took him to Ropar and there he enrolled himself as a spiritual disciple of Hazrat Syed Mohammed Azam. He lived in his company and acquired the graces of spiritual life. Subsequently, his spiritual guide and teacher conferred upon him the robe of caliph and entrusted all his spiritual disciples to him, and he attended to all their moral and spiritual requirements.

After his spiritual guide and teacher died, he left Ropar and went to Manikpur and settled there permanently. He devoted himself to the training of his spiritual disciples. To some he would suggest *commemoratio cordis*, to others loud repetition of the name "Allah," suggesting a ritual or spiritual practice to each according to his need. He would hold training classes both in the morning and the evening. If any of his spiritual disciples did not attend these circle he would inquire why and if the response did not satisfy him, he would turn him out of the monastery.

The mystery

He had a dog called Kalwa which used to live on the doorsteps of the monastery and there would be regularly fed. One day the dog disappeared. On inquiries being made, Hafiz Sahab was told that the dog had gone out to loiter with others in the vicinity. He instructed the inmates of the monastery not to allow the dog to enter the monastery again.

After sometime the dog returned, and was turned out by Hafiz Sahab. The dog went off another, search for him was made, but he was not found. In the evening, the dog was found dead and in accordance with Hafiz Sahab's orders was covered in a white cloth and buried.

Death

He passed away on the sixteenth of Ramazan in AH 1247 and was buried in Manakpur.

Caliphs

Hafiz Syed Mohammed Husain was his most outstanding caliph.

A gem of truth

He says that the grave of the spiritual guide is the chest of the spiritual disciple.

Traits of character

Hafiz Sahab was humble and kind, and shunned publicity. He disliked and condemned formalities and did not wish that anyone to praise, admire, or extol him.

He had great regard and respect for seekers of truth and paid special attention to his guests, to whom he would extend great courtesy and kindness.

Hafiz Sahab was generous. He used to receive *fatuhat* (unsought gifts) but he would spend all the money so received on the maintenance and upkeep of the dervishes and distribute all the gifts. If any money remained, this would be sent to widows, orphans, and the handicapped.

He was a man of simple habits and had a forbearing nature, taking any criticism in his stride. When his spiritual guide and teacher passed away he, after conducting his funeral prayers, returned to his tenement. People criticised him vehemently for this, but he was unmoved, only remarking that they did not understand the reality.

81

Hazrat Shah Niyaz Ahmad

Hazrat Shah Niyaz Ahmad was a renowned saint and founded the Niyazi Order. His forefathers belonged to the royal family of Bukhara. One of his forefathers, Ayat-ul-lah Ulwi, migrated to India and settled in Multan. His grandson Azmat-ul-lah Ulwi left Multan and settled in Sirhind.[1]

Hazrat Niyaz Ahmad was an Ulwi Syed from his paternal family and a Rizvi Syed from the maternal side. His father, Shah Mohammed Rehmat-ul-lah, who earned the title of "Hakim-e-Ilahi," left Sirhind and settled in Delhi in AH 1160 and accepted the post of Qazi.

His mother, Bibi Ladoo, was known and addressed as "Bibi Gharib Nawaz." She was the daughter of Syed Maulana Sa'id-ud-din, who traced his descent from Hazrat Iman Musa Raza. He was a spiritual caliph of Hazrat Shaikh Kalim-ul-lah of Shahjahanabad (Delhi). Hazrat Bibi Gharib Nawaz was the spiritual disciple of Hazrat Shaikh Mohi-ud-din Giyasnami of the Qadiri Order.

He was born in Sirhind. His name was Raz Ahmad, but he was better known as Niyaz Ahmad. He came to Delhi alongwith his parents and settled there. He was well-educated and well-trained completing his education, when he was fifteen years old.

Initiation into the Sufi Order

His mother, Hazrat Bibi Gharib Nawaz, entrusted him to the care of Hazrat Maulana Fakhr-ud-din, better known as "Fakhre Jahan," who imparted to him inner training. He used to call him as "Miyan." At his request, Hazrat Maulana Fakhre Jahan initiated him as his spiritual disciple, at the initiation asking him to clasp lower garment[2] in a ceremony known as Bait-e-Talbi.

One day, Hazrat Maulana Fakhre Jahan told him that Hazrat Shaikh Abd-ul-Qadir of Jilan, better known as Ghous-ul-Azam Piran-e-Pir, had introduced him to a certain person who would be sent to initiate him as a spiritual disciple. Hazrat Ghous-ul-Azam had added that the person who was being sent was closely related to him and that Hazrat Maulana should have him (Hazrat Niyaz Ahmad) accepted by him.

Time passed while he expectantly awaited the arrival in Delhi of this individual. After the passage of six months, Hazrat Maulana said one day, that Hazrat Ghous-ul-Azam had informed him that the person had reached Delhi three days earlier. He was traced at the Central Mosque in Delhi where he was staying and Hazrat Maulana was fully satisfied that his features matched those of the individual who Ghous-ul-Azam had indicated.

Hazrat Maulana placed a trayful of sweets on his head and holding Hazrat Niyaz Ahmad's hand in his right hand, left for the Central Mosque. Seeing the person from Baghdad, he at once recognised him and placed the tray before him. Hazrat Shah Niyaz Ahmad was initiated as a spiritual disciple therein the arch of the mosque. After accepting him as one of his spiritual disciples, Hazrat Syed Abdullah of Baghdad suggested that he undertake certain rituals and practices.

Hazrat Shah Niyaz Ahmad also received spiritual blessings from the following saints from various Sufi Orders. Syed Abdullah of Baghdad and Hazrat Mohi-ud-din Giyasanami who both belonged to the Qadiri Order; in the Suhrawardi Order from Hazrat Maulana Fakhre Jahan; in the Chishti-Nizami Orders from Hazrat Maulan Sa'id-ud-din Rizvi and Hazrat Maulana Fakhre Jahan; and in Chishti-Sabri-Naqshbandi Orders from Hakim-e-Ilahi Shah Rahmat-ul-lah.

Marriage and children

He married the daughter of Hazrat Syed Abdullah of Baghdad who died after some years leaving no issue. He married again and had two sons, Hazrat Shah Nizam-ud-din Husain and Shah Nasir-ud-din.

Death

Hazrat Shah Niyaz Ahmed passed away on the sixth of Jamadi-us-Sani in AH 1250. His tomb in Bareilly is an object of veneration for myriads of people.

Caliphs

His eldest son, Hazrat Shah Nizam-ud-din Husain, was his premier caliph and *sajjadanashin*. He left a large number of caliphs prominent among whom are: Syed Mohammed Sani of Badakhshan, Maulvi Abd-ul-Latif of Samarqand, Maulvi Nemat-ul-lah of Kabul, Maulvi Yar Mohammed of Kabul, Mulla Jan Mohammed of Kabul, Maulana Ewaz Mohammed of Badakhshan, Maulvi Mohammed Husain of Mecca, and Mirza Asad-ul-lah Beg of Bareilly.

Traits of characters

He nurtured deep love, regard, and respect for the Syeds. He would wake up in the middle of the night and devote himself to prayer, rituals, and spiritual practices.

He was a very learned man, great mystic, an inspired dervish, and an enlightened saint. A very good poet, his poetic pseudonym was "Niyaz."

Supernatural powers

- Once fire broke out in the city. When it reached the Qutb ward in which he lived, his eldest son informed him of this while he was resting. He at once came out and saw that the horses of Risaldar Amir Khan were being taken out from the thatched stable. On seeing him, the Risaldar asked the servants to stop taking out the horses and saying: "If His Holiness wishes to save them, they will be saved. Otherwise let them be burnt befqre him." Hearing these words, he underwent a transformation and when he lifted his eyes, the fire took a different direction and was extinguished. The next day his eldest son inquired what he had recited. He replied: "What? I did not recite anything. Becoming à sea, one spout of my water extinguished the blaze."
- Once one of his disciples requested him to show his real face. He rubbed his hand over his face, which suddenly became radiant like the sun. Nobody could see it. Allah Bakhsh Khan, who had made the request found himself in an exalted condition. When he recovered consciousness Hazrat Niyaz Ahmad told him: "O brother! This is sufficient for you."
- Once, a certain person left Kabul for Bareilly with the idea of becoming his spiritual disciple. Before entering the city, somebody asked him where he had come from and where he was bound. He disclosed that he had come from Kabul and was going to Hazrat Niyaz Ahmad to enrol himself as a

spiritual disciple. Thereupon the stranger told him that he himself was Niyaz Ahmad. He initiated him as his spiritual disciple then and there on the river bank. He directed him to the monastery and informed him, that he would reach there soon. When the stranger arrived at the monastery, he was surprised to see that prayers were being offered on the third day and that Hazrat Niyaz Ahmad had already passed away. He then realised that he had been accepted by Hazrat Niyaz Ahmad as his spiritual disciple after he had expired.

References

1. *Karamat-e-Nizamiya*, p. 3.
2. Ibid., p. 17.

82
Hazrat Shah Mohammed Afaq

Hazrat Shah Mohammed Afaq, born in AH 1160, is a famous saint of the Indian subcontinent. He was the spiritual disciple of Hazrat Khwaja Ziaullah Naqshbandi and subsequently became his caliph. Hazrat Shah Mohammed Afaq went to Afghanistan and there propagated the Gospel of Truth. Many people there got themselves enrolled as his spiritual disciples. The king of Afghanistan, Zaman Shah, became his devotee and disciple.

Death
He passed away on the seventh of Muharram in AH 1251 and was buried in Delhi.

Caliphs
His prominent caliphs were Hazrat Maulana Fazl-ur-Rahman of Ganj Moradabad and Hazrat Maulana Nasir-ud-din.

Traits of Character
He was among the absorbed, over lost in meditation, and was overpowered by love of God. He was well-acquainted with the divine secrets and strictly adhered to the tenets of the Holy Prophet Mohammed, and a perfect dervish.

He was very gifted spiritual guide, and teacher and had no equal in spiritual knowledge. He was an embodiment of piety, purity, trust in God, contentment, hope, belief, and faith, deriving deep pleasure from prayers and ascetic practices.

An idea can be formed of his spiritual perfection by the fact that Hazrat Shah Ghulam Ali used to send some of his spiritual disciples who had undergone training and education to him to seek his blessings. They were considered fully equipped only when he found them to have attained his exacting standards of perfection.

Teachings

The Mujaddadi order to which he belongs, lays emphasis on the repetition of the negative and positive aspect (*La ilaha illàllah*—There is no deity but God) and on the repetition of the name of God. The attention of the spiritual guide requires him to turn his heart towards that of his disciple so that the light of remembrance illuminating his heart enters the heart of the spiritual disciple.

83
Hazrat Shah Abu Sa'id

Hazrat Shah Abu Sa'id was an eminent saint of the Naqshbandi Order. He traces his relationship from Hazrat Shaikh Ahmad of Sirhind, better known as Mujaddid Alif Sani.[1] His father was Shaikh Safi-ul-Qadr.

He was born in Mustafabad (Rampur) on the second of Ziqada in AH 1196. Hazrat Shah Abu Sa'id committed the Holy *Quran* to memory when he was ten years old and learnt rhythmic recitation of it from Nasim who was well-versed in the art. He acquired the certificate of *hadis* from Shah Abd-ul-Aziz.

Initiation into the Sufi Order

After completing his education, he took to self-purification and self-illumination, first from his father and later with his father's blessings, he went to Hazrat Shah Dargahi and requested him to accept him as a humble spiritual disciple. The request was granted. In a very short time, Hazrat Shah Dargahi authorised him to enrol and accept disciples. He gave him the robe of caliph and bade him farewell.[2]

Hazrat Abu Sa'id left Rampur for Delhi and from there wrote to Hazrat Qazi Sanaullah of Panipat seeking advice about the path to further spiritual perfection. The latter suggested the name of Hazrat Shah Ghulam Ali and wrote that in his opinion there was no one better than him to guide him along the path to spiritual perfection and enable him to achieve his goal. He accepted the suggestion and became the spiritual disciple of Hazrat Shah Ghulam Ali, but this in no way interfered with or diminished in anyway the respect, reverence, and regard that he nurtured for Hazrat Shah Dargahi.

The great assignment

He describes how his spiritual guide and teacher assigned him his place:[3] "Thank God, that after a long time, my spiritual guide and teacher indicated to me in the month of Jamadi-ul-Awwal in AH 1233, that I will be assigned high office and said, that since he had received the inspiration, he had conveyed the good news to him."

He called him from Lucknow. He wrote to him:[4]

> I am seeing that you have been assigned the last rank of the status of this august family. Before this, I had seen in dream during the course of my last illness, that you were sitting on my bed and you were assigned the high rank. There appears to me nobody able and fit for these strange and curious attractions except you. So, seeing this letter, start at once towards this direction all alone and leave Ahmad Sa'id there in your place. . . .

In another letter, he wrote:[5]

> I have been receiving inspiration that Abu Sa'id should be summoned. The blessed soul of Hazrat Mujaddid insists on this. I have seen in dream that I have made you sit on my right thigh and I have assigned to you the rank, the details of which will be revealed to you in near future.
>
> Hazrat Shah Abd-ul-Aziz and some prominent people of the city, impressed by your unimpeachable moral character and by your humble ways, spirit of renunciation, simple habits, honesty and integrity, devotion to the remembrance of God and by your patience, perseverance and forbearing nature, justify my calling you and treat it as correct.
>
> I have also received inspiration, that you alone are fit and able for this work. Live here and popularise your order and leave the means of subsistence and the source of income in the hands of God. God is sufficient and he is a good supporter. The promise of God is sufficient.

In accordance with of his spiritual guide's mandate, he came to Delhi, and succeeding him devoted himself to the propagation of truth.

Advice

His spiritual guide and teacher gave him the following words of advice:

- Forever protect your inner affiliation.
- Engage yourself in presence and attention.
- Do not give up remembrance at anytime and under any circumstance.
- Adhere to the Holy Prophet in all your actions.
- Pass all your time in genuflexions and prayer, and offer prayer with the concomitant requisites. Take delight in other rituals, practices, remembrances, recitation of the Holy *Quran*, benedictions to the Holy Prophet Mohammed, and in the seeking the pleasure of God and seeking forgiveness for your sins.
- The object of treading the spiritual path is the attainment of the right conduct, noble character, and to be ever attentive in the presence of God. His outward condition should be bound by the *Sunnah* of the Holy Prophet and his inward state should not admit anyone besides God. He should be exclusively absorbed in and entirely devoted to God Almighty.

Death

Hazrat Shah Abu Sa'id left for a pilgrimage to Mecca in AH 1249 and later went to Medina to pay his respects to the sacred tomb of the Holy Prophet Mohammed. He returned to India and reaching Tonk on the twenty-second of Ramazan, he stayed there because he became ill. His condition took a return for the worse and he passed away on the 'Id-ul-Fitr in AH 1250. He was buried in Tonk. Forty days after his death, his coffin was brought to Delhi, where his dead body was taken out and reburied there.

Caliph

His eldest son, Shah Ahmad Sa'id, was his premier caliph and *sajjadanashin*.

Traits of character

Hazrat Shah Abu Sa'id underwent the trials and tribulations of the world with patience and courage, never complaining about the hardships of life. He was proud of his poverty and faithfully followed the injunctions of his spiritual guide and teacher. He was a learned man and a perfect dervish. He was also a man of literary taste and the author of an important book entitled *Hidayat-ut-Talebeen* written in Persian.

Teachings
He says:[6]

> The difference between the apparent name and the inward name is this, that in the manifestation of the apparent name there appear the qualities pertaining to self, without consideration of the self. Whereas, in the manifestation of the inward name, though there appear the qualities of the name of qualities, but sometimes the sacred and holy self also appears.
>
> My spiritual guide and teacher paid attention to the physical body of this humble being and conferred upon me the grace of the perfection of prophethood, i.e., permanent personal manifestation. The knowledge and insight of this station constitute this only, that knowledge and insight are wiped off and all the conditions of the inward state are not to be recognised, and this station is characterised by colourlessness and statelessness, and faith and devotion gain strength of every type. . . .[7]

Sayings

> When God Almighty is kind to any person, he cause him to reach to anyone of his friends.
>
> The person who cannot discover with his conscious wisdom, does not deserve to be given the indication of the stations and the good news. To do so, would be to defame the way of the dervishes and to create misunderstanding about it.

Supernatural power
Forty days after his death, his dead body was brought to Delhi. When it was taken out of the coffin there were no signs of mutilation. It appeared as if it had been bathed then and was fresh and the cotton sheet placed beneath the body had a very good aroma.[8]

References

1. *Hidayat-ut-Talebeen,* p. 1.
2. *Anwar-ul-Arefeen,* p. 497.
3. *Hidayat-ut-Talebeen,* p. 95.
4. Ibid., pp. 96-97.
5. Ibid., pp. 98-101.
6. Ibid., p. 53.
7. Ibid., pp. 61-62.
8. *Anwar-ul-Arefeen,* p. 499.

84

Hazrat Hafiz Syed Mohammed Husain

Hazrat Hafiz Syed Mohammed Husain was the spiritual caliph of Hazrat Hafiz Musa. His forefathers settled in Rampur, and he was born there. He was named Mohammed Husain and bore the pseudonym "Hafiz Bankey." The reason for his pseudonym was, that in his early years he used to wear a solider's uniform. Once his spiritual guide and teacher, Hazrat Hafiz Musa, seeing him dressed in this way, called him "Bankey," and from there on, he came to be known as "Hafiz Bankey."

He committed the Holy *Quran* to memory at a very early age and went to Delhi for further education. He was fortunate in having as his teacher the renowned scholar and saint Hazrat Shah Abd-ul-Aziz, under whose guidance and supervision he completed his education.

Initiation into the Sufi Order

He set out in search of God. He met many saints in Delhi and also came in contact with saints living elsewhere but he did not derive any inner satisfaction. Eventually, he reached Manakpur and was accepted as a spiritual disciple by Hazrat Hafiz Musa. He lived in his company for sometime, engaging himself in the attainment of spiritual perfection through spiritual practices of various kinds including renunciation.

His efforts were rewarded. He began to see various types of light, not visible to the worldly. He ignored such manifestations and very soon traversed the path from the world of *nasut* to that of *lahut*, and began to see one in many. Subsequently, he was honoured by his spiritual guide and teacher by being appointed as his spiritual caliph.

Death

Hazrat Hafiz Syed Mohammed Husain came to Ajmer to settle there permanently. He occupied a secluded place in the Dargah of Hazrat Khwaja Moin-ud-din Hasan Chishti whose spiritual blessings he sought to derive. He was however summoned to Jaipur to participate in a symposium concerning mysticism held by members of both the Hindu and Muslim communities. He refused saying, that he had permanently settled in Ajmer and he would not go anywhere else. That very night he received the mandate that he should go to Jaipur as that was the city marked out for his eternal rest. He accordingly, left for Jaipur the following morning. On the way he contracted fever, and the day he reached Jaipur, people flocked to him with many inquiries. The next day, i.e., on the first of Zilhijj in AH 1280 he passed away and was buried in Jaipur.

Caliph

Shah Nasir-ud-din is one of his eminent caliphs.

Traits of character

Hazrat Hafiz Syed Mohammed Husain underwent various ascetic practices. He was devoted to the remembrance of god.

He was an accomplished man of letters and was well-versed in religious ceremonies. He had specialised in logic, philosophy, commentaries on the Holy *Quran* and the *hadis*. He had a fairly sound knowledge of the Vedas and Shastras. He is the author of a book entitled *Tohfat-ul-Mohaqqeqeen*.

Supernatural power

Once he went to Amroha. He learnt of a Maulvi who lived there who did not believe in mysticism and who abused the sufis. Hearing this, he went to a mosque and asked a certain person to convey to the Maulvi, that a dervish sat in the mosque claiming to be God. He also asked him to suggest to the Maulvi, that he should invite the dervish to his house on some pretext and beat him.

The Maulvi invited Hafiz Sahab to his house. Some of his devotees, suspecting foul play, did not want him to go alone, but Hafiz Sahab chose to do so.

A discussion ensued between him and the Maulvi. He advanced arguments in support of mysticism and subsequently caught hold of the Maulvi's shoulder and told him that what he had so far said had been theoretical but he should also see their practical manifestation.

Thereupon, the Maulvi fell at his feet and together with all his family members, became his spiritual disciple.

85

Hazrat Shah Nasir-ud-din

Hazrat Shah Nasir-ud-din was the spiritual caliph of Hazrat Hafiz Syed Mohammed Husain. His pseudonym was "Mohammed Nasir Khan."

Initiation into the Sufi Order

Initially, he went to Maulana Derail and in his company he acquired certain spiritual graces and received the robe of caliph from him pertaining to the Faqiriya Order, and from Shah Ali Naqi, received the robe of caliph pertaining to the Qadiri Order.

Reaching Delhi, he went to Hazrat Hafiz Syed Mohammed Husain and became his spiritual disciple. He lived in his company for sometime, and at his behest engaged himself in ascetic practices and rigours.

Once, during his stay in Firozabad, he went with him to the tomb of Patanga Shah, situated outside the city accompanied by Ali Naqi Shah and others. There at the tomb, he placed on his head the turban given to him by Hazrat Hafiz Musa and thus appointed him as his spiritual caliph successor. He also gave him the deed of caliphate, the deed of will, and the *waqf* deed.

Addressing him, he told him that half of Akbarabad (Agra) and the whole of Firozabad formed part of his domain and was to be his concern. It was for him to decide where he wanted to live, whether in Akbarabad or Firozabad. Then he disclosed very many spiritual secrets to him and acquainted him with many implications concerning the ascension of the Holy Prophet.

Death

Hazrat Shah Nasir-ud-din breathed his last on the twenty-second of Shawwal in AH 1295 and was buried in Firozabad, U.P.

Caliphs

His outstanding caliphs are: Shah Ghazi-ud-din, Maqsud Ali Shah of Shahjahanpur, Shah Wajid Ali of Sandiliya, Syed Qazi Enayat Ali, Subhan Ali of Firozabad, and Abd-ur-Rahman of Shikohabad.

Traits of character

Hazrat Shah Nasir-ud-din kept himself aloof from worldly people, preferring to live outside the city all day. He spent his nights in the mosque engaged in prayers. He ate frugally and at night, he ate only five or six morsels. He fasted for years all through the year and kept awake all night. He was, at times, deeply absorbed in contemplation.

He was very humble and meek, kind, courteous, and entertaining. Whosoever came into contact with him found him greatly attracted towards him.

He reposed his utmost trust in God. At the approach of Muharram each year he used to distribute all the goods of his monastery to the needy, the poor, and the indigent retaining nothing but a wrapper.

Once a dervish came to his monastery and stayed overnight. Seeing him spending lavishly, he was surprised and asked what the source of his income was. The dervish said that provided he promised on oath, not to reveal the secret to others he would let him know a way of preparing alchemy. He inquired of the dervish whether it was the alchemy of hand or of tongue. He replied, that he knew that of the hand only, which he would show him. Thereupon Hazrat Nasir-ud-din said that such a type of alchemy might be learnt by an individual who did not repose his trust in God. He reposed his trust in God and God was sufficient for him. He showed the utmost concern for his spiritual disciples. He confined himself almost entirely to the monastery where he lived and seldom ventured out.

Supernatural powers

- He himself says, that once he was engaged in prayers in the middle of the night. He saw two absorbed saints coming to him, i.e., Harman Shah of Firozabad and Maulvi Karamat Husain of Shikohabad. They said that his prayer had been accepted and disappeared immediately afterwards.
- One of his devotees fell ill. In a state of despondency, he exclaimed: "O, Hazrat! should I die now." After he had uttered the words, he saw him standing near him and recovered from his illness. His recovery greatly astonished the physicians.

86

Hazrat Syed Mohammed Ghous Ali Shah

Hazrat Syed Mohammed Ghous Ali Shah belonged to all the four principal Orders of the sufis. He is a Hasni and Husaini, i.e., he traced his relationship from Hazrat Imam Hasan and Hazrat Imam Husain. His father, Syed Ahmad Hasan, alias Ahmad Ali, was a great spiritual figure of his time. His mother had acquired spiritual graces from her father. He was born in AH 1219 in Asthawan.[1]

When he attained the age of discretion, his father called him to Delhi. He was engaged in acquiring knowledge and learning. He counted among his teachers such outstanding learned men as Shah Abd-ul-Aziz and Maulana Shah Mohammed Ishaq, who taught him the *hadis*, jurisprudence and other branches of outward knowledge. Maulana Fazle Imam of Khairabad taught him logic and theology. Maulvi Qalandar Ali of Jalalabad taught him the *Masnavi* of Maulana Rumi.

Initiation into the Sufi Order

In line with his family traditions, he initially became his father's spiritual disciple. His grandfather took him to Haji Lal, who was in Delhi then and who was a spiritual caliph of Hazrat Maulana Fakhr-ud-din, Fakhre Alam Chishti-Nizami. Haji Lal, told him: "I have been waiting for you for a long time. Whatever I hold in trust for you, please take from me." He showed him the utmost kindness.

His father later took him to Syed Fida Husain Rasool Shahi, who accepted him as his spiritual disciple. He thus was a member of the Suhrawardi Rasool Shahi Order of the sufis. Mir Azam Ali Shah also accepted him as his spiritual disciple, giving him membership of the Qadiri Order. He also became a spiritual disciple of Miyan Habibullah Shah of the Naqshbandi Order so he was also affiliated with the Naqshbandi Order. He went to Hazrat Amir-ud-din Shah Chishti and became his spiritual disciple, thereby gaining entry to the Chishti Order too.

Tours and travels

He toured and travelled extensively visiting virtually every part of the Indian subcontinent. He even went overseas visiting Egypt, Baghdad, Jerusalem, Najaf, Mecca, Medina, Syria, Hijaz, and other places. He was very fond of meeting perfect dervishes, and during the course of his tours and travels, he met eighty-nine who were considered to have attained spiritual perfection. Besides the dervishes, he also met many *sanayasis* and saints from other religions.

Death

He passed away on the twenty-sixth of Rabi-ul-Awwal in AH 1297 and was buried in Panipat.

Caliphs

Mohammed Yusuf and Maulvi Gul Hasan were his two prominent caliphs.

Traits of character

He was a *qutb* entrusted with the domain of the Indian subcontinent. He was deeply absorbed in contemplation. He professed the creed of the Qalandars and he firmly believed in *Tauhid,* or the unity of God. He was unique in outer and inner perfection, eloquent in speech, kind courteous, and polite. He did not hanker after this world and the world hereafter. He was indeed perfect.

Teachings

He condemned misappropriation and breach of trust. He frowned on those who created disturbances, detested backbiting. In short, he deprecated all immoral acts.

He emphasised that an individual should scrutinise him self at least once every twenty-four hours to analyse, what mistakes of omission and commission he has made. An individual should then seek to reform himself.

Sayings

- The world and everything in it are useless. To be engrossed in its temporary and short-lived beauty and splendour deprives one so engaged of eternal life.

- The world entangles an individual in its met through various different means.
- It is foolish to be proud of wealth, goods, and beauty, as one day they will vanish.
- Patience and perseverance constitute imperishable wealth for an individual.
- Jealousy is opposed to faith. A jealous person is always involved in grief.

Supernatural powers

- A rich person, Ata Mohammed, had no issue. He had grown old, but the desire for a son had not waned. He had great faith in Hazrat Ali Shah and told him that God in his grace had given him everything, but unfortunately he had not been blessed with a son. He requested him to pray for one.
  He told the person that God is omnipotent. One should not be disappointed of His Grace. God Willing, you will have a son. When a son was born to him after sometime, Ata Mohammed brought him to Hazrat Ali Shah who placed one of his hands on the head of the child and placing the other hand on the head of Ata Mohammed, recited a couplet. Whenever the child fell ill, his father would bring him Hazrat Ali Shah who would smile and recite the same couplet.
- There was a Naib-Tehsildar in Panipat, who was a great devotee of Hazrat Ali Shah. Once he submitted to him that he had appeared in an examination and that he wanted permanent tenure in his job, and requested he pray that this should happen. Hazrat Ali Shah smiled and told the Naib-Tehsildar: "Such good news is initially conveyed by the father." When the Naib-Tehsildar went home he found a letter from his father conveying the good news.

Reference

1. *Seerat-e-Ghosiya*, p. 6.

87

Hazrat Maulana Shah Fazle Rahman

Hazrat Maulana Shah Fazle Rahman is a leading saint of the Indian subcontinent. He traced his relationship from Hazrat Shaikh Mohammed, better known as Misbah-ul-Ashiqeen, who was buried in Mila-e-van, a town at some distance from Ganj Moradabad. His father, Shaikh Ahilullah, son of Shaikh Fayyaz, was a spiritual disciple of Hazrat Maulana Shah Abd-ur-Rahman of Lucknow, who conveyed the glad tidings of his birth to his father. His mother, Bibi Basirat, traced her descent from the first caliph of Islam, Hazrat Abu Bakr Siddique, through Hazrat Shahab-ud-din Umar Suhrawardy.

He was born in Mila-e-van in AH 1208.[1] When he was six years old, his father took him to his spiritual guide who kissed him and said: "This boy will be a Qutb of India."[2]

Childhood

Once when playing with children of his own age, a carriage passed that way which ran him over and lost him one ear. As he grow up, he began to imbibe and exhibit the wisdom of a mature mind. Once he was going with his father who had a bird in a cage with him. Passing through a field his father plucked some grain and gave it to the bird with the owner's consent. His father moved on, but he stayed rooted there. His father called him, but he refused to accompany him, saying that until the owner of the field came and he had sought his pardon, he would not leave. His father, finding him adamant, took the grain and threw it away, and it was only then that he was willing to leave.

Education

He went to Lucknow for his education. Maulana Nur taught him *Sharah Wiqaya* and Hazrat Maulana Ishaq taught him *Sihah-us- Sittah*. Coming to Delhi, which was then considered the centre of learning he took to the study of the *hadis*. In a short time, he was able to got a certificate from Hazrat Maulana Shah Abd-ul-Aziz of Delhi.[3]

Initiation into the Sufi Order

When he was in Delhi, he heard a great deal about Hazrat Shah Afaq. Once he went to him and found him a man with a magnetic personality. He continued this contact and would go to him occasionally. Eventually, he made up his mind to become Shah Afaq's spiritual disciple, and was accepted by him as such with prophetic words: "In the last years of his life, he will become famous." Shah Afaq was very kind to him. Subsequently, he appointed him as his spiritual caliph. Some of the spiritual disciples of Hazrat Shah Afaq felt jealous of him, complaining that they were his old devotees and disciples and had served him for long, out in spite of that, he paid greater attention to Maulana Fazle Rahman. To this Hazrat Shah Afaq replied: "It may be true. I am anxious that you may become something. But in this case, it is the decree of God and the decree of God always triumphs."

Marriage and children

He married twice. His first wife, the daughter of Shaikh Badle, passed away, leaving two sons, Maulvi Abd-ur-Rahman and Maulvi Abd-ur-Rahim, who died during their father's lifetime. His second marriage was solemnised with Raisa Bibi in Ganj Moradabad. After this marriage, he shifted from Mala-e-van and settled in Ganj Moradabad. This marriage gave him a son, Ahmad Miyan, and a daughter, Bibi Shafqat.[4]

Death

He made a will that just before his death the *hadis* should be read over to him.[5] A little before he died he called his son Ahmad Miyan and whispered something in his ear. Then he withdraw his hand and continued to look towards him and closed his eyes. He breathed his last on the twenty-second of Rabi-ul-Awwal in AH 1313 just after sunset[6] and was buried in Ganj Moradabad.

Caliphs

His son, Hazrat Ahmad Miyan, and Maulvi Syed Mohammed Ali of Kanpur were his prominent caliphs.

Traits of character

He felt proud of his poverty. His worldly possessions comprised a bed, a small *chowki* covered with a mat upon which he offered his prayers, an earthen jar, and two pitchers of water. He had no bedding and sat on a mat. He ate barley bread, and his food was cooked in earthen pots. He had given up meat. He reposed great trust in God and whatever he received as a gift or *fatuhat* would be spent that very day. He was generous, hospitable, and courteous but would not allow guests to stay with him for more than two days at a stretch. He was extremely happy to be visited by the *ulama*,[7] and paid utmost respect to his spiritual guide and teacher. He was hot tempered. He was ever engaged in the remembrance of God and in meditation. He offered pre-dawn prayers regularly.

Teachings and sayings

He recommended the reading of the *Masnavi* by Maulana Rumi. Even reading it without understanding it is useful.[8]
Some of his sayings are:

- Real sainthood is constituted by a passion for the manifestation of God.
- Adherence to the tenets of the Holy Prophet is equivalent to the rank of a *ghous* or a *qutb*.
- To be the spiritual disciple of one having an affiliation with God is a source of salvation for, on the Day of Judgment, the blessings showered upon him will have their effect on his spiritual disciples and therefore, all his spiritual disciples will enter paradise with him.

Supernatural powers

- Once two persons came to him and submitted that the summons they had received showed that their case had been fixed for that day in the district courts. Given the distance of these, how could they reach the court in time. He asked them to close their eyes. They did so, and when they opened their eyes, they found themselves in Court premises.[9]
- He suggested a ritual to one of his spiritual disciples in a dream. After the lapse of a few years, the disciple came to him and requested him to suggest some ritual. Hazrat Fazle

Rahman replied that many years earlier he had suggested a ritual to him and he repeated the same one that he had suggested in dream.

- A certain person coming to meet him had to cross a river. His horse got stuck in the mire. The person invoked Hazrat Fazle Rahman's help and immediately his horse struggled out of the mire. When this individual reached in his presence, he found him lying in the tenement, covered with a sheet. Seeing him, Hazrat Fazle Rahman remarked about the way people troubled him and showed his back. The signs of mud and the feet of the horse were visible on it.[10]

References

1. *Masalek-us-Salekeen,* vol. II, p. 179.
2. Ibid., p. 180.
3. Ibid.
4. Ibid., p. 181.
5. Ibid., p. 190.
6. Ibid., p. 179.
7. Ibid., p. 186.
8. Ibid., p. 195.
9. Ibid., p. 191.
10. Ibid., p. 193.

88

Hazrat Maulana Syed Waris Ali Shah

Hazrat Maulana Syed Waris Ali Shah was a prominent saint. His ancestors migrated from Nishapur to India. His father, Syed Qurban Ali Shah, was a rich man,[1] and lived in Deva.

Hazrat Waris Ali Shah was born in AH 1232 and named Waris Ali. Being an orphan, he laboured under various handicaps. He was however admitted in a *maktab* when he was five years old and committed the Holy *Quran* to memory at the age of seven.

Initiation into the Sufi Order

From childhood he had of a mystic turn of mind and would go out and pass the nights in desolate and deserted places. He was restless. His brother-in-law, Hazrat Syed Khadim Ali Shah was an accomplished sufi, and generally stayed in Lucknow. He called him and accepted him as one of his spiritual disciples. After his death, on the thirteenth of Safar in the year AH 1252, Hazrat Waris Ali Shah was accepted as his spiritual successor.

Tour and travels

Receiving the mandate from his spiritual guide, who told him in a dream "Go on Travels," he set out on the thirteenth of Rabi-ul-Awwal in AH 1252 and reached Ajmer via Jaipur. When in Ajmer, he went to the tomb of Hazrat Khwaja Gharib Nawaz, he wanted to enter the tomb, when someone pointed out to him, that he should take off his shoes, he did so and never wore them again for the rest of his life. He also visited Bombay and Jeddah. He then went to Mecca and, after performing the pilgrimage, went to Medina where he stayed for sometime. He also visited Jerusalem, Syria, Damascus, Beirut, Baghdad, Kazman, Najaf, Karbala, Iran, Constantinople, and parts of Europe.

Returning to his hometown, Deva, he found that his house was in a dilapidated state and that his relations had taken possession of his property. He resumed his travels again visiting nearby places.

Death

He passed away on the thirteenth of Muharram in AH 1323 corresponding to sixth of April 1905.

Disciples

Hazrat Waris Ali Shah had a huge following. His spiritual disciples were spread throughout Asia, Europe, and Africa. Sultan Abd-ul-Majid was one of his spiritual disciples and prominent among the others we may mention: Shaikh Mazhar Ali, Shams-ud-din, Baadnam Shah, and Miyan Jahangir Shah.

Traits of character

Hazrat Waris Ali Shah was a bachelor with a generous disposition. He renounced every comfort and took to asceticism, his attire comprising only a wrapper and his meals very frugal. He was deeply absorbed in contemplation. He went about on foot, covering great distances, and it was only when he had to cross a river or the sea would he travel in a boat or ship.

Teachings

He said that a woman whose husband was living with her, is not worried about the necessities of life. The husband himself looks after her and provides her maintenance. Similarly, when God is so close to us, an individual should not worry at all about sustenance.

He condemns jealousy and says that he who is not jealous is indeed blessed.

Supernatural power

- When he went to perform the pilgrimage to Mecca for the first time, he starved himself for several days. The ship suddenly halted and notwithstanding all the captain efforts the ship would not move.

  One night, the captain saw the Holy Prophet in dream telling him: "The passengers are hungry, and you eat to your heart's content. This mishap is the result of that." The following day the captain entertained all the passengers on board the ship, but Hazrat Waris Ali Shah did not join the feast. Again the captain received the same warning in a dream and again entertained all the passengers. This time too Hazrat Waris Ali Shah did not attend and engaged in the remembrance of God. The captain received the same warning a third time. This time he was a little more cautious. He took a roll call of all the invitees and learnt thereby that one of the passengers was absent. The captain ran up to him and presented him sundry delicacies. Then the ship resumed its journey.

- One of his devotees Ali Mohammed Khan, a Risaldar in the army was transferred to Egypt. He went to Hazrat Haji Waris Ali Shah and implored his aid. The latter told the Risaldar, that wherever he might be, he would always be with him. The Risaldar submitted that he had been ordered to go to Egypt. Hazrat Waris Ali Shah responded: 'Egypt is famous for its knives. Ali Mohammed is it not true that if some Indian officer renders distinguished service, the Queen may show him great respect? Vilayat (England) is a good country.' Having said this, he asked him to leave.

The Risaldar received recognition for his services in Egypt. He was sent to England where he had an audience with the Queen Victoria, who treated him with great respect. On his return from his visit to Egypt and England, the Risaldar brought the Hazrat some beautiful knives.

Reference

1. *Hayat-e-Waris.*

89

Hazrat Syed Malik Mohammed Alam

Hazrat Syed Malik Mohammed Alam was born in Kubke, also known as Khabaki, which is situated in Shahpur district. He is known and invoked as "Sayeen Gudri Shah Baba." His father, Malik Sher Mohammed Khan, had acquired considerable property when the Sikhs ruled. After his father's death, he underwent a transformation and began wandering around in jungles.

Hazrat Sayeenji enjoyed the company of Moazzam Shah, who was buried in Sialkot. He visited many holy and sacred places, travelling on foot. When he arrived in Ajmer, he settled there permanently. He passed away on the tenth of Ramazan in AD 1909 and was buried at the Chilla of Khwaja Gharib Nawaz in Ajmer. It is said, that he lived up to the age a hundred and twenty-five years.

Sayings

- Acquaint thyself with the divine secret and bid farewell to thy rosary.
- Whatever belongs to a dervish is for the goods of all.
- Overcome the devil of inordinate desires, so that you may become worthy to receive the blessings of God.

90

Hazrat Qazi Abd-ur-Rahim Shah

Hazrat Qazi Abd-ur-Rahim Shah is better known and addressed as "Qazi Gudri Shah Baba." His father, Shaikh Ali Bakhsh, initially lived in Kashipur and subsequently took up residence in Meranpura. Hazrat Abd-ur-Rahim Shah was brought up under the vigilant care of his father in Meranpura and went to Ajmer when he was twenty-seven years old. He lived in the company of Hazrat Syed Malik Mohammed Alam, better known as Sayeen Gudri Shah Baba and served him for about twenty-five years.

Hazrat Qazi Sahab died at the age of sixty-four years on the fifth of Shawwal in AH 1344 and was buried at the Chilla of Khwaja Gharib Nawaz in Ajmer.

Sayings

- A dervish is wedded to God.
- Love is above all speech.
- Man achieves something only when he dies before his physical death.
- A dervish is tongue-tied.
- A dervish does not yield to temptations. His passions are under his control.

91

Hazrat Nawab Gudri Shah Baba

Hazrat Mohammed Khadim Hasan Shah Sahab Zuberi Moini Gudri Shahi, better known as Nawab Gudri Shah Baba, shone brightly in the spiritual firmament of modern India. He was born with a silver spoon in his mouth in a respectable family in Moradabad, Uttar Pradesh. He traced his descent from Hazrat Mus'ab, the illustrious son of a distinguished companion of the Holy Prophet Mohammed, Hazrat Zubair, and from Hazrat Makhdum Sama-ud-din Suhrawardi, an eminent saint of the Suhrawardy Order. His father, Mazhar Hasan Sahab, was a leading landlord of Moradabad district and a spiritual disciple of Hazrat Maulana Fazl-ur-Rahman Sahab, an outstanding saint of the Naqshbandi Order. His mother, Bedar Khanam, traced her descent from the Moghul royal family. On learning of his birth, Hazrat Maulana Sahab named him "Khadim Hasan" and congratulated his father on the birth of a son in his house who, as Hazrat Maulana Sahab prophesied, would be a guide to wayward travellers in search of their destination and would be the source of a fountain of spiritual blessings.

His father passed away in 1910. Hazrat Gudri Shah Baba joined the Muir Central College at Allahabad, where he was unable to complete his studies. He visited Ajmer for the first time in 1911 and offered his reverence and respects at the tomb of Hazrat Khwaja Moin-ud-din Hasan Chishti, better known as Khwaja Gharib Nawaz. That very year a call came from Mecca and he left to perform the pilgrimage. From Mecca he went to Medina and offered his reverence and respects at the tomb of the Holy Prophet Mohammed. Subsequently he paid short visits to Cairo, Jerusalem, and Damascus. On his return, he began to live at Moradabad and got married, but he was not satisfied with the life he led and but was in quest of a higher and better one leading the path of spiritual illumination.

In 1921, when he was in Ajmer, he met an accomplished saint named Hazrat Qazi Abd-ur-Rahim Shah, better known as Qazi Gudri Shah Baba. He was so taken with him that abandoning all he cast his lot with him, and became his spiritual disciple.

Hazrat Qazi Gudri Shah Baba was a spiritual disciple and *sajjadanashin* of Hazrat Malik Mohammed Alam, better known as Sayeenji Gudri Shah Baba, who belonged to the Qadiri and Chishti Orders, and it is to him that the Order known as the Gudri Shahi owes its existence.

After his initiation, Hazrat Nawab Gudri Shah Baba spent a considerable length of time every year in Ajmer in the company of his spiritual guide. In 1926, when Hazrat Qazi Gudri Shah Baba breathed his last at Ajmer, which was his permanent abode.

In 1935, he performed the pilgrimage to Mecca a second time and as a mark of his devotion also paid his respects at the tomb of the Holy Prophet Mohammed in Medina. That time too he paid his respects to the tomb of Maula Ali in Najaf-e-Ashraf and to the tomb of Hazrat Imam Husain in Karbala, and to many other tombs of saints in Baghdad. He is the author of many reputed books in Urdu, and these contributions to knowledge and learning include: *Moinul Arwah; 'Id Milad-un-Nabi wa Sulhaye Ummat; Haqiqi Hukmrani; Ausaf-e-Ali; Maratab-e-Ali; Wilayat-e-Ali; Nazul-e-Rahmat;* and *Syed-us-Shuhada*. He was also a poet and wrote under the poetic pseudonym "Khadim." The volume containing his poetry is entitled *Naghma-e-Dard*, which is a collection of verses written in honour of the Holy Prophet Mohammed and of saints and others dealing with mysticism. He breathed his last on the twenty-ninth November 1970. His tomb at the Usmani Chilla in Ajmer still attracts adherents.

Hazrat Nawab Gudri Shah Baba was essentially a man with a mission. His ideal was a better life for the downtrodden. He worked ceaselessly for a cause: of moulding, reshaping, and reconstructing humanity into a better mould of love, piety, contentment, trust in God, hope, belief, and faith, on the one hand and sincerity, service, sharing, and sacrifice on the other.

According to him, love is absorbing and makes a man unmindful of the self, is a blessing endowed by God Almighty. The path of love leads inexorably towards God. He emphasised that one should meet people with a cheerful smile and warned those desirous of treading the spiritual path, that they should first try to change their habits.

To him a saint is more than a king. Empires rise and fall but the spiritual empire knows no fall; the crown that a saint wears cannot be snatched away. It is a sign and a symbol and an epitome of a life nobly lived with dedicated devotion to the service of God Almighty.

92

Hazrat Data Ganj Bakhsh

Hazrat Data Ganj Bakhsh illumined the spiritual firmament of the Indian subcontinent. He traced his descent from Hazrat Imam Hasan, son of Hazrat Ali, son-in-law of the Holy Prophet Mohammed which makes him a Hasni. His father, Syed Usman, was the son of Syed Ali and was born in Ghazni.

Hazrat Ganj Bakhsh's name is Ali. He is called Makhdum Ali Hujweri. Hujwer is not the name of a village, town, or city but the name of a mohalla or ward of Ghazni. He is invoked and addressed as "Data Ganj Bakhsh, the giver of bounties." The title was given to him because while living in Lahore he visited the tomb of Hazrat Khwaja Moin-ud-din Hasan Chishti, stayed there at a secluded place, and derived spiritual blessings from it. At the time of his departure, he recited the following couplet in Moin-ud-din Chishti's honour:

> The giver of bounties, the benefactor of the world [and]
> manifestation of the light of God,
> To the imperfect a perfect spiritual guide
> and to the perfect a guide.

Since that day he came to be known as "Data Ganj Bakhsh."

Initiation into the Sufi Order

He was accepted as a spiritual disciple by Hazrat Shaikh Abul-Fazl, son of Hasan Junaid of Hambal. Hazrat Shaikh Abul-Fazl was the spiritual caliph of Hazrat Syedna Khizrmi, who was a spiritual disciple and caliph of Hazrat Syedna Shaikh Shibli. He also derived spiritual blessings from the company of Hazrat Shaikh Abul-Qasim Gorkani, Hazrat Shaikh Abu Sa'id Abul-Khair, and Hazrat Shaikh Abul-Qasim Tashiri.

The mandate

One night he saw in a dream his spiritual guide and teacher Hazrat Shaikh Abul-Fazl saying to him: "O, my son! we have appointed you as the *qutb* of Lahore. Be prepared and start forthwith for Lahore." In the dream, he submitted to this injunction, saying: "Your Holiness has already appointed Khwaja Hasan Zingani as the *qutb* of Lahore. What is the need for this humble being in his presence there? What is the importance, significance, and implication of the order of your holiness?" Thereupon his spiritual guide and teacher said: "O my son! do not argue with me and leave for Lahore without loss of time."

He accordingly left Ghazni for Lahore. When he had reached the outskirts of the city, it had grown dark. He stayed outside the city and entered it in the morning. To his great surprise, he saw a funeral. On his inquiring, he learnt that it was the funeral of Hazrat Shaikh Khwaja Hasan Zingani, who had passed away the previous night. He led the funeral prayers. He settled in Lahore at a place where his tomb is now situated and spent the rest of his days there guiding, teaching, and inspiring the people and preaching and propagating the doctrine of truth.

Death

Hazrat Data Ganj Bakhsh passed away in AH 465 and was buried in Lahore. His *'urs* takes place on the twentieth and the twenty-first of Safar every year.

Teachings

Hazrat Data Ganj Bakhsh was very unassuming and simple. He was a perfect dervish and an accomplished man. He wrote several books, the most famous of which is entitled *Kashf-ul-Mahjub* in which he has discussed various aspects of mysticism. According to him there are seven types of lust, which are deep-rooted in an individual.[1] An individual should guard himself against them. The lust of the eye is to see, of the ear to hear, of the nose to smell, of the tongue to speak, of the mouth to taste, of the body to touch, and of the heart to think. A seeker should protect himself and learn to discipline himself.

About the efficacy and characteristic of love he says:[2]

When love takes its abode in any heart, it does not change with presence or absence, trial or tribulation, comfort or pleasure, separation or unity. Love is called love because it removes from the heart all else except the beloved. . . . And the love of God for an individual is this, that he may give him very many blessings and good things in this world and in the world hereafter, may protect him from torture, prevent him from committing sin, may award him a high and dignified position, may turn his face towards him instead of allowing him to look towards others, may confer upon him his eternal grace, so that the individual may remain aloof from all and may alone to seek His will and pleasure. . . .

The love of an individual for God is a quality that appears in the heart of a submissive faithful in the shape of respect and remembrance, so that he may seek the Will of the beloved. In the fondness of seeing Him, he may be restless and in the desire to win his nearness; he may be impatient. He may have no other desire except to be united with Him. He may draw solace from the remembrance of God and abstain from the remembrance of anyone else besides Him. He may have absolutely no rest or respite. He may hold himself aloof from the things he loved, may give up greed and may accept the relation of friendship. He may be ever prepared to carry out his behest. He may recognise God by the qualities of perfection.

It is not becoming that the love of God for him be of the same types of love that people have for one other. . . .

Zakat or charity is one of the divine commandments. Whosoever can afford it, should not avoid it. But charity becomes obligatory upon the completion of a blessing. . . . There is also the charity relating to status or position, just as there is charity relating to wealth, for status is also a complete blessing. The Holy Prophet has said: 'Verily, God has made obligatory upon you the charity relating to status as the charity relating to your wealth.' The Holy Prophet has also said: 'There is a charity pertaining to all things and the charity of home is the guest-house.'

The reality of giving in charity is offering thanks to God with the blessings of the kind. Health is also a great blessing. There is a charity for all the limbs of the body, and such charity is this that all the limbs of the body may be ever kept engaged in prayer and remembrance and not allowed to be engrossed or engaged in pastime, frivolity, or idle chatter, so that they may be among those paying the charity concerning the blessing.

There is also *zakat* or charity for inner blessings. Due to its abundance, its reality cannot be circumscribed. There is thus charity for it, which is becoming it. And it is the enlightenment of the outer and the inner blessings. Once an individual has realised that God Almighty has conferred very many blessings upon him, thanksgiving for these abundant blessings then must be abundant charity. . . .[3]

Sayings

- The knowledge of extinction is this, that thou may'st know that the world is mortal and the knowledge of permanence is this, that thou may'st know that the world hereafter is lasting.
- The position of a dervish in the path to God is very great indeed.
- Sufi is one who has annihilated his self, who lives in the fondness of God, who is released from the limitations of mood, and who is united with the reality.
- Censure is very effective in true friendship, as if the people of God were marked out for censure.

Supernatural power

After he had permanently settled in Lahore, he constructed a monastery for himself and also a mosque. When the mosque was under construction, the *ulama* of the city raised a storm of opposition to the effect that the mosque was not exactly aligned towards *qibla*. He remained unconcerned about this opposition and objection. When the mosque was complete he invited the *ulama*, sufis, saints, and leading citizens to it and they all offered prayers behind him. After the prayers were over, he addressed all those present, saying: "People have expressed doubt concerning the alignment of the mosque. I request you to close your eyes and meditate and then decide whether it is correct or not." Thereafter he meditated and the curtains were removed from the eyes of the people. All of them saw that the sacred Ka'ba was before their eyes and that the mosque direction had been correctly aligned.

References

1. *Kashf-ul-Mahjub*, p. 233.
2. Ibid., p. 350.
3. Ibid., p. 357.

93

Hazrat Shah Mohammed Yusuf Gurdezi

Hazrat Shah Mohammed Yusuf of Gurdez was one among the prominent saints of the Indian subcontinent. His family migrated from Baghdad in the fourth century AH and settled in a village named Gurdez situated near Ghazni. His grandfather, Hazrat Shah Qasur, was one of the spiritual disciples of Hazrat Bayazeed of Bustam. His father was Syed Abu Bakr.

Hazrat Mohammed Gurdezi was born in AH 462, though some believe he was born in AH 450.[1] His parents gave him a good education and training, making him well-versed in outer knowledge. He was a spiritual disciple of his grandfather, Hazrat Syed Shah Qasur.[2] It is said, that his mother directed him to go to Multan where he reached in AH 481 and settled there permanently.

Death

He died in AH 547 and was buried in Multan though some hold that he passed away in AH 531.

Traits of character

He had a magnetic personality which drew many people to his fold. He was pious, gentle and courteous. He had surrendered his will to the Will of God and was extremely devoted to prayers and ascetic practices.

Supernatural power

Once he passed through a city where the people were afraid of a lion that killed a man daily. The people of the city sought his help in the matter. He went to the jungle and greatly surprised everyone when he returned riding the lion. It had been tamed and did not attack anyone thereafter.

References

1. *Jamal-e-Yusufiya.*
2. *Irshad-us-Salekeen; Jamal-e-Yusufiya.*

94

Hazrat Shaikh Jalal-ud-din

Hazrat Shaikh Jalal-ud-din of Tabriz was a perfect dervish and a renowned saint of the Indian subcontinent. He was a spiritual disciple of Shaikh Abu Sa'id of Tabriz, and when one of his spiritual guide and teacher expired, he served Hazrat Shaikh Shahab-ud-din Suhrawardi. The latter went on pilgrimage every year and did not like the food that was available on the way. Hazrat Shaikh Jalal-ud-din of Tabriz would carry his tiffin basket on his head and would offer him hot food. In short, he served him as no ordinary spiritual disciple could have done.[1] Delighted with his devotion and service, Hazrat Shaikh Shahab-ud-din Umar Suhrawardi conferred upon him very many spiritual blessings.

Tours and travels

Hazrat Shaikh Jalal-ud-din travelled and toured extensively, often with Hazrat Shaikh Baha-ud-din Zakariya of Multan. When he met Shaikh Farid-ud-din Attar and praised him highly and even forgot to mention the name of Hazrat Shaikh Shahab-ud-din Suhrawardi to him, they parted company.

He arrived in Delhi during the lifetime of Hazrat Khwaja Qutb-ud-din Bakhtyar Kaki and was on friendly terms with him. It is said, that he, not liking the city, did not stay in Delhi for long. He said:[2] "When I came to this city, I was pure gold. Now I am silver. Let us see what comes next."

One day, when he was sitting at the main entrance of his house in Budaun, a person selling curd passed that way. He belonged to a gang of dacoits. When he saw him sitting there he was attracted to him. Shaikh Jalal-ud-din cast a look upon him and he immediately embraced Islam. The former named him "Ali."

Shaikh Najm-ud-din Sughra, who was the Shaikh-ul-Islam, brought a serious charge against him, with the result that he was forced to leave for Bengal where he passed the remaining days of his life.

Death
Hazrat Shaikh Jalal-ud-din passed away in AH 642 and was buried in Dev Mahal Bandar (Sylhet), Assam.[3]

Traits of character
He was very pious. His piety can best be appreciated by the fact that once he gave a pomegranate to Hazrat Baba Farid-ud-din Ganj-e-Shakar, who was quite young then and was known as "Qazi Bachchan Divana,"[4] who was then fasting. The latter distributed the pomegranate among those present there. By chance one seed of the pomegranate was found to be lying there when the time came to break his fast. He broke his fast with that one seed and found himself that day to be spiritually improved and purified. Hazrat Baba Sahab thought to himself that it would have been very nice to have taken the whole pomegranate. When he went to Hazrat Khwaja Qutb-ud-din Bakhtyar Kaki, he narrated what had transpired. Whereupon Hazrat Qutb Sahab said: "Baba Farid, whatever there was for you was contained by that one grain." Hazrat Jalal-ud-din did not hanker after worldly pleasures, steadfastly believing in renunciation and asceticism.

Teachings
In a letter addressed to Hazrat Baha-ud-din Zakariya of Multan he wrote: "Whoever, indulged in the pleasure of the senses will never be benefited." Also: "Whosoever is interested in industry, becomes a man of the world."

Supernatural power
One day, when he was sitting by a river bank during his days of exile he suddenly got up, did his ablutions, and said to those present: "Come, let us offer funeral prayers for the Shaikh-ul-Islam of Delhi. He had just died." This had actually occurred. After offering prayers, he addressing those present there thus saying: "The Shaikh-ul-Islam of Delhi turned me out of the city. Our spiritual guide turned him out of the world."

References

1. *Akhbar-ul-Akhiyar.*
2. *Fawaid-ul-Fu'ad.*
3. *Gangena-e-Sarwari,* better known as *Gang Tarikh,* p. 45; *Gulzar-e-Abrar,* p. 66.
4. *Jawami'-ul-Kilam.*

95

Hazrat Baba Farid-ud-din Mas'ud Ganj-e-Shakar

Hazrat Baba Farid-ud-din Mas'ud Ganj-e-Shakar was an eminent saint of the Indian subcontinent. He was the caliph and spiritual successor of Hazrat Khwaja Qutb-ud-din Bakhtyar Kaki and the spiritual guide and teacher of Hazrat Nizam-ud-din Auliya.

He was related to Farrukh Shah, king of Kabul. When the Ghazni dynasty assumed political supremacy, the kingdom of Kabul lost its sovereignty and thereby suffered an eclipse, his ancestors continued to live in Kabul. With the rise of Chingiz Khan however and the fall of Ghazni and Kabul, his ancestors had perforce to leave Kabul. His great grandfather was killed in the battle of Kabul.

His grandfather Qazi Shuaib, alongwith his three sons left Kabul and came to India. He stayed in Qasoor, situated near Lahore, and was extended a warm welcome by the Qazi there. The Qazi of Qasoor informed the king of his arrival in Qasoor and recommended that some suitable provision should be made for his maintenance. The king was greatly pleased to learn of his accomplishments and showed his willingness to help him in any possible way. To this offer Hazrat Qazi Shuaib replied: "I do not desire any worldly object, but for the simple reason that whatever is lost to me, I do not hanker after its shadow." His appointment as the Qazi of Kehatwal was in recognition of his merit and attainments. Consequently, Hazrat Shuaib shifted to Kehatwal and began to discharge the duties appertaining to his high office with courage and even handedness.

His father, Jamal-ud-din Sulaiman, was related to Sultan Mahmud of Ghazni; his mother was the sister of the Sultan's mother. He shifted to and settled in Multan at imperial command. His mother, Qulsum Khatoon, was the daughter of Maulana Wajih-ud-din Khagand. He had two brother. His elder brother's name was E'zaz-ud-din and that his younger brother Najib-ud-din Mutawakkil. He was born in AH 569 in Kehatwal and named as Mas'ud.[1] It is said that Farid-ud-din Attar called him after his own name and it was then that he began to be known as "Farid-ud-din." There are others however, who believe that Farid-ud-din is not his name as alleged, but is a title conferred on him by God Almighty.

Title

Hazrat Baba Sahab is invoked and addressed as "Ganj-e-Shakar." The reasons are as follows: Under the instructions of his spiritual guide and teacher, he kept a fast that was unbroken for three days. As the time approached to break the fast, there was nothing to eat. By midnight, he became restless. Not finding anything else, he picked up some dust and put it in his mouth. The dust tasted sweet. He took it out of his mouth and threw it away.

After sometime, seized by acute hunger, he again picked up some dust and put it in his mouth. That too turned sweet. In order to satisfy his doubts, he put some more dust into his mouth and took it out again three times. Each time it tasted sweet. This he thought had been so ordained by God.

Subsequently, when he went to his spiritual guide and teacher, he was given a word of encouragement. "You did well. It was ordained by God. Go and live and be sweet like sugar." From that day he became famous and came to be known as "Ganj-e-Shakar."[2] According to others there is another reason for his title. A certain merchant was carrying bags of sugar. Hazrat Baba Sahab asked him for some sugar. The merchant thereupon informed him that contrary to his belief the bags contained salt and not sugar. They agreed to check, and when the bags were opened to his astonishment the merchant found they actually contained salt. The merchant ran up to Hazrat Baba Sahab and apologised, implored his forgiveness, and requested him to pray that this be reversed. He prayed and the bags of salt turned into bags of sugar. It is said, that this supernatural power earned for him the title of "Ganj-e-Shakar."[3]

Initiation into the Sufi Order

At the age of eighteen years, he went to Multan which was then an important seat of learning. He committed the Holy *Quran* to memory and attended the lectures of Maulana Minhaj-ud-din Tirmizi on the famous book entitled *Nafeh.*[4] One day, when he was studying *Nafeh,* Hazrat Khwaja Qutb-ud-din Bakhtyar Kaki suddenly entered the mosque.

He saw him studying the book and was attracted to him. He inquired what he was reading to which he respectfully responded: "I am reading *Nafeh*, sir." Thereupon Hazrat Khwaja Qutb-ud-din Bakhtyar Kaki said: "Do you know me." Hazrat Baba Sahab replied, "I will be benefited by your looks of grace and kindness alone." Saying thus, he stood up and placed his head at the feet of Hazrat Qutb-ud-din Bakhtyar Kaki, who honoured him by accepting him as his spiritual disciple.

Pursuit of knowledge

Hazrat Khwaja Qutb-ud-din Bakhtyar Kaki left for Delhi and was accompanied by Hazrat Farid-ud-din for three stations; when his spiritual guide and teacher bade him farewell instructing him to concentrate on the pursuit of knowledge and learning so very essential to a dervish. He was advised by his spiritual guide that after completing his education, he should come to him in Delhi for inner purification and illumination.

He obeyed. In pursuance of the instructions issued, he left for Kandhar where he stayed for five years, acquiring knowledge and learning. Subsequently, he went to Baghdad and there enjoyed the inspiring company of such eminent saints and sages as Hazrat Shaikh Shahab-ud-din Umar Suhrawardi, Saif-ud-din Bakhzai, Sa'idi Hamvi, Hazrat Baha-ud-din Zakariya of Multan, Shaikh Ohad-ud-din of Kirman, and Shaikh Farid-ud-din Mohammed of Nishapur.

Hazrat Baba Sahab came to Delhi to offer his respects to his spiritual guide and teacher, who was greatly pleased to see him and greeted him cordially. He began to live in Delhi near Ghazni Gate, took to ascetic practices and rituals, and devoted himself to meditation and the remembrance of God. He used to meet his spiritual guide and teacher once every two weeks.[5]

Receiving the blessings of Hazrat Khwaja Gharib Nawaz

Hazrat Khwaja Moin-ud-din Hasan Chishti reached Delhi from Ajmer in AD 1214 and stayed in the monastery of Hazrat Khwaja Qutb-ud-din Bakhtyar Kaki. During his stay in Delhi, Hazrat Khwaja Gharib Nawaz conferred his spiritual blessings on very many people, and one day himself asked Hazrat Qutb Sahab whether all his followers and spiritual disciples had received his spiritual blessings and had been otherwise benefited. To this Hazrat Qutb Sahab replied that among his spiritual disciples a person called Farid-ud-din, who was at a secluded place had not so far been able to receive his spiritual blessings. Both of them went to him, and when they opened the door of his tenement they found him extremely weak, so much so that he was unable to stand up to pay them respect. With all humility and due deference, tears overflowing, he put his head upon the ground. Seeing his condition, Hazrat Khwaja Gharib Nawaz was greatly moved and asked Hazrat Qutb Sahab how long he would subject him to such extreme stress and how long his ascetic practices would continue. "Come," said Hazrat Khwaja Gharib Nawaz, "let us confer some blessings upon him." Khwaja Gharib Nawaz then took his left hand and Hazrat Qutb Sahab his right and in this way helped him to stand. Khwaja Gharib Nawaz then raising his head high up towards the sky, prayed: "O God Almighty! Accept our Farid and make him a perfect dervish," and in response a voice was heard to the effect: "We have accepted Farid. He will be a great dervish of his time." Hearing these words Hazrat Baba Sahab's condition underwent a transformation. Khwaja Gharib Nawaz then suggested to Hazrat Qutb Sahab that preach to him the gospel handed down from the Khwajas of the Chishti Order, and through this he learnt the mystery of inner life.

Khwaja Gharib Nawaz conferred a robe upon him and Hazrat Khwaja Qutb Sahab gave him a turban and other articles. Khwaja Gharib Nawaz made a prophecy about him and addressing Hazrat Qutb Sahab said: "Thou has brought a big hawk in the net. His nest will undoubtedly be in the highest heaven." A poet, who was there composed the following couplet, at the spur of the moment:[6]

> The benefits of both the worlds, conferred by the Shaikhs,
> has been received by Farid;
> He has indeed got the kingship from the kings of the world.

The last meeting

Hazrat Farid-ud-din described his last meeting with his spiritual guide and teacher:[7]

> One day, when I was present in the company of my spiritual guide and teacher Hazrat Khwaja Qutb-ud-din Bakhtyar Kaki, I suddenly stood up to seek his permission to go to Hansi. He, with

tears in his eyes, gazing towards me said: 'O, Maulana! I known that you will go to Hansi.' I submitted: 'I am at your service, Sir. Whatever it be, I will obey and abide by the your Holiness's command.' Thereupon he said: 'It has been ordained by God, that you will not be present here at the time of my death.' Later, addressing those present he said: 'Let all of us invoke blessings for this dervish and pray for him to God Almighty, that he may in his mercy and grace confer upon him blessings of this, world and of the world hereafter and recite the *sura* of purity of faith.' All those present did so. Later, he gave his special praying carpet and stick to this humble dervish. He then said: 'I will handover your trust, i.e., the robe of caliphate, turban and the sandals, which have been handed down to me by the spiritual guides of the Chishti Order to Qazi Hamid-ud-din of Nagore. He will hand over these to you within five days of my death. You should keep them with you with all the respects due to them. Know that my place is just your place.' Those present, hearing these words, began to weep and all of them accordingly prayed for me.

Receiving the holy relics

One night, when in Hansi, he dreamt that he was being summoned by his spiritual guide and teacher Hazrat Khwaja Qutb-ud-din Bakhtyar Kaki and immediately realised that he had expired. He left for Delhi, and on the way there, at met Mohim, met the person sent by Hazrat Qazi Hamid-ud-din of Nagore to inform him of what had occurred.

On the fourth day, he reached Delhi and on the fifth day he paid his respects to the grave of Hazrat Khwaja Qutb-ud-din Bakhtyar Kaki. Hazrat Qazi Hamid-ud-din of Nagore and Hazrat Shaikh Badr-ud-din of Ghazni, entrusted to him the robe of caliphate and the other holy relics that had Hazrat Qutb Sahab handed over to them to be given to Hazrat Baba Sahab and he received all the holy relics and offered his prayers on the prayer carpet he had received, donned the robe given to him by his spiritual guide and teacher, and stayed in his house.[8]

Change in residence

Hazrat Baba Sahab did not stay in Delhi for more than six days,[9] leaving for Hansi. He did not like the huge crowds of people that waited upon him, being averse to publicity. He felt that this disrupted his prayers, rituals, ascetic practices, and remembrance of God. He moved on to a town called Ajoodhan, now called Pak Pattan, and began to live there. The people of Ajoodhan were then steeped in ignorance and followed a way of life characterised by bad morals and ignoble practices nurturing little need or regard for the sufis, saints and *ulama*.

Marriage and children

Hazrat Baba Sahab had four wives. He married Bibi Nehar Buza the daughter of Sultan Ghiyas-ud-din Balban. His other wives were Bibi Umme Kulsum, Bibi Sharoo, and Bibi Sakr. Bibi Nehar Buza gave birth to five sons and three daughters. The eldest son was named Shaikh Shahab-ud-din, his second son Badr-ud-din Sulaiman, who became the *sajjadanashin* of his illustrious father. His third son, Shaikh Nizam-ud-din, was killed in battle his fourth, Shaikh Yaqub, disappeared, and his fifth, Shaikh Abdullah, died in infancy. He had three daughters, Bibi Mastura, Bibi Sharifa, and Bibi Fatima who was given in marriage to Maulana Badr-ud-din Ishaq.

Death

Before his death, he made a will to his son-in-law Hazrat Badr-ud-din Ishaq to the effect that: "After my death, gave my robe which I received from my spiritual guide and teacher Hazrat Khwaja Qutub-ud-din Bakhtyar Kaki to Nizam-ud-din."

He passed away on the fifth of Muharram in AH 670.[10] A voice was heard to the effect: "The friend has been united with the Friend." His tomb is situated in Pak Pattan.

Caliphs

Hazrat Baba Farid had many spiritual caliphs. Prominent among them were:[11] All his four sons, namely, Shaikh Shahab-ud-din, Shaikh Badr-ud-din Sulaiman, Shaikh Nizam-ud-din, and Shaikh Yaqub; Shaikh Nasir-ud-din whom he brought up like a son; Shaikh Jamal-ud-din of Hansi, Hazrat Nizam-ud-din Auliya, Shaikh Badr-ud-din Ishaq, Shaikh Najib-ud-din Mutawakkil, Shaikh Mohammed Siraj, Ali Shakar Reez, Dhanni, Shaikh Zain-ud-din of Damascus, Jamal of Kabul, Shaikh Rukn-ud-din, and Hazrat Ali Ahmad Sabir.

Traits of character

Hazrat Baba Sahab was an eminent saint and a very learned man.

He was very fond of travelling and visited many places in the Indian subcontinent. He went abroad and visited Sewistan, Iraq, Arabia, and Palestine. During the course of his tours and travels, he came into contact with some eminent saints and outstanding scholars. He met Shaikh Saif-ud-din Bakhavzi in Bukhara, who gave him the following piece of advice:[12] "O, dear one, in this path be a stranger to all so that you may become familiar with God."

He also met Sa'd-ud-din Samooya, Shaikh Mahmud of Sewistan, and Shaikh Ohad-ud-din of Kirman. He was very happy to meet Hazrat Shaikh Shahab-ud-din Umar Suhrawardi who revealed to him the following: "When God Almighty wants to confer the blessings of his friendship on anyone, He opens the door of his remembrance for him."

In the course of his travels in Baghdad, he was once in the company of Hazrat Shaikh Baha-ud-din Zakariya of Multan, Shebaz Qalandar, Shaikh Dawood Mokadi, and Shaikh Mahmud Behragi.[13] He also met Shaikh Farid-ud-din Mohammed Attar of Neshapur.

Hazrat Baba Sahab performed a great many ascetic practices and rituals and kept fasts lasting three days at a time.

In this way, he passed thirty years with little rest or respite and ate very little. Hazrat Baba Sahab paid the utmost respect to his spiritual guide and to his spiritual ancestors and their relations. He was fond of music and passed his days in utter poverty. His book entitled *Fawaid-us-Salekeen* sets out the discourses of his spiritual guide and teacher Hazrat Khwaja Qutb-ud-din Bakhtyar Kaki. He was also a poet.

Teachings

His discourses are contained in a book entitled *Rahat-ul-Qulub* compiled by his spiritual disciple and premier caliph Hazrat Nizam-ud-din Auliya.

He says *inter alia*:[14]

> To conceal the faults and shortcomings of others constitutes sainthood. A dervish must then adopt four things. If he possesses these four things, then he will be entitled to be called a dervish, otherwise not. Firstly, he must close his eyes so that he may not see the faults of the people. Secondly, he must close his ears so that he may not hear anything undesirable. Thirdly, he should keep his tongue tied so that he does not say anything undesirable. Fourthly,

he should keep his legs and his feet tied, so that his self does not carry him to a place undesirable or without any necessity. If the dervish may possess these four things, then alone will he be counted among the dervishes, otherwise he is a liar pure and simple.
Perseverance is a virtue that characterises the way of the saints. Ordinary perseverance is not sufficient and should extend to the utmost limit; so much so that even if someone places an unsheathed sword upon his neck or strikes it, he should evince joy. He should not curse the person who so treats him.

According to him, "fast is a secret between an individual and God Almighty." He says: "The month of Ramazan is a blessed month. In this month, Satan is confined in iron chains. . . ."

He lays great stress on the service rendered and respect shown to saints. According to him, whosoever got the blessings of both the worlds earned them by virtue of service rendered and respect shown to the saints. If a person serves the saints with all sincerity and devotion for a week, he in turn gets the reward of prayers performed for seven hundred years. He says that a sufi is one who makes all things pure and nothing impure.

Sayings

- Planning implies trouble and submission denotes safety.
- He alone is sincere in love, who is engaged at all times in the remembrance of the beloved.
- Love becomes perfect by remembrance (of God).
- Nothing is better than the recitation of the Holy *Quran*.
- A sufi should be periodically engaged in the remembrance of God. So long as he does so and is absorbed in this, he is alive and when he abandons the practice, he is dead.
- Whosoever may come to a dervish, whether he be rich or poor, should not be allowed to leave empty handed.
- Sainthood implies contentment. If a dervish does not receive an unsought gift, he should not complain about it.
- He who does not know his own self runs after other people, but when he realises the love of God, even if the angels and the eighteen thousand worlds pursue him, he does not look towards them.

Supernatural powers

- Once an old woman came to him and said that her son had disappeared some twenty years ago and that his whereabouts had not been traced since then. She requested him to pray for her son's return. He went into a trance and after some contemplation told to the old woman: "Go, your son has reached home." The old woman was overjoyed to learn this and met her son on her way home.
- The officer-in-charge of Lahore sent him one hundred Dinars through someone. The man kept fifty Dinars for himself and offered the remaining fifty to him. Accepting the fifty Dinars he told him: "Indeed, you have divided them equally well." The man was ashamed. He returned the fifty Dinars to the man too, warning him that criminal breach of trust is a sin that render's all prayers futile and ineffective.
- A man came to him once and submitted that he had no son, and requested him to pray for one. Thereupon, Hazrat Baba Sahab said that he had given him seven sons. A person overhearing the conversation said: "O, Shaikh! know you well, that it amounts to a claim to be God and not a mere boast." He remained silent. After some years, the person came to him again, but this time, he was not alone, but accompanied by his seven sons.

References

1. *Siyar-ul-Aqtab.*
2. *Siyar-ul-Auliya.*
3. *Akhbar-ul-Akhyar; Anwar-ul-Arefeen.*
4. *Tarikh-i-Firishta,* vol. II, p. 383.
5. *Tarikh-i-Firishta.*
6. *Siyar-ul-Auliya,* p. 72; *Siyar-ul-Arefeen,* p. 23; *Siyar-ul-Aqtab,* p. 166; *Masalek-us-Salekeen,* vol. II, p. 320.
7. *Siyar-ul-Aqtab,* p. 73; *Rauzat-ul-Aqtab.*
8. *Masalek-us-Salekeen,* vol. II, p. 312.
9. *Jawahar-e-Faridi.*
10. *Masalek-us-Salekeen,* vol. II, p. 312.
11. *Jawahar-e-Faridi.*
12. *Rahat-ul-Qulub.*
13. Ibid.
14. Ibid.

96

Hazrat Baha-ud-din Zakariya

Hazrat Baha-ud-din Zakariya was one of the foremost saints of the Indian subcontinent and belonged to the Suhrawardi Order. He influenced the life and thought of myriads of people. He was Quraishi, Asadi, and Hashimi[1] and is said to have belonged to the house of Aswad, son of Muttabb, son of Asad.[2] Some have called him "Quraishi-ul-Asadi."[3] It is also said, that he traced his relationship from Asad Qurshi, who was one of the forefathers of Hazrat Ali, son-in-law of the Holy Prophet Mohammed.[4] He traced his descent from Asad, son of Hashim.[5] His grandfather, Shaikh Kamal-ud-din Ali Shah, migrated from Mecca and reached Khawarizm. Subsequently, he shifted to Multan.[6] His father, Shaikh Wajih-ud-din, married Bibi Fatima, the daughter of Maulana Husam-ud-din Tirmizi who, tired of the Tartars, had settled in Kote Karrore. It is also said, that his father, Shaikh Wajih-ud-din, went to a city, named Hama and there Hazrat Shaikh 'Isa, who was one of the descendants of Hazrat Shaikh Abd-ul-Qadir of Jilan, better known as Ghous-ul-Azam, gave his daughter Bibi Fatima in marriage to him.[7] He lived there for sometime and then returned to Kote Karrore. Hazrat Baha-ud-din Zakariya was born in the morning on Friday the twenty-seventh of Ramazan in AH 566 in Kote Karrore.[8] "Abu Mohammed" and "Abul Barkat" are his pseudonyms.[9]

Early life and education

He was born a saint. From his very childhood he showed the signs of spiritual greatness as if marked out for a great spiritual destiny. When his father recited the Holy *Quran*, he would abandon his milk and listen to the recitation of the verses of the Holy *Quran* very respectfully and attentively. He committed the Holy *Quran* to memory at the age of seven and also learnt the seven rhythmic methods of reciting it. At the age of twelve he lost his father, but he continued his education. After his father's death he went to Khorasan,[10] and there engaged in acquiring the outward knowledge and in attaining the inward graces. He spent seven years in this. Subsequently, he went to Bukhara and completed his education. There he was called "Baha-ud-din Firishta."[11]

He then went on to Mecca and Medina, living in Medina for five years. He wanted to continue his studies, and pursuit of knowledge took him to Shaikh Kamal-ud-din Mohammed of Yemen, who was considered an authority on the *hadis* and had spent fifty-three years there. He acquired the knowledge about the *hadis* and was subsequently awarded a certificate by Shaikh Kamal-ud-din.[12] From Medina, he went to Jerusalem, and from there to Baghdad.

Initiation into the Sufi Order

When in Baghdad, he heard a great deal about the name, fame, and spiritual attainments of Hazrat Shaikh Shahab-ud-din Umar Suhrawardi and wanted to be his spiritual disciple. He went and requested him to accept him as such. The request was granted. He lived in the company of his spiritual guide and teacher for seventeen days. During this period, he received very many blessings.[5] The other spiritual disciples were surprised and were even jealous of this new entrant. Hazrat Shaikh Shahab-ud-din Umar Suhrawardi could read their thoughts. He smiled and said: "You people need not worry in the least, because you are like wet wood, whereas Baha-ud-din Zakariya is like dried wood. You must know that dried wood catches fire soon."

After being enrolled as a spiritual disciple, he was anxious to be elevated to the position of a caliph.[13] One night, he dreamt of a house of light in which the Holy Prophet Mohammed was seated with his spiritual guide Hazrat Shaikh Shahab-ud-din Umar Suhrawardi standing respectfully in his presence. There was a rope upon which several robes were hung. He was summoned and presenting him saw, that his spiritual guide taking him by the hand and to the Holy Prophet and asking him to pay his respects. He also dreamt that the Holy Prophet pointed to a certain robe and said: "O, Umar, take this robe and cause Shaikh Baha-ud-din to wear it. He took the robe from where it was hung and asked him to wear it, then caused him to bow down and touch the feet of the Holy Prophet. When he awoke, he pondered over the dream and construed it as a foretaste of things to come."

He was summoned early the following morning. When he entered the house, he found it mirrored that which he had seen in his dream the previous night. His spiritual guide and teacher asked him to come close to him, took the same robe from the hanger that had been pointed out by the Holy Prophet, and caused him to wear it with his own hands, and then said: "Baba Baha-ud-din! all these robes belong to the Holy Prophet. I am only an intermediary and I cannot cause anyone to wear it without the permission of the Holy Prophet, as you yourself witnessed in your dream last night."

Departure from Baghdad

Hazrat Baha-ud-din Zakariya was allowed to leave and was instructed to go to Multan and settle there permanently. He was accompanied by Shaikh Jalal-ud-din of Tabriz. When they reached Neshapur they parted. Shaikh Jalal-ud-din of Tabriz went to Hazrat Farid-ud-din Attar. On his return, Hazrat Zakariya asked him who he considered the best among the dervishes of the day.

He replied: "Undoubtedly Hazrat Farid-ud-din Attar is the best." He then inquired about the conversation they had. He replied that as soon as Hazrat Farid-ud-din Attar saw him, he inquired whence the dervishes had come, to which he replied that he had come from Baghdad. Hazrat Farid-ud-din Attar then inquired which dervish was most absorbed in the remembrance of God. He said that he had not replied and had remained silent. Hazrat Baha-ud-din Zakariya suggested that rather than remaining silent he should have replied, and mentioned the name of Hazrat Shaikh Shahab-ud-din Umar Suhrawardi. Hazrat Jalal-ud-din of Tabriz responded that the eminence of and respect for Hazrat Farid-ud-din Attar had so greatly overwhelmed and influenced him that he forgot to mention his name. This was sufficient to annoy and irritate Hazrat Zakariya and they parted company.[14]

Meeting Qalandars

On the way to Multan, he reached a place where there was no *sarai* (inn) so he stayed under some trees. Nearby there was a party of Qalandars also staying there. They were all awake, but one was asleep. The one who was seated saw a light shining from his head up to the sky and was quite amazed. He was a very learned man named Syed Abd-ul-Quddus and belonged to Mosul. He had been initiated into the Order of the Qalandars at the grave of Syed Jamal-ud-din Mujarrad, and was attired in their characteristic attire. Hazrat Zakariya inquired from him what he was doing among the Qalandars. He replied: "O, Zakariya! know that there is an outstanding person in every sect and God Almighty in his grace grants salvation to the sect through him." Hazrat Baha-ud-din Zakariya rescued him from the Order of the Qalandars, freed him from his attire, and caused him to reach the place of enlightenment. The path of the Qalandars is the path of the libertines and this would make it impossible for a learned man like Abd-ul-Quddus to progress in a way consisted with his personal capabilities.

Arrival in Multan

After traversing the long distance and undergoing innumerable privations and an arduous journey, he eventually reached Multan. Then Multan was a very important place. Besides being the centre of learning, it was also the abode of very many outstanding and accomplished dervishes.

His arrival in Multan received very wide publicity. People talked about him a great deal and flocked to him in large numbers. The dervishes and saints living in Multan did not want him to stay there fearing that he might eclipse them. They therefore thought of a plan to get rid of him, jointly sending him a cup of milk full to the brim. This implied that the city afforded no further scope for any more dervishes.

When he received the cup he understood it and appreciate the implications. Plucking a flower and placing it on the cup of milk he returned the cup. This implied that his place in the city would be just like the flower on the milk. They all were greatly surprised by his depth of vision, intelligence, and his courteousness. Initially his stay in Multan was uneventful. He spent the period in equipping himself for the great task that awaited him, leading a life of seclusion. Seclusion is said to be the nurse of enthusiasm and enthusiasm is necessary to accomplish and great work. He devoted himself to prayers, remembrance of God, meditation, and ascetic practices. Later, he began to preach and propagate the doctrine of truth.

The charge

Nasir-ud-din Kubacha, who was in-charge of Multan, brought a charge against him. The facts are that Sultan Qutb-ud-din Aibek had freed Shams-ud-din Iltutmish and has nominated him as his successor. He entrusted Ochha and Multan to the care of Nasir-ud-din Kubacha and made a will to that effect that he should be loyal to Shams-ud-din Iltutmish. When Sultan Qutb-ud-din Aibek died it appeared that Nasir-ud-din Kubacha did not extend to Iltutmish his unflinching loyalty and allegiance and began to hatch a plot against him. Besides, it was said, he failed to conform to the dictates of Islam.

Hazrat Baha-ud-din Zakariya and Qazi Sharf-ud-din, who was Magistrate of Multan, secretly informed Sultan Shams-ud-din Iltutmish of this. The two letters conveying the information and addressed to the Sultan were intercepted. Nasir-ud-din Kubacha summoned them both. He first showed the two letters to Qazi Sharf-ud-din of Asfahan, who seeing them was unable to offer any explanation. Kubacha, furious, had him executed then and there. Then he turned towards Hazrat Zakariya and asked him what he had to say about the matter. Not disowning the letters, he said that he had written the letter in accordance with divine mandate. Hearing this, Kubacha began to tremble and asked him to go away.[15]

The appointment

Though he had a distaste for service and worldly honour, yet forced by circumstances he was obliged to accept a post which he held for sometime.

Hazrat Shaikh Jalal-ud-din of Tabriz arrived in Delhi and was given a rousing reception with Sultan Shams-ud-din Iltutmish receiving him outside the city. He was held in high esteem and became very popular in the city.

Najm-ud-din Sughra, who was Shaikh-ul-Islam then, became jealous of him, apprehending that the deep respect and social status enjoyed by Hazrat Shaikh Jalal-ud-din, coupled with his growing popularity, would one day prove detrimental to him.

He hatched a plot. He persuaded a prostitute named Gohar to bring a charge of adultery against him. It was agreed that she would receive two hundred and fifty gold coins in advance and an equal amount after she had performed her task. The prostitute did as she was directed to do. Sultan Shams-ud-din Iltutmish found himself in a very awkward situation. As a fountain of justice he was expected to dispense justice without fear or favour.

He summoned all the leading *ulama*, the saints and the law-givers. Hazrat Baha-ud-din Zakariya, also received an invitation to visit

Delhi in this connection. Besides the *ulama* and the law-givers, over two hundred saints assembled in Delhi for the purpose. The ecclesiastical council was held on Friday after prayers in the Minar mosque. Sultan Shams-ud-din Iltutmish was himself present.

The Sultan directed Shaikh Najm-ud-din Sughra to choose someone among the saints to function as an arbitrator. He, believing that Hazrat Baha-ud-din Zakariya and Hazrat Jalal-ud-din of Tabriz were not on cordial terms as they had parted company in Neshapur, suggested the name of Hazrat Baha-ud-din Zakariya.

The prostitute came and reaffirmed the charge. When Hazrat Jalal-ud-din of Tabriz entered the mosque, all those present stood up in respect. Hazrat Baha-ud-din Zakariya immediately went up to him and touched his shoes. All those present were amazed by this great honour being extended. Sultan Iltutmish expressed the opinion that it appeared that the matter had been finally decided as the arbitrator himself has shown him so much honour and respect.

To this Hazrat Zakariya said, that it was obligatory upon him to show him respect and honour, for he had lived in the company of his spiritual guide and teacher Hazrat Shaikh Shahab-ud-din Umar Suhrawardi and had served him at home and in travels for seven long years. The truth was known only to God Almighty, but that notwithstanding, it was necessary that the real facts should be revealed.

Addressing the prostitute, he said: "O, woman! State the true facts, otherwise thou shalt be overtaken by the wrath of God." The prostitute disclosed the conspiracy, surprising everyone by her statement. Shaikh Najm-ud-din Sughra fainted.

Sultan Shams-ud-din Iltutmish dismissed him from the post he was holding and appointed Hazrat Baha-ud-din Zakariya in his place as Shaikh-ul-Islam.[16] He discharged the duties of his office for sometime and then returned to Multan and devoted himself exclusively to the remembrance of God, to prayers, penances, ascetic practices, and the pursuit of a higher and abiding life.

Marriage and children

Hazrat Baha-ud-din Zakariya married in Multan and had seven sons: Hazrat Shaikh Sadr-ud-din Arif, Shaikh Burhan-ud-din, Shaikh Zia-ud-din, Shaikh Ala-ud-din, Shaikh Shahab-ud-din, Shaikh Quwwat-ud-din, and Shaikh Shams-ud-din.[17]

Death

He had a prolonged illness. On the day of his death, he was lying in his tenement with his son, Hazrat Shaikh Sadr-ud-din Arif seated at the door. A person with an appearance brought a sealed letter and asked Hazrat Sadr-ud-din to deliver it to his father. He did so and then went out but did not find the bearer of the letter there. A voice was heard to say: "The friend has been united with the Friend." When his son, Hazrat Sadr-ud-din, re-entered in the tenement he found him dead. Thus, came to an end to a noble and illustrious career on Thursday the seventh of Safar in AH 666.[18]

He was a hundred years old then. His tomb, situated in Multan, is an object of veneration.

Caliphs

His prominent caliphs are: Hazrat Shaikh Sadr-ud-din Arif, Hazrat Syed Jalal-ud-din Surq of Bukhara, Hazrat Shaikh Hasan Afghan, Hazrat Syed Usman better known as Lal Shehbaz of Sindh, Hazrat Shaikh Fakhr-ud-din Ibrahim of Iraq, and Hazrat Syed Sadr-ud-din Ahmad better known as Syed Husain.[19]

Traits of character

Hazrat Baha-ud-din Zakariya reposed his utmost trust in God he led a simple life. He ate frugally with a preference for a nutritious diet, and after doing so took a little pill and drank a little water. He showed utmost respect and regard for the *ulama* and the saints. If they were his guests, he would greet them cordially. He would feed the needy.

It is said, that at the outset of his spiritual career he fasted daily for twenty years. When breaking a fast, he would eat a little bread and drink a little water. It is also said, that during the latter years of his life, he fasted daily.[20]

He was a rich man and engaged in trade and commerce on a large scale. He also derived an income from land, on which many people worked.

Hazrat Baha-ud-din Zakariya ran a free kitchen and gave large sums of money in charity. He was very generous. Once the stock of grain of the officer-in-charge of Multan was exhausted so he requested Hazrat Zakariya to send him some. He sent a large quantity to him. In which some silver coins were recovered. The officer returned the amount so recovered from the grain, but he refused to take it back.

He used to complete the whole of the Holy *Quran* each night and slept very little. When one-third of the night remained he would get out of bed and devote himself to prayer till the break of dawn. After performing the morning prayers, he would again engage himself in prayers. He was a very successful preacher and would accompany the funeral processions of devotees, disciples, admirers, acquaintances, and even of strangers.

He had forbearing nature. Once when some Qalandars came to him to ask for something he ignored them. They abused and threw stones at him. He remained unmoved and said: "You must know, that I have not sat here myself. I have been caused to sit hereby the perfect saint named Hazrat Shahab-ud-din Suhrawardi." All the Qalandars then fell at his feet.

His love of God knew no bounds. Once he bowed down in reverence about a hundred times.

He was so deeply absorbed in concentration that for several days he would not eat anything or say anything. One day it happened that he went into a state of spiritual exaltation. Emerging from the monastery, he roamed throughout the city proclaiming that whosoever saw his face that day would not enter hell. People flocked to him to do so.

He was also fond of music. Once a *qawwal* named Abdullah came to him. He listened to his singing and gave him a robe and twenty *tankas* of silver. Sometimes, when listening to music he would go into a state of rapture. He was himself a poet.

Teachings

- The wealth of the world, howsoever much it may be, is but little. The company of the snake is dangerous for and detrimental to the man who does not know of an antidote.
- The loss and gain of the wealth of the world make no difference to dervishes. They do not feel sorry at its going and they do not feel happy at its coming.
- Love means that one does not see anyone else but God. One so consumed should turn his face away from heaven, hell, relations, and dependants.

Sayings

- One should not be attached to every door and person but hold fast to one door and one alone.
- Real love implies that when one rises in the morning, one does not remember what transpired during the night, and at the approach of night, one does not remember anything of the day.
- Piety consists of three things. He who is not endowed with them cannot be said pious. Firstly, there is the recognition of the right of the world and to renounce it; secondly, there is the service of God and being mindful of the ways of respect; thirdly, there is the desire for the world hereafter and to demand it.
- It is obligatory upon a *mureed* (spiritual disciple) to take to meditation and should eradicate all else there is in his heart besides God and should shun the company of people and should derive pleasure in being close to God.
- If the repetition of the remembrance of God is lacking, then an individual cannot even smell the love of God.
- The safety of the body lies in eating less; the safety of the soul lies in sleeping less; and the safety of religion lies in prayer.

Supernatural power

Hazrat Syed Jalal-ud-din Surq of Bukhara came to Multan during the summer and stayed in his monastery. He was used to the cold climate of Bukhara, where snow fell and cold winds blew. Tired of the hot wind and scorching heat of Multan, he was reminded of the refreshing climate of Bukhara.

Hazrat Zakariya could read his thoughts. He sent one of his devotees to the monastery and directed him to remove the praying carpets and to sweep the courtyard of the mosque. Suddenly a dark cloud appeared and enveloped the monastery. There was a heavy downpour of rain accompanied by a thunderstorm but not a drop fell outside the monastery. At the time of Zuhr (afternoon prayers) Hazrat Zakariya came to the mosque and, seeing Hazrat Jalal-ud-din Surq of Bukhara, he smiled and said:

'Tell me, O Syed, which among the two is better: the snowballs of

Multan or the snow of Bukhara?' Responding, Hazrat Jalal-ud-din Surq respectfully said that under the circumstances it appeared that the snowballs of Multan were far better than the snow of Bukhara. That very day Hazrat Jalal-ud-din was honoured by being appointed a spiritual caliph.

Khwaja Kamal-ud-din Mas'ud of Shiraz, one of his spiritual disciples, was a dealer in costly jewels and precious stones. Once, when on board a ship, he experienced such a storm, that he lost all hope of reaching the shore. The ship began to drift. He invoked Hazrat Zakariya's assistance. Suddenly, he appeared on the ship and the passengers actually saw him. He assured them of a safe landing and eventually they reached Aden safely. All the passengers on board the ship gave one-third of their goods to Khwaja Kamal-ud-din Mas'ud of Shiraz to be offered to Hazrat Baha-ud-din Zakariya. Khwaja Kamal-ud-din added half his jewels to these goods and asked his sister's son Khwaja Fakhr-ud-din of Jilan, to deliver all the gifts. The latter arrived in Multan not having seen him before except on that one occasion when he had appeared on the ship. Seeing him, he at once recognised him and found him wearing the same clothes in which he had appeared on the ship.

Khwaja Fakhr-ud-din offered him all the goods and the precious stones, valued at about seventy lakh Tankas. Hazrat Zakariya distributed all the goods within three days. Seeing him do so Khwaja Fakhr-ud-din also distributed his own goods and got himself enrolled as his spiritual disciple. Subsequently, he received the robe of caliph.[21]

One day Hazrat Baha-ud-din Zakariya was sitting with Hazrat Baba Farid-ud-din Ganj-e-Shakar. Suddenly, he stood up and began weeping, Hazrat Baba Sahab was surprised and inquired why he was doing so. He asked him to stand up and see for himself. Hazrat Baba Sahab saw, that the pall of Hazrat Shaikh Sa'd-ud-din Hamoya was being carried and funeral prayers being offered in front of the mosque at Baghdad. Later, news arrived that Hazrat Shaikh Sa'd-ud-din Hamoya had passed away that very day.[22]

References

1. *Anwar-e-Ghosiya.*
2. *Tazkarat-ul-Auliya.*
3. *Akhbar-ul-Akhiyar; Mukhbir-ul-Waseleen.*

4. *Takmila Siyar-ul-Auliya.*
5. *Masalek-us-Salekeen,* vol. II, p. 509.
6. *Siyar-ul-Arefeen; Masalek-us-Salekeen,* vol. II, p. 511.
7. *Anwar-e-Ghosia;* Manuscript copy of "Kholasat-ul-Waseleen."
8. *Masalek-us-Salekeen,* vol. II, p. 511.
9. Ibid., p. 509.
10. *Siyar-ul-Arefeen.*
11. *Masalek-us-Salekeen,* vol. II, p. 511.
12. *Fawaid-ul-Fu'ad.*
13. *Siyar-ul-Arefeen.*
14. *Masalek-us-Salekeen,* vol. II, p. 512.
15. Ibid., p. 513.
16. Ibid., p. 515.
17. Ibid., pp. 523-24.
18. Ibid., p. 509.
19. Ibid., p. 520.
20. *Siyar-ul-Arefeen.*
21. *Israr-ul-Auliya.*
22. *Masalek-us-Salekeen,* vol. II, pp. 521-22.

97

Hazrat Shaikh Badr-ud-din Sulaiman

Hazrat Shaikh Badr-ud-din Sulaiman was the most famous among the sons of Hazrat Baba Farid-ud-din Ganj-e-Shakar.

Initiation into the Sufi Order

He was the spiritual disciple and caliph of his distinguished father Hazrat Baba Sahab.

Once two prominent persons, Khwaja Zore and Khwaja Ghore, came to Ajoodhan from Chisht. They both belonged to the Chishti Order. When Hazrat Baba Sahab learnt of their arrival, he was delighted, showed them the utmost respect, and extended a very warm welcome to them. He gave them a grand feast and entertained them lavishly.

Hazrat Baba Sahab presented his two sons, Maulana Shahab-ud-din and Shaikh Badr-ud-din Sulaiman, to them with the request that they might be so good as to bless them. He also requested the distinguished guests to place on their heads the cap denoting discipleship. The two guests apologised and were reluctant to do so. They told Hazrat Baba Sahab that it would be impertinent to do so in the presence of a spiritual sovereign like him. To this, Hazrat Baba Sahab responded by saying that whatever spiritual blessings he possessed had been derived from and conferred upon by their family alone and so he wished them to be kind enough as to accept his humble request.

The two distinguished guests, finding Hazrat Baba Sahab adamant, agreed and asked him to fetch two caps for the purpose. Hazrat Baba Sahab asked his son-in-law Hazrat Maulana Badr-ud-din Ishaq to fetch these. Hazrat Baba Sahab, as requested by the two distinguished guests, touched the caps with his hand, straightened them and gave them to the two persons. They placed one cap on the head of Maulana Shahab-ud-din and the other on the head of Shaikh Badr-ud-din Sulaiman.[1]

Hazrat Baba Sahab having had the caps placed on their heads accepted them as his own spiritual disciples.

After the death of his father, Hazrat Shaikh Badr-ud-din Sulaiman, was unanimously accepted as his father's spiritual heir.

Death

Hazrat Shaikh Badr-ud-din was buried in Pak Pattan close to his father.

The successor

His son, Shaikh Ala-ud-din, sat on the *sajjada* of his father at the age of sixteen. He was very pious, and prayed only at the Central Mosque. He did not mix with the noblemen and the kings and would fast throughout the year. He was very generous.[2]

He was buried in Pak Pattan.

References

1. *Siyar-ul-Auliya*, pp. 188-89; *Akhbar-ul-Akhyar* (Urdu trans.), p. 153; *Jawahar-e-Faridi*, p. 285.
2. *Akhbar-ul-Akhyar* (Urdu trans.), pp. 206-7.

98

Hazrat Shaikh Sadr-ud-din Arif

Hazrat Shaikh Sadr-ud-din Arif was the son, spiritual disciple, caliph, spiritual successor, and *sajjadanashin* of his father—Shaikh-ul-Islam Hazrat Baha-ud-din Zakariya of Multan. His name was Shaikh Sadr-ud-din, and his pseudonym "Abul-Mughanim." He is addressed and invoked as "Arif" (enlightened). The reasons for calling him "Arif" are firstly, that when reading the Holy *Quran* he would ponder over the meaning and implications of all he read, and his heart and mind and soul were illumined.[1] Secondly, as stated by Makhdoom Jahanian-e-Jahan Gasht, every time he read the Holy *Quran*, he discovered a new meaning and a new implication, different from those he had previously discovered.[2]

He was brought up under the vigilant care of his father and received his education from him. He committed the Holy *Quran* to memory, acquired and perfected a knowledge of ritual, and mastered theology. He attributed his inner and spiritual training to his father. On his father's death, the family assets were distributed. His personal share in cash alone amounted to seventy lakh Tankas. The very day he received the goods and the money, he distributed them all to the poor, the indigent, and the handicapped. A certain dervish inquired what the reason for this was. His reply was that his father had overpowered the world and hence the presence of silver and gold could do him no harm. Though, he himself had to a considerable extent overpowered the world, yet despite this he suffered occasional lapses. Afraid that some day the world might overpower him, he thought it best to rid himself of the worldly goods and the gold and silver and thereby free himself of an impending threat.

Marriage

Hazrat Shaikh Sadr-ud-din Arif was married. His son, Hazrat Shaikh Rukn-ud-din Abul-Fath, was his spiritual successor.

Death

He passed away on the twenty-third of Zilhijj in AH 684 and was buried besides his father in Multan.

Caliphs

His outstanding caliphs are: Hazrat Shaikh Rukn-ud-din Abul-Fath, Hazrat Shaikh Jamal-ud-din Khandan of Ochha, Hazrat Shaikh Ahmad Mashooq, Hazrat Shaikh Salah-ud-din Durvesh, Hazrat Shaikh Ala-ud-din, better known as Mahboobullah, and Hazrat Shaikh Husam-ud-din Badavli.[3]

Traits of character

Hazrat Shaikh Sadr-ud-din Arif was unique in his piety, purity, and simplicity. He disliked publicity, and his life was characterised by a spirit of renunciation and abstinence. He was ever absorbed in the remembrance of God, had a generous disposition, and was very hospitable and entertaining. He was an accomplished man of letters and discharged his duties as *sajjadanashin* for a full eighteen years with ease, grace, and distinction.

Sayings

- Whatever happens before death is not lasting. The pen of extinction is certain to be turned over it.
- The sign of perfect faith is the ability to derive pleasure from good and abhor evil.
- The permanence of faith means that one's love of God and his apostle is supreme.

Supernatural powers

Maulana Imam-ud-din Mubarak states that one day Hazrat Shaikh Sadr-ud-din and his son Hazrat Shaikh Rukn-ud-din Abul-Fath went to a river at some distance from Multan. He was busy making ablutions in the river when a herd of deer passed that way. His son, who was seven years old then, was attracted by a baby deer in the herd.

In the meanwhile Hazrat Arif, having completed his prayers called his son to impart a lesson to him. A noticeable change occurred that day. Hazrat Shaikh Rukn-ud-din Abul-Fath used to commit a part of the Holy *Quran* by reciting it three times only. That day, he repeated it ten times yet failed to commit it to memory. Hazrat Arif inquired why this was so and was told about the young deer. Hearing this, he asked for the direction in which the herd of deer had left. On being told, he focused his attention in that direction and instantaneously the herd returned. His son caught the baby deer and took it to the monastery. In a state of exaltation he committed one part of the Holy *Quran* to memory rather than his usual quota.[4]

One day, when he was coming out of the tomb of his father Hazrat Baha-ud-din Zakariya, one of his admirers and devotees, Maulana Husam-ud-din, thought that he should ask for a piece of land for his grave in the compound of his father's tomb. Hazrat Arif was able to read his thoughts and said: "It will not be in the least difficult for me to allot to you a piece of land for your grave. I have no objection to that but the Holy Prophet Mohammed has suggested a place for your burial in Budaun, and therefore, you will be buried in Budaun. That is exactly what happened."

Maulana Husam-ud-din, when in Budaun, dreamt of the Holy Prophet making ablutions at a certain place. When he awoke the following morning he found the place wet. He made a will to the effect that he should be buried at that very spot.[5]

References

1. *Masalek-us-Salekeen,* vol. II, p. 523.
2. *Jame'-ul-Uloom.*
3. *Masalek-us-Salekeen,* vol. II, p. 524.
4. Ibid., pp. 524-25.
5. Ibid., p. 525.

99

Hazrat Shaikh Rukn-ud-din Abul-Fath

Hazrat Shaikh Rukn-ud-din Abul-Fath was the son, spiritual disciple, caliph, and *sajjadanashin* of his father Hazrat Shaikh Sadr-ud-din Arif.

His mother, Bibi Rasti, was an accomplished woman of her time. She was very pious and had committed the Holy *Quran* to memory and would recite the Holy *Quran* everyday. She was accepted by her father-in-law Hazrat Baha-ud-din Zakariya as his spiritual disciple. Once, during the seventh month of her pregnancy, his mother went to her father-in-law to offer her respects to him. Seeing her, Hazrat Baha-ud-din Zakariya stood up. His mother was greatly surprised at this unusual gesture and told father-in-law that she did not deserve such honour and respect being according to her. In response Hazrat Baha-ud-din Zakariya said that he had stood up to accord respect to the child in her womb. He will be the pride of the family. Hazrat Rukn-ud-din was born on the ninth of Ramazan in AH 649.[1] His grandfather, Hazrat Baha-ud-din Zakariya, named him Rukn-ud-din. His pseudonym was "Abul-Fath" and was addressed as Fazlullah.

Early life and education

One day when he was only four years old, his illustrious grandfather Hazrat Baha-ud-din Zakariya was sitting on his bed leaning against a pillow, his turban placed on the bed. Hazrat Rukn-ud-din was playing in the room. Suddenly he approached the bed, took hold of the turban and placed it on his head. His father, seeing this, forbade him not to do so and asked him to take it off. His grandfather smiled and said:[2] "Baba Sadr-ud-din, do not forbid him. There is nothing wrong with what he has done because he has worn the turban as of right. I entrust this turban to him." The turban was therefore stored in a box and when he became the *sajjadanashin* he wore that very turban. His grandfather, Hazrat Baha-ud-din

Zakariya oversaw his education and training, and his upbringing was in the family tradition. He acquired a very sound knowledge of the *hadis*, jurisprudence, commentaries on the Holy *Quran*, logic, literature, metaphysics, and history. After completing his education, he engaged himself in acquiring inward knowledge and the spiritual graces.

Initiation in Sufi Order

When he grew up he wanted to be initiated into the Sufi Order and became a spiritual disciple of his father. A few days before his death, his father appointed him as his spiritual caliph and entrusted his father i.e., Hazrat Baha-ud-din Zakariya's robe and other holy relics to him and in doing so and accepted him as his successor.[3]

Relations with Hazrat Nizam-ud-din Auliya

His relations with Hazrat Nizam-ud-din Auliya, for whom he nurtured great respect and love, were extremely cordial. He paid occasional visits to Delhi to meet him, coming five times during the lifetime of Hazrat Nizam-ud-din Auliya with the express purpose of meeting him. When Hazrat Nizam-ud-din Auliya fell ill, he came to Delhi to inquire about his health.[4]

Relations with the Imperial Court

He commanded great influence. The king, an admirer and devotee of his, held him in high esteem and frequently invoked his spiritual assistance and blessings. People, would often submit their grievances to the king through Hazrat Rukn-ud-din. Whenever he visited Delhi, Sultan Ala-ud-din would send a sum of two lakh Tankas to him as an offering the day he arrived. On the day of his departure from Delhi, he would offer him a sum of five lakh Tankas. Whenever he visited the king, he would be received by him at the third door and be conducted to the royal apartment.

Marriage and children

Hazrat Shaikh Rukn-ud-din Abul-Fath had no issue.

Death

Three months before he died he had severed all connections with the public, devoting himself exclusively to the remembrance of God. When his condition became critical and all hope of recovery appeared to have been lost, one of the devotees suggested organising some charitable work and prayers for his recovery. He did not permit this because he knew that his end was fast approaching.

On the day he passed away, he called one of his chief devotees, Maulana Zahir-ud-din, inside the tenement and asked him to make preparations for the funeral. Having offered the sunset prayers, he bowed in adoration and passed away on the sixteenth of Rajab in AH 735.[5] His tomb in Multan is an exquisite piece of architecture.

Caliphs

His prominent caliphs are: Hazrat Syed Jalal-ud-din of Bukhara, better known as Makhdoom Jahanian-e-Jehan Gasht, Hazrat Shaikh Usman Sayyah, Hazrat Haji Shaikh Sadr-ud-din *alias* Haji Chiragh Hindbun, Hazrat Maulana Imad-ud-din Isma'il, Hazrat Shaikh Hamid-ud-din better known as Sultan-ut-Tarekeen Qarsi Al-Hankari.

Traits of character

He had a towering personality and brought it to bear over men and affairs. By the sheer force of his personality and spiritual attainments he brought about a new orientation in the thinking of the people over whom he exercised a marvellous influence.

During his lifetime the Suhrawardi Order reached the pinnacle of its influence in the Indian subcontinant and brought the church and state close to each other. The Order received fresh impetus and innumerable people thronged to join it, making it a powerful instrument for social, moral, ethical, and spiritual advance. Eminent saints and sages, like Makhdoom Jahanian-e-Jahan Gasht, accepted his creed, invoked his blessings, became his spiritual disciple, and entered the Order which underlines the magnetic force of the Order and the strength of Hazrat Abul-Fath's personality and spirituality which won the devotion of commoners and the king alike.

Hazrat Makhdoom Jahanian-e-Jahan Gasht states that he had seen his prayer carpet in Ka'ba close to that of the Holy Prophet and that the prayer carpet of Hazrat Nasir-ud-din Chiragh of Delhi was behind it by four yards. He states that he asked Hazrat Imam Abdullah Yafai, why this was so he replied that Hazrat Rukn-ud-din's rank was nearer and closer to the Holy Prophet than that of

Hazrat Nasir-ud-din Chiragh of Delhi. Hazrat Makhdoom Jahanian-e-Jahan Gasht used to offer prayers in Ka'ba behind the two praying carpets.

Hazrat Rukn-ud-din was unique in prayer, piety, purity, asceticism renunciation, abstinence, and self-surrender. He was generous, kind-hearted, and sympathetic. His love and advice extended to all.

He was very courteous and accommodating, free from advarice, malice, and greed. From the age of seven, he prayed punctually and fasted regularly. Besides the five obligatory prayers, he also offered Tahajjud, the pre-dawn prayer, the Ishraq, and Chasht prayers, and genuflected.[6] Hazrat Rukn-ud-din regularly undertook ascetic practices. He was able to read the thoughts of individuals and could rapidly traverse long distances through the force of his spiritual powers and could foretell the future course of events.

As an example, it may be related that once a person came to him and requested him to accept him as a spiritual disciple. He refused. When he insisted that he should be so honoured, Hazrat Rukn-ud-din suggested that he should patiently wait for sometime and then approach him again. The man began to weep and continued to insist. His brother, Maulana Imad-ud-din, asked him why he would not accept him as his spiritual disciple in the face of such insistence and anguish. His response was that he would not accept him as his spiritual disciple because he was yet to commit some sins. His partook of a simple nutritious diet. Whatever he received as an offering, whether in cash or kind, he would immediately have it distributed among the poor and needy. He reposed his utmost trust in God and took pleasure in fulfilling the wants of others. He would not allow anyone to leave his door in need or empty handed.

In spite of his high position, spiritual attainments, inward illumination, he did not feel proud of his power, wealth, or prestige. He was so humble that sometimes when he got out of a palanquin, he would have both his arms extended, when asked why he did this he replied: "This is because it is quite likely the hand of someone who has attained salvation may touch mine and I may also be benefited and thereby attain salvation." He held the *ulama;* the dervishes, and sages in high respect.

He had great regard for others. Once a rich man came to him and became his spiritual disciple, firmly resolving not to commit sins again. Hazrat Rukn-ud-din gave him his own cap to him. A certain dervish who was there raised an objection to this saying that he had given his cap to a person who was still engrossed in worldly affairs.

To this the response was. "O, dear one! if he is able to refrain from committing sins through receipt of a cap and attain salvation on that account, then why should I not give him the cap." In short, his traits of character, marked him out for spiritual greatness.

Supernatural powers

One of his devotees, who belonged to Sindh, went to Mecca on a pilgrimage. There he found the cost of living and the soaring prices beyond his means. He had earlier bought four loaves of bread daily, but now it became difficult for him to buy even one. Once, in the course of conversation, he mentioned to a dervish that he was not happy there he was not getting what he had formerly done. He mentioned that the kindness and benevolence that Hazrat Shaikh Rukn-ud-din had extended to him had made him very happy. The dervish informed him that Hazrat Rukn-ud-din Abul-Fath came every Friday night to Mecca and actually showed him the place where he offered prayers and engaged himself in the remembrance of God. The devotee was anxious to meet him and to offer his respects. On the appointed day he went to the specified place and actually found him. He made his *salaams* and offered his respects. Hazrat Rukn-ud-din in acknowledged these and asked him in the dialect of Multan why he was so confused and perplexed. His devotee described the adverse circumstances in which he was living and said that he longed to return to Multan as he was not getting enough to eat. Having heard his grievance, Hazrat Rukn-ud-din said that he should stop worrying because henceforth here too he would receive what he had received in Multan. From that very day till he returned to Multan he regularly received loaves of four bread and two cups full of vegetable everyday.[7]

Once, when the Mughals reached the outskirts of Multan he was beseeched by the people to avert the danger of Mughal invasion. He lowered his head for a while contemplated a little, and then said that the Mughals had fled scattering after then reached the river bank. A devotee inquired what had happened to the Mughals, to which he replied that God Almighty in his grace and mercy had sent an army of angels who had routed and scattered the Mughals.[8]

One of his spiritual disciples was engaged in the remembrance of God in the tenement of the monastery in Multan. Once in a dream he saw a person who suggested that he should go on a pilgrimage to Mecca. The next morning he came to meet Hazrat Rukn-ud-din, and as soon as he saw him, he told him that Satan was responsible for his dream and that Satan wanted to deprive him of the remembrance of God. He added that pilgrimage was not obligatory upon him as he was a poor man and a *faqir*.

Sayings

- A human being is the combination of shape and quality, and what counts is the quality and not the shape.
- On the Day of Resurrection, the reward will be in accordance with the deserts. The tyrant will see his face like that of a wolf and one who is proud will see his face turned into that of a tiger, and the miser and the greedy will find themselves turned into the shape of swine.
- So long as an individual does not practice self-control and does not achieve a purification on his heart, he remains within the fold of the beast and beastly qualities continue to govern his life.
- Self-control is not possible without prayer and the help of God.
- The sign of His grace and mercy is that an individual is acquainted with the shortcomings of the self and the light of his mercy illumines his heart through which love of the world and people of the world is eradicated. He finds evil deeds abhorrent and wishes to imbibe angelic qualities. Hence, rather than tyranny, anger, greed, miserliness, and lust he exhibits the qualities of forgiveness, forbearance, hospitality, generosity, and sacrifice. This relates to the desire to win over the world hereafter. However, the case of those seeking the ultimate truth is different from the better and higher than the rest.
- The meaning of harmony of the deeds is this, that the limbs may come under control. So that the, prohibited and unlawful, anti-Islamic acts are not to be performed and ignoble society, idle chatter, and the company of the hypocrites are shunned.

- One who is not a seeker is in fact a hypocrite.

Rituals and practices

Hazrat Rukn-ud-din Abul-Fath took a delight in meditation and practised *commemoratio cordis.*

References

1. *Masalek-us-Salekeen,* vol. II, p. 527.
2. *Siyar-ul-Arefeen.*
3. *Masalek-us-Salekeen,* vol. II, p. 524.
4. *Siyar-ul-Auliya.*
5. *Masalek-us-Salekeen,* vol. II, p. 527.
6. *Anwar-e-Ghosiya; Masalek-us-Salekeen,* vol. II, p. 530.
7. *Jame'-ul-Ulum.*
8. *Masalek-us-Salekeen,* vol. II, p. 533-34.

100

Hazrat Syed Jalal-ud-din Surq Bukhara

Hazrat Syed Jalal-ud-din Surq of Bukhara is the grandfather of Syed Jalal-ud-din of Bukhara, better known as Makhdoom Jahanian-e-Jahan Gasht.

He came from Bukhara and settled in Multan.[1]

Initiation into the Sufi Order

He was accepted as a spiritual disciple by Hazrat Baha-ud-din Zakariya of Multan and was subsequently honoured by being appointed a caliph.

Marriage and children

The Holy Prophet directed him in dream to marry the daughter of Syed Badr-ud-din of Bhekar. Syed Badr-ud-din received a similar mandate to give his daughter in marriage to Hazrat Syed Jalal-ud-din Surq of Bukhara. The marriage was accordingly solemnised.

He had three sons, Syed Ahmad Kabir, Syed Baha-ud-din, and Syed Sadr-ud-din, better known as Mohammed Ghous.

Arrival in Ochha

At the command of his spiritual guide and teacher, Hazrat Baha-ud-din Zakariya of Multan, he left for Ochha and settled there. He died and was buried there.

REFERENCE

1. *Siyar-ul-Arefeen.*

101

Hazrat Makhdoom Jahanian-e-Jahan Gasht

Hazrat Makhdoom Jahanian-e-Jahan Gasht was one of the leading spiritual figures of the Indian subcontinent and occupies a unique position amongst the saints and sages who have by their precept and practice brought about a transformation in human society. He was one of the most widely travelled saints, bearing up cheerfully with the inconveniences of travel in those times. He visited every part of the then Islamic world. He met saints, sages, dervishes, and doctors of law wherever he went. He came into contact with the high and the low and with people engaged all the various pursuits of life.

He refused to be governed or swayed by the traditions and conventions of mystic life as they then obtained. He did not confine himself to the blessings of one Sufi Order alone, believing that loyalty to a cause is quite different from loyalty to an individual. He believed that every Order was endowed with some inherent spiritual greatness and therefore joined every Order that then existed.

His teachings and his principles, his method and his approach, his vision and his design, and his deals and his pursuit of them led to the birth, of a new Order, that came to be known as the "Jahanian Order" after his name.

He belonged to Bukhara. He traced his relationship from Hazrat Imam Husain, son of Hazrat Ali, son-in-law of the Holy Prophet Mohammed. That makes him a Husaini. His father, Syed Ahmad Kabir, was the son of Shaikh Jalal-ud-din Surq of Bukhara, and was an accomplished man. He too was a sufi and a saint whom Hazrat Gasht succeeded.

Hazrat Makhdoom Gasht was born on the fifteenth of Sha'ban in AH 707 and was named Jalal-ud-din Husain. His pseudonym is "Abu Abdullah," and he is addressed and invoked as "Makhdoom Jahanian-e-Jahan Gasht," meaning "the respected globe-trotter." One reason for his title is, that he travelled very widely and extensively in times when the means of communications were very primitive and therefore it was unusual to travel so much. Another reason given is that once, on the night of a certain 'Id he went to the tomb of Hazrat Baha-ud-din Zakariya and engaged in prayer. Subsequently, he went to the tombs of Hazrat Sadr-ud-din Arif and Hazrat Rukn-ud-din Abul-Fath. On all the three shrines he asked for the gift of 'Id, and at all the three shrines, he heard himself being addressed by the title.[1] From that day on, he began to be known, addressed, and invoked as "Makhdoom Jahanian-e-Jahan Gasht."

To complete his antecedents, it may be mentioned that he had one brother, Shaikh Sadr-ud-din, better known as Raju Qattal, who was his spiritual disciple and caliph.

Early life

When he was seven years old his father took him to Shaikh Jamal-ud-din Khandan of Ochha, a spiritual caliph of Hazrat Shaikh Sadr-ud-din Arif. He, as directed by his father, kissed Shaikh Jamal-ud-din's hands and touched his feet and sat down respectfully. In the meanwhile, a tray full of dried dates was brought in and distributed among all those present. He was given his share and ate the dates with the seeds. All those present were surprised. Some thought that he had not eaten dried dates before and therefore did not know that the seed was not supposed to be eaten. Hazrat Shaikh Jamal-ud-din Khandan of Ochha smiled, and unable to restrain himself, eventually asked him "why he was doing so." He responded: "Your Holiness! not only have the dried dates, I have received here been blessed, but also the kernels within them. To throw them away would be an act of disrespect and would deprive me of half the blessings. How can I throw them away?" The reply delighted the Shaikh who then prayed for his future welfare and conferred upon him very many spiritual blessings.[2]

Education and training

He took great pains to acquire knowledge and learning. The outstanding scholar of his time Qazi Baha-ud-din of Ochha acted as his teacher, but his education was still incomplete when his teacher died. After his death, it became a problem for Hazrat Gasht to continue his education. Ochha being a small place, there were no facilities for further education.

He thought of going to Multan, which was then a centre of knowledge and learning. He wanted to complete *Hidaya* and *Bazoodi*. Reaching Multan, he was faced with the problem of boarding and lodging. The problem was soon solved. Hazrat Shaikh Rukn-ud-din permitted him to stay in the *madrasa*. He was fortunate to be taught by such eminent scholars as Shaikh Musa and Maulana Mujadd-ud-din and soon completed *Hidaya* and *Bazoodi*. He studied some other books too during his one year stay in Multan.

Return to Ochha

On the expiry of a year, he was ordered by Hazrat Shaikh Rukn-ud-din Abul-Fath to return to Ochha. The reason he had sent him back to Ochha so soon was that the Shaikh was given to understand that Hazrat Makhdoom's father was not on good terms with Hazrat Jamal-ud-din Khandan of Ochha and that he did not pay him the respect due to him. The Shaikh conveyed through Hazrat Makhdoom his mandate that his father should seek reconciliation with Hazrat Jamal-ud-din and should extend every respect and honour. He honoured the former by sending him in his special boat. When he reached Ochha, he conveyed the Shaikh's order to his father, who accordingly went to Hazrat Shaikh Jamal-ud-din Khandan and apologised for his behaviour, embraced him, and asked for forgiveness.

Initiation into the Sufi Order

Hazrat Makhdoom did not confine himself to one Order or to one person.[3] He derived spiritual ecstasy from the company of all the saints he met, and sought and received their blessings.[4] It is said that he was initiated as a spiritual disciple into and received the robe of caliph from fourteen sects.[5] He first became his father's spiritual disciple and received the robe of caliph from him. Thereafter, he became a *mureed* (spiritual disciple) of Hazrat Shaikh Rukn-ud-din Abul-Fath.

The sundry robes of caliph he received were as follows:[6]

He states that he received the robe of caliph from Hazrat Ali in dream which he had received from the Holy Prophet.

He received the robe of caliph from his father Syed Ahmad Kabir which he had received from Hazrat Shaikh Baha-ud-din Zakariya. A third robe of caliph was granted by Hazrat Shaikh Rukn-ud-din Abul-Fath in dream which when he awoke, he found to be on his head.

Again, he received a robe of caliphate from Hazrat Nizam-ud-din Auliya in dream, but when he awoke it was not there. He also received one from Hazrat Shaikh Qiyam-ud-din, who was the spiritual caliph of Hazrat Shaikh Rukn-ud-din Abul-Fath, and others from Qutb-ud-din Manawwar, Hazrat Nasir-ud-din Chiragh of Delhi who was the spiritual caliph of Hazrat Nizam-ud-din Auliya, Imam Abdullah Yafai, Hazrat Abdullah Ali Mutri, Hazrat Fakhneema Bisal, Shaikh Abu Ishaq Kazarooni, Shaikh Amin-ud-din and also from his brother Shaikh Imam-ud-din. He is also said to have received the robe of caliph form Shaikh Hamid-ud-din and from Shaikh Sharf-ud-din Mahmud Shah Tashtari, a spiritual caliph of Hazrat Shaikh Shahab-ud-din Suhrawardi.

He asserts that Syed Ahmad Kabir Rifai, Shaikh Najm-ud-din Sinyani, and Shaikh Najm-ud-din Kubra also conferred spiritual blessings upon him as well as the robe of caliph. He also refers to Hazrat Khizr, Hazrat Ohad-ud-din Hasni, and Hazrat Shaikh Nur-ud-din as having honoured him by conferring upon him the robe of caliph.[7]

It is said that he was most attracted and attached to the Qadiri Order than to the rest.

The appointment

For sometime he had to shoulder the encumbrance of office. During the reign of Sultan Mohammed Tughlaq Shah he was appointed Shaikh-ul-Islam of Sewistan and the adjoining areas but did not hold the office for long. As directed by Hazrat Shaikh Rukn-ud-din Abul-Fath he resigned his post and left for Mecca to perform the pilgrimage.

After the pilgrimage

After performing the pilgrimage he reached Medina to offer his respects at the tomb of the Holy Prophet. It is said that when he went to the tomb of the Holy Prophet, he addressed him as follows: "Peace be on you, O, My forefather!" A voice from the tomb acknowledged the greetings: "Peace be also on you, O my son."[8] He utilised his time in Medina in studying books besides deriving spiritual blessings from the tomb of the Holy Prophet. He spent about two years with Shaikh Afif-ud-din Abdullah Al-Mutri, who taught him the *Awarif* and other books. After Hazrat Makhdoom had performed the pre-dawn prayers, Shaikh Abdullah Al-Mutri would come to him with food in one hand and a lamp in the other hand and teach him *Sahah* and *Awarif* and impart lessons on mysticism and divine philosophy.[9] He later received the robe of caliph from Shaikh Abdullah Al-Mutri.

One day it so happened that when he went to offer prayers, the Imam was not therein the mosque. People asked him to lead the prayers. Acting as an Imam, he stood in a row behind the place where the Holy Prophet used to stand and conducted the prayers. The deference and regard thus shown to the place where the Holy Prophet had stood evoked admiration and praise from Shaikh Abdullah Al-Mutri.

From Medina he returned to Mecca, and during his stay there came in close contact with Imam Abdullah Yafai, who also conferred the robe of caliph upon him. During the course of this journey, he also met Syed Sadr-ud-din Kamash and Shaikh Hamid-ud-din son of Mahmud al-Hasni of Samarqand. He returned in AH 752 and met Hazrat Nasir-ud-din Chiragh of Delhi and received the robe of caliph from him.

Tours and travels

Besides performing the pilgrimage he visited many other countries and places including Yemen, Palestine, Iraq, Syria, Iran, Transjordan, and Khorasan. He also visited many places in the Indian subcontinent. It is said, that during the course of his extensive tours and travels he came into contact with over three hundred saints and sages.

Death

In the twilight of his life he kept indifferent health and after a prolonged illness, passed away on the tenth of Zilhijj in AH 788. He was buried in Ochha (Multan).

Caliph

Qazi Abd-ul-Malik, better known as Shah Ajmal, is his outstanding caliph.

Traits of character

He was devoted to prayers and ascetic practices and regularly genuflected five hundred times every twenty-four hours. He recited the Holy *Quran* and practised his daily rituals without fail. Even in old age, he used to offer a hundred genuflections daily. He was conversant with all the seven rhythmic methods of reciting the Holy *Quran,* and would recite the name "Allah" aloud. He was deeply absorbed in contemplation in the closing years of his life. He dressed simply and did not listen to music, though some hold that he did. When meals were served, he would stop talking.

He paid utmost respect to the saints and the dervishes. One day when Hazrat Shaikh Rukn-ud-din was descending some steps he laid down below one step so that he might place his foot upon him. The former was greatly pleased by his spirit of devotion and humility. Taking Hazrat Makhdoom's hand in his he rubbed it against his chest, thereby transmitting to him spiritual blessings.

On another occasion, he again showed his spirit of devotion. Hazrat Shaikh Rukn-ud-din Abul-Fath was bathing and the water splashing down. He himself bathed in that water. When Hazrat Rukn-ud-din learnt of this he conferred upon him the choicest spiritual blessings.

He did not accept at all and sundry as his spiritual disciples. When he did accept someone, he initiated him in the Order on behalf of the saint who had empowered him to do so, and would say that he was only an intermediary, so to say a pleader, and nothing more. It is also said that when he accepted anyone as his spiritual disciple, he used to address him as follows:

> I am not among those, who are competent enough to accept anyone as a spiritual disciple. I only establish the Fraternity of Faith as ordained by the Holy Prophet to the effect that: 'Increase the brotherhood of faith.' God is Merciful. It is beyond his mercy, that he may put men to torture before the very eyes of their brethren.

The procedure he followed when accepting anyone as his spiritual disciple was to catch hold of the hand of the seeker, to offer repentance, and then to say that they were both repenting and then to place the disciple's hand upon his chest.

He never wished anyone ill-will. As a mark of his humble disposition, it may be pointed out that he would pray with his cap on and would say that the turban was meant especially for "men" and he was not a "man."

He had a forgiving disposition, was forbearing, and tolerant bearing with courage and patience any ill-treatment meted out to him by people.

Sultan Firoz Shah was one of his devotees. His vizir Khan-e-Jahan did not however extend to him any courtesy or regard. Once the vizir sentenced the son of a clerk to undergo imprisonment. The clerk, who was one of his devotees, went to him and implored his blessings and sought his assistance, and persuaded Hazrat Makhdoom to go to the minister and plead his case. When he did so, but was not only refused an audience, but was turned away with foul language. He tried again with the same result. This happened nineteen times. When he went again a twentieth time, in the minister conveyed to a message that as a Syed, he should feel ashamed to have come so many times fruitlessly. His response was: "O, dear one! everytime that I come, I get the spiritual relief. I want to have freed one upon whom tyranny has been perpetuated by your hand, so that you too may'st attain spiritual relief and blessings." On receipt of this response the minister came out bareheaded with a rope tied around his neck, fell upon his feet, and apologised. He implored his blessings and became his spiritual disciple. He set the clerk's son free and gave him a robe and a horse. The minister gave *nazrana* (offering) to Hazrat Makhdoom who accepting it and passed it on to the clerk's son.

Teachings

- He thought that for the spiritual development of an individual, travel was necessary as they afforded the person an opportunity to see and appreciate the handiwork of God Almighty. When travelling an individual comes into close proximity with nature. The hardships and privations of the journey make an individual indifferent towards the tribulations of life, while also strengthening his belief and faith.
- Detachment towards home, hearth, relations, and friends is necessary for spiritual development. By living a long at one place an individual finds himself attached to his environment.
- He believed that spiritual blessings are not in the nature of temporal or transitory gains. They are abiding and everlasting. Abiding virtues cannot be the monopoly of anyone person, group, sect, or Order.

- Spiritual blessings are in the nature of a universal truth. Truth does not admit of geographical boundaries, caste, colour, or nationality. Spiritual blessings can both be acquired, and conferred.
- Every Sufi Order derives its inherent strength from the precepts and practice of those belonging to that Order who have attained spiritual perfection. Every Order and every saint has something to offer in the nature of spiritual ecstasy, spiritual blessings, spiritual exaltation, inner purification, and inward illumination. Hence, according to him, there is nothing wrong in being the spiritual disciple of more than one person and there is absolutely no harm in being affiliated with or attached to more than one Sufi Order. There is not and cannot be any question of a clash of loyalty for the simple reason that every saint or Order must convey something different.
- Association and environment have their own effect.
- Perfect spiritual advancement does not admit of differential treatment. The varieties of absolute truth should sought for and found. The blessings of every saint and of every Order should be received and enjoyed.
- It is not enough to be a spiritual disciple or to receive the robe of caliph. What is important and useful is that the spiritual disciple should live in the company of his *pir* (spiritual guide) and teacher for at least sometime.
- *Khirqa* is of two kinds. One is known as *khirqa-e-tasawwuf* (the robe of mysticism) and the other as *khirqa-e-tashabbo* (the robe of sacredness). The former makes the company of the spiritual guide obligatory, the latter which has a bearing on mysticism does not enjoin or make the company of the spiritual guide necessary. It denotes sanctity.
- Spiritual good and social good are not opposed to each other. Individual good is dependant on guidance, sweetness, grace, and light and therefore cannot be opposed to spiritual good.
- The mystics and the saints show the light. The light of guidance constitutes the spiritual heritage of mankind.

Sayings

- The enlightened should be so engaged that his ritual is not disrupted by association, society, or seclusion. People should be viewed as minerals. Practice and ritual should not be abandoned on account of people.

- He who treads the path of spiritual perfection, should not allow anything else besides God to enter his heart.
- An action that may not yield its fruit in this world, will be of no consequence in the world hereafter.
- The dervish, provided he follows the Holy Prophet in speech, action, and intention is a saint but not otherwise.
- Patience is of three kinds, namely, common, uncommon and most uncommon. Common patience implies one's controlling oneself when confronted with something unpleasant though it may appear difficult. Uncommon patience implies that one tolerates something unpleasant without a murmur. The most uncommon form of patience implies that one derives pleasure when facing trouble or adversity.
- Meditation implies the realisation that God knows everything about him and is seeing him rather than just sitting down with one's head bowed.
- He who treads the spiritual path, unless and until he is freed from the lust of this world and the world hereafter, does not reach the place of unity.
- Faith is of three kinds. One type relates to relying on outward manifestations, e.g., one may see the sky and think and ponder that it is hanging and is without pillars. There must be somebody who has made it. Hence, an individual must bring his faith to bear and believe it. The second type of faith is that of the follower. Whatever the Holy Prophet has said must be believed to be true. The third type of faith relates to actually seeing; as when the glance of a saint is focused on heaven and hell, the throne and the chair, the slate and the pen he at once realises that there is someone who has created it. When this station is reached, one sees through asceticism undergone the vision of God Almighty by the eye of the heart.
- There are two things for he who treads the spiritual path. The first is awareness and the second unconsciousness. He should therefore be ever watchful and aware lest he fall down and lower himself. This is indeed perfection.
- He who treads the path of enlightenment occupies two stations, namely, beginning and extreme end. The beginning implies offering repentance in the correct way. It is done in

two ways. One relates to the repentance offered for the sins against the *shari'at* and *tariqat* and to that offered for taking partners of God. The station of the extreme end is the realisation of God which implies achievement of the desired goal.

- He indeed is not wise who is engrossed in the blessing and unmindful of the donor of the blessing.
- Saints get intuition though this may only be momentary.
- Inner remembrance of God is with the heart and soul and not with the tongue, and opposed to it is outward remembrance of God.
- To avert and to remove the will are different. A thing that does not exist is said to be averted and one that is in existence is said to be removed.
- For perfect sainthood three things are necessary. Without these sainthood is not possible. The first condition precedent is the person should be well-versed in the three branches of knowledge, namely, that of *shari'at, tariqat*, and *haqiqat*. The second condition is that the wise people of his time accept him and become his devotees and disciples. The third condition is that he seek nothing except the vision of God.
- Keep yourself aloof from illiterate sufis because they are thieves of religion and the plunderers of Mussulmans.
- For the divine knowledge, piety is necessary as ablutions are necessary for prayers.
- Piety is of three kinds, namely, common, uncommon, and the most uncommon. Common piety is that of refraining from idolatry, sin, and superstitions. Uncommon piety means abstaining from things that cannot do good or many causing injury. The most uncommon piety is that of abstaining from all but God.
- He who treads the spiritual path should possess great courage and he should not seek anything from God other than him alone.
- The seeker should take to seclusion so that he may rid himself of confused ideas and become calm and collected.
- It is obligatory upon the faithful, that he should acquire knowledge first and subsequently engage himself in its practice.
- The seeker cannot do without a spiritual guide and teacher.
- The qualities characterising one treading the spiritual path are that he speaks and he is motionless; exists and does not

exist is present and is absent.

- Contact with some saintly person or the company of some spiritual guide or the society of the one who has acquired divine knowledge is far better and more useful than to sit on the prayer carpet and engaged in rituals.
- Unless one has severed all one's worldly connections, one will not emerge victorious.
- The saints are not afraid of any man or anything except God Almighty.
- Every breath that passes bears the price of both the worlds.
- So long as the abuse and praise of the people do not appear to be the same to him who is treading the spiritual path he does not become perfect.
- Satan is not afraid of a person who is disobedient.
- It is *tariqat* to save the heart from the rancour of human beings.
- It is *haqiqat* to save the heart from all else besides God.
- It is *shari'at* to turn one's face towards the *qibla*.
- To turn one's face towards God is *tariqat* and to be so absorbed constitutes *haqiqat*.
- He who treads the spiritual path should not talk of the stations which he has not reached.
- Three acts are best, namely to sever connections with the world, to keep an eye on realities, and to discover the universal truth. He who is not endowed with these three qualities cannot claim to be a sufi.
- In the beginning, there is nothing better for him who is treading the spiritual path than to take to seclusion.
- Seclusion is best for the remembrance of God.

Supernatural powers

He exhibited a great many supernatural powers. Some are related below:

- Once there was no rain in Delhi. People approached him and requested him to pray for the rain. He did so and the city experienced a very heavy downpour. It rained incessantly and people found it troublesome and requested him to pray that it stopped. He smiled and prayed; the rain stopped soon after.
- Once when he was sitting in a secluded place in the Central Mosque of Ochha during the month of Ramazan, the officer-

in-charge of Ochha named Somera came there and turned all the people out of the mosque. Unable to tolerate this he told the officer: "O Somera! art thou gone mad, that thou art giving trouble and causing inconvenience to the dervishes." As soon as he uttered these words, Somera went mad and notwithstanding the best medical treatment available, he did not recover. Eventually his mother learnt the cause of his madness. She brought her son to him and sought his forgiveness and requested that he show mercy, grace, and kindness to her son. This appeal had its effect. He asked the mother to bathe her son and clothe, him and then take him to the tomb of Hazrat Shaikh Jamal-ud-din Khandan for blessings and then to bring her son back to him. She acted accordingly. When Somera was brought into his presence, he kissed his feet and tendered an unconditional apology to the dervishes and fully recovered.

- His son, aged four, was once playing in the vicinity of his prayer carpet when he was offering the Chasht prayers. After he had finished his prayers, he said the child's play had diverted his attention and went on to say that it appeared to him that the child would not live long. That very night the child died.[10]

References

1. Firishta.
2. *Akhbar-ul-Akhyar.*
3. Firishta.
4. *Akhbar-ul-Akhyar.*
5. *Masalek-us-Salekeen,* vol. II, p. 426.
6. *Siyar-ul-Arefeen.*
7. *Masalek-us-Salekeen,* vol. II, p. 429.
8. Ibid., p. 436.
9. Ibid.
10. Ibid., p. 437.

102

Hazrat Maulana Badr-ud-din Ishaq

Hazrat Maulana Badr-ud-din Ishaq was the spiritual caliph and son-in-law of Hazrat Baba Farid-ud-din Ganj-e-Shakar. He traced his relationship from Hazrat Imam Husain, son of Hazrat Ali, son-in-law of the Holy Prophet Mohammed which means he is a Husaini.[1] His father Khwaja Ali was the son of Khwaja Ishaq.

He received his education in Delhi, and became well-versed in various branches of knowledge. Seeking further education, he left Delhi for Bukhara. On his way there he reached Ajoodhan where Hazrat Baba Farid-ud-din Ganj-e-Shakar lived.

Initiation into the Sufi Order

Hearing the name and fame of Hazrat Baba Sahab, he was attracted to him and visited him to pay his respects. He was greatly impressed by his personality, and in the course of conversation, Hazrat Baba Sahab solved his difficulties relating to certain branches of knowledge. Believing that he had achieved the object for which had set off for Bukhara, he abandoned the idea of going there for further study. He began to live in Ajoodhan and serve Hazrat Baba Sahab with all his heart and the latter, at his request, accepted him as one of his spiritual disciples. Subsequently, he honoured him by accepting him as his caliph.

Marriage and children

He married Bibi Fatima, the daughter of Hazrat Baba Farid-ud-din Ganj-e-Shakar and had two sons. Khwaja Mohammed and Khwaja Musa.

Death

When he died he was buried in the central mosque of Ajoodhan.

Traits of character

He was a very pious and gentle person. He loved his spiritual guide and teacher and served him with devotion. He taught the Holy *Quran* to Syed Mohammed of Kirman, Khwaja Yaqub and Shaikh Ala-ud-din. He had very cordial relations with Hazrat Nizam-ud-din Auliya.

He was a poet and an author. He has written a book entitled *Tasreef-e-Badri* in verse.[2] Another book by him entitled *Israr-ul- Auliya* contains the discourses of the spiritual guide and teacher Hazrat Baba Farid-ud-din Ganj-e-Shakar.[3]

Supernatural power

The officer-in-charge of Dipalpur, Malik Sharf-ud-din Kabdar, once went to Hazrat Baba Farid-ud-din Ganj-e-Shakar and requested him to accept him as one of his spiritual disciples. Hazrat Badr-ud-din Ishaq was directed by Baba Sahab to initiate the officer as his spiritual disciple. He did so.

After sometime the officer was arrested at the order of the king and sent a man with a letter to him requesting him to pray for his release and to purchase and deliver some watermelons alongwith it.

The messenger acted accordingly. At that time some admirers and devotees were there, among them Qazi Sadr-ud-din, who was officer-in-charge of Ajoodhan. Maulana Badr-ud-din Ishaq asked him to distribute the watermelons. He gave to each his share and placed Malik Sharf-ud-din Kabdar's share before him too. He did so. Maulana Badr-ud-din Ishaq took off his turban and placed it by the side of the watermelon. Having done so, he said, "We will not eat this watermelon, nor shall we wear this turban until Sharf-ud-din comes and when he comes we shall consume it with him." He was then engrossed in conversation. An hour later Sharf-ud-din Kabdar arrived there and informed him that he had been released by the king. Hazrat Maulana Badr-ud-din Ishaq then wore his turban and began to eat the watermelons.[4]

References

1. *Jawahar-e-Faridi*, p. 338.
2. *Siyar-ul-Auliya*, p. 173.
3. *Akhbar-ul-Akhyar*, Urdu trans., p. 145.
4. *Siyar-ul-Auliya*, p. 175; *Jawahar-e-Faridi*, pp. 341-42.

103

Hazrat Shaikh Jamal-ud-din Ahmad

Hazrat Shaikh Jamal-ud-din Ahmad of Hansi traced his relationship from Hazrat Imam Abu Hanifa and was a prominent spiritual disciple and caliph of Hazrat Baba Farid-ud-din Ganj-e-Shakar. The deeds of caliph-hood granted by Hazrat Baba Sahab were sent to him for approval. If he approved, the deed received the final sanction of Hazrat Baba Sahab. If it was rejected, Hazrat Baba Sahab would not give his final sanction and would say: "that which is torn by Jamal cannot be sewn by Farid."

Marriage and children

He had two sons. One of them, Shaikh Burhan-ud-din Sufi, received the spiritual blessings of Hazrat Baba Farid-ud-din Ganj-e-Shakar. Hazrat Baba Sahab also honoured him by appointing him as one of his caliphs and confided to him his prayer carpet and the stick.[1] Hazrat Shaikh Jamal is the other son, who had been in a trance most of the time. Hazrat Nizam-ud-din says that he come out of his trance occasionally, and once, when he did so, he uttered the words: "Knowledge is a great curtain of God." When asked to explain this he said thus: "Knowledge is a stranger to God and what is stranger to God is a curtain of God."

Turning point in life

Since the day, he heard the *hadis,* which translated means "the grave is one of the gardens of heaven or it is one of the ditches of hell, he showed signs of a transformation and led a life of restlessness."

Death

He was buried in Hansi.

Traits of character

His spiritual guide and teacher, Hazrat Baba Farid-ud-din Ganj-e-Shakar, loved him intensely which caused him to stay in Hansi for twelve long years.

Hazrat Baba Sahab would say about him: "Jamal is indeed our manifestations." Sometimes, Hazrat Baba Sahab would say: "Jamal, I want to go round you." Hazrat Jamal-ud-din was a great speaker. When he was a spiritual caliph by Hazrat Baba Sahab, he renounced his worldly possessions, starved himself underwent privation, and took to an ascetic way of life. He was an author and a poet. His book entitled *Mulhemat* is a collection of sayings.

Teachings

To him sainthood represents noble character and produces such virtues as contentment, trust in God, patience, perseverance, forgiveness, service, sharing and sacrifice, generosity, submission, self-surrender, sincerity, hope, belief, and faith. The *faqir* who possesses these qualities demonstrates these virtues is indeed perfect, and if he does not, he is not entitled to be called a *faqir*.

Supernatural power

Once there was scarcity of rain and famine conditions prevailed. He was requested to pray for the rain. He remained silent and suddenly rain began to fall.[2]

REFERENCES

1. *Akhbar-ul-Akhyar*, (Urdu trans.), p. 149.
2. *Jawahar-e-Faridi*, p. 264.

104

Hazrat Lal Shehbaz Qalandar

Hazrat Lal Shehbaz Qalandar was a prominent saint of the Indian subcontinent. He traced his relationship from Hazrat Imam Jaffer Sadiq. His father Kabir, son of Shams-ud-din was a saintly man. Hazrat Lal Shehbaz was born in Marvind and was named Mohammed Usman. He is also known as "Usman of Marvind," "Lal Surkh." It is said that he did not adhere strictly to religious injunctions and precepts, following the way of the censured and as he wore red clothes, he came to be known as "Lal Shehbaz Qalandar." He completed the Holy *Quran* and acquired a sound knowledge of the *fiqh* and *hadis*.

Initiation into the Sufi Order

He was a spiritual disciple and caliph of Hazrat Shaikh Baha-ud-din Zakariya of Multan,[1] and also received spiritual blessings from Hazrat Shaikh Mansur and Shaikh Baba Ibrahim.

Arrival in Sind

Sind was demarcated as the area for his spiritual, moral, and social activities. Arriving there he settled in Sarwali and began to preach the doctrine of truth. By his precept and practice, he brought about a change in the life of the people by condemning ignoble local practices and customs. He did so not through any coercion but by persuading people to lead a good life. By good life he meant a life of beauty, harmony, and truth based on love and mutual regard.

Death

He died in AH 724 and was buried in Sewhan in Sindh.[2]

Traits of character

He had all the outward and inward graces of life. He was an

accomplished man, a perfect dervish. It is however said that he did not follow *shari'ah* strictly and did not observe some of its injunctions.[3]

He was a good Arabic and Persian poet. He is ranked among the outstanding saints like Hazrat Baba Farid-ud-din Ganj-e-Shakar and Hazrat Shah Bu Ali Qalandar.

References

1. *Tazkarat-ul-Fuqra,* p. 32.
2. Ibid., p. 33.
3. *Ma'arij-ul-Vilayat.*

105

Hazrat Qutb-ud-din Munawwar

Hazrat Qutb-ud-din Munawwar was the grandson of Hazrat Jamal-ud-din of Hansi and a spiritual disciple and caliph of Hazrat Nizam-ud-din Auliya.

The gift of his spiritual guide
Hazrat Nizam-ud-din Auliya, after he had appointed him as his caliph, told him:

> Your illustrious grandfather, Maulana Qutb Jamal of Hansi, once gave me a book entitled *Awarif*. When I went to him after being appointed caliph by Hazrat Baba Sahab, he told me that Hazrat Baba Sahab had given him the book alongwith many others. Now I present this book to you in the hope that when one of my sons will come to you for blessings, you will give the book to him and also confer upon him many blessings.

He took the book and thanked Hazrat Nizam-ud-din for it.

Death
He died in AH 760 and was buried in Hansi.

Traits of character
He was well-known for his piety, purity, knowledge, and learning, simple habits and ascetic temperament. He forever engaged in ascetic practices and lived a secluded life paying little attention to the world or people of the world. He reposed his trust in God and rarely went out of his house except of offer Friday prayers or to meet the saints. He exhibited a marvellous spirit of renunciation.

106

Hazrat Syed Sadr-ud-din Raja Qattal

Hazrat Syed Sadr-ud-din Raja Qattal was a brother of Hazrat Makhdoon Jahanian-e-Jahan Gasht. His father was Syed Ahmad Kabir. He is known as "Raju Qattal" one who wages war against his self. Since his forefathers came from Bukhara, he is known as "Raju Qattal Bukhari."

Initiation into the Sufi Order

He became a spiritual disciple of his father Syed Ahmad Kabir and received the robe of caliph from him.[1] It is also said that he was a spiritual disciple of his brother, Hazrat Syed Jalal-ud-din Husain, better known as Makhdoom Jahanian-e-Jahan Gasht and that he also received the robe of caliph from him. Some people traced their affiliation with Hazrat Makhdoom Jahanian-e-Jahan Gasht through him. Others however trace their affiliation through his son Nasir-ud-din Mahmud.[2]

Death

He breathed his last on the sixteenth of Jamadi-ul-Akhir in AH 827 and was buried in Ochha.[3]

Traits of character

He was ever lost in meditation, and was so absorbed in this that he was unaware of what was going on around him. He was a man with magnetic personality, but kept himself aloof from people. Whatever he said, whether good or bad, actually happened. Hazrat Makhdoom Jahanian-e-Jahan Gasht used to say that he was engaged with the people, but Hazrat Raju Qattal, by a divine decree was drawn towards God.[4]

Supernatural power

It is said that if a person visits his tomb for a few days continuously, his wish will be fulfilled.

References

1. *Anwar-e-Sufiya*, p. 324 (Urdu trans. of *Akhbar-ul-Akhyar*).
2. *Tarikh-e-Muhammedi.*
3. *Takmila Siyar-ul-Auliya*, p. 32.
4. *Mirat-ul-Israr.*

107

Hazrat Syed Kabir-ud-din Hasan

Hazrat Syed Kabir-ud-din Hasan was amongst the leading saints of Ochha who spent his life in preaching and propagating the Gospel of Truth. He travelled widely.

Death
He died in AH 896 and was buried in Ochha. It is said, that he was one hundred and eighty years old at that time.

108

Hazrat Makhdoom Shaikh Mohammed

Hazrat Makhdoom Shaikh Mohammed occupied a high position amongst the saints of his time. He traced his descent from Hazrat Imam Husain, son of Hazrat Ali, son-in-law of the Holy Prophet Mohammed which makes him a Husaini. He also traced his relationship from Hazrat Shaikh Abd-ul-Qadir of Jilan, better known as Ghous-ul-Azam, Piran-e-Pir. His genealogy is as follows: Syed Mohammed, son of Syed Shah Amir, son of Syed Ali, son of Syed Mas'ud, son of Syed Ahmad, son of Syed Safi-ud-din, son of Hazrat Shaikh Saif-ud-din Abd-ul-Wahab, son of Hazrat Shaikh Mohi-ud-din Abi Mohammed Abd-ul-Qadir of Jilan.

Arrival in Ochha
He left Rum for Khorasan. From Khorasan he went on to Multan and then to Ochha to settle permanently. He became very popular and commanded great influence.

Marriage and children
He had three sons, namely, Shaikh Abd-ul-Qadir, who is known as Makhdoom Sani, Syed Abdullah, and Syed Mubarak.

Death
He was buried in Ochha.

Traits of character
He was a perfect dervish and was also well-versed in outer knowledge. He was a poet. His poetic pseudonym is "Qadiri." He has written some verses in honour of Hazrat Shaikh Abd-ul-Qadir of Jilan and also left a collection of his other poems.

109

Hazrat Makhdoom Shaikh Abd-ul-Qadir

Hazrat Makhdoom Shaikh Abd-ul-Qadir was the eldest son of Hazrat Makhdoom Shaikh Mohammed. His mother was a Syeda, and the daughter of Shaikh Abul-Fath, who was related to Syed Safi-ud-din Gazarooni. He was born in AH 862 and is addressed and invoked as "Shaikh Abd-ul-Qadir Sani," and "Makhdoom Sani."

The turning point in life

He was brought up in a well-to-do family and led a life of ease and comfort, and was devoted to luxuries whenever he went out he took musical instruments laden on camels, alongwith him. Once when he went to hunt in Ochha forest he happened to see a partridge crying strangely. A dervish was passing the way and seeing him said: "Praise be to God, the day will come when this young man, out of love of God, will be crying like this partridge." Hearing the words, he underwent a transformation and began to nurture a distaste of mundane affairs and became enamoured with the pursuit of a higher life. He renounced comforts and luxuries and took to seclusion and the remembrance of God. After his father's death he succeeded him as his spiritual caliph and *sajjadanashin*.

Relations with the Imperial Court

He resigned his post and this displeased the king. That did not bother him. He returned all the documents and the *farmans*, he had received to the king, saying that he did not require them and thus refused to be benefited by the favours and he had been given by the king. After sometime the king wrote to him seeking his forgiveness for his mistakes of omission and commission and requested him to honour him by visiting him Hazrat Makhdoom refused to do so.

Marriage and children
He had two sons. The eldest son, Shaikh Abd-ur-Razzaq, became his *sajjadanashin*. His second son, Syed Zain-ul-Abedeen, died during his lifetime.

Death
He died on the eighteenth of Rabi-ul-Awwal in AH 940 and was buried in Ochha.

Traits of character
He derived spiritual blessings from Hazrat Shaikh Abd-ul-Qadir of Jilan and placed great faith on this affiliation. Initially, he used to listen to music but when he succeeded his father, he stopped doing so. If he ever heard music by chance, he would undergo a state of ecstasy and would weep. He passed many years of his life in poverty and penury. He used to tolerate the bad treatment meted out to him by the people and showed wonderful equanimity in times of difficulties. He had healing touch. Whenever he placed and rubbed his hand over an invalid, the latter recovered from illness.

Supernatural power
Once a plague took a heavy toll of human life in Multan. The people plucked the grass that grew at the spot where he used to do his ablutions and rubbed it at the spot that showed symptoms of the disease. The grass worked wonders and patients recovered.

110

Hazrat Shaikh Dawood

Hazrat Shaikh Dawood was an eminent dervish. He took to ascetic practices and rigours at a comparatively early age. Sometimes he would pass the night in prayers. He demonstrated enormous self-control denying himself of all the pleasures and comforts of life. His ascetic practices yielded him rich dividends in terms of mental peace and inner satisfaction. Then he sought to be initiated into the Sufi Order.

Initiation into the Sufi Order
On an inner indication, he went to Hazrat Makhdoom Shaikh Hamid and requested him to accept him as one of his humble disciples. This the latter acceded to and subsequently conferred upon him the robe of caliph.

Death
He died in AH 982 and was buried in Shergarh.

Caliph
Shaikh Abul-Ma'ali was his spiritual caliph.

Traits of character
He was a restless and a very learned man. He would sometimes turn his face towards the direction of Baghdad, where the tomb of Hazrat Shaikh Abd-ul-Qadir of Jilan, better known as Ghous-ul-Azam, is situated, which points to the close affiliation, he had with the latter.

111

Hazrat Miyan Mir

Hazrat Miyan Mir was a great *pir* of the Indian subcontinent and is considered an outstanding saint and an eminent mystic. He traced his relationship from the second caliph of Islam Hazrat Umar Faruq. His grandfather was called Qazi Qalandar and his father, Qazi Sayeen Data, belonged to the Qadiri Order of the sufis. His mother, Bibi Fatima was the daughter of Qazi Qadan, and a very accomplished woman of her time. He had four brothers, Qazi Bolan, Qazi Mohammed Usman, Qazi Tahir, and Qazi Mohammed. He was his father's youngest son and all his brothers became his spiritual disciples. He had two sisters, Bibi Jamal Khatoon and Bibi Hadi.

Initiation into the Sufi Order

After his father's death he relied on his mother, from whom he continued to derive spiritual blessings till eventually he achieved perfection in inward knowledge and severed his connection from the world and the people of the world. Having sought his mother's permission he left his home in search of truth and undergoing many hardships and ascetic practices. His search was finally rewarded when he was accepted as a spiritual disciple by Hazrat Shaikh Khizr, an enlightened saint of the Qadiri Order who roamed the jungles and mountains and had wholly renounced the world. Hazrat Miyan Mir was greatly benefited by his company. The secrets of divine mystery were disclosed to him and he became wholly devoted to a quest for the higher life and disenchanted with the mundane world. He felt disgusted with the world, its ways and methods. Hazrat Shaikh Khizr, finding him spiritually perfect permitted him to go wherever he wanted.

With this permission and the blessings of his spiritual guide and teacher, he left for Lahore where he engaged himself in acquiring the outward knowledge and learning. He counted Maulana Sa'dullah as his teacher. The latter, who was considered to be one of the leading learned men of his time, paid him special attention. It is also said that he passed some years in the company of Maulana Ne'matullah, who imparted to him knowledge and who, as he himself says, was quite unaware of his spiritual attainments and inner purification.

Departure for Sirhind

He did not like the huge crowds of people and the large number of devotees and admirers who waited upon him day-in and day-out and therefore left Lahore for Sirhind. There he fell seriously ill, and the illness was prolonged without any apparent hope of recovery. One night he invoked the aid of Hazrat Shaikh Abd-ul-Qadir of Jilan, better known as Ghous-ul-Azam, Piran-e-Pir. The request did not go unheeded. Hazrat Ghous-ul-Azam and Hazrat Khizr, his spiritual guide appeared and inquired about his health. He requested the former to restore him to health. Hazrat Ghous-ul-Azam showed him kindness and rubbed his hand over the body of Hazrat Miyan Mir, and gave him a cup of water to drink it. As soon he did so he felt fully recovered with no trace of illness left. When he had been ill Haji Ne'matullah of Sirhind served Hazrat Miyan Mir with the greatest devotion, which greatly pleased the latter. He inquired from Haji Ne'matullah whether he would like to receive spiritual blessings from him, which might transform him completely and thus would make him an enlightened saint. The latter expressed his willingness to be spiritually benefited. Hazrat Miyan Mir transformed him completely within a week, enabling him to reach a high position in the spiritual domain.

After he had wholly recovered, he left Sirhind for Lahore where he settled permanently and began to preach and propagate the doctrine of truth.

Relations with Imperial Court

Hazrat Miyan Mir did not like meeting anyone but sometimes he was prevailed to do so. Emperor Jahangir reposed faith in saints and was fond of meeting Hazrat Miyan Mir. Once the Emperor sent a special messenger to him requesting him to honour him with a visit and at the same time, regretting his inability to visit him due to distance and the pressing demands of the business of state.

Hazrat Miyan accepted request and went to the royal palace and was accorded the utmost respect by the emperor. His inspiring company had such a great effect on the latter, that he sought his permission to abdicate and devote himself exclusively to the remembrance of God. The emperor also said that he drew no distinction between gold, silver, precious jewels, and bricks and stones. Hazrat Miyan Mir thereupon said: "A perfect sufi is one, who does not draw any distinction between stone and jewel. Since you say that you draw no such distinction, you are a sufi." The emperor responded that in so arguing he wanted to kill himself. Thereupon Hazrat Miyan Mir replied: "Your existence is necessary for the welfare of the people. By the blessings of your justice, the *faqirs* are concentrating on their work."

The emperor implored him to pay him attention. He told the emperor: "First of all find a conscientious and an able person like you to serve the people, thereafter, I will take you with me and get you engaged in the remembrance of God." His reply was greatly appreciated by the emperor. The latter wanted to whether Hazrat Mir required anything. His Holiness replied that he required nothing, but wanted his permission to leave. The emperor bade him farewell with all the honour due to him.

Emperor Shah Jahan, like his father, also showed him great respect. The emperor twice visited him in his monastery and found him to be a perfect saint. On the occasion of his first visit, he was accompanied by four persons. Hazrat Mir advised the emperor to tend to the welfare of his people and the affairs of state. He should not indulge in pleasure and should be just to all. He should spend all his time in the service of the people, for if the people are satisfied, they will be happy and the coffers of state will also be full. On the occasion of his second visit, the emperor submitted that he should pay him some attention. Thereupon his Holiness replied: "It is advisable that when you perform some good deed and make others happy you pray at that time. Do not ask anything from anybody except God."

Dara Shikoh had mystic turn of mind and loved the company of saints and mystics. He reposed faith in Hazrat Mir's spiritual powers and met him number of times. The letters written by Hazrat Mir and addressed to Dara Shikoh are revealing and searching, as they point to sad events, that actually occurred resulting in the catastrophe of Dara Shikoh being beheaded.

Death

He breathed his last on the seventh of Rabi-ul-Awwal in AH 1045, corresponding to the eleventh August AD 1635 at the age of eighty-eight years. He was buried near Lahore Cantonment.

Caliphs

Of his outstanding spiritual caliphs the following may be mentioned:

Hazrat Mulla Shah. He was the spiritual guide and teacher of Dara Shikoh and he belonged to Badakhshan. In the prime of youth he left his home in search of truth. He visited Kashmir and from there he went to Agra. During his stay in Agra, he heard a great deal about the spiritual perfection of Hazrat Miyan Mir and therefore left for Lahore where he sought to be accepted as a spiritual disciple. Hazrat Mir advised him to first acquire knowledge and learning and then to come to him. He therefore engaged in the pursuit of knowledge for the next ten years and was then accepted as a spiritual disciple by Hazrat Miyan Mir. In a very short time, he attained spiritual perfection.

He was very pious and saintly. He did not marry. He was also a good poet. His poems have been collected in a book entitled *Diwan-e-Mulla Shah.*

He took to renunciation for long thirty years, he lived in darkness. When one night Dara Shikoh visited him, he had the lamp in his home lighted for the first time after thirty long years.

Shaikh Nattha. He belonged to Lahore. He died in AH 1027 and was buried in Lahore Cantonment.

Shaikh Isma'il. He was a perfect dervish who derived spiritual blessings from Hazrat Miyan Mir.

Shaikh Ne'matullah of Sirhind. He was a saint upon whom Hazrat Miyan Mir showered his spiritual blessings.

Mulla Abd-ul-Ghafoor. He died during the lifetime of his spiritual guide and teacher. He was a teacher in Lahore. Giving up all worldly interests and resigning his post, he went to Hazrat Miyan Mir. Hazrat Mir initially paid him no attention which greatly saddened him. Very soon however he was able to win Hazrat Mir's affection and the latter confided the divine secrets to him and acquainted him with various manifestations of spiritual science. In this way, through the blessings of Hazrat Mir he achieved spiritual perfection. He was buried in Kala Nur. Miyan

Hamid Qadiri and Miran Shah Sa'id were his two other caliphs.

Traits of character

Hazrat Miyan Mir had a retiring nature and disliked publicity. He used to devote himself to prayer and remembrance of God in desolate and deserted place and did not like mixing with the people. He had such great breath control that for sometime he breathed only once at night. When he grew old, he used to breathe four times during the night. He accepted only a few people as spiritual disciples. He was a man of faith. He exhibited marvellous self-control, sometimes not eating anything for weeks together. For thirty years, nothing was cooked in his house. Contentment was his armour. In the closing years of his life he allowed one kind of food to be cooked in his house which his devotee would to cook in earthen pots for him. He ate very little. He was ever in meditation unconcerned about the weather, the month, the day, or the year. He slept little, talked very little, and mixed very little with the people. He would not go to anyone's house on the ground that someone who did not like people to visit his house, would not wish to visit anyone else's house. He did not care for anyone because he was lost in the thought of the friend. One of his devotees requested that he remember him at an opportune time. Hazrat Mir replied: "Woe be to the time when I remember you." He did not dress like the dervishes or *faqirs*, wearing ordinary clothes without a robe or a cloak. He had great respect and regard for the dervishes and *faqirs*, was not very fond of music, and was very courteous and kind.

Teachings

According to him there are two ways of reaching up to God. One way is to be absorbed in meditation and thus to be united with him. The one, who is drawn by God towards Him, becomes united with Him. The other way is that of a *salik* treading upon the spiritual path, which is a stairway to God, either through asceticism, rigours, or through the assistance of some saint.

He says that search for God is not easy thing and reaching him entails hardship. Unless one is lost in His search, the seeker will be unable to find Him simply because he has only one heart, and within single heart only one thing can be contained. It is therefore necessary to pursue the ideal with single-minded devotion in the pursuit of which he should sever his connection with the world and take to renunciation because by being entangled in the world, he cannot pay undivided attention to the goal and achieve enlightenment. He prescribes for those treading the spiritual path, that they should eat little, talk little, and sleep little. He holds that the apparel of a dervish should resemble that of the common people so that he is able to pass unnoticed.

Sayings

- The lover of the renunciation of the world is he indeed who does not achieve his object.
- A sufi is one who does not exist, i.e., he is united with God.
- The thought of anyone else besides God reduces the degree of renunciation and asceticism.
- The urge for submission to God and of doing good is greater when the saints are young and it increases during the period of old age. So it is that the urge to get a thing when an individual is young increases during the period of old age.
- The self as reformed by *shari'at,* the heart is reformed by *tariqat,* and the soul is reformed by *haqiqat*.
- The influence of the saints is the same after their death as it was during their lifetime.
- When a *faqir* becomes perfect and his heart is cleared of doubt, then nothing can cause him harm or injury. He himself becomes a king then and pays little attention to the king, rather the kings are overpowered by him.

Supernatural powers

- One of his devotees once entered his tenement in the night to place a jug of water for making ablutions. The devotee did not find Hazrat Mir on the bed. He searched him, but in vain. A little later the devotee found him on the bed and felt some concern over his mysterious disappearance. Initially Hazrat Mir remained silent but on repeated inquiries from the devotee replied: "We had been to the cave of Hira for prayers."
- Once his brother visited him from his home town after a long time. He received his brother cordially, but unfortunately, he had nothing in his house that day and was unable to entertain

him. He asked his brother to be seated and himself went to the garden and there offered prayers. After the prayers were over, he prayed: "Oh, Great God! I have received a guest and reposing my faith in Thy Grace, I have caused him to sit in my house. I have not one else except Thee to help me." A voice was heard to the effect, "We have fulfilled thy want before thou asked." In the meanwhile, his brother came to him in the garden and informed him that just after he had left the tenement, a certain person brought food and was waiting for him. Hazrat Mir returned to his tenement accompanied by his brother and was surprised to see a handsome young awaiting him. The young man made a *salaam* to Hazrat Mir and humbly conveyed that God Almighty in His Grace and Kindness had sent the food for him and had also sent something in cash and had assured him, that he would give him whatever he asked for. His Holiness asked the handsome young man who he was. He replied, that he was just an ordinary person. Hazrat Mir ate with his guest but the young man, on the pretext that he was keeping a fast, did not join them. Hazrat Mir, after he had finished eating, handed over the tray to the young man. After the young man left, it became apparent that he had been an angel.

112

Hazrat Madhu Lal Husain

Hazrat Madhu Lal Husain was an eminent saint who was born in AH 945 in Lahore. His father, Shaikh Usman, was a weaver.

Initiation into the Sufi Order

Hazrat Madhu Lal Husain joined a *maktab* where he committed to memory six parts of the Holy *Quran*. Hazrat Behlul, who was a Qutb of his time, receiving a mandate from Hazrat Imam Musa Raza, left Meshed to impart spiritual training to him. When he reached *maktab*, he asked Hazrat Husain to bring some water for ablutions. He did so. Hazrat Behlul, after the ablutions, prayed for him: "O Great God! make this boy an enlightened one."

Addressing his teacher, Hazrat Behlul told him that in the approaching month of Ramazan, Hazrat Husain would recite the Holy *Quran* in entirety. As he had so far committed to memory only six parts of the Holy *Quran*, it was thought to be impossible for him to recite the whole of it so soon.

Hazrat Behlul told him, that he should not be down-spirited but should go to the river and fetch some water. He told him that on the river he would meet a saint and that he should obey him in all respects. Hazrat Husain went to the river and was trying to fill the jug with water when suddenly he saw a saintly man who asked him to pour water from the jug over his hand. Hazrat Husain obeyed. The saint, sprinkled some of the water on his face and allowed him to leave.

On his return, he narrated all that had transpired to Hazrat Behlul. The blessing of that saint enabled Hazrat Madhu Lal Husain to recited the whole of the Holy *Quran* in the month of Ramazan.

After living for sometime in the company of Hazrat Behlul, he eventually left. Hazrat Behlul directed that he should not miss paying respects to the tomb of Hazrat Data Ganj Bakhsh as this would spiritually benefit him. He acted accordingly.

Prayers and asceticism

He used to go to the tomb of Hazrat Data Ganj Bakhsh everyday and offer prayers there, passing the night on the river bank engaged in prayer and recitation of the Holy *Quran*. It is said that he passed twenty-six years exclusively engaged in prayer and remembrance of God.

One day, when he was offering respects to the tomb of Hazrat Data Ganj Bakhsh, a certain saintly figure came and told him: "I am Ali of Hujwer. You have served me for a long twelve years. As a reward of your services, I have by the command of God made you a saint. You will periodically be intoxicated with the wine of unity."

The transformation

Hafiz Abu Bakr oversaw his education and training. During the period of ascetic practices, he did not stop acquiring knowledge and learning. In the afternoon, he used to attend lectures by Shaikh Sa'dullah on the commentaries on the Holy *Quran*.

One day, the lecture related to a certain *ayat* of the Holy *Quran*, which implied that "the life in this world is but pastime and play." He was greatly moved and began to dance. His teacher asked him why he was dancing. He replied: "When knowledge is bereft of practice, then merrymaking is better than that knowledge." He added that in a mystic way that "God has called the world a pastime, so one should be engaged in it."

Now he was transformed. He came out of school dancing, and threw his books into a nearby well. His class-fellows, observing this were angry and rebuked him. He laughed and addressing the water in of the well said: "Please return my books. My class-fellows are displeased with me on that account." As soon as he had uttered these words, the water of the well rose up. The books were there and were not wet. He picked them out and handed them over to his class-fellows and himself moved on.

The new way of life

This unintended manifestation of supernatural power placed him in a position that he did not like. He became the topic of conversation in the town and people began to be attracted towards him. He abhorred the publicity. In order to counteract the growing faith and devotion of the people, he invented a new strategy. He adopted a new way of life. He would utter impolite words and behave in an indecent manner so that the people might believe that he was a mad and show him contempt and hatred. That day, he had his beard shaved and used to carry about a goblet and wine, and was found singing in an intoxicated state and roaming aimlessly about thus in the lanes, streets, and markets of Lahore.

His spiritual guide and teacher, Hazrat Behlul, who was in Chenwat then, learnt his condition and came to see him and found him in an absorbed state. He took his hand in his hand, paid him special attention, and uttering the words "Praise be to God" went away.

The magic touch of love

One day he happened to be passing through Shahdara near Lahore in an absorbed state when he saw a young Hindu boy named Madho, the son of a Brahmin. He saw in Madho a manifestation of divine beauty and fell in love with him. He would wander around Madho's house and would not leave without seeing him. In this way he passed sixteen years.

Hazrat Madho was also attracted to him and they both became close companions, spending most of their time together. The silken cords of immortal love united them to such a degree, that their identity fused and Hazrat Husain came to be known and became famous as "Hazrat Madho Lal Husain." He is remembered as such to this day.

Relations with the Imperial Court

Some people complained to Emperor Akbar about his free movements and his peculiar way of living. The emperor summoned him to his presence and haughtily asked him: "O dervish! it has been heard that you have reached up to God." Hazrat Husain replied: "Certainly your Majesty." The emperor then asked him: "How did you reach up to God?" Hazrat Husain replied: "O king! I did not reach up to God, but God has reached up to me."

The emperor was apparently not satisfied with the reply. A courtier intervened and asked him whether he had any proof of what he was saying. He smiled and pondered a little and then, addressing the emperor, said: "O great and powerful sovereign of

India! it does not require much thinking. If Your Imperial Majesty had not so wished how could this humble being have reached up to Your Majesty?"

The emperor was delighted with the reply and, taking both Hazrat Husain's hands in his hand kissed them out of devotion and faith.

Prince Salim, who ascended the throne as Jahangir, held him in high respect and had great faith in his spiritual powers. He was so fascinated and influenced by him, that he appointed a person called Bahadur Khan to write his diary, which was published under the title *Baharya.*

The prophecy

He liked two placed in Lahore, Baghbanpura and Shahdara. In Shahdara he had a well dug at a certain place and had some trees planted there too. He made a remarkable prophecy of what was going to happen after his death. He said: "Here will be my grave. But thirteen years after my death a flood will come. Our devotees will take out our corpse from the grave and will bury it in Baghbanpura. After my death, Madhu will sit as my *sajjadanashin* in my place for thirty-five years. His grave will just be close to my grave." His prophecy came proved to be exact.

Death

He died in AH 1008 at the age of sixty-three. He was buried, as he had prophesied, first in Shahdara and subsequently thirteen years later in Baghbanpura, Lahore.

The sajjadanashin

After his death, Hazrat Madhu succeeded him as his spiritual heir, functioning as his spiritual caliph and *sajjadanashin.* Hazrat Madhu, having witnessed some of Hazrat Husain's supernatural powers had reposed his faith in him and embraced Islam, under the name "Miyan Mahboob-ul-Haq." He is however famous and is known to this day as "Madhu."

After he had become the *sajjadanashin,* he began to so resemble Hazrat Husain that it became difficult for people to distinguish between the two. So long as he lived, he paid no attention to worldly affairs. He died in AH 1056 and was buried close to Hazrat Madhu Lal Husain.

Traits of character

He followed the way of the censured. He used to engage in merrymaking and pastimes; would dance and sing. Once when asked who he really was, replied: "Neither I am among those who stay and neither among those who travel. I am neither a Mussulman nor given to idolatry." It is also said that he allowed himself the use of intoxicants and would celebrate the festival of Basant.

He was a quick-witted man. Once the city Qazi inquired of him the ingredients of Islam. He replied: "There are five ingredients of Islam, namely, unity, prayer, fast, *hajj*, and *zakat* (charity)." Then addressing the Qazi, he said:

> In the unity of God Almighty, you and I both are included. All the people believe in and bear a testimony to the unity of God. Of the remaining ingredients, you have missed two of them, namely, *hajj*, and *zakat*. I, on my part, have omitted two of them, namely, fasting and prayer. Now the balance is equal between you and me. We both sail in the same boat. How then am I to be blamed alone?

Supernatural powers

Once, he passed through a certain village. There the people were expecting rain, but no rain had fallen so a condition of famine was developing. When the *lambardar* of the village learnt of his arrival, he went to see him. At that time he was out. The *lambardar* caught hold of those who had accompanied him and locked them in a room. When Hazrat Husain asked the *lambardar* what he happened. The *lambardar* said that if he was a true *faqir*, he should pray for rain, and alone then would his companions be freed.

He told the *lambardar*, Bahadur Khan, that he should first entertain them and offer them all baked bread and chicken and then he would pray. The *lambardar* did so. After eating the food, Hazrat Husain gazed towards the sky and said: "What is the delay now?" No sooner had he uttered these words than clouds appeared in the sky and rain began to fall. The *lambardar* was greatly impressed and became his disciple and devotee.

Madho, at Hazrat Husain's behest, had joined Raja Man Singh's army. The Deccan expedition resulted in failure. Somebody pointed out to him that Madho was a saint and should be approached, and this was done. Madho, in turn, referred the matter to Hazrat Husain, who was then engaged in merrymaking. Hazrat Madho Lal Husain at once stood up, reached the Deccan by dint of his spiritual powers, and told Madho that he should ask the Raja to invade as it was an opportune time. Raja Man Singh's forces emerged victorious.

113

Hazrat Shah Abul-Ma'ali

Hazrat Shah Abul-Ma'ali, of the Qadiri Order of the sufis has an assured position among the saints of the Indian subcontinent. He traces his relationship from Hazrat Syed Musa Al-Burqa, son of Hazrat Imam Mohammed Taqi Al-Jawwad. One of his ancestors, Syed Faizullah Baqi, left Kirman alongwith his son, Syed Mubarak of Kirman, for India in AH 796 and settled in Ochha. Subsequently, he left Ochha and began to live in Dawood Jal near Multan. His father Syed Rahmatullah, left Dawood Jal for Sankhara in AH 930, and sometime, went to Shergarh and settled there permanently.

Hazrat Abul-Ma'ali was born in Shergarh on the tenth of Zilhijja in AH 960. His name is Abul-Ma'ali and titles are "Asad-ud-din" and "Shah Khair-ud-din." His poetic pseudonyms are "Ghurbati," "Muslami," and "Ma'ali." He acquired the outward knowledge from his father and completed his education at a very early age.

Initiation into the Sufi Order

After completing his education, he felt such an attraction to and love for Hazrat Shaikh Abd-ul-Qadir of Jilan, better known as Ghous-ul-Azam, Piran-e-Pir, that he left home, and began roaming around in jungles and deserted places without rest or respite. He went to Delhi in AH 980 when he was twenty years old. One day, quite by chance, he met an absorbed saint in an inn who looked towards him, smiled, and then said: "The people of the world go to Shaikh Dawood today for inner illumination and purification, and for his spiritual blessings, and here are some people, who leaving the imperishable wealth at home and go out." Moved by these words, Hazrat Abul-Ma'ali left Delhi for Shergarh. When he went to Hazrat Shaikh Dawood, he, seeing him, at once said: "Ma'ali come before me and tell me what the absorbed saint on seeing thee said and what did thou hear?" When told Hazrat Shaikh Dawood advised him to live in his company and thus be benefited by his spiritual blessings. He did so and was ever engaged in his service. His spiritual guide and teacher's pleasure became his delight.

Kindness of spiritual guide

One day he was restless. The desire to see Hazrat Shaikh Abd-ul-Qadir of Jilan, better known as Ghous-ul-Azam, Piran-e-Pir, seized him. He wanted to be blessed with a vision of Ghous-ul-Azam. His spiritual guide and teacher could read his thoughts and conveyed the following good news: "Ma'ali, either today or tomorrow I will take thee and present thee before Hazrat Ghous-ul-Azam, Piran-e-Pir. Wait for the auspicious hour." These words were to him as *manna* from heaven. He voluntarily gave up food and sleep and began to eagerly await the propitious hour.

One night, when it so happened that he was half awake and half asleep, his spiritual guide took his hand in his hand and led him to the blessed presence of Hazrat Ghous-ul-Azam, Piran-e-Pir. His spiritual guide Hazrat Shaikh Dawood took his seat on the left side of Hazrat Ghous-ul-Azam and Abul-Ma'ali of Iraq sat to his right. He says that seeing them sitting I wondered whether the person sitting to the right of Hazrat Ghous-ul-Azam was superior in rank and status to my spiritual guide. As soon as the thought entered his mind, Hazrat Ghous-ul-Azam, Piran-e-Pir looked towards him and said: "O Abul-Ma'ali, your Shaikh is my heart and the heart is ever on the left side."

Arrival in Lahore

At the behest of his spiritual guide and teacher, he settled in Lahore after the former passed away. Arriving in Lahore in AH 1011, when he was about fifty years old, he began to preach and propagate the doctrine of truth.

Death

Hazrat Shah Abul-Ma'ali breathed his last on the sixteenth of Rabi-ul-Awwal in AH 1024 and was buried in Lahore.

Traits of character

He was a Qutb of his time. He had merged his self in that of his spiritual guide and teacher and lost himself in the ocean of divine reality. He was a great mystic poet. He was forever restless in the love he bore for Hazrat Ghous-ul-Azam, Piran-e-Pir.

Teachings

- He did not believe that the bond of love ceased to exist after an individual died. On the contrary, he held that love did not admit of time or space. Our love for an individual who is dead does not die *ipso facto.*
- Enjoining opposition to self, he says that such an opposition is useful and profitable. The self should be overpowered.
- He preferred solitude and seclusion. He himself says: "When I love the beloved with all my heart and soul and when I am shown kindness by the beloved, then I do not require any stranger."
- He emphasises that the image of the manifestation of the beloved should be engraved on the heart of the lover. In the absence of this he is not a true lover.

114

Hazrat Sultan Bahu

Hazrat Sultan Bahu was a man with a mission. He had a vision of a better world, but he was not visionary. It has been said that "where there is vision, the people perish." Of him, it can be said that he was a vision to the people and rescued them from self-destruction. His asceticism, renunciation, faith, hope, and belief place him in the first rank of the sufi saints of the Indian subcontinent. His unflagging zeal, dogged determination, and purity of faith, and above all his humanism continue to inspire.

Hazrat Sultan Bahu was born into the Awan tribe known for its organisation and discipline, obedience to the patriarch, valour, education, and fear of God. He traced his descent from Hazrat Ali, the son-in-law of the Holy Prophet Mohammed.

His father, Bayazeed Mohammed, served emperor Shah Jahan as officer-in-charge of Kohistan.[1] He had committed the Holy *Quran* to memory and was thus a Hafiz. He was a learned man of his time, and adhered strictly to the tenets enjoined by Islam. His father was very unhappy with the position he held and therefore left Kohistan for Multan. When ordered to return, he tendered his resignation. After spending sometime in Multan, he migrated to Shore Kote and settled there permanently. In lieu of his meritorious services rendered, he was granted land for his maintenance.[2] He died there. His mother was known for her piety and religious fervour. Hazrat Bahu was born at Shore Kote in AH 1039 and was named Bahu. He was proud of his name. When still an infant, he did not drink milk during the day in the month of Ramazan as if keeping a fast. His childhood was passed in Shore Kote. He received his education and training at home. His mother brought him in accordance with the fashions of the time: one of plain living and high thinking. Intuition, inspiration, and observation were his real teachers.

The dream

After he had attained majority, one night he had a dream in which he saw himself being presented in the Court of the Holy Prophet Mohammed by no other than Hazrat Ali. The Holy Prophet took his hand in his and thereby honoured him by initiating him. He himself acknowledged all those blessings, that ensued. He says: "I attained so many and such stations and exalted positions, which cannot be described." Subsequently, the Holy Prophet entrusted him to Hazrat Shaikh Abd-ul-Qadir of Jilan, better known as Ghous-ul-Azam.[1] The dream brought about a noticeable transformation in him. He became indifferent to mundane affairs and lost interest in his surroundings. He was ever absorbed in the manifestation of the glory of God Almighty and was lost in the beauty of the absolute.

Advice

His mother observing this advised that he get himself initiated in to some Sufi Order. He was reluctant to do so and frankly told his mother, what he had in mind: "Why? Where is the need to be initiated again? The Holy Prophet has already honoured me thus. That is enough, is it not?" His mother gave him a patient hearing and then said: "My dear son, you must know, that the world in which we live is undoubtedly a place where cause and effect, act and react, and where external means and ostensible circumstances are required and are necessary. You should therefore get yourself initiated into some Sufi Order." He submitted this argument: "If that is the case, then you are sufficient unto me. You are, I am sure, the best person to accept me and to act for me as my spiritual guide." His mother smiled and regretted her inability to act as his spiritual guide, and said: "Women are not allowed to initiate anyone into the Sufi Order." He then asked his mother: "Where a spiritual guide is to be found? And where should I go in search of him?" His mother pointed towards the East.

Search

Hazrat Sultan Bahu left home and went out in search of a spiritual guide. He had heard of the great spiritual attainment and powers of Hazrat Shah Habibullah so he went to him and revealed the object of his visit. To this Hazrat Habibullah responded by saying: "Know thou, that for a seeker of truth, it is necessary that he should have peace and tranquillity. If his attention is diverted, then success is doubtful. It is therefore better that he should first try to be free himself of the lust of gold and silver and then set foot on this path." He was greatly moved by this advice and returned home and acted upon it. Later he returned to Hazrat Shah Habibullah and began to live with him. Time passed. One day, Hazrat Habibullah told him: "Frankly I tell you that I am incapable of conferring the types of blessings upon you that you deserve. But I can point out the way to the destination. If you go there, I am sure you will achieve your object. I suggest that you should go to my spiritual guide Hazrat Shaikh Syed Abd-ur-Rahman Qadiri and clutch his garment. That will be sufficient for you."

He thereupon went to Delhi and became a spiritual disciple of Hazrat Shaikh Syed Abd-ur-Rahman Qadiri, and later, his spiritual guide conferred upon him the robe of caliph, thus enabling him to accept spiritual disciples. After living in Delhi for sometime, he returned to Shore Kote and began to preach the Gospel of Truth. He called his Order "Qadiriya Masrooriya."[3] Among his caliphs the following may be mentioned: Hazrat Nou Rang; Hazrat Mulla Ma'ani; and Hazrat Momin Shah.

Marriage and children

He had four wives who bore him eight sons. His youngest son, Sultan Hayat Mohammed, died in childhood. His seven other sons were:[4] Sultan Noor Mohammed; Sultan Wali Mohammed; Sultan Latif Mohammed; Sultan Saleh Mohammed; Sultan Ishaq Mohammed; Sultan Fath Mohammed; and Sultan Sharif Mohammed.

Character and literary pursuits

He was ever absorbed in meditation and indifferent to mundane affairs. He would cultivate the land, but would not reap the crop. He is the author of many books: *Ain-ul-Faqr; Gang-ul-Israr; Kalid-ut-Tauhid; Noor-ul-Huda; Mahabat-ul-Israr; Shams-ul-Arefeen; Aurange Shahi; Israre Qadiri; Taufiq-e-Hidayat; Majalistun-Nabi; Tegh-e-Berehna; Risala Rahi; Qurb-e-Didar; Kalid-e-Jannat; Miftah-ul-Ashiqeen; Kashf-ul-Israr; Amir-ul-Kaunain; Jam-e-Israr; Ain-un-Nijat; Qutb-ul-Aqtab;* and *Hujjat-ul-Israr.*

Teachings

His teachings serve as a code for life, useful to all. He writes:[5]

> 'Woe to those persons who are content to live in darkness.' God Almighty says: 'O ye people! come towards God.' But, what to say of coming towards God, they run to avoid this. They take themselves to be enlightened even though the ray of enlightenment may not have fallen upon them. But, in fact, they are far from truth and are for ever proud of their so-called spiritual attainments.

About *faqr* (poverty), he says:[6] 'It has three words, the one meaning extinction of self, the second meaning is wrath on self, and the third meaning is submission to the divine will. . . .'

Sayings

- By practising generosity, obligations towards the people of the world are discharged.
- Generosity and kindness are the two qualities, that unite an individual with God.
- Greed and jealous lead but to depredation and humiliation.
- The people of the world are slaves to the world and to silver and gold, but the world itself and the silver and gold are slaves to the saint.
- With four selves, kill four birds, i.e., the cock of sensuality, the crow of greed, the peacock of decoration, and the pigeon of avarice.[7]

Supernatural power

One day a certain person came to him to demand some money from him. He was at that time ploughing the land. The person, seeing him doing so wanted to return. As soon as Hazrat Bahu saw him, he called him and said: "O you have come from so far off, how is it, that you are leaving without meeting me?" He asked the person to plough the land while himself went to urinate. When he returned, he threw all the pebbles that he had removed on the ground and lo! they turned into gold. Addressing the person, he said: "You had come for money. I did not want to disappoint you. Now, take as much gold as you wish." The person picked up a large quantity of gold and returned a very happy man.

Death

He breathed his last on the first of Jamadi-us-Sani in AH 1102. His tomb in Shore Kote draws myriads of devotees from far flung places.

References

1. *Manaqib-e-Sultani.*
2. Ibid., p. 45.
3. *Ain-ul-Faqr.*
4. *Manaqib-e-Sultani.*
5. Ibid., pp. 43-44.
6. *Gang-ul-Israr,* (Urdu trans.), p. 7.
7. *Kashf-ul-Israr,* (Urdu trans.), p. 15.

115

Hazrat Bulleh Shah

Hazrat Bulleh Shah was an eminent saint. His father, Syed Sakhi Durvesh Mohammed, left Ochha to settle permanently in Malikwal. He was engaged in teaching and preaching. At that time Hazrat Bulleh Shah was six years old.

His name was Abdullah Shah and his pseudonym and poetic name is "Bulleh Shah." He received his early education from his father who was well-versed in Arabic and Persian, and then went to Qusur to complete his education.

Initiation into the Sufi Order

After completing his education, he thought of getting himself initiated into the Sufi Order and ran from pillar to post in search of a spiritual guide. One day, in the course of the search he was tired and wanted to rest. He sat down under the shade of a tree and was overcome by sleep. While he slept, he dreamt that the throne of one of his ancestors descended from the air. Hazrat Syed Abd-ul-Hakim, who sat on the throne inquired who he was. He replied, that he was a Syed. On his inquiring again, he revealed his name and his father's name. Hazrat Abd-ul-Hakim said: "O my son! I am feeling thirst." Hazrat Bulleh Shah offered him a cup full of milk. He drank a little out of it and gave what remained to Hazrat Bulleh Shah. As soon as he had drunk it, he became restless and absorbed. He had been spiritually purged, purified, and illumined. Then Hazrat Abd-ul-Hakim said: "O my son! I had with me your share, which I have now given to you. From today onwards, you will receive ten rupees a day. Go and seek out your spiritual guide." He awoke quite exalted and returned home and narrated the dream to his father. His father, thereupon pointed out to him, that he committed an error. Since he had met such a great saint, he should have submitted to him, that having found him, why should he seek any other spiritual guide and teacher. Hazrat Bulleh Shah realised that his father was right and asked him where he would find the saint. His father meditated a little and then told him that at that time he would find the saint in a village called Sanda. He immediately left for Sanda and there found Hazrat Syed Abd-ul-Hakim. He repeated the words suggested to him by his father, whereupon Hazrat Syed Abd-ul-Hakim directed him to go to Hazrat Shah Inayatullah Qadiri for initiation as a spiritual disciple. He returned home and informed his father of what had transpired and sought his father's permission which was granted. He gave him some money and a turban to be presented to Hazrat Shah Inayatullah Qadiri.

He reached Lahore and met Hazrat Shah Inayatullah Qadiri in a mosque situated in Bhati Darwaza and revealed the object of his visit, imploring him to accept him as one of his humble spiritual disciples. Hazrat Shah Inayat placed one condition on such enrolment. He showed his willingness to run at his bidding and anxiously inquired what he wanted him to do. Hazrat Shah Inayat asked him to bring a sum of five hundred rupees in cash, a horse worth five hundred rupees, a pair of gold bracelets worth five hundred rupees, and an apparel worth five hundred rupees.

Hearing this, he was stunned and felt desperate. He was not hopeful that he could ever fulfil the condition. Lost in such thoughts, he reached the banks of the river Ravi and thought of drowning himself in the river. He was about to leap to do so when he heard a voice. He turned his head and saw a person with a veil over his face coming on horseback. Coming close to him, the person said that he wanted to bathe in the river and requested him to hold of his horse and to look after his belongings. He agreed, so the veiled man, entrusted to him a purse containing rupees five hundred. Next, he entrusted to him his pair of gold bracelets and then handed-over his horse to him. The person got into the river and did not emerge again. He waited a long time for him and then eventually left the river bank and came to Hazrat Inayatullah Qadiri with all the things he had asked him to bring. His quest and devotion were finally rewarded. Hazrat Shah Inayatullah Qadiri accepted him as one of his spiritual disciples. He lived in the company of his spiritual guide and teacher for sometime, until, as instructed by his spiritual guide and teacher, he went to the banks of the Chenab, where he engaged himself in prayer and remembrance of God. He later shifted to Qusur and settled there permanently.

Visit to Gwalior

On one occasion his spiritual guide and teacher was displeased with him so he went to Gwalior and availed of the opportunity to offer his respects to the tomb of Hazrat Shaikh Mohammed Ghous of Gwalior. There he acquired proficiency in music. By the grace of Hazrat Shaikh Mohammed Ghous, his relations with his spiritual guide were also restored.

Death

Hazrat Bulleh Shah breathed his last in AH 1171 and was buried in Qusur.

Traits of character

He was a perfect dervish and loved his spiritual guide and teacher very much. He was a poet and has an assured position among the mystic poets of the Indian subcontinent. He was very fond of music and sometimes, when listening to it would go into a state of rapture.

Supernatural power

Hazrat Bulleh Shah was so to say born a saint. One day, when still a boy, he took his cattle out to graze. He left the cattle in the jungle and rested under a tree. The cattle strayed into another field whose owner, seeing them, went to find their owner. He found Hazrat Bulleh Shah sleeping under a tree with a snake with upraised hood casting its shadow upon him.

Jiwan Khan, the owner of the field, was greatly perturbed. He ran up to his father and informed him that the cattle had destroyed his field and that his son lay dead under a tree with a snake beside him. His father, alongwith some other men, rushed to the spot, and found that the snake had slipped away and then Hazrat Bulleh Shah woke up. His father told him that the Jiwan Khan had complained to him that his cattle had destroyed his field. Hazrat Bulleh Shah replied, "First, see for yourself that the field has not been destroyed, but is thriving better than it was earlier. This was actually the case. Jiwan Khan, seeing this manifestation of his supernatural power, was so much impressed that he offered Bulleh Shah's father the entire field."

116

Hazrat Shah Abd-ul-Latif

Among the saints and mystic poets of the Indian subcontinent Hazrat Shah Abd-ul-Latif occupies a prominent position. He came from a Syed family. His great-grandfather Hazrat Syed Abd-ul- Karim Shah was a renowned saint of Sind who is still remembered and invoked as "Shah Karim." Hazrat Shah Abd-ul-Latif was born in a village situated in Hyderabad (Pakistan) in AD 1689.

Childhood
From childhood he showed the traits of the exceptional personality that he was subsequently to develop. He was consumed by a vision of divine unity. When he was four years old, he was sent to a *maktab* to learn the alphabet. The teacher told him that the first letter of the alphabet is "Alif" (A). When teaching him the second letter, he flatly refused to say "Bay" (B), denying its very existence. The teacher complained about this disobedient behaviour to his father, but the latter, was not angry at all. He understood that his son would not go beyond the "Alif," which stands for God, who is one without a second and which is the symbol of God and unity.

The turning point
Once it happened that the daughter of a nobleman, named Mirza Mughal Beg was seized by a malady, that threatened her life. Her father was a great devotee and admirer of Hazrat Abd-ul-Latif's father, Shah Habib and in times of difficulty or stress would seek his spiritual blessings, and assistance. On this occasion too he sent a message requesting him to come to his house and give his blessings and offer prayers at the bedside of his ailing daughter. As Shah Habib could not go. He sent Shah Abd-ul-Latif, then in prime of youth, instead. The Mirzas enjoyed a privileged position. Their womenfolk, as was customary in aristocratic families, observed

purdah and were thus kept in strict seclusion. No one was allowed to enter the inner apartments reserved for women only. The case with the members of Shah Habib's family was however quite different. They had access to the inner apartments, and when they entered the ladies of the household wrapped themselves up in their mantles. Shah Abd-ul-Latif, when he reached the house was taken inside the inner apartment where the ailing girl, known for her charm and beauty was lying. Shah Abd-ul-Latif caught hold of her little finger which, according to the custom in Sind, implied calling the girl his own. The Mirza was greatly displeased; so much so that Shah Latif's family was compelled to leave the place. The beginning of the romance brought about a change and transformation in Shah Abd-ul-Latif's life and proved to be a stepping stone to the real love: the love of God. He began to compose mystic verses bearing on the anguish and mental and spiritual torment of the lover being separated from his beloved.

Death

Hazrat Shah Abd-ul-Latif breathed his last in AD 1752. His tomb in Bhit draws a huge concourse of his devotees and admirers.

Traits of character

Hazrat Shah Abd-ul-Latif was essentially a mystic and from childhood exhibited traits of his unusual and marvellous personality. He had a meditative turn of mind and always appeared to be lost in contemplation. He brought to bear this thoughtful outlook on the problems besetting him and humanity at large, which turned him away from mundane affairs. He liked to be solitary and nurtured and developed an enthusiasm for union in solitude wandering alone through jungles and deserted places.

He drew solace, comfort and inspiration from the company of saints, sages, and mystics who interpreted the divine mystery and pursued their ideals in complete contrast to worldly people. He led an ascetic life renouncing all comforts. He deprecated cruelty to animals, denounced physical or mental or spiritual pain being inflicted upon an individual. He was an inspired mystic poet. Nature was his teacher. He was a peerless poet of Sind. His poetical works have been collected and published in a book entitled *Risalo.* In his poems, he has touched upon every aspect of life, and lucidly described hills, lakes, valleys and plains, deserts, woods, and pastures, flowers and animals, and all the other varied manifestations of nature. In his poems, he has immortalised Suhni and Mehar, Sasni and Punhu, Momul and Rano, and Heer and Ranjhe.

He was a man of the highest integrity with a gentle and humble disposition who rose above the distinctions of caste, creed, colour, or country. He was very fond of music, which touched his very soul and tuned it with the infinite. How, to what degree and in which way he was sensitive to the influence of music he expressed in his own words: "In my heart, there is a tree of divine love that dries up, unless I sing or listen to music. I am restless without it, but with it I commune with the Creator."

Teachings

He adhered strictly and faithfully to the tenets of sufism. He belonged to a fraternity that knew no distinction between man and man, but only asked: "Are you thirsty, O traveller? Enter then and drink." He stood for complete tolerance in thought and action, leaving everyone to themselves.

He emphasised divine love and union. To him love was everything. According to him, an individual should seek the truth and that there was no use in running after the world. Substance is better than shadow. Real pearls are better than brittle glassware. An individual should assiduously pursue the goal and not pleasure, that sidetrack him or her from the path of love and truth. All his tales have a spiritual significance. The heroines, namely, Suhni, Sasni, Momul, and Heer stand for the seeker. The Beloved, in each case, is God.

Once, he retired to the trunk of a tree and sat there telling beads and repeating the name of God. Two milkmaids arrived, sat under the shade of the tree and began to talk. One of them asked the other: "Sister, I have met my lover many times this month. What about you? How many times have you met yours this month?" The other milkmaid replied: "Sister, why inquire the number of times? Why should we keep an account with our lovers?"

Hazrat Shah Abd-ul-Latif was overhearing this dialogue and was greatly impressed by what the second milkmaid had said. He threw away his rosary and said: "Indeed, why keep an account with our lover (God)."

He held that an individual should pursue his object with zeal and single-mindedness.

He treated nature as a moving symbol of the spirit, and emphasises the souls quest is for beauty that is God.

Hazrat Shah Abd-ul-Latif did not believe in philosophic mysticism. The mysticism of ardent love runs through all his poetry.

He emphasised the unit of God is the unity of all experience and he also stressed the importance of sinking individuality into the ocean of divine union.

Sayings

- He is not there, where you thought Him to be.
- Simple ones. Count up and sacrifice all the corners of the houses; do not go and seek far, as He is within.
- Bend low in humility and look.
- Anger is woe.
- All happiness lies in patience.
- Do not fling back abuse at those who cast it upon you.
- Read only the word "Alif." Forget all the learning from the books.

Supernatural power

A blind man came to seek his blessings. At the time Hazrat Shah Abd-ul-Latif was lost in meditation. The blind man sat silently there and after a while regained his eyesight and his joy was unbounded. Hazrat Shah Abd-ul-Latif then came out of his contemplation and inquired why he was so joyful. The man replied: "Sire, I came here blind to seek your blessings. Now, by your favour and kindness, I have received light in my eyes." Hearing this he told the man that it was not due to his favour or kindness, God had heard his prayer. All Praise, Thanksgiving, and Gratitude should be to God, who is Merciful. He recited the following verse:

> The same God, sometimes He cancels the path,
> Sometimes He is a Guide on the path.
> He degrades and He exalts.

117

Hazrat Shaikh Dawood Jhani Wal

Hazrat Shaikh Dawood Jhani Wal was a prominent saint. His ancestors belonged to Arabia. Leaving home, they came to India and permanently settled here. Hazrat Dawood was born in Sibtpur and was named Shaikh Dawood. Jhani is a town near Lahore. He received his education from Maulana Isma'il Aja, who was one of pupils of Maulana Abd-ur-Rahman Jami. Even at an early age, he was able to read *Asfahani* without difficulty.

Initiation into the Sufi Order

It is said that initially he had the Owasia affiliation. He used to be spiritually benefited by Hazrat Shaikh Abd-ul-Qadir of Jilan, better known as Ghous-ul-Azam, Piran-e-Pir. Having spiritually received the indication and mandate of Ghous-ul-Azam, Piran-e-Pir, he became a spiritual disciple of Hazrat Shaikh Hamid Qadiri, son of Shaikh Abd-ul-Qadir Sani.

Death

He passed away in AH 982 and was buried in Shergarh near Jhani.[1]

Traits of character

He occupied a high position among the saints of his time. His noble disposition and his spirit of renunciation earned for him respect and influence.

REFERENCE

1. *Safinat-ul-Auliya*, p. 193.

118

Hazrat Shah Bilawal

Hazrat Shah Bilawal belonged to the Qadiri Order of the sufis and was born in AH 976 in Shekhood Ahan in Punjab. He became a spiritual disciple of Hazrat Shaikh Shams, who was a spiritual disciple of Shaikh Abu Ishaq. Who in turn was a spiritual disciple of Hazrat Shaikh Dawood Jhani Wal.

Death

He breathed his last on the twenty-eighth of Sha'ban in AH 1046 at the age of seventy.[1] He was buried in Lahore.

Traits of character

He attained mastery of both the outward and inward knowledge. He fasted throughout the year, would keep awake in the night, and undertake ascetic practices and undergo rigours. Hazrat Shah Bilawal was distinguished by his piety and purity.[2] His hospitality extended to all, and he would entertain people. People used to come to him to seek his spiritual blessings. People would bring water to him and he would offer prayers over it and return it to them to be given to invalids and the sick. It is said that led the latter to recover the water.

REFERENCES

1. *Safinat-ul-Auliya,* p. 199.
2. Ibid., p. 198.

119

Hazrat Shah Kamal

Hazrat Shah Kamal was the spiritual disciple of Hazrat Kakra Beg Suhrawardi. He was born in Sialkot and traced his descent from Hazrat Imam Husain. This makes him a Husaini.

He was a saint and a scholar combined. Throughout his life, he was engaged in preaching and teaching, and had a large number of pupils. Prominent among them were Hazrat Ahmad Mujaddid Alif Sani, Allama Abd-ul-Hakim of Sialkot, and Nawab Sa'dullah Khan who became the Prime Minister of Emperor Shah Jahan.

Hazrat Shah Kamal was buried near Achhra.

120

Hazrat Shah Jamal

Hazrat Shah Jamal was the younger brother of Hazrat Shah Kamal. He was a Husaini. He went to Lahore during the reign of Emperor Akbar and settled near Achhra. He was a great saint and sufi of his time.

Death

One day he went down into an underground section of his monastery, where he went to meditate, and did not emerge again. He sent a message that he was dead and that his grave should be built. He passed away in AH 1049 and was buried near Achhra.

Supernatural powers

Hazrat Shah Jamal built himself a monastery with seven storeys. Just close to it, there was a palace, garden, and the tank belonging to Nawab Sultan Begam, Emperor Akbar's daughter. She was displeased at having this stately monastery in her neighbourhood, eclipsing her palace. She conveyed a message to him that he being a dervish, should demolish some portion of it. If he did not do so, his monastery would be forcibly demolished. He replied that he would demolish some portion of his monastery, but it should be known that the royal buildings would not survive for long. At night, when a music concert was being held, he struck his foot on the ground with the result that the royal building was buried beneath the ground leaving no trace.

A person, a Khattri by caste, came to him and submitted that he had no issue and requested that Hazrat Jamal pray that he have one. Hazrat Jamal gave him two watermelons and then began to offer prayers. The person thought that he had been given the two watermelons to eat. He cut one watermelon and ate it up. After completing his prayers Hazrat Jamal saw that the person had eaten up one watermelon. He told him: "What you have done? I had given you the two watermelons so that you and your wife would share them and that the blessings they conferred. God Almighty would have given you two sons. Now take this one home. Two sons will be born to you. One will be Hindu and the other will be a Mussulman. The son who is Mussulman will become my spiritual disciple.' This is what actually happened. One of the sons, named Fakhr-ud-din, became the *sajjadanashin*, when Hazrat Jamal passed away.

121

Hazrat Shah Chiragh

Hazrat Shah Chiragh belonged to the Qadiri Order of the sufis. He is the son of Syed Abd-ul-Wahab. At the time of his birth, his grandfather exclaimed in joy: "A lamp has been born in our house." Since that day, he came to be known as "Shah Chiragh." He was his father's spiritual disciple.

Hazrat Shah Chiragh travelled widely and derived spiritual blessings from many saints. Emperor Shah Jahan was one of his devotees. He breathed his last on the twenty-second of Ziq'ada in AH 1068 and was buried in Lahore.

A certain person suffering from leprosy came, Hazrat Chiragh rubbed his finger to the entrance leading to his future place of burial and uttering the word *gurlarya*, placed it on the white spot, believing it to be a perfect medicine. So, it proved. The patient recovered and the white spot soon disappeared.

122

Hazrat Shah Abu Ishaq

Hazrat Shah Abu Ishaq belongs to the Qadiri Order of the sufis and came from Bukhara.

He was buried in Lahore. His tomb was constructed by a merchant named Abdullah, son of Abd-ul-Qadir. The merchant was one of his spiritual disciples. Once he was travelling to Arabia on a ship that was overtaken by a storm. He invoked Hazrat Ishaq's assistance. He suddenly saw the latter appeared and pushed the ship out of the storm and later disappeared. The merchant was able to sell his goods and earn a tidy profit. When he returned home he was informed of Hazrat Ishaq's death and as a token of his gratitude, constructed his tomb.

123

Hazrat Dargahi Shah

Hazrat Dargahi Shah was a prominent saint of the Qadiri Order. He was buried in Lahore. There is a well close to his tomb. It is said that its water serves as a cure for pimples on the body. People suffering from pimples, come to the well, bathe in it and are cured.

124

Hazrat Khwaja Nur Mohammed

Hazrat Khwaja Nur Mohammed was a caliph and spiritual successor of Hazrat Maulana Fakhr-ud-din Fakhr-e-Jahan. His forefathers belonged to the Panwar tribe. The Panwar sect was a compact community. His father was named Hindal and belonged to the Kharral sect, which was an offshoot of the Panwar tribe. His father lived in Mahar, which is situated near Bhawalpur.

Hazrat Nur Mohammed was born in Chotala which is situated three miles away from Mahar on the fourteenth of Ramazan in AH 1142.[1] He was named Suhail.[2] He was addressed as "Nur Mohammed." The reason for this title is as follows. His spiritual guide and teacher Hazrat Maulana Fakhr-ud-din Fakhr-e-Jahan loved him dearly. He had prayed so much and had undergone such ascetic practices as could not be undertaken by ordinary human beings. His spiritual guide and teacher found him the radiated light and hence addressed him as "Nur" or graceful light.

Education and training

He committed the Holy *Quran* to memory at the age of sixteen. He counts among his teachers the famous Hafiz, named Mohammed Mas'ud of Mahar, through whose efforts he was able to commit the Holy *Quran* to memory.[3]

For further education, he had to leave his natal town and go to Lahore. When in Lahore, he used to hear that Delhi was the centre of learning, where not only the outstanding saints lived, but also eminent scholars and the *ulama*.

He left Lahore and reached Delhi in search of knowledge and learning. Hearing the news of the arrival of Hazrat Maulana Fakhr-ud-din Fakhr-e-Jahan, he went to him and lived in his company for sometime, acquiring the outward knowledge.

Initiation into the Sufi Order

He was so profoundly influenced by the personality of Hazrat Maulana Fakhr-ud-din Fakhr-e-Jahan, that he determined to enlist himself as his spiritual disciple. Once, on the occasion of the *'urs* of Hazrat Nizam-ud-din Auliya, he went to him and requested him to accept him as his spiritual disciple. His request was granted. It is said that he was the first to enlist himself so as his spiritual disciple in Delhi. After he had attained perfection, he was made a spiritual caliph.

His spiritual guide and teacher spent thirty-four years in Delhi and he stayed in his company for six months each year. He accompanied his spiritual guide to Pak Pattan. He was deeply devoted to him and served him so wonderfully that Maulana Fakhr-ud-din showered his blessings upon him and used to say that whosoever became the spiritual disciple of Khwaja Nur Mohammed, in fact, became his own disciple. He got Hafiz Sharf-ud-din to enlist himself as the disciple of Khwaja Nur Mohammed.

Marriage and children

Hazrat Khwaja Nur Mohammed married and had three sons, namely, Nur-us-Samad, Nur Ahmad, and Nur Hasan.

Death

He passed away on the third of Zilhijja in AH 1205 and was buried in Mahar. He had led a simple life, his only object being how best he could please his spiritual guide and teacher.

Teachings

He believed, that love served as the panacea of all ills. Once, during the course of conversation, he revealed some of the implications of the theory of negative existence. He said, that in the early years of his spiritual career, Sultan Bahu fell in love with the son of a zamindar. He left home and began to live in an underground cell, which he had himself constructed near his house.

One day he was seized with a longing to see the boy. By midnight the desire became irresistible. The boy was sleeping inside the house so it was virtually impossible to see him. He though of a plan. He set his own cell on fire, to draw out people from their houses. The boy also came out and thus Sultan Bahu was able to see him.

Sayings

- The eye of the *ulama* is cast on the idolatry of the idol worshippers and the eye of the saints is cast on the manifestation and reality and not on idolatry.
- Most people feel the dangers of the connections of wife, son, agriculture, trade, and commerce, and other worldly pursuits. One should avoid such dangers.
- One should eat less, sleep less, talk less, and have less social intercourse.
- A saint, subject to attention, comes to know of the present, the past and the future.
- A perfect individual is the life of knowledge and his death is in fact the extinction of the world.

References

1. *Anwar-ul-Areefeen.*
2. *Manaqib-e-Mahboobeen.*
3. *Anwar-ul-Areefeen.*

125

Hazrat Abdullah Shah Qadiri

Hazrat Abdullah Shah Qadiri was an outstanding saint of the Qadiri Order. He died in AH 1212 and was buried in Lahore. Once a person approached him and asked whether there was any truth in alchemy or was it just quackery. He demonstrated how alchemy could be effected and asked him to take all the gold that had been prepared. The person thereupon said that he did not require the gold, but only wanted to know how it could be effected. To this Hazrat Abdullah responded: "This alchemy is quite easy to effect. Devote yourself to prayers and remembrance of God. If you do so with a sincere heart, the touch of your hand will turn the earth into gold. The enlightened turn iron into gold merely with a glance of their eyes."

Shaikh Faiz, one of his devotees, wanted to undertake alchemy but failed in the attempt. The following, Hazrat Abdullah went to meet him, and said: "How is it Shaikh ji, that you also try to undertake alchemy? If you busy yourself with such things, how will you find God?"

126

Hazrat Khwaja Shah Mohammed Sulaiman

Hazrat Khwaja Shah Mohammed Sulaiman, born in AH 1184 in Garh Googi, was a prominent spiritual figure of the Indian subcontinent. He belonged to the Jaffarya clan of Afghanistan. His father, Hazrat Zakariya, son of Abd-ul-Wahab, son of Umar Khan, died when he was an infant.

Education and training
After his father's death, he was entrusted to the care of his mother who looked after his education and training. At the early age of four, he learnt fifteen parts of the Holy *Quran* from Mulla Yusuf Jaffer. Miyan Hasan Ali taught him the remaining fifteen parts. He also taught him the book written by Shaikh Farid-ud-din Attar and the two Persian classics entitled *Gulistan* and *Bustan* written by Shaikh Sa'di of Shiraz, and also some other books.

He moved to Langh and there joined Maulvi Wali Mohammed's study circle and there completed his Persian education. His quest for knowledge took him to Kote Mathan where he joined the Madrasa of Qazi Mohammed Aqil and studied the prescribed Arabic books.

Initiation into the Sufi Order
On hearing the news that Hazrat Khwaja Nur Mohammed of Mahar had come to Ochha, went thereto be initiated as his spiritual disciple. At that time he was sixteen years old. He acquired spiritual knowledge from his spiritual guide which eventually led to his inner purification and illumination. At the age of twenty-two he was appointed as a spiritual caliph by Hazrat Khwaja Nur Mohammed.

Arrival in Tonsa
Receiving the command of his spiritual guide and teacher, he left

Garh Googi permanently and settled in Tonsa. In Tonsa, many people entered his fold. Amir Iqbal Khan became his spiritual disciple. With Hazrat Khwaja's permission he constructed a house for him in which he began to live. The ruler of then Bhawalpur State, Nawab Bhawal Khan, also had the honour of being initiated as his spiritual disciple. He built a mosque in Tonsa. Hazrat Khwaja Shah Mohammed Sulaiman established a school in Tonsa for religious education. He used to teach himself.

Death

His two sons, Khwaja Gul Mohammed and Khwaja Durvesh Mohammed, died during his lifetime. Hazrat Khwaja Shah Mohammed Sulaiman breathed his last on the seventh of Safar in AH 1267 and was buried in Tonsa. His grandson, Hazrat Allah Bakhsh, became his spiritual heir and successor (*sajjadanashin*).

Traits of character

He had the greatest respect and love for his spiritual guide and teacher. Initially, he used to spend a month in his company. When seized by the desire to see him, he would go there on foot to pay his respects.

He was a very learned man, well-versed in the *Quran, hadis, fiqh,* and other religious topics.

He passed the early years of his life in straitened circumstances. Subsequently, he began to receive *fatuhat* (unsought gifts) but would retain nothing, spending all that he received. His *langar* (free kitchen) was open to all. Besides feeding them he also helped the dervishes and students financially.

He was ever engaged in prayer and remembrance of God and also in renunciation and self-abnegation. He would read the Holy *Quran* everyday and led a simple life.

Teachings

He laid stress on adherence to the tenets of the Holy Prophet, the importance of cultivating good manners and good habits, and avoidance of bad company. He deprecated vanity and pride, and pleaded for tolerance and social justice.

According to him an individual should be humble, gentle, and meek and to regard himself or herself as the lowliest. He said that one should try to abstain from backbiting and slander.

To him, the object of life was nothing but the remembrance of God. An individual, he emphasised, should repose his utmost trust in God. He stressed that the love of the world and the company of the people of the world should be avoided and shunned.

Glossary

chilla	Sitting in a secluded place; prayer and meditation in a secluded place for forty days.
chowki	A wooden platform with four legs, generally made of wood.
dal	A kind of food, cooked pulses.
farman	Royal decree.
fatwa	Judgement in accordance with the mandates of Islam.
ghous	The one who is empowered to hear complaints and grievances.
goolar	A kind of fruit.
haqiqat	Reality.
'Id	A festival celebrated by Muslims. There are two principal festivals celebrated. One is 'Id-ul-Fitr and the other is 'Id-ul-Azha.
'Idgah	The place earmarked for prayers conducted on the occasion of the two 'Ids.
jabrut	It literally means greatness; awe of God; unity of God. But according to the enlightened the status of the qualities of God, namely, *haqiqat* (reality).
Kalima-e-Taiyibah	"There is no deity but God and Mohammed is the Prophet of God." An article of faith for Muslims.
khanqah	Convent; monastery.
lahut	The world of the person of God, in which the illumined soul attains the station of extinction in God, namely *marifa*.
malkut	Kinship; omnipotence; world of angels and to the sufis world of souls.

marifat	Enlightenment.
mashhood	Present; presented.
millat	Group; community; refers to Islamic brotherhood.
miqraz	A pair of scissors.
Mohammed Kasa-e-lais	Mohammed, greedy for more and more blessings.
muhaddis	One who recites the sayings of the Holy Prophet Mohammed.
nasut	The world in which we live; sufis imply the *shari'at*.
Owaisi	The one having affiliation with Hazrat Owais Qarni, who lived during the life time of the holy Prophet Mohammed, but could not meet the Holy Prophet. His love for the Holy Prophet is well-known.
qutb	A saint, so-called to denote his place in the spiritual hierarchy, working as leader and guide.
shari'at	The way pointing towards the path of God; implies the Islamic code.
tariqat	Path to enlightenment.

Bibliography

PRIMARY SOURCES

Abd-ul-Haq Muhaddis Dehlavi, Shaikh, *Akhbar-ul-Akhyar,* Delhi, 1914.
Amir Khurd, *Siyar-ul-Auliya,* Delhi, 1885.
Dara Shikoh, *Safinat-ul-Auliya,* Kanpur, 1900.
al-Ghazzali, Abu Hamid Muhammad ibn Muhammad ibn Ahmad, *Ihya'u Ulum-id-din,* Cairo, 1957.
Hujwiri, Abu'l-Hasan, *Kashf-ul-Mahjub,* Lahore, 1923.
al-Isfahani, Abu Na'im, *Hayat-ul-Auliya,* 10 vols., Cairo, 1932-38.
Jami, 'Abd-ur-Rahman Nuruddin, *Kitab Nafahat al-Uns,* Tehran, 1918.
Lodi, Sher Khan, *Mir'at-ul-Khayal,* Bombay, 1906.
Makki, Abu Talib, *Quwwat-ul-Qulub,* 2 vols., Cairo, 1888.
Maneri, Sharafuddin, *Maktubat-e-Sa'di,* Lucknow, 1870.
al-Qushayri, *Risalat fi 'ilm at-Tasawwuf,* Karachi, 1964.
al-Sarraj, Abu Nasr, *Kitab-ul-Luma fi'l-Tasawwuf,* London, 1963.
as-Suhrawardi, Shihabuddin Abu Hafs 'Umar, *Awarif al-Ma'arif,* Cairo, 1957.

GENERAL SOURCES

Abdel-Kader, A.H., *The Life, Personality and Writings of al-Junayd,* London, 1962.
Addas, Claude, *Ibn 'Arabi ou la Quête du Soufre Rouge,* Paris, 1989.
al-Alawi, Shaikh, *Knowledge of God,* Norwich, 1981.
Amuli, Sayyid Haydar, *Inner Secret of the Path,* Shaftesbury, 1989.
Ansari, Abdullah, *Chemin de Dieu,* Paris, 1985.
—, *Intimate Conversations,* New York, 1978.
Ansari, Muhammad Abd-ul-Haq, *Sufism and Shari'ah,* Leicester, 1986.
al-Aqili, Muhammad M., *Ibn Sheerin's Dictionary of Dreams,* according to Islamic Inner Traditions, Philadelphia, 1992.

Arberry, A.J., *Sufism*, London, 1969.
—, *The Doctrine of the Sufis*, Lahore, 1966.
Ardalan, Nader, and Laleh Bakhtyar, *The Sense of Unity*, Chicago, 1973.
Arifi, *The Book of Ecstasy*, London, 1980.
Attar, F., *The Conference of the Birds*, Middlesex, 1984.
—, *Le Livre Divin*, Paris, 1961.
—, *Le Mémorial des Saints*, Paris, 1976.
—, *Le Livre de L'Epreuve* (*Musibatnama*), Paris, 1981.
—, *Le Livre des Secrets*, Paris, 1985.
Austin, R.W.J., *Sufis of Andalusia*, Sherborne, 1988.
Bakhtyar, Laleh, *Sufi Expressions of the Mystic Quest*, London, 1976.
Baldick, Julian, *Mystical Islam*, London, 1989.
—, *Imaginary Muslims—The Uwaysi Sufis of Central Asia*, New York, 1993.
Baljon, J.M.S., *A Mystical Interpretation of Prophetic Tales by an Indian Muslim*, Leiden, 1973.
Barnabas, *Het Evangelie van Barnabas*, Haarlem, 1990.
Bencheikh, J.E., *Le Voyage Nocturne de Mahomet*, Paris, 1988.
Birge, John Kingsley, *The Bektashi Order of Dervishes*, London, 1994.
Bommel, A. van, *Kom tot het Gebed*, Den Haag, 1989.
Bonaud, Christian, *Le Soufisme al-tasawwuf et la spiritualité islamie*, Paris, 1991.
Browne, E.G., *A Literary History of Persia*, 4 vols., Bethesda, 1197.
Burckhardt, Titus, *Alchemy*, Shaftesbury, 1987.
—, *An Introduction to Sufi Doctrine*, Lahore, 1971.
—, *Mirror of the Intellect*, Albany, 1987.
Burton, Sir Richard F., *Personal Narrative of a Pilgrimage to al-Madinah and Meccah*, 2 vols., New York, 1964.
—, *The Kasidah of Haji Abd el-Yezdi*, London, 1974.
Charaf, Cheikh Sadik Mohammad, *Le Rappel et l'Invocation de Dieu*, Kuwait, 1987.
Chebel, Malek, *Dictionaire des symboles musulmans—Rites, mystique et civilisation*, Paris, 1995.
Chittick, William C., *The Sufi Path of Knowledge*, Albany, 1989.
—, *The Sufi Path of Love*, Albany, 1983.
—, *Faith and Practice of Islam*, Albany, 1992.
—, *Imaginal Worlds, Ibn al-'Arabi and the Problem of Religious Diversity*, Albany, 1994.
—, *The Self-Disclosure of God, Principles of Ibn al-'Arabi's Cosmology*,

Albany, 1998.
Chodkiewicz, Michel, *Le Sceau des Saints*, Paris, 1986.
—, *Un Océan Sans Rivage*, Paris, 1992.
Corbin, Henri, *Die Smaragdene Vision*, München, 1989.
—, *Spiritual Body and Celestial Earth*, Princeton, 1977.
—, *Avincenna and the Visionary Recital*, Princeton, 1988.
—, *Creative Imagination in the Sufism of Ibn Arabi*, Princeton, 1969.
Cornell, Vincent J., *The Way of Abu Madyan—The Works of Abu Madyan Shu'ayb*, Cambridge, 1996.
Currie, P.M., *The Shrine and Cult of Mu'in al-din Chishti of Ajmer*, Bombay, 1989.
Darqawi, Shaykh Mawlay al-'Arabi, *The Darqawi Way—The Letters of Shaykh Mawlay al-'Arabi ad-Darqawi*, Norwich, 1981.
Deikman, Arthur J., *The Observing Self: Mysticism and Psychotherapy*, Boston, 1982.
Dermenghem, Emile, *Vies des saints Musulmans*, Paris, 1981.
Devos, Claire, *Qawwali—La musique des maîtres diu soufisme*, Paris, 1995.
Dierl, Anton Josef, *Geschichte und Lehre des anatolischen Alevismus-Bektasismus*, Frankfurt, 1985.
Dunn, Ross E., *The Adventures of Ibn Battuta*, Beckenham, 1986.
During, Jean, *Musique et extase: L'audition mystique dans la tradition soufie*, Paris, 1988.
Elahi, M., *The Couplets of Baba Farid*, Lahore, 1976.
Elias, Jamal J., *The Throne Carrier of God*, New York, 1995.
Emre, Y., *The City of the Heart*, Shaftesbury, 1992.
—, *Laten we liefhebben en onszelf geliefd maken*, Rotterdam, 1991.
Eric ,Winkel, *Mysteries of Purity—Ibn al-'Arabī's asrār al-tahārah*, Notre Dame, 1995.
Ernst, Carl W., *Words of Ecstasy in Sufism*, Albany, 1985.
—, *Eternal Garden*, Albany, 1992.
—, *Ruzbihan Baqli—Mysticism and the Rhetoric of Sainthood in Persian Sufism*, Richmond, 1996.
—, *The Shambhala Guide to Sufism*, Boston and London, 1997.
Fadiman, James, and Robert Frager, eds., *Essential Sufism*, Edison, 1998.
Fahd, Toufic, *La divination arabe*, Paris, 1987.
Fani, Mohsin, *The Religion of the Sufis*, London, 1979.
Farhadi, A.G. Ravan, *Abdullah Ansari of Heart—an Early Sufi Master*, Richmond, 1996.

Faruqi, Burhan Ahmad, *The Majaddid's Conception of Tauhid*, Lahore, 1979.
Field, C., *The Confessions of Al-Ghazzali*, Lahore, n.d.
Field, R., *Dansend near God*, Wassenear, 1977.
Frembgen, Jürgen, *Derwische—Gelebter Sufismus*, Köln, 1993.
Friedlander, Ira, *The Whirling Dervishes*, London, 1975.
Friedmann, Yohanan, *Shaykh Ahmad Sirhindi*, Montreal, 1971.
Ghazali, Ahmad, *Sawanih*, London, 1986.
Ghazali, M., *Le Tabernacle des Lumières*, Paris, 1981.
—, *Das Elixier der Glückseligkeit*, Köln, 1984.
—, *Inner Dimensions of Islamic Worship*, Leicester, 1983.
—, *The Ninety-Nine Beautiful Names of God*, Cambridge, 1992.
—, *Invocations and Supplications*, Cambridge, 1990.
Gimaret, Daniel, *Les noms divins en Islam*, Paris, 1988.
Gramlich, Richard, *Islamische Mystik*, Stuttgart, 1992.
—, *Die Gaben der Erkenntnisse des 'Umar as-Suhrawardi (Awarif al-ma'arif)*, Wiesbaden, 1978.
—, *Das Sendschreiben al-Qušayris über das Sufitum*, Wiesbaden, 1989.
—, *Schlaglichter über das Sufitum*, Stuttgart, 1990.
Gray, Elizabeth T., *The Green Sea of Heaven*—Fifty *ghazals* from the *Diwan of Hafiz*, Ashland, 1995.
Gudri Shah Baba, Nawab Mohammed Khadim Hasan, *The Path of Tasawwuf*, Ajmer, 1990.
Hafiz, *Diwan of Hafiz*, Melbourne, 1986.
—, *L'amour, l'amant, l'aimé*, Paris, 1989.
Hallaj, Mansur, *The Tawasin*, Berkeley, 1974.
—, *Diwan*, Paris, 1991.
Hamadani, 'Ayn Al-Quzat, *Les Tentations Métaphysiques*, Paris, 1992.
Haveri, Shaykh Fadhlulla, *The Sufi Way to Self-unfoldment*, Shaftesbury, 1987.
Hirtenstein, S., *The Unlimited Mercifier—The Life and Thought of Ibn 'Arabi*, Oxford, 1999.
—, and M.Tiernan, eds., *Muhyiddin ibn 'Arabi*, Shaftesbury, 1993.
Ibn Arabi, Muhyiddin, *Fusus al-Hikam*, Ismail Hakki Bursevi's translation and commentary, 4 vols., Oxford, 1985.
—, *Divine Governance of the Human Kingdom*, Louisville, 1997.
—, *Les Illuminations de la Mecque*, Paris, 1988.
—, *The Tarjuman-ul-Ashwak*, London, 1978.
—, *La Profession de Foi*, Paris, 1995.
—, *Le Livre de l'Extinction dans la Contemplation*, Paris, 1984.

—, *La Parure des Abdāl*, Paris, 1992.
—, *Traité de l'Amour*, Paris, 1986.
—, *L'Arbre du Monde*, Paris, 1990.
—, *La Vie Merveilleuse de Dhûl Nûn l'Egyptien*, Paris, 1988.
Ibn 'Ataullah, *Traité sur le nom Allah*, Paris, 1981.
—, *The Key to Salvation*, A Sufi Manual of Invocation, Cambridge, 1996.
—, *The Book of Wisdom*, New York, 1978.
Ibn Hazm, *The Ring of the Dove*, London, 1994.
Ibn 'Ibad (of Ronda), *Letters on the Sufi Path*, Mahwah, 1986.
Ibn Tufayl, Abu Bakr Muhammad, *Wat geen oog heeft gezien—De geschiedenis van Hayy ibn Yaqzan*, Amsterdam, 1985.
Iqbal, A., *The Life and Works of Jalaluddin Rumi*, London, 1983.
Iraqi, Fakhruddin, *Divine Flashes*, New York, 1982.
Izutsu, Toshihiko, *Sufism and Taoism*, Berkeley, 1983.
—, *Creation and the Timeless Order of Things, Essays in Islamic Mystical Philosophy*, Ashland, 1994.
Jami, *Yusuf and Zulaikha*, London, 1980.
—, *Lawa'ih*, London, 1978.
al-Jerrahi, Shaikh Muzaffer Özak, *Irshad—Wisdom of a Sufi Master*, Warwick, 1988.
al-Jilani, Shaikh 'Abd-ul-Qadir, *The Sublime Revelation*, Houston, 1992.
—, *The Secret of Secrets*, Cambridge, 1992.
Jurji, Edward Jabra, *Illumination in Islamic Mysticism*, Lahore, n.d.
Kadri, Yakup, *Flamme und Falter*, Köln, 1986.
Khalili, K., *Quatrains of Khalilullah Khalili*, London, 1981.
Khan, Khan Sahib Khaja, *Studies in Tasawwuf*, Lahore, 1973.
Lapidus, Ira M., *A History of Islamic Societies*, New York, 1989.
Lawrence, Bruce B., *Notes from a Distant Flute*, Tehran, 1978.
Lewison, Leonard, ed., *Classical Persian Sufism: from its Origins to Rumi*, London, 1993.
Lings, Martin, *What is Sufism*, London, 1975.
—, *Muhammad*, London, 1983.
—, *A Sufi Saint of the Twentieth Century, Shaikh Ahmad al-Alawi*, Berkeley, 1973.
Litvak, Stuart, *Seeking Wisdom*, Maine, 1984.
Lory, Pierre, *Les Commentaires ésotériques du Coran d'après 'Abd al Razzāq al-Qāshāni*, Paris, 1980.
Maneri, Sharafuddin, *The Hundred Letters*, New York, 1980.
Mason, Herbert W., *Al-Hallaj*, Richmond, 1995.

Massignon, L., *The Passion of al-Hallaj*, vol. 1, Princeton, 1982.
—, *Essay on the Origins of the Technical Language of Islamic Mysticism*, Notre Dame, 1997.
Meier, Fritz, *Die Fawa'ih al-Gamal wa-Fawatih al-Galal des Nagm ad-Din al-Kubra*, Wiesbaden, 1957.
Mirza, M.W., *The Life and Works of Amir Khusru*, Lahore, 1962.
Monawwar, M.E.E., *Les Etappes Mystiques du Shaykh Abu Said*, Paris, 1974.
Muhiyuddin, M.R. Bawa, *Questions of Life—Answers of Wisdom*, vol. 1, Philadelphia, 1991.
al-Muqaddasi, *Revelation of the Secrets of the Birds and Flowers*, London, 1980.
Murata, Sachiko, *The Tao of Islam*, Albany, 1992.
—, and William C. Chittick, *The Vision of Islam*, London and New York, 1996.
Nakosteen, M., *The Rubáiyyát of Bábá Táhir Oryán of Hamadán*, Boulder, 1967.
Nasafi, *Le Livre de l'Homme Parfait*, Paris, 1984.
Nasr, Seyyed Hossein, *Living Sufism*, London, 1980.
—, *An Introduction to Islamic Cosmological Doctrines*, London, 1978.
—, *Sadr al-Din Shirazi and His Transcendent Theosophy*, Tehran, 1978.
—, ed., *Islamic Spirituality*, 2 vols., New York, 1985-91.
Netton, Ian Richard, *Allah Transcendent*, Richmond, 1994.
Nicholson, R.A., *Studies in Islamic Mysticism*, Cambridge, 1985.
—, *A Literary History of the Arabs*, Richmond, 1993.
—, *Kashf al-Mahjub*, Lahore, 1976.
—, *The Mathnawi of Jalalu'ddin Rumi* (text, translation, and commentary), 8 vols., London, 1971-85.
Niffari, *Le Livre des Stations*, Combas, 1989.
Nizami, *Das Alexanderbuch*, Zürich, 1991.
—, *Chosrou und Schirin*, Zürich, 1980.
—, *Die Sieben Geschichten der Sieben Prinzessinen*, Zürich, 1959.
—, *Leila und Madschnun*, Zürich, 1963.
Nurbakhsh, Javed, *Sufism*, 15 vols., New York and London, 1982.
—, *The Psychology of Sufism*, London, 1993.
—, *The Truths of Love*, London, 1982.
—, *Divan-i Nurbakhsh*, New York, 1980.
Nwyia, Paul, *Ibn 'Ata' Allah 709/1309) et La naissance de la confrérie šadilite*, Beyrouth, 1990.
—, *Exégèse Coranique et Langage Mystique*, Beyrouth, 1991.

O'Fahey, R.S., *Enigmatic Saint: Ahmad ibn Idris and the Idrisi Tradition*, Evanston, 1990.

Omar Khayyam, *Quatrains*, Paris, 1983.

Ozelsel, Michaela, *Forty Days, The Diary of a Traditional Solitary Sufi Retreat*, Brattleboro, 1996.

Padwick, Constance, *Muslim Devotions*, London, 1960.

Pourafzal, Haleh, and Roger Montgomery, *The Spiritual Wisdom of Haféz*, Rochester, 1998.

al-Qadi, Imam 'Abd-ur-Rahim ibn Ahmad, *Das Totenbuch des Islam*, Bindlach, 1991.

Qureshi, Regula Burckhardt, *Sufi Music of India and Pakistan*, Cambridge, 1986.

Radtke, Bernd, *Drei Schriften des Theosophen von Tirmid*, Beirut and Stuttgart, 1996.

Rauf, Bulent, *Addresses*, Robertson, 1986.

ar-Razi, Fakhr-ud-din, *Traité sur les noms divins*, 2 vols., Paris, 1986-88.

Razi, N.D., *The Path of God's Bondsmen from the Beginning to the Return*, Delmar, 1982.

Renard, John, *All the King's Falcons, Rumi on Prophets and Revelation*, Albany, 1994.

Ridder, A.J., *De Rechtgeleide Kaliefen*, Den Haag, 1987.

Ridgeon, Lloyd, *'Aziz Nasafi*, Richmond, 1998.

Ritter, Helmut, *Das Meer der Seele*, Leiden, 1978.

Rizvi, Saiyid Athar Abbas, *A History of Sufism in India*, 2 vols., New Delhi, 1978-83.

—, *Shah Wali-Allah and His Times*, Canberra, 1980.

Rückert, Friedrich, *Dreiundsechzig Ghaselen des Hafis*, Schweinfurt, 1988.

Rumi, *Von Allem und vom Einen*, München, 1988.

—, *De Middernachtelijke Zon*, Zoetermeer, 1999.

Sa'di, M., *The Bustan of Sa'di*, Lahore, n.d.

—, *The Gulistan or Rose Garden of Sa'di*, London, 1964.

Sakkakini, W.E., *First among Sufis: The Life and Thought of Rabia al-Adawiyya*, London, 1982.

Sanai, *The Enclosed Garden of the Truth*, New York, 1975.

Schimmel, Annemarie, *My Soul is a Woman*, New York, 1997.

—, *Gärten der Erkenntnis*, Köln, 1985.

—, *A Dance of Sparks*, Den Haag, 1979.

—, *Islamic Names*, Edinburgh, 1979.

—, *And Muhammad is His Messenger,* Chapel Hill and London, 1985.
—, *Nimm eine Rose und nenne sie Lieder,* Köln, 1987.
—, *As through a Veil,* New York, 1982.
—, *The Triumphal Sun,* Den Haag, 1978.
—, *A Two-Colored Brocade,* Chapel Hill and London, 1992.
—, *Make a Shield from Wisdom,* London, 1993.
—, *Mystische Dimensionen des Islam—Die Geschichte des Sufismus,* München, 1992.
Schuon, Frithjof, *Understanding Islam,* London, 1976.
—, *Sufism—Veil and Quintessence,* Bloomington, 1981.
Selimovic, Meša, *Der Derwisch und der Tod,* Salzburg, 1994.
Shabestari, M., *La Roseraie du Mystère,* Paris, 1991.
Shafi', Mohammad, *Freedom from the Self: Sufism, Meditation and Psychotherapy,* New York, 1995.
Shah, Amina, *The Assemblies of al-Hariri,* London, 1980.
Shah, Idris, *Knowing how to know,* London, 1998.
—, *Learning how to learn,* London, 1978.
—, *Tales of the Dervishes,* Frogmore, 1973.
—, *The Way of the Sufi,* Harmondsworth, 1992.
Shah, Omar Ali, *The Sufi Tradition in the West,* New York, 1994.
Shakoor, M., *The Writing on the Water,* Shaftesbury, 1988.
Sharib, Z.H., *The Culture of the Sufis,* Southampton, 1999.
—, *The Qur'anic Prayers,* Southampton, 1997.
—, *Reflections of the Mystics of Islam,* Southampton, 1996.
—, *The Meditations of a Sufi Saint,* Southampton, 1995.
—, *Sarmad and His Rubaiyat,* Southampton, 1994.
—, *Hafiz and His Rubaiyat,* Southampton, 1993.
—, *Abu Sa'id Abu'l-Khair and His Rubaiyat,* Southampton, 1992.
—, *The Psalm of Love,* Southampton, 1990
—, *The Psalm of Light,* Southampton, 1990.
—, *The Psalm of Life,* Southampton, 1990.
—, *Live,* Southampton, 1981.
—, *Khawaja Gharib Nawaz,* Lahore, 1975.
—, *Innerliske Vrede,* trans. into Dutch by Gulnar and Siraj, Zoetermeer, 1999.
—, *Soefi Trilogie,* trans. into Dutch by Gulnar and Siraj, Zoetermeer, 1995.
—, *De Roos van Bagdad,* trans. into Dutch by Gulnar and Siraj, Zoetermeer, 1994.
—, *De 99 schone Namen van Allah,* trans. into Dutch by Gulnar and

Siraj, Den Haag, 1992.
—, *De Navolging van Moehammad,* trans. into Dutch by Gulnar and Siraj, Krimpen aan den IJssel, 1989.
—, *Khawaja Moinuddin Chishti: De Geliefde van Allah,* trans. into Dutch by Gulnar and Siraj, Den Haag, 1979.
—, *Suggerimenti per una Vita Positiva,* trans. into Italian by Q. Corrado and H. Corrado, Trieste, 1993.
Shushud, Hasan, *Masters of Wisdom of Central Asia,* Moorcote, 1993.
Sijzi, Amir Hasan, *Nizam-ud-din Awliya—Morals for the Heart,* New York, 1992.
Simsar, Muhammed A., *The Cleveland Museum of art's Tuti-Nama/ Tales of a Parrot,* Graz, 1978.
Siraj-ud-din, Abu Bakr, *The Book of Certainty,* Cambridge, 1992.
Sakali, Faouzi, *La Voie Soufie,* Paris, 1985.
Smith, M., *An Early Mystic of Baghdad:* A Study of the Life and Teachings of Harith b. Asad al-Muhasibi, London, 1977.
Sohravardi, S.Y., *Le Livre de la Sagesse Orientale,* Lagrasse, 1986.
Sohrawardi, A.N., *A Sufi Rule for Novices,* Cambridge, 1977.
Sorley, H.T., *Shah Abdul Latif of Bhit,* Lahore, 1966.
Stoddart, William, *Soefisme,* Den Haag, 1982.
as-Sufi, 'Abd-ul-Qadir, *Indications from Signs,* Norwich, 1979.
as-Sulami, Ibn al-Husayn, *La Lucidité Implacable,* Paris, 1991.
—, *The Book of Sufi Chivalry,* New York, 1983.
Sviri, Sara, *The Taste of Hidden Things,* Inverness, 1997.
Taeschner, Franz, *Zünfte und Bruderschaften im Islam,* Zürich and München, 1979.
Tahir, Baba, *A Fool of God,* London, 1979.
Takeshita, Masataka, *Ibn 'Arabi's Theory of the Perfect Man and its Place in the History of Islamic Thought,* Tokyo, 1987.
Teufel, J.K., *Eine Lebensbeschreibung des Scheichs Ali-i-Hamadani,* Leiden, 1962.
Thackston, W.M., *The Mystical and Visionary Treatises of Suhrawardi,* London, 1982.
Topper, Uwe, *Sufis und Heilige im Maghreb,* München, 1991.
Trimingham, J.S., *The Sufi Orders in Islam,* Oxford, 1973.
Troll, Christian W., *Muslim Shrines in India,* Bombay, 1989.
Tweedie, *Daughter of Fire,* Nevada City, 1986.
'Uthman Dan Fodio, Shaikh, *Handbook on Islam, Iman and Ihsan,* Norwich, 1978.
Valad, Sultan, *Maitre et Disciple,* Paris, 1982.

Valiuddin, Mir, *Contemplative Disciplines in Sufism*, Den Haag, 1980.
—, *Love of God—The Sufi Approach*, New Delhi, 1968.
Vaughan-Lee, Llewellyn, *The Face Before I was born, A Spiritual Autobiography*, Inverness, 1998.
Vitray-Meyerovitch, Eva de, *Rumi and Sufism*, Sausalito, 1987.
Walbridge, John, *The Science of the Mystic Lights*, Cambridge, 1992.
Wali-Allah, *Full Moon Appearing on the Horizon*, Lahore, 1988.
—, *Sufism and the Islamic Tradition*, London, 1980.
—, *The Sacred Knowledge of the Higher Functions of the Mind*, London, 1982.
Weischer, B.M., and Peter Wilson, *Heart's Witness—The Sufi Quatrains of Awhaduddin Kirmani*, Tehran, 1978.
Wilson, P.J., and Pourjavady, *The Drunken Universe*, Grand Rapids, 1987.
Yagan, M., *I come from behind Kaf Mountain*, Putney, 1984.